Earline's Pink Party

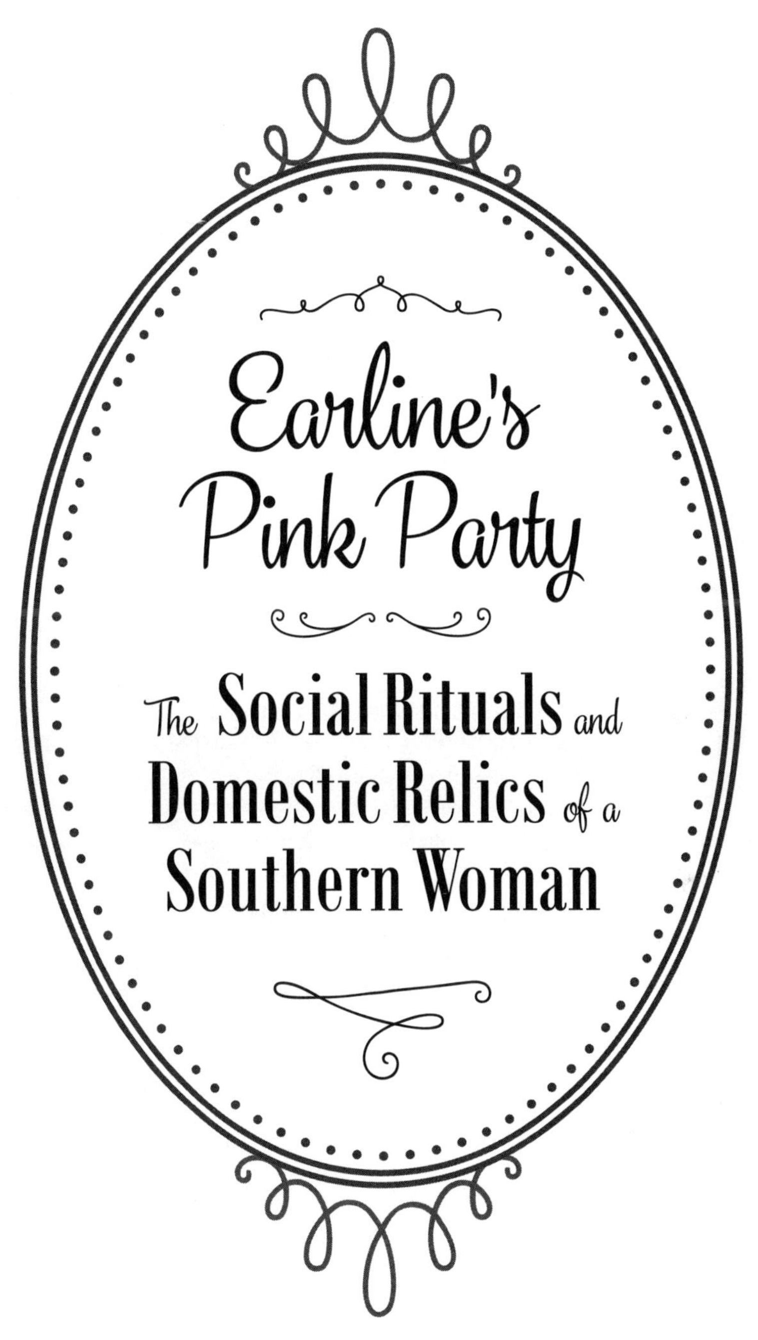

Earline's Pink Party

The Social Rituals and Domestic Relics of a Southern Woman

ELIZABETH FINDLEY SHORES

The University of Alabama Press
Tuscaloosa, Alabama 35487-0380
uapress.ua.edu

Typeface: Scala Pro

Cover design: Michele Myatt Quinn

Library of Congress Cataloging-in-Publication Data

Names: Shores, Elizabeth F., author.
Title: Earline's pink party : the social rituals and domestic relics of a Southern woman / Elizabeth Findley Shores.
Description: Tuscaloosa : The University of Alabama Press, [2017] | Includes bibliographical references and index.
Identifiers: LCCN 2016032549| ISBN 9780817319342 (cloth : alk. paper) | ISBN 9780817390686 (e book)
Subjects: LCSH: Findley, Annie Earline Moore, 1896–1953. | Women, White—Alabama—Tuscaloosa—Biography. | Women, White—Alabama—Tuscaloosa—Social life and customs—20th century. | Tuscaloosa (Ala.)—Social life and customs—20th century. | Tuscaloosa (Ala.)—Race relations—History—20th century.
Classification: LCC F334.T9 S55 2017 | DDC 976.1/84063092 [B] —dc23
LC record available at https://lccn.loc.gov/2016032549

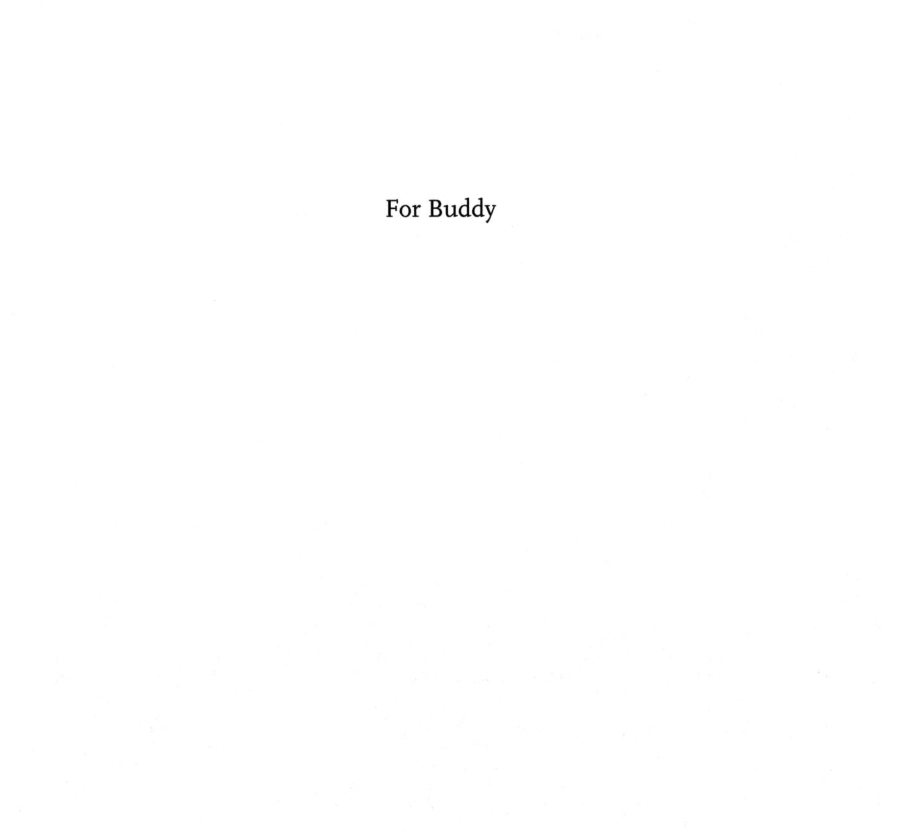

For Buddy

Contents

Figures follow page 95.

Acknowledgments

Many relatives and friends helped me assemble this story of the life of my grandmother Annie Earline Moore Findley. First and foremost, my husband, Finos Buford ("Buddy") Johnson Jr., drove on trips to Alabama, found and gave me a fragile copy of the University Club cookbook, and supported this project in every possible way. Our sons, Findley Shores Johnson and Layet Spigner Johnson, adventurous and creative young adults, helped me reach an understanding of how the bungalow was Earline's life's work. Layet also transformed my sketches into clear maps and diagrams. My aunt Margaret Koster Findley of Tuscaloosa, Alabama, provided numerous primary and secondary sources and patiently answered many questions for several years. She also organized an expedition, with my cousins Lynn Findley and Louise and Don Bailey, to the Christopher Chapel and Robertson-Stone cemeteries in 2010. My distant cousins Joan Christopher Mitchell of Montgomery, Alabama, Velma Ruth Moore Kynerd of Bailey, Mississippi, Claude Bowman Slaton of Baton Rouge, Louisiana, and Anita Kenerson Prickett of Chichester, New Hampshire, shared information about their branches of the Christopher, Moore, and Findley families. Lynn Findley helped compile bibliographic information about the family library, and Melissa Macdougall did bibliographic research for me in Austin and Llano County, Texas. Helen Maroon, formerly of Chattanooga, Tennessee, kindly shared information about Virginia Killingsworth Moore. Elna Bolding Shugerman of Birmingham, a contemporary of my mother, shared her impressions of the Findleys. My cousin by marriage Angela Raper Clevenger of Ashdown, Arkansas, permitted me to explore her bungalow. Three dear friends, Elizabeth Moody Steele of Richmond, Virginia, Nelle Hogan Peck of Grand Rapids, Michigan, and Susan Fountain Bettoli of Cookeville, Tennessee, gave me unflagging moral support. The beautiful Patricia Amos, Betty Canan, Elna Shugerman, and Geraldine Woodson of Birmingham provided hospitality and encouragement when I made trips to Alabama. My aunt Linda Shores of Grand Haven, Michigan, shared my experience of being a distant Shores.

Librarians and archivists gave me essential help during the research. Mary Bess Paluzzi, associate dean for special collections at the University of Alabama, and her staff, including Kevin Ray, Donnelly Lancaster Walton, and Gates W. Winters III, were always friendly, helpful, and highly professional. In the Central Arkansas Library System (CALS), the employees of the interlibrary loan office, Leland Razer, Jennifer Clark, Jenifer Hamel, and Kelly Hirrel, were absolutely vital to my work, and all of the employees of the Adolphine Fletcher Terry Branch Library were helpful as I came in several times a month, for a period of three years, to pick up books. In the Arkansas Studies Institute, a division of CALS, Linda Pine, Kay Lundgren, Frances Morgan, and Colin Woodward were helpful, as was Lauren Jarvis of the Arkansas History Commission. Professor Esther Moore Howard of the University of West Alabama (UWA) made it possible for me to spend two days exploring the campus and examining materials in the university archive. Sheila Blackmon Limerick of archives and special collections at UWA pulled materials for me to examine and gave me useful insights about the early days of the Alabama Normal School. The staff of the Tuscaloosa County Record Room helped me locate deeds. Meredith McLemore and Norwood A. Kerr, archivists at the Alabama Department of Archives and History (ADAH) in Montgomery, provided valuable assistance. Mary Beth Newbill at the Birmingham Public Library was cordial and responsive to my requests. My distant cousin A. J. Wright, associate professor and clinical librarian in the University of Alabama at Birmingham (UAB) School of Medicine, operated a listserv on Alabama history that was a source of many valuable leads. In Tuscaloosa, Katie Neidhardt of the University Club searched for a record of my grandfather's membership, and James and Wendy Tucker, the current owners of the house that Lyman and Margaret Findley built, graciously allowed me to photograph the cast-iron trim that was reinstalled there after the demolition of the Findley bungalow.

The following people were very helpful in arranging permanent homes for portraits and other artifacts of the Findleys: at the University of Alabama, Mary Bess Paluzzi, Charles E. Hilburn, assistant to the president, and Jessica Lacher-Feldman, curator of rare books and special collections; the Hon. Judge Scott Donaldson of the Sixth Judicial Circuit, Alabama; Linda L. Overman and Sherrie Hamil of ADAH; and Tim L. Pennycuff, assistant director of historical collections for the UAB Lister Hill Library.

I thank John Kvach and the members of the program committee for the Alabama Historical Association conference in 2012 for permitting me to give a paper about the conceptual basis for *Earline's Pink Party*. Joan Mitchell reviewed several draft chapters and made extremely helpful suggestions and corrections. Jane Hedrick Beachboard of Little Rock read the entire manuscript and gave me smart, frank advice that made it a much better book. She also shed light on Anne's piano lessons and combed old cookbooks to help me speculate on the canapés and sweets that Earline served at the Pink Party. Jane and her husband, James Paul Beachboard, encouraged my interest in material culture, particularly books and vernacular furniture; I am very happy that some of my grandfather Herbert's volumes of military and political history have a home in Jim's library. Adrienne Ames of Nashville, Tennessee, Melissa Macdougall of Valley Spring, Texas, Harriet Swift of New Orleans, Cheri Thriver of Little Rock, and Anneke Wambaugh of Seattle read portions of the manuscript, giving me feedback that was essential in making it a more coherent book.

My deepest thanks go to Donna Cox Baker and Daniel Waterman of the University of Alabama Press for their belief in *Earline's Pink Party*. The anonymous reviewers provided encouragement and excellent advice, particularly for the hierarchy of ideas in my conclusions about Earline's motivation. The editors Joanna Jacobs and Jenn Backer added immeasurably to the clarity of the manuscript. It should go without saying that although I have benefited from the help and advice of many individuals, all errors in *Earline's Pink Party* are my own.

The historian Johanna Miller Lewis of the University of Arkansas at Little Rock (UALR) introduced me to material culture studies in 1993. Two other historians at UALR, C. Fred Williams (1943–2013) and Stephen L. Recken (1947–2010), gently and persistently encouraged me to stop being an editor and start being an historian. I would not have found my way as a writer without them.

Earline Moore Findley's Family

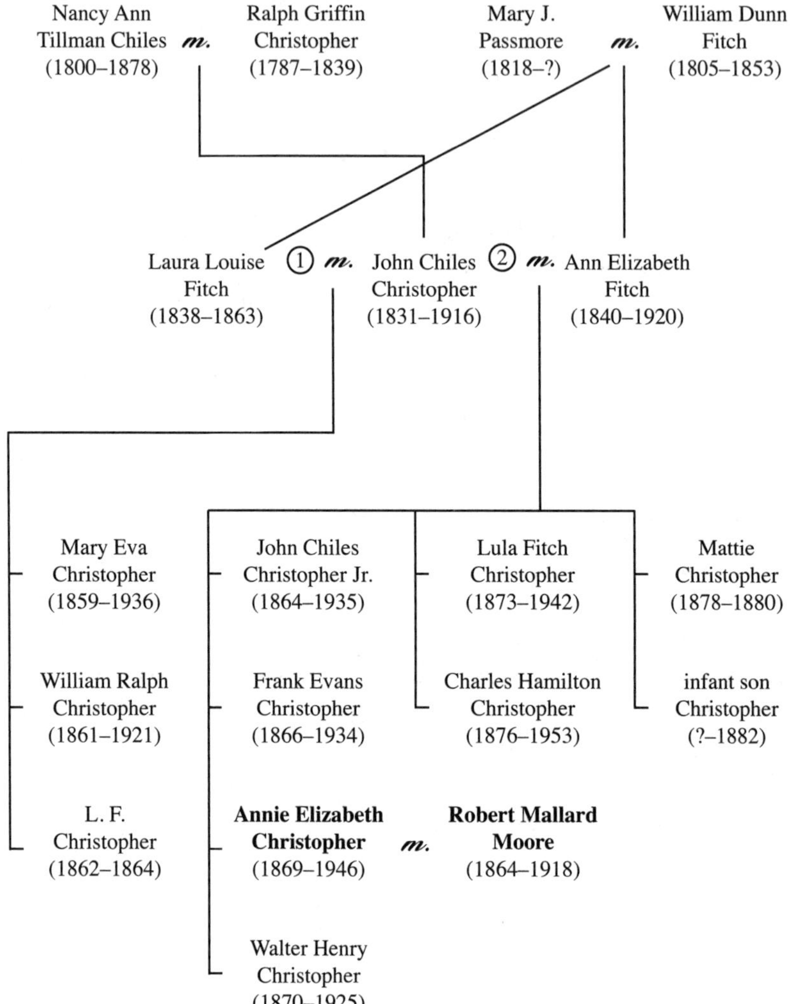

Family tree shows the two marriages of Earline Moore Findley's maternal grandfather John Chiles Christopher (upper left); the marriage of her parents, Annie Elizabeth Christopher and Robert Mallard Moore (boldface); and the early deaths of her great-aunt Laura Louise, her aunts and uncle L. F., Mattie, and an unnamed baby boy, and her brother Mallard Lester. (Design by Layet Johnson.)

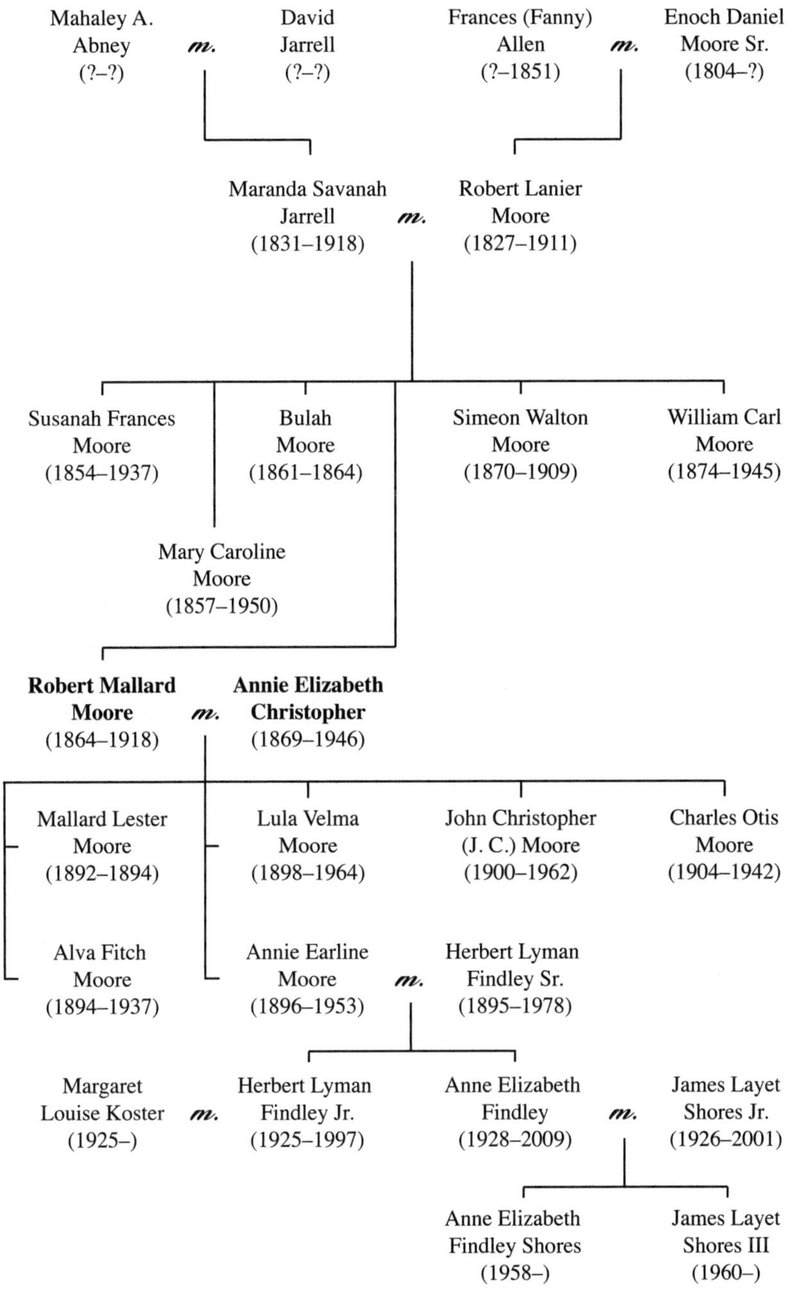

Mahaley A. Abney (?–?)
m.
David Jarrell (?–?)
Frances (Fanny) Allen (?–1851)
m.
Enoch Daniel Moore Sr. (1804–?)
Maranda Savanah Jarrell (1831–1918)
m.
Robert Lanier Moore (1827–1911)
Susanah Frances Moore (1854–1937)
Bulah Moore (1861–1864)
Simeon Walton Moore (1870–1909)
William Carl Moore (1874–1945)
Mary Caroline Moore (1857–1950)
Robert Mallard Moore (1864–1918)
m.
Annie Elizabeth Christopher (1869–1946)
Mallard Lester Moore (1892–1894)
Lula Velma Moore (1898–1964)
John Christopher (J. C.) Moore (1900–1962)
Charles Otis Moore (1904–1942)
Alva Fitch Moore (1894–1937)
Annie Earline Moore (1896–1953)
m.
Herbert Lyman Findley Sr. (1895–1978)
Margaret Louise Koster (1925–)
m.
Herbert Lyman Findley Jr. (1925–1997)
Anne Elizabeth Findley (1928–2009)
m.
James Layet Shores Jr. (1926–2001)
Anne Elizabeth Findley Shores (1958–)
James Layet Shores III (1960–)

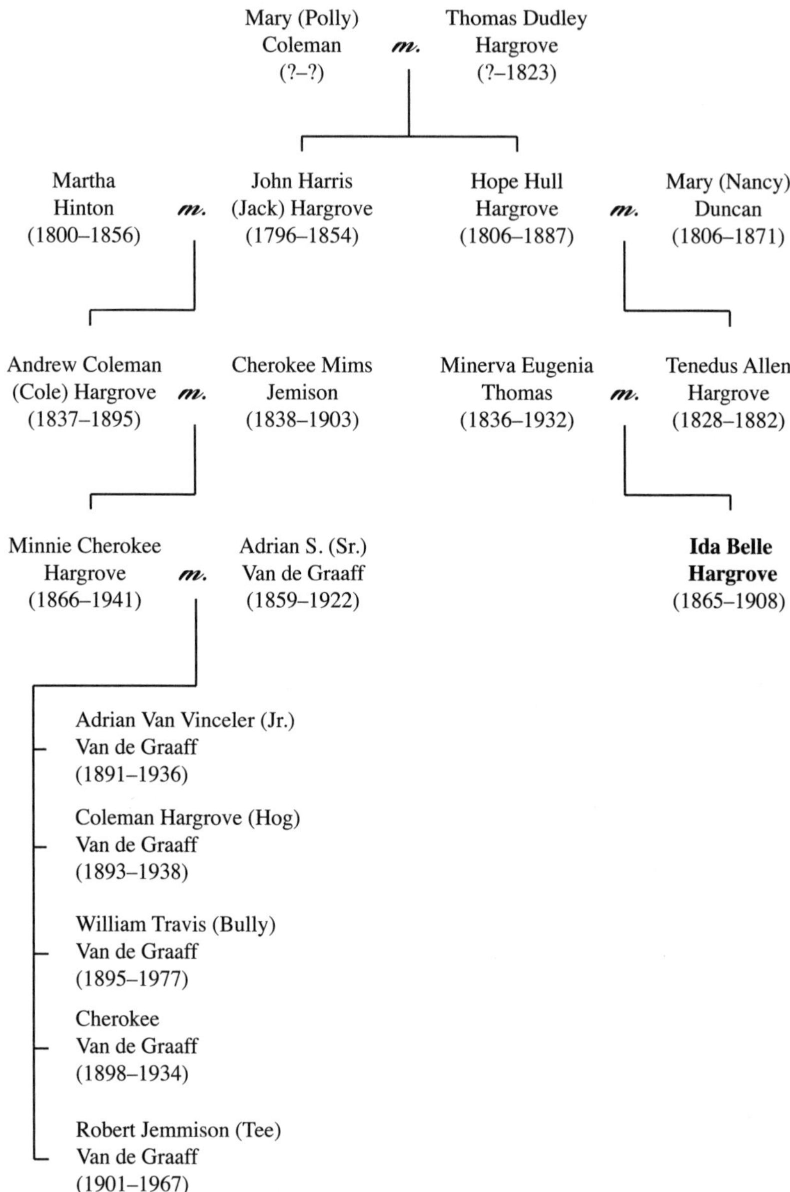

Family tree shows the marriage of Herbert Lyman Findley Sr.'s parents, Ida Belle Hargrove and Kenneth Murchison Findley Jr. (in boldface). (Design by Layet Johnson.)

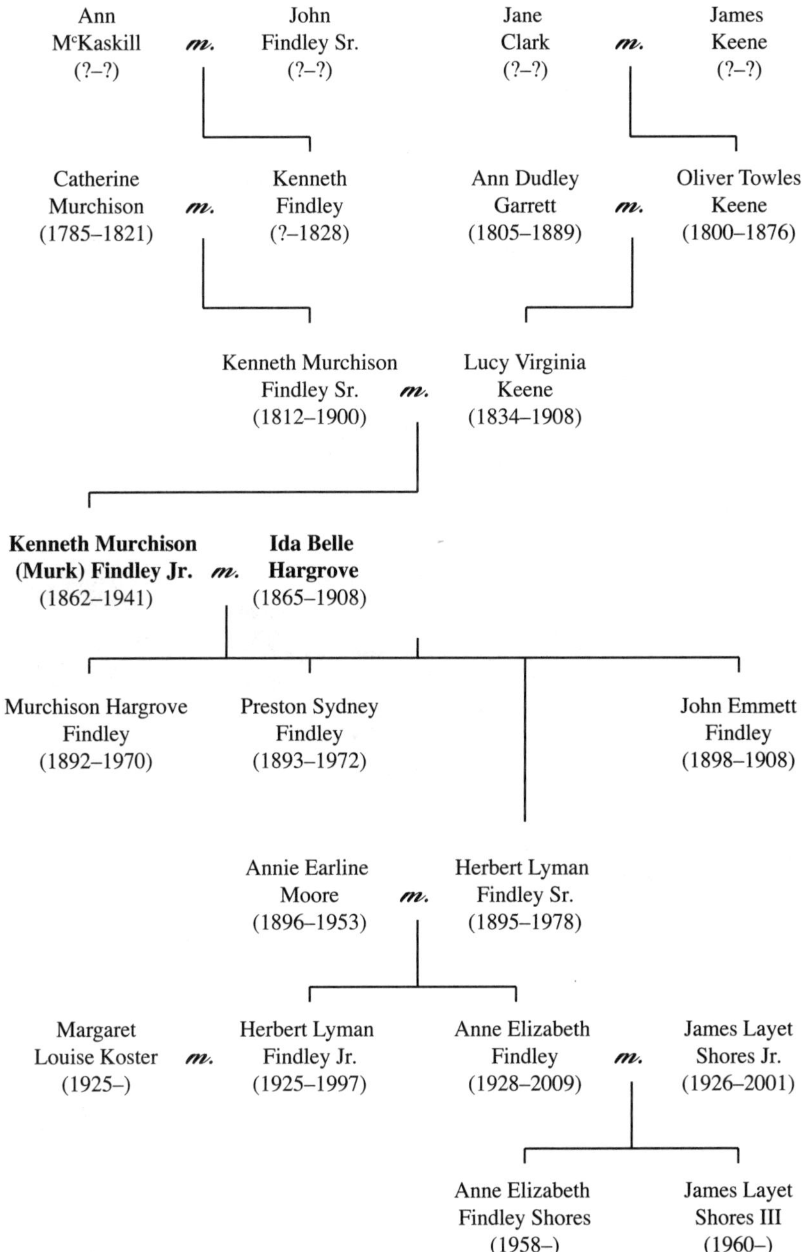

Ann McKaskill (?–?)
m.
John Findley Sr. (?–?)
Jane Clark (?–?)
m.
James Keene (?–?)
Catherine Murchison (1785–1821)
m.
Kenneth Findley (?–1828)
Ann Dudley Garrett (1805–1889)
m.
Oliver Towles Keene (1800–1876)
Kenneth Murchison Findley Sr. (1812–1900)
m.
Lucy Virginia Keene (1834–1908)
Kenneth Murchison (Murk) Findley Jr. (1862–1941)
m.
Ida Belle Hargrove (1865–1908)
Murchison Hargrove Findley (1892–1970)
Preston Sydney Findley (1893–1972)
John Emmett Findley (1898–1908)
Annie Earline Moore (1896–1953)
m.
Herbert Lyman Findley Sr. (1895–1978)
Margaret Louise Koster (1925–)
m.
Herbert Lyman Findley Jr. (1925–1997)
Anne Elizabeth Findley (1928–2009)
m.
James Layet Shores Jr. (1926–2001)
Anne Elizabeth Findley Shores (1958–)
James Layet Shores III (1960–)

Earline's World, Tuscaloosa, circa 1953

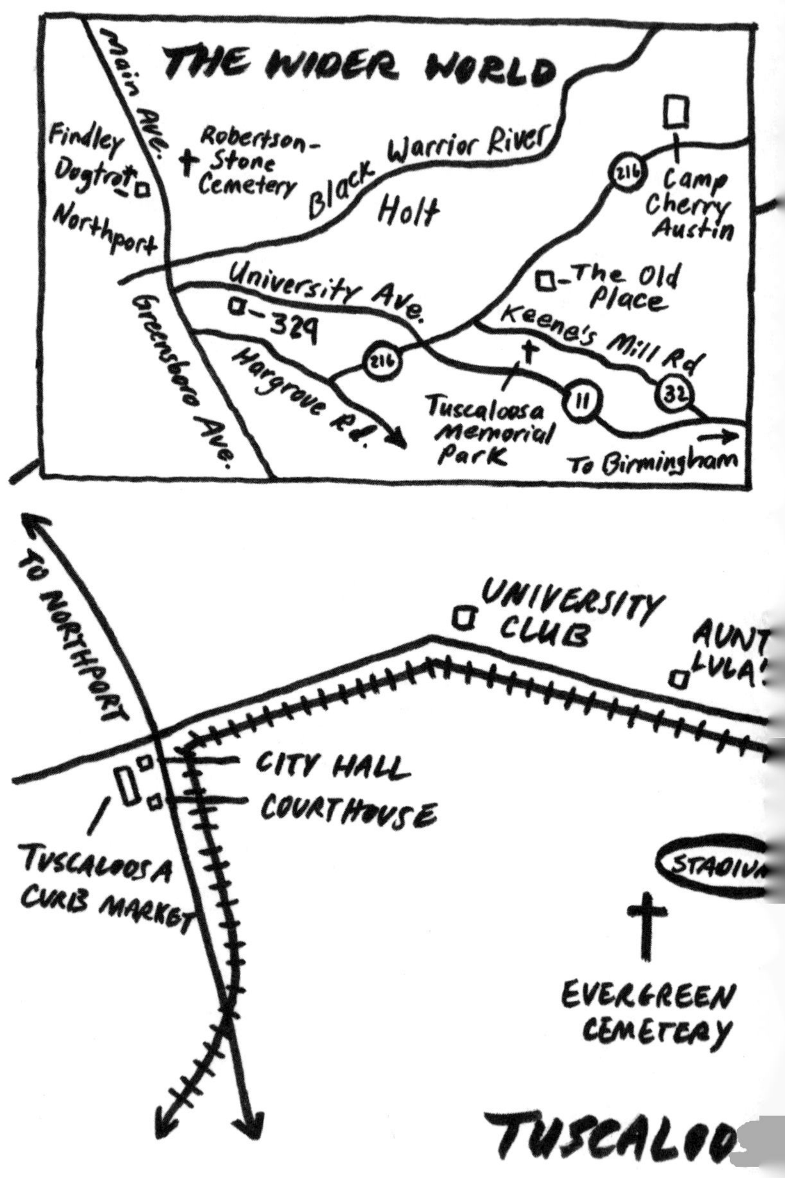

Sources: M. H. Findley, Map of Northport, Alabama (copy of unpublished original), 1919; A. C. Parker, Map of the City of Tuscaloosa, 1942; Branscomb Drive-It Co., University of Alabama (map), 1943; E. B. Thurston, City of Northport, Tuscaloosa County, Alabama (unpublished city plat map), 1946; R. V. Hawkins, Map of City of Tuscaloosa,

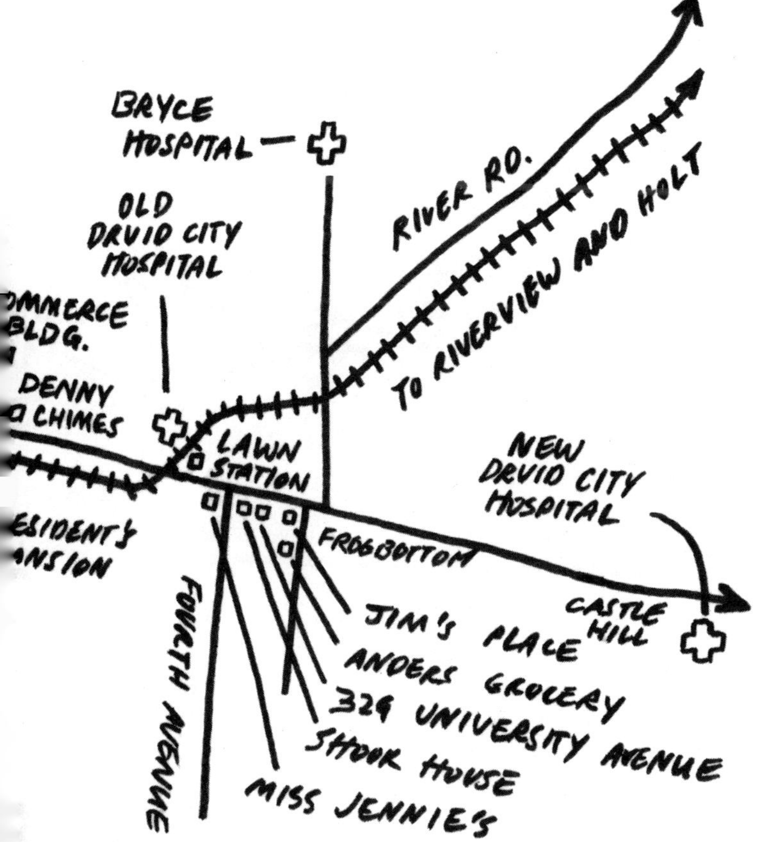

Tuscaloosa County, Alabama, 1957, all from University of Alabama Map Library, www.alabamamaps.ua.edu; U.S. Geological Survey, Tuscaloosa Quadrangle (map), 1926. (Map by Layet Johnson.)

Earline's Pink Party

Introduction

The Female Elemental

THIS IS THE SECOND BOOK TO GROW out of my study of my maternal grandparents' house in Tuscaloosa, Alabama. On each visit to that house, from the time I was permitted to roam the property on my own until it was demolished when I was fifteen, I explored almost every square foot, walking through the rooms and noticing changes, of which there were few. I went into the attic, discovering the handmade pasteboard models of houses that were the beginning of my biography of the botanist Roland McMillan Harper.[1] I inspected the yard, walkway, and porches of the neighboring house. At the time, I was reconnecting, literally, with the place that felt most like home, but in retrospect I was searching for a maternal figure, the grandmother who arranged the furnishings in the house and gardens outside and who died five years before I was born. Earline was absent but intensely, if for the most part silently, remembered. I rarely heard her mentioned, but we ate and talked and read and listened to the radio and watched the television and slept in spaces she created. The memory of her was in every cabinet and on every shelf, in the dishes we used and the sheets and towels that my grandfather's maid washed and hung on the backyard clothesline. Earline's oblong crystal bowl was always placed in the center of the dining table as if to remove it would be to remove her. Yet I had no memory of her.

Like Roland Harper, who was a roomer in the house during my mother's childhood, I hunted for wildflowers and tried to document them in a sketchpad with pencils and watercolors. Like Harper and my grandmother, I tried to create a house, using scraps of balsa wood that I salvaged from my brother's model airplane kits to make a tiny, square, one-room model. Working at a card table that I set up in my bedroom in Birmingham, I glued the scraps together in panels and cut the panels into four walls. After riding to the hobby shop on my bicycle to purchase tiny pots of paint, I added scenes of furniture and flower arrangements on the interior sides of the walls. I waited for the paint to dry, turned the panels over, and painted the exterior sides of the house, one with a front door. I made two more panels for a pitched roof and a final pair for the gables. It was a poor job and I did not make a second model house.

When my grandfather decided to move out of the Tuscaloosa bungalow, the family divided the contents of the house. My mother, Anne, moved most of her share to Birmingham, using some objects in the same ways her mother had—keeping stamps in a small writing box, placing two lavender lamps, a small vase hand-painted with violets, and a satin coverlet in her bedroom. She arranged some things in new ways, hanging her paternal grandfather's university diploma and T-square together in the hall. She hid an oil portrait of herself. By the time of our last visit to the bungalow before it was torn down, I had moved from drawing to photography as a way of emulating Dr. Harper, so I took my Kodak Pocket Instamatic to Tuscaloosa and took a few pictures of the exterior of the house. Then my mother, standing in the driveway beside me, suggested I stop. When it was time to move on, she said in her customary somber way, it was best to not look back. I stopped taking pictures and the only shot that turned out was a blurry image of a mockingbird perched on the roof, but I did not follow Anne's advice. In fact, her words made the sentimental aura of the doomed bungalow seem even more mysterious. I was determined to answer the question, what was she like? How did she view her world? The postmodernist philosopher Jean-François Lyotard advocated studying the lives of obscure individuals. As he would have asked, what was Earline's *petit récit*?[2]

Eventually Anne's Tuscaloosa heirlooms became mine and I incorporated them into my home, studying each piece as if I could find an explanation of Earline on the back of a painting or in the stitches of a half-completed crazy quilt. My aunt sent me a copy of an unpublished memoir, a series of short profiles of many of the lawyers in Tuscaloosa County by the late Artemas K. "Temo" Callahan, a fiddle-playing, square dance–calling lawyer and off-and-on legislator in Tuscaloosa who was a few years younger than my grandfather. Later, I began reading current magazines about interior decoration to learn more about that subject. Opening an issue of *House Beautiful* one month, I found a brief interview of a New York designer named Temo Callahan. How extraordinary this was! He described his bedroom as "a comforting cave" and mentioned the sheets he inherited from a relative. I learned that he was indeed the son of Temo Callahan the lawyer and had once written a letter to the *Tuscaloosa News* suggesting the town name a bridge for the enslaved bridge-builder Horace King.[3] This seemed to be a sign. Perhaps my idea of exploring the interior and grounds of a nonexistent house for clues about my long-dead grandmother's take on race relations was not completely far-fetched.

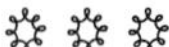

Annie Earline Moore Findley led an ordinary life in western Alabama, becoming a teacher and marrying a man with a modestly aristocratic lineage. She raised their children in a home on one of Tuscaloosa's main thoroughfares. Because she could employ some domestic help, she enjoyed leisure time that she used to create beautiful clothes and costumes for her children, to prepare special desserts, and to decorate the family home. Earline was, as the historian Catherine M. Howett described a wealthier and more prominent North Carolina matron, "a woman of the American South . . . who . . . devoted herself—as did most women of her class and place—to home, family, church, and community." The scholarship on the American South is deep and wide, but there has been relatively little attention paid to the day-to-day lives, much less the perspective and motivation, of women like Earline.[4] To understand her as an example of these women is challenging because she left very little in the way of a written record of her ideas and feelings: brief captions beneath a few photographs, recipes scribbled on the backs of envelopes, and short notes to her daughter Anne.[5] Although she was a schoolteacher for a few years, Earline was not an adept writer, misspelling simple words and friends' names. Even if she had kept a diary throughout her life, it is not likely that she would have recorded her sentiments on the civil rights movement or any other controversial subject, for the most powerful commandment for elite white women like Earline was to "be nice." Instead, Earline usually wrote to Anne about the matters that were significant to her: domestic tasks such as sewing and supervising the maids and gardener; social activities; the cattle husbandry her husband undertook after he retired; and, most notably, her fear that Anne would contract polio.

Because Earline wrote so little, the books on her shelves, the pictures on her walls, the passed-down furniture, relics of her mother-in-law, textiles and tableware, the photographs and newspaper clippings that the family saved, the objects that Earline herself made, and even her decorative color schemes must serve as clues to her view of the southern world. Her life remains "manifest," as the anthropologist Elizabeth Hallam and the sociologist Jenny Hockey might put it, in the furniture and decorative objects that her survivors saved, but her placement of those objects over time gave them greater meaning. Her house was both her work, as she was responsible for its appearance and upkeep, and her world, the setting for rituals of family and social life—in the words of Hallam and Hockey, her "emotional realm." "Decorating" was a pejorative term when early feminist scholars regarded women's domestic lives merely as evidence of sexual oppression, but by the 1990s some scholars began to reconsider the decorative arts, recognizing that the choices women made, particularly in creating the domestic interior, reflected their view of the exterior world. The historian Thomas J. Schlereth, one of the founders of American material culture studies, proposed that the home is "a complicated environment of social behavior," an "artifact of artifacts embodying interactions between genders, classes, and generations." The art historian Kenneth L. Ames, another leading scholar of material culture, advised that furnished homes, "as a genre of artifacts[, are] likely to give us access to the female elemental" and that domestic activities "like making music and needlework [are not] incidental or trivial, but central and important." The paths and plantings outside a house are evidence too of what Pierce Lewis called "a form of cultural autobiography." The folklorist Michael Owen Jones declared "personal decoration of space" a genre of folklore, arguing that creative domestic activities reflect the maker's *response* to her physical environment and her relationships. We must look, Jones suggested, for the homemaker's "motivations for creating things." The cultural historian Bernard L. Herman drew on Claude Levi-Strauss's concept of "the *bricoleur,* the archetypal putterer with a message," to understand assemblages of objects in situ. Our responsibility, according to Herman, is to "render observations of the ordinary into explanatory narrative." Regrettably, for the purposes of this study, Earline's house is not whole. To explore her psyche, then, we must reconstruct her world, reading the "text between the lines" of her vanished home, as the cultural historian Peter Burke advised, noting particularly the changes that she made to her house and garden over time because, as Jones argued, a person's choices in *redesigning* personal space may reflect a need for "a sense of authority and degree of control," or even the role she sought, revealing "what one thinks one is or wishes one were or hopes others think one is."[6]

The second category of evidence about Earline's life is documentary.

Many of the public records I cite are available in digital archives. Except where noted, genealogical data was found on Ancestry.com. Newspaper articles that the Findleys clipped indicate their civic and social interests.[7] The *Tuscaloosa News* minutely reported the activities of elite white women during the decades when Earline lived in Tuscaloosa, making it the richest primary source about her family and social circle. While I was conducting the research for this book, a digital archive of the *Tuscaloosa News*, from the July 1, 1929, issue to the present, was available online. As important, the *Tuscaloosa News* was the primary source of information *for* Earline and her friends, the subject as well as the medium. The newspaper was not merely a mirror of local culture but a performer and director in its continual enactment.[8] For example, in 1933, a writer for the paper referred to little girls at a birthday party as "future belles."[9] Thus, the *Tuscaloosa News* is a deep well of information about the events and people that interested Earline.[10] Another fascinating newspaper source was a series of articles by two architecture scholars engaged by the Historic American Buildings Survey (HABS), a federal initiative during the Great Depression, to document antebellum houses in Alabama. Their articles demonstrate some of the preoccupations of elite white women in twentieth-century Alabama, particularly their interest in domestic interiors.[11] For describing Earline's visual environment, that survey, other archives of historic photographs, and the University of Alabama digital archive Alabama Maps were crucial.

Several social scientists conducted detailed studies of particular communities in Alabama and Mississippi during Earline's lifetime. For example, the anthropologist Morton Rubin studied the upper-middle class in Wilcox County, Alabama—people who lived in the same neighborhoods as the upper class and might marry into that class if they possessed enough "physical attractiveness[,] manners, education, family background, [and] property." Rubin found the upper-middle-class housewife "supervises cooks and nurses and yardboys; she shops downtown . . . to visit with friends and to 'see what is going on.'" The husbands tended to participate in politics, the wives in Sunday school and church circles. The women might join a lineage organization such as the United Daughters of the Confederacy (UDC), which raises an interesting question about Earline that we shall consider later.[12] Allison Davis and Burleigh and Mary Gardner made similar observations in Natchez, Mississippi. White middle-class wives spent their weekday afternoons in "recreation with other wives" and "participate[d] in associations, church clubs, and informal group activities. . . . Wives of Masons usually join[ed] the Eastern Star; wives of American Legionnaires, the Legion Auxiliary." Davis and the Gardners characterized the social network of white middle-class couples as a "clique. . . . To be accepted they must behave according to the standards of the group."[13] Two other investigators, Hortense Powdermaker and John Dollard, studied Indianola, Mississippi.[14] It is from these and other scholars' work that I know Earline was typical of white women in the upper-middle class. The writer James Agee and photographer Walker Evans were participant-observers of another kind; their impressionistic records of poor tenant families in Hale County, south of Tuscaloosa, provide a different view of the cultural landscape that Earline occupied.[15]

Family Bibles, with blank pages for recording births, marriages, and deaths, provide many clues about family history.[16] The Christopher family Bible, which Earline's maternal grandparents apparently purchased around the time of their first child's birth, was a large, leather-bound 1864 edition.[17] Someone began the records on the "Births" page with Earline's maternal great-grandparents, "R. G. Christopher" and "Ann T. Christopher." Other sources show that "R. G." was Ralph Griffin Christopher, a minister and physician with a background of colonial ancestors in Virginia. He married Nancy Ann Tillman Chiles, or "Ann T.," and they migrated to Alabama in 1823, around the same time as Nancy Ann's parents, some of her siblings, and possibly some of the Chiles family's slaves.[18] The Chiles-Christopher family was solidly part of the small-planter class on Alabama's frontier.[19] With Griffin at various times preaching and practicing medicine as well as farming, the family lived in Greensboro (Hale County) and then in a community in Choctaw County known as Harris Crossroads, Barbour, and finally DeSotoville,[20] where the Methodist church, Christopher Chapel, was named for him. In Greensboro, their neighbor Sarah Haynesworth Gayle marveled at Griffin's "fine, full voice!" when he officiated at the home funeral for "Mrs. Clarke's little baby" in 1827: "He gradually [sang] louder, and louder, until the words were lost in the harmony of sound, while the female voices rose softly and clearly, as if below him, somewhere."[21] Child and maternal deaths were a fact of life in antebellum Alabama. So much could go wrong during the perinatal period, killing mother, infant, or both. Inexperienced physicians or midwives might use unclean instruments or excessive force to pull infants from their mothers, dismembering the babies. Women could die from puerperal fever, which no one knew how to prevent. Yellow fever, cholera, diphtheria, dysentery, smallpox, and typhoid fever killed many children.[22]

The faint, spidery writing in the record pages of the Christopher Bible shows that, like the grieving Mrs. Clarke, generation after generation of Christopher women suffered the deaths of young children. Griffin and Nancy Ann's last two children apparently died when they were five and four years old.[23] The first wife of their son John Chiles, Laura Louise Fitch, died soon after the birth of her third child. John next married Laura's sister Ann Elizabeth Fitch, who took up the care of her sister's children and probably purchased the Bible. Then Laura's third child died, no more than twenty-four months old and remembered only as "L. F.," the same year that Ann Elizabeth had her first baby.[24] Ann Elizabeth and John had five more children including Earline's mother, Annie Elizabeth, but their two youngest babies also died, the only evidence of their lives a few faint pencil lines in the margin of the Bible records, written in a different hand as if Ann Elizabeth was too cautious to record her children's births before they passed their second birthdays and too grief-stricken to note their deaths. She could have still been in mourning for her fifth child when the sixth died. She also may have had lingering health problems; many women in nineteenth-century Alabama suffered chronic illnesses as they bore child after child. As Earline's mother came of age, witness to her mother's pregnancies and the deaths of her youngest siblings, fears of pregnancy, childbirth, and disease pervaded the rural South.[25] Annie's sister-in-law Viola had lost an infant son and while Annie was pregnant her half sister Mary Eva lost her sixth child, an eighteen-month-old boy.[26] Then Annie's own first baby died. These experiences must have affected Annie's ability to mother her surviving children, including Earline. Some mothers expressed "calm resignation" when their children died while others retreated into long periods of melancholy and seclusion. Some delayed naming their children for fear they would not live long.[27] We find our first clue to Earline's interior life in the family's record of death and fear.

In addition to artifacts and documentary sources, the third major category of evidence about Earline's world is memories. They include ex-slave narratives that provide the attitudes of African Americans who lived around her. As for memories of Earline and her family, the passed-down stories that I heard—some as a child and some after beginning this study—are clues about the facts of family history, but more importantly they suggest how the members of her family *regarded* the past. The historian Elizabeth H. Pleck characterized "the telling of the family story" as a "commemorative act,"[28] but commemoration is not always accurate. A story that my grandfather

Herbert Lyman Findley Sr. repeated, of a state senator's fight against secession, is an example of the pitfall of memory. In my hazy recollection, Herbert spoke of Robert Jemison Jr. as he would a relative. Perhaps he felt related to Jemison because Jemison had a hand in building the Findley home known as Riverview, or because Herbert's relative Andrew Coleman "Cole" Hargrove married Jemison's daughter, or for both reasons. At any rate, I did not realize the figure who opposed secession was not actually a relative until I began this research. In these pages, I try to tease apart fact and meaning in this and other family stories and ponder why I heard so few about Earline's forebears.

Even more so than my memories of family stories, my memories of Earline's house have been crucial for envisioning her world. Fortunately, my aunt Margaret Koster Findley confirmed or corrected my recollections, elaborating on some. Throughout this book, where I describe or refer to family stories and to the fixtures or contents of the house and grounds without any attribution, I have relied on my own memory. My version of Earline's home is like a memory painting—not, I hope, too sentimental a view but one that resists, as the art scholar Roger Cardinal put it, "the temptation to prettify the past, [that] turns an honest and unblinking eye upon remembered scenes."[29]

At the time Earline was growing up, purveyors of an imaginary Old South created a fantastical canon that dominated cultural ideas and values.[30] Parthenia Hague recalled "the faint tinkle of bells as 'the lowing' herds wound 'slowly o'er the lea,'" wondering "if any part of the world could be more beautiful." In 1905, when Earline was nine years old, Virginia Clay-Clopton wrote that Tuscaloosa in the 1830s was a "bucolic" place; Anna M. Gayle Fry wrote in 1908 of a plantation with a "long lane of three miles bordered on each side by a tall rail fence and shaded occasionally by peach trees, which in springtime presented a pretty picture—the brilliant pink blossoms [and] the green, waving corn." The literary scholar Lucinda H. MacKethan called this romantic vision of antebellum life the South's "favorite illusion."[31] As Earline became a teacher, the UDC encouraged its members to write their own reminiscences "of faithful slaves," publishing those pieces in an anthology that went through six printings in the 1920s.[32] Other writers produced fiction in the tradition of the wildly popular nineteenth-century novelist Sir Walter Scott.[33] One of the key fictional works in the fantastical canon was Thomas Nelson Page's *Social Life in Old Virginia before the War*, published the year after Earline was born. Page and writers like him, born into the pre-Emancipation elite or descended from it, invented a tradition of southern noblesse oblige, entrancing their readers with the idea that by forcing former slaves back into economic serfdom, the white ruling class restored balance in the southern world.[34]

Through the first half of the twentieth century—Earline's lifetime—historians contributed to this illusion. The Georgian Ulrich Bonnell Phillips advanced the idea that slavery was mutually beneficial for whites and blacks.[35] The leading historian of Alabama, Walter L. Fleming, similarly characterized slavery as a happy time for African Americans: "The sound of fiddle and banjo, songs and laughter was always heard in the 'quarters.' . . . The slaves were on the whole happy and content." Although most white historians of Fleming's time admired him as an outstanding scholar, the black historian W. E. B. Du Bois called Fleming's work "pure propaganda."[36] Earline was personally acquainted with another historian who was an apologist for slavery in Alabama. James Benson Sellers was her principal when she was a schoolteacher. He left school administration to earn a PhD in history from the University of North Carolina, returned to Tuscaloosa County in 1943 to teach at the University of Alabama, and the next year was appointed a steward of Earline's church, just a few years after Earline's husband held the same position. Sellers produced monographs on the history of their church, the university, and Prohibition in the state, but his major work was *Slavery in Alabama*. As a later Alabama historian, Harriet E. Amos Doss, noted, Sellers perpetuated the idea of Phillips and Fleming that slave owners treated their slaves well. "When old age came," Sellers wrote, "most plantation Negroes could count on being pensioned and allowed to live out their lives without working as part of the plantation family."[37]

To argue that elite white women in the South collaborated with mythmakers to perpetuate the fantasy of southern nobility, some scholars adopted the idea, which the sociologist Erving Goffman introduced in 1959, that individuals tend to perform roles in social rituals.[38] For example, the textile scholar Shirley Pribbenow Foster commented that antebellum white women in Tuscaloosa County were "trained like actors for, literally, the role of a lifetime," and the seminal scholar of southern memory, W. Fitzhugh Brundage, called southern white social rituals "memory theater." In this interpretation, the upper classes before and after Emancipation used rituals to continually reassert the rightness of southern society's archetypal roles.[39]

In the first of those roles, the Anglo-Saxon white master ruled the southern world.[40] The more slaves he owned, the more powerful he was.[41] He governed his domain with chivalry and justice, "treating the negroes well," according to Fleming, and bestowing gifts upon them[42] and, as Earline's principal James Sellers emphasized, providing them with homes and food even when they were too old to work. The historian H. E. Sterkx found that magical thinking about masters became embedded in Alabama during the Civil War.[43] The actual defeat of the Confederacy did not diminish the white master's rule. To the contrary, his descent from slaveholders practically assured his ongoing social prominence and civic and economic power. The notion that Old South planter families were the nobility of the American slave economy justified the entire post-Emancipation economic and political structure. Ruling-class white men regained power over local economies and society by entering manufacturing, banking, and the professions, activities that gave them the same aura of gentility and power that slaveholding did previously. Rubin described a twentieth-century planter as "the absolute ruler of his little empire . . . by virtue of his economic wealth, social prestige, political power, educational background, and intellectual achievement and know-how," an aristocrat because of his lineage of earlier wealthy planters.[44] "The assumption persists," the journalist W. J. Cash observed in 1941, "that the great South . . . was the home of a genuine and fully realized aristocracy."[45] A judgeship, empowering the post-Emancipation white man to interpret laws and rule on the fates of individuals and even entire families, was most like the role of antebellum planter. Indeed, lawyers in Alabama tended to run for elected judgeships as much for the honorific of "Judge" as for the salary.[46]

The archetypal white mistress bore the next generation of noble southerners while engaging in elaborate hospitality rituals to help maintain her family's status. Consider, for example, the stories of Anna Fry, who described house parties in her memoir of antebellum life, providing the barest possible hint of the slave labor that made the parties possible. While the men roamed the countryside, inspecting crops or on a foxhunt, the hostess saw that her female guests, each "tastefully dressed in the fashion of the day[, their] smooth, beautifully braided hair (which . . . required a full hour for a maid to arrange)[,] spent the morning hours . . . in reading, conversation, or fine needlework."[47] The third archetypal player, the planter's daughter, was the axis of the slaveholding class. Nursed and nurtured by slave women but trained in the social graces by her mother, she was the means by which her father could strengthen and expand his financial legacy because her marriage into an equally wealthy and aristocratic family ensured that the next generation of children would inherit twice as much wealth and social status.[48] The daughter had to be an attractive marriage prospect, so she was alluring, but she had to be selective, so she was coquettish. She was the star of every social event, the centerpiece of every scene. As young women married sons of planters, they were transformed into archetypal plantation mistresses; thus the cycle of southern life went on. From such daughters, Page created the archetypal belle, "a creature of peach-blossom and snow."[49] Historians have demonstrated that, like the other southern archetypes, the belle was based on a genuine type in southern society. Anne Firor Scott described the belle's central importance: a young woman was expected to be "the most fascinating being in creation." Beauty was necessary for a great match, but if she was not naturally beautiful, she could compensate with charm and accomplishments such as playing the piano. Carol K. Bleser and Frederick M. Heath observed that belles "were sought after by men, both young and old, who expected them to be pretty, unmarried, affluent, charming, fashionable, and flirtatious." Giselle Roberts found a standard of great beauty truly existed in antebellum culture, quoting one young woman who "was obsessed with what she considered her 'ugliness' and declared that she knew all too well that 'ugly people are not liked'" and another who "was perfectly shocked to read that her sister had gained weight[, writing,] 'Emma it's horrible the way you increase in weight. . . . A short fat woman is awful.'"[50] Here, in the cruel, relentless pressure to be beautiful, we have the second clue to Earline's perspective and motivation.

The last figure in the quartet of archetypes was the servant who, if he was wise, convinced his master that he enjoyed his place in the southern world order. Goffman called "the ignorant, shiftless, happy-go-lucky" affectation of African Americans in the modern South "a performance," and many historians have applied this performative interpretation to the interactions between slaveholder and slave. Bertram Wyatt-Brown referred to the "mask of obedience." David Goldfield described the "stage Negro" who pretended to be "childlike" in ritual encounters with whites. Concerning weddings that some slaveholders staged for slaves, Pleck noted that all of the players recognized the ceremonies were not genuine: "No matter how lavish, the ritual offered no guarantee of permanence and none of the rights of legitimacy of offspring and guardianship of children that legal marriage provided." David W. Blight concluded that although some former slaves certainly were steadfast employees and even ancillary members of the white family, the fantastical view of the pre-Emancipation South overlooked "the 'defections' or 'betrayals' of . . . trusted slaves." The reality that African Americans sought escape from slavery was "lost to near oblivion in white memory." In their place, the happy servant emerged in the "Southern imagination."[51] John Massey of Choctaw County, a contemporary of Earline's grandfather John Christopher, recalled a man named John who usually assisted white men and boys on hunts. "We called him 'Kimbo,'" Massey wrote, with no explanation for this nickname. John "was a good man" who "took as much care of us as if we had been his own children," Massey added, with no apparent recognition that in a genuine child-parent relationship, the child would not address the parent by a name such as "Kimbo." Being acquainted with John was the experience that "began my friendship for the negroes," Massey reminisced, revealing, in his final words on the kindly Kimbo, the performative nature of John's conduct on those hunts: "The negro has wonderful power to attach himself to the white man when he chooses to exercise it."[52]

Married to a minor local judge who resisted civil rights for African Americans, Earline was part of what the historian Fred Arthur Bailey called a "patrician cult," one of the "ruling white oligarchs of the South," to use the journalist John Egerton's term. The cheap labor of the black underclass made possible virtually every aspect of her privileged existence. She was the kind of elite white woman whose activities reflect, in Brundage's view, a fundamental commitment to preserving segregation.[53] Her life was bracketed by the two definitive judicial rulings in the history of American racial segregation, *Plessy v. Ferguson* (1896) and *Brown v. Board of Education of Topeka* (1954). In *Plessy*, the US Supreme Court upheld separate accommodations for black and white rail passengers, finding they did not "stamp . . . the colored race with a badge of inferiority." This ruling was the foundation for legal segregation of public facilities throughout the South. The Findley family's naming practices, the meals Earline planned, the clothes she made, the books she read and the music she enjoyed, her gardening and decorating choices, and her participation in church and civic groups all can be interpreted as cultural acts intended to preserve the fantastical status quo and thus preserve segregation. Not until thirteen months after her death did the Supreme Court strike down the *Plessy* "separate but equal" doctrine, directly attacking, in *Brown*, the southern way of life by ruling unanimously that separate schools were "inherently unequal." One of the justices was an Alabamian, Hugo Black, who shook off the segregationist beliefs of his upbringing as neither Earline nor her husband ever did.[54]

The "inter-racial situation," the anthropologist Hortense Powdermaker observed, pervaded "every aspect of life for every individual of the community," yet to actually *refer* to racial subjugation was in poor taste so the best performers never acknowledged the divide in what the cultural historian Robin Bernstein called "the performance of not-noticing."[55] The problem with this performative interpretation of the elite white woman in the post-Emancipation South is that if she never acknowledged her performance, how are we to know whether she was acting? Was Earline a willing actor or a witless puppet in the continual enactment of the Old South fantasy? Did she accept that "Lost Cause religion," to use the term coined by the historian Charles Reagan Wilson?[56] Did she truly believe in the vision of "early Alabama life [and] a great white house set in widening grounds" of which Virginia Clay-Clopton wrote?[57] This is my second question about Earline, the same one Goffman raised about any individual who attempts to project an identity she has chosen: Was she "fully taken in" by her role as gracious mistress, or did she recognize that she was performing?[58] If the latter, did she realize that the servants also were performing, and if she knew the servants only pretended to be grateful, did she nonetheless feel that her world was safe and beautiful? In her monumental work *Within the Plantation Household: Black and White Women of the Old South*, the historian Elizabeth Fox-Genovese made explicit value judgments about Sarah Gayle, the Alabama woman who was a neighbor and friend of Earline's great-grandparents. Gayle's "finest qualities," Fox-Genovese wrote, "cannot be divorced from her willing complicity in a social system that permitted her to flourish through the enslavement of others. . . . Her experience and perceptions as a woman depended upon the social system in which she lived."[59] In confronting the life of my maternal grandmother, I can do no less than Fox-Genovese. Earline was a party to the systematic post-Emancipation subjugation of African Americans, a beneficiary of the terrorism that imprisoned many black day laborers almost as much as if they were slaves. But merely to brand Earline a racist, even to describe the entire history of our family's involvement with slavery and segregation, is not to understand *how* any such woman could occupy an ugly, dangerous world without trying to change it. As we will see, some privileged white women and men in Earline's world stood up to racial tyranny. My third fundamental question is: Why didn't she?

Looking into the life of my grandmother opens a new window on the interior lives of privileged white women in the South of the twentieth century.[60] By examining objects from the bungalow and connecting them to my memories, we can move through Earline's world, entering the living room as her guests did, seeing her assemblages of furniture and decorative objects in her beloved pink-and-green color scheme. We can pass through the hallway to the bedrooms and kitchen that were the heart of her home. One of the artifacts that I inherited was Earline's cookbook, including some recipes she wrote by hand and tucked between the pages, some with the notation that they came from "Hatchett." Learning Hatchett's identity and exploring their relationship pointed me to one of the most horrific periods in Tuscaloosa's history of racial terrorism, showing just how close Earline lived to the edge of madness, violence, and death.

One

Unpainted Houses

THE EARLIEST ARTIFACTS OF EARLINE MOORE'S childhood in Choctaw County are two photographs of her and her siblings that probably were taken at their home in the small community of Jachin around 1901 and 1905. At the time, door-to-door photographers traveled over country roads, stopping at houses to offer family portraits. The appearance of a photographer was an important event in the life of a rural family, encompassing the novelty of the stranger's arrival and his mysterious equipment, the ritual of posing during a twenty-second exposure, and the opportunity to preserve an image of the family and send copies to faraway relatives. Mothers dressed their children carefully and arranged them as if they were posing for a painted portrait.[1] For the first Moore photograph, four children sat on the front steps of an unpainted wooden house. Alva wore a short dark suit and held the baby, John Christopher, upright on the step above him. The girls, Earline and Velma, wore white dresses and dark stockings and boots. Both had blonde hair that had been parted in the middle and styled in ringlets with bows. Each girl held a flower. Velma ducked her head slightly and sucked a thumb. Earline stared at the photographer without smiling, her feet together and hands in her lap. In the background, a woman stood on the porch, only her feet and skirt visible in the photograph, a pile of linens or clothing on a rocking chair. In the later photograph, Alva, J. C., Earline, and Velma stood on the porch, Earline in the center and holding the new baby, Otis, so he would not fall from his perch on a box. The girls' hair had become dark.[2]

As the older daughter in a household with little domestic help, Earline often had to watch the younger children, making sure babies did not roll off a bed and toddlers did not bump against the hot stove. To escape the heat, noise, and chores inside the house, she must have sometimes slipped out to the front porch. This was farm and timber country, traversed by wagon or carriage over poor roads past fields and barren expanses of longleaf pine stumps, the roads so rutted from heavy log wagons, and so slick after a rain, they sometimes were impassable.[3] Oxen and mules pulled the wagons around the bend and out of sight, bells jingling, wheels creaking, the animals' droppings quickly attracting flies in their dusty wake. Cicadas thrummed loudly and fields of corn, cotton, and sweet potatoes, a landscape of nothingness, blended into the blinding blue sky.[4]

Magazines and catalogs encouraged women to beautify the inside of their homes,[5] but there are no clues to the interior of Earline's childhood home. Her paternal uncles' homes, however, were modest. Will Moore and his wife, Bettie, lived near Jachin in an unpainted frame house that sat on brick piers in a bare dirt yard. He farmed on some of the Moore family property and raised hogs and kept a cow, a calf, and a couple of horses in a rough pen and barn. Bettie tended chickens, did the housework, and sold hats and bonnets.[6] Since Will and Bettie apparently worked all of the time to make ends meet, they probably did not have luxurious furnishings. Sim Moore and his wife also lived in an unpainted house, a dogtrot cabin constructed of longleaf pine that smelled of oozing sap.[7] The lack of paint on the three Moore brothers' houses was a clear sign of their low economic and social status. From the beginning of white settlement in the Old South, paint on the exterior of a white family's house was an important symbol, as essential as a second story and a front porch for signifying the family's achievements.[8] Whitewash on slave dwellings had been a symbol of the order and control that slaveholders tried to maintain;[9] white paint on the homes of emancipated African Americans signified a higher social class within black society.[10] Clement Wood, an Alabama writer, evoked Camelot in describing the first view that newly emancipated African Americans had of painted houses in Birmingham, "houses such as they had never seen in the Black Belt; not so grand as the big houses of the masters, and yet white and clean . . . perched up on whitewashed stilts along the mountain-side."[11] Although Earline's mother, Annie Elizabeth Christopher Moore, did her best to present her children as well kept and fashionable for the porch photographs, she could not change the significance of the unpainted exterior of their home.

☼ ☼ ☼

Like the Christophers, Annie's in-laws maintained a Bible with genealogical information that Annie, who outlived her husband by almost thirty years, left to Earline.[12] Earline's children shared the Moore Bible, her son and his wife carefully transcribing the information in it for the benefit of genealogists, her daughter keeping it in a family secretary at her house in Birmingham. The earliest entries suggest that Enoch Daniel Moore and Frances Allen "Fanny" Moore purchased the Bible shortly before they migrated from North Carolina to Alabama in 1836. Settling near the Christophers, they joined a Baptist church but Enoch worked with Griffin Christopher's son-in-law to build the DeSotoville Male and Female Academy for white children in the vicinity.[13] The Moores' son Lanier grew up to live a life like his father's, farming and becoming a deacon. He joined Griffin's son John in the Fraternal Order of Masons, a national organization that functioned as a network of social and business contacts invaluable for men looking for a step up in society. Lanier married Maranda Savanah Jarrell, a daughter of landed slaveholders who belonged to Christopher Chapel. They had six children including Robert Mallard. Neighbors regarded Lanier as a good citizen, if rather inflexible, one admirer calling him "a man of strong personality[,] upright in life, chaste in his conversation."[14]

Three of Annie's brothers became physicians and her half sister, Mary Eva Christopher, married a man with an aristocratic background who also was a physician,[15] but Annie apparently did not have the same romantic options. She and Mallard probably attended the DeSotoville school together; it was so near the Christopher home, her parents rented rooms to students from outside the area.[16] A portrait of Mallard as a young adult shows that his most noticeable physical feature was an offset right eye, which he tried to counter with a full moustache, fastidiously combed hair, and dapper clothes, but his overall effect must have been negligible because two different chroniclers of the Christophers reported no information about Mallard even as they extensively described the spouses of Annie's siblings.[17] Mallard's mother's membership in Christopher Chapel and his father's standing in Lodge #178 probably helped make the match acceptable to the Christophers. He and Annie were married in 1891, about two weeks before her twenty-third birthday.[18] When their first child was born the next year, Annie and Mallard named him Mallard Lester.

Mallard received a federal appointment as the postmaster of a new post office near Clear Creek in 1894. He named the post office Jachin, a name so central to the culture of Freemasons that an immensely popular manual for earning the basic degrees of Masonry was titled *Jachin and Boaz.*[19] Annie's father and brothers probably used political connections to get Mallard the job. Men in the Christopher family had been obtaining postmaster appointments for three generations, typically to supplement income from farming or a profession.[20] To help Annie and her son would have been motivation enough, but as fellow Masons, the Christopher men had a fraternal obligation to help Mallard, and it was common in small southern communities for Masonic chapters to subsidize the construction of post offices, with the group's meeting room upstairs and Masonic emblems displayed on the exterior. Post offices even did triple duty as general stores, and Mallard later worked full-time as a merchant, so it is likely that he operated a mercantile business inside the Jachin post office, selling clothing, candy and drugs, packaged foods, inexpensive jewelry, and household items.[21]

Annie's child Lester died soon after Mallard began the postmaster job, while she was pregnant with their second child. Before they buried him in the cemetery at Christopher Chapel, she clipped a lock of his blond hair, tied it with a tiny blue ribbon, and tucked it inside a twofold greeting card that came from a department store, probably one of Mallard's vendors. The small die-cut card was embossed with purple violets. Annie wrote "Lock of hair of Mallard Lester Moore taken at death" in the card and placed it inside a large Bible.[22] When her next child was born three months later, she named him Alva Fitch, the middle name her mother's maiden name, establishing a pattern of combining a fashionable name with a name from her birth family. There followed Annie Erline, named for Annie herself; Lula Velma, for Annie's sister Lula; John Christopher, his entire name in honor of her father; and Charles Otis, for her brother Charles.[23]

In a family of seven, in a house that probably did not have electricity or running water, Earline and Velma had to help their mother in endless rounds of cleaning, gardening, tending chickens, cooking, sewing, and laundry.[24] Annie was not as desperate as the southern women whom the journalist Walter Hines Page famously described in 1897 as "clad without warmth or grace, living in untidy houses, working from daylight till bed time at the dull round of weary duties, the slaves of men of equal slovenliness, the mothers of joyless children."[25] However, like her Moore sisters-in-law Bettie and Viola, and unlike most of her sisters and sisters-in-law on the

Christopher side, she had no live-in domestic servants.[26] If she could employ a maid for just one chore, it probably was for washing the clothes, diapers, and linens.[27] Laundry was an exhausting job that involved boiling dirty clothes and linens in well water, rinsing them (with white items going in a separate tub for the "bluing" stage), cranking a wringer to squeeze the water from the sodden cloth, hanging everything on lines to dry, and ironing or stretching all of it.[28] It was thirsty work, but the water could have tasted foul; a visitor described water in the nearby town of York as having "a very strong bitter taste like Epsom salts," and at another spot nearby the water tasted "as if a dirty gun barrel had been washed in it."[29] Hanging the laundry, sweeping the porch and bare dirt yard, or watching the younger children play, hot even in the shade, Earline must have wished they had more help.[30] In the old days, the Christopher family had numerous slaves. Two slaves who attended Christopher Chapel in 1854, Barber and Rose, were held by Annie's grandmother Nancy Ann Christopher, and thirty-one others belonged to families that became aligned by marriage with the Christophers. (A family story is that church members had "a slave balcony . . . added, so that the slaves of the church members could attend church with their masters, and . . . many Negro slaves [were] buried in the northwest corner of the cemetery." Some of those slaves apparently continued living and working nearby after Emancipation: Hager Thompson, who lived next door to the Christophers' friends Daniel and Elizabeth McCall, probably was the church member named Hager; a couple named Jacob and Sibby DeLoach must have been the enslaved members recorded as Jacob and Libby.)[31] To have such help not only eased the labors of white women, it conveyed social status. Having a cook, a maid, and a nurse for one's children was part of the white woman's identity, a sign that she was the peer of other elite white women.[32]

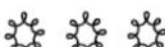

The Moore family's neighborhood was primarily populated with poor African American farmworkers, so Earline had few playmates except Velma. Going to her father's post office on an errand for her mother might have been her most frequent break from the domestic routine. Rural mail delivery did not exist, so anyone who expected a letter or needed to mail one came into Mallard's post office, but black and white customers usually stood apart without greeting each other. There was little friendship between the races. As an African American in Choctaw County sang in an old slave song, blacks would "rather be a nigger than a poor white man."[33]

Racial fear was a contagion in the Alabama countryside that had passed from one generation to the next. Less than a month before Earline's maternal grandfather married his first wife, a newspaper in the nearby town of Livingston (Sumter County) reported an alleged conspiracy, by several hundred slaves in west Alabama, to revolt during the Christmas holidays. In 1888, when Earline's parents were coming of age, Parthenia Hague wrote "in any section where the negro forms any very great part of the population, . . . white men or women are in danger of murder, robbery, and violence." During Earline's adolescence, Anna Fry recalled a riveting story of murder by slaves. Supposedly, a slave lured a white woman outside by sending "the cook to tell her he had found a turkey nest." As Fry retold the story, the unsuspecting mistress "arose, put on her bonnet, and went with the negro, followed by the cook, another trusted servant. Just as she leaned over to remove the eggs from the nest the man struck her on the head with an ax and killed her instantly."[34] Some former slaves in west Alabama also told vivid stories of slavery that a folklorist, Ruby Pickens Tartt of Livingston, documented. Tartt, who may have been distantly related to Earline through the Chiles line, was an outspoken advocate for her black neighbors. As an employee of the Federal Writers Project, she interviewed former slaves in Sumter County, which is adjacent to Choctaw County and within six miles of DeSotoville.[35] Earline's relatives undoubtedly knew some of Tartt's interview subjects as well as the former slaveholders whom they described.[36] Ex-slave narratives can be problematic as historical sources because most of the surviving former slaves were young children before Emancipation and did not have extensive or detailed memories of the slavery system. Moreover, African Americans still living in the South were understandably cautious about speaking ill of white families. They might recite the fantastical stories they believed whites expected them to tell. Some interviewers even asked leading questions intended to elicit positive statements about slavery.[37] However, Tartt's informants trusted her and spoke very frankly, passing on damning stories. Using phonetic spelling to preserve the men's and women's deep drawls, Tartt apparently made few changes to obscure their horrible memories.[38] Their stories were brief, incomplete, not always verifiable, and perhaps not the most typical or representative experiences of the period, but they demonstrate that African Americans who lived in the vicinity of the Christophers and Moores during Earline's childhood vividly recalled being treated like animals and living under a constant threat of torture and murder.

Amy Chapman said her parents "was driv' down to Alabamy lak cattle" and a planter bought them. Laura Clark was sold away from her mother when she was six or seven years old and carried in a wagon from North Carolina to Alabama. She remembered an overseer who whipped and murdered slaves: "Iffen you didn't do what you git tole, de overseer . . . hit you in de haid . . . till he kilt you. Den de mens would dig a hole . . . and throw 'em in hit right dere in de fiel' jes' lak dey was cows—didn't have no funeral no nothin'." Charlie Johnson remembered how slaveholders would "bell" slaves with an "iron band roun' de waist, en another iron band roun' de neck, en a thing stick up de back, way up, wid de bell on hit." Martha Jackson described a leather strap and the terror of slaves who were helpless to stop the beatings: "De holes in de strop de sucks flesh up thoo 'em, and de nigger's a hollerin' en ev'ybody so skeered." The brutality drove some slaves to insane acts. Chapman told Tartt that after a white man "whupped a cullid woman near 'bout to death," the woman "got so mad at him dat she tuk his baby chile whut was playin' roun' de yard and grab him up an' th'owed it in a pot of lye."[39] Some slaves tried to escape, but slaveholding men served regular shifts on "patrol," riding the countryside with bloodhounds running alongside to catch and return slaves who left their holders' property.[40] "Honey, dem nigger dogs; they sho' did run," Charity Grigsby said.[41] George Young equated being chased by bloodhounds to wild game hunts: slave catchers set "de nigger dogs on [runaway slaves] lak fox houn's run a fox today." When Young's brother Harrison tried to escape, slave hunters caught him. "Den dey turned de dogs loose on him," George Young told Tartt, "and sich a screamin' you never hyared. He was all bloody an' Mammy was a-hollerin', 'Save him, Lord, save my chile, an' don' let dem dogs eat him up!' Mr. Lawler said, 'De Lord ain't got nothin' do wid dis here.'"[42]

Despite all of the risks of running, in 1846 a man named Anthony who lived in Choctaw County escaped from Allen C. Yates, a wealthy planter whom the Christophers probably knew since his wife was a colorful and well-liked Methodist. Anthony fled five hundred miles before he was arrested some months later in South Carolina. After serving a jail sentence, he was auctioned and a local farmer bought him. Again he escaped; again he was arrested and presumably returned to the same farmer.[43] Yates petitioned the South Carolina legislature in 1859 for compensation for the loss of Anthony's labor. (Annie's great-uncle Judge Anderson Crenshaw presided over similar claims in Russell County, Alabama.)[44] John Massey, who grew up near the Yates farm, recalled while Earline was in college that two women on Yates's plantation eventually murdered him, "crushing his head with their hoes." One of Yates's descendants told a different version in 1982: Yates was "on horseback . . . hunting for a runaway slave," and when he "got off his horse to rest by the river" the runaway killed him.[45] Another planter, Burwell Boykin, who had a farm about twenty miles from DeSotoville, also was "killed by [a] Negro." The Boykin family passed down a story that relatives lynched "a buck slave" named Sham after he killed Boykin with a hoe.[46]

Whether or not the story of the revenge killing of Sham is accurate, fear of slaves and rage against them were deeply entrenched in white culture, and lynchings were commonly accepted. James Sellers, the historian who was Earline's principal, gave this example from Sumter County in 1855: "A group of some seventy-five to one hundred men" seized from the jail a slave suspected of murdering a young white girl. "The slave was tied to a stake, with fat 'light-wood' piled around him, and the torch was applied. The local paper estimated that two thousand persons saw him die."[47] During the Civil War, white fear of attack by retaliatory slaves mounted.[48] A woman left alone with an infant and forty-three slaves on an Alabama plantation wrote that she could be "murdered by negroes at any time."[49] After the war, as former slaves walked away from the farms and plantations they had worked and former slaveholders struggled to regain control of their labor force, rumors of planned insurrections by freedmen often spread. Lynchings became ritualistic spectacles in Alabama.[50] Slave "patrollers" or "paterollers," some of them bands of Ku Klux Klan members, still roamed on horseback, terrorizing, assaulting, and murdering African Americans. The violence became so notorious that a subcommittee of the US Congress held field hearings in Livingston and other Alabama towns in 1871 to collect information about the situation.[51] The testimony of local citizens to the subcommittee provides a fuller sense of the racial climate in Annie and Mallard's world when they were very young. The lawyer Reuben Chapman Jr., whose father, Samuel Chapman, probably purchased the slave Amy Chapman and whose uncle and namesake was an early governor of the state,[52] described several incidents in Sumter County of white men murdering black men. In response to pointed questions, he confirmed other incidents of harassment, abduction, murder, and lynching. The chairman of the subcommittee asked Chapman, "Did you ever hear the case of Amanda Childers, a girl about ten years old, whipped to death by a man named Jones?" Chapman acknowledged the death of the girl but claimed the girl's father said she died from an infection.

When the chairman asked, "Is it not quite possible" that her father "got frightened out of . . . prosecution?" Chapman's blasé response was, "I have no idea of it, sir."[53]

The terrorism came even closer to Earline's parents. In 1871, when a black man named Abe Lyon of DeSotoville supposedly threatened to retaliate against white men who had whipped his nephew, he was murdered. Daniel McCall described the incident in the congressional field hearing, testifying that he found Lyon's body on his property and went to "Squire Christopher" to call for an inquest. "Squire" was an honorific for a justice of the peace, a local elected official who could preside over civil and criminal inquiries. This squire almost certainly was Annie's father.[54] John Christopher and McCall were both family men in DeSotoville, members of Christopher Chapel with young children, Annie and Daniel Thompson, born a year apart; by 1880, they were next-door neighbors. As McCall described the inquest, Squire Christopher questioned Lyon's wife. She told him a posse came to the door of their cabin and demanded that Lyon come out, seized him, took him some distance away, and shot him.[55]

Annie and Mallard were too young to clearly remember Lyon's lynching, but they had to sense the innate white fear of violent insurrection by blacks,[56] particularly during the public panic, rage, and lynching of Jack Turner in 1882. This episode began with twelve-year-old Daniel Herd Brown of DeSotoville, a boy whom Annie and Mallard certainly knew, considering that the three youths were just six years apart in age.[57] Daniel discovered a package of documents in the road outside his family's house. The papers appeared to be minutes of meetings at which blacks in the county planned to massacre whites. Ostensibly they identified Jack Turner as a leader of the plot. Turner, whose very name echoed that of the infamous Nat Turner, was well known for an incident eight years earlier when he supposedly led a gang of armed black men into the nearby county seat, the village of Butler. Although very little actually occurred, the Butler newspaper warned that the safety of white families was "dangerously threatened by war-like demonstrations on the part of some negroes." Since then, Turner had bought property, learned the rudiments of reading, and become a leader of the Reconstruction-era Republican Party in the county. He was admired by many blacks, and even by some whites, but his encouragement of black voters threatened white political power. As alarmed talk about Daniel's discovery spread, the circuit judge issued warrants for Turner and several of his associates. The sheriff arrested the men but allowed vigilantes to take two out of the jail and torture them to extract confessions. One suspect first denied there was any conspiracy, but after he was whipped and hung from a tree, he sobbed and agreed that Turner was leading a plot to attack whites. A crowd gathered on the courthouse square and voted, by shouting, in favor of a motion to hang Turner. Seizing the jail keys from the sheriff, the mob took Turner from a cell and hung him from an oak on Butler's town square. The *Atlanta Constitution* and the *New York Times* questioned the authenticity of the documents that implicated Turner, but newspaper editors in Alabama tended to accept the massacre conspiracy and endorse the lynching. "An outraged people," the Butler *Courier* declared four days later, "took the law in their own hands and Jack Turner sleeps the everlasting sleep, and will never again ruffle the current of this people's happiness."[58]

By the time Earline was born, the white view of black men was focused on their supposed threat as sexual predators, and many white women and girls absorbed the idea that violence was necessary for their protection. Manhunts, in which mobs of white men hunted black men like animals, still occurred during her childhood and adolescence, with southern law enforcement agencies sometimes hiring trackers with trained "nigger dogs" to hunt for escapees from jail. The sound of the dogs traveled for miles. Clement Wood, the white novelist who imagined how freedmen viewed painted houses on a Birmingham ridge, was born in western Alabama just eight years before Earline. He described "the hollow baying" of bloodhounds at night: the sound "set the silence trembling. . . . The deep, solemn tones, booming out of the distance, entered and filled the room, throbbing and pulsing." Coming closer, "the voice of the dogs changed. . . . Nearer now—it was at the nearest end of the field. . . . The undergrowth complained at the leaping insult of heavy bodies crashing through." Once the lead dog reached a terrified black family's home, "there was a whirling, writhing tumult of dogs [that] whined and worried around the shack; one, growling, teased at a loose board." For blacks, the sound was the threat of being chased, pinned, mauled to death, whipped, or lynched in what the sociologist Arthur Raper called the "man-hunt tradition." For whites, the baying of the hounds was a reminder of the widely held belief that all black men were potential rapists and murderers. This was the milieu of Earline's childhood. Not only did pregnancy, childbirth, and disease threaten women and children with death, one could be raped or murdered by black bogeymen loose in the countryside. In a continual reenactment of slavery, blacks and whites in Alabama lived with the fear of violent attack, torture, and death.[59]

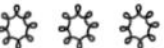

Earline's inscriptions in one of her childhood textbooks, *A Wonder Book for Girls and Boys*, hint at the dislocations of her childhood. Beneath her original inscription, "Erline Moore, Jachin, Choctaw, Ala.," she added, "Earline Moore, Isney, Ala." While some relatives moved to Mississippi and some to the nearby community of Lisman, her family had followed her maternal uncles from Jachin to Isney, a remote farming community without even a railway depot, about forty miles away in the southwestern corner of the county. The move took place around 1909 when Annie's sister Lula took over the Jachin post office from Mallard. In Isney, Mallard and Annie bought a house near her brother and sister-in-law Frank and Susie Christopher. Mallard had a new job selling "general merchandise," possibly at Frank's pharmacy in nearby Silas.[60] To be a mere storekeeper was not prestigious so this must have been a humiliating step down from postmaster, made worse if Mallard was beholden to his wife's family for the job. Mallard may have developed a drinking problem. No stories about this came down through the family, but merchants had easy access to alcohol when they went on shopping trips to cities like Mobile where wholesalers entertained them with dinners and drinks. Drinking was a common activity in their stores, too; they kept barrels of whiskey, serving drinks in tin dippers, and even sold laudanum, opium, morphine, and paregoric openly. The large Bible in which Annie kept Lester's lock of hair contained a fill-in-the-blank certificate with elaborate banners and ornate borders, in the form of a "Family Temperance Pledge" to "by the help of God . . . abstain from the use of all intoxicating drinks"—yet the lines for signatures are blank. One of Mallard's sons became an alcoholic and as an adult Earline demonstrated a strong antipathy to drinking. When Mallard's father, Lanier, died in 1911, Annie's brother Walter, by then a member of the Choctaw County board of health, and two other local men wrote a tribute for the *Choctaw Advocate* that someone in the family carefully clipped and saved. They praised Lanier as a loyal member and officer of the local Masonic lodge, adding some advice for Lanier's descendants: "We would say, emulate his example, who said he had never sworn an oath and was never drunk." Mallard was the only possible target of this embarrassing public advice. Of Lanier's sons, Sim had been known to enjoy a drink but he had been dead two years, and Will was upright enough that Lanier's widow Savanah moved into his home. Adding to the indignity of Walter's insult, Mallard, by then forty-six years old, apparently hoped to inherit a share of his father's land but as his brother Will's wife, Bettie, explained in a letter to his brother Sim's widow, Viola, "everything" in Lanier's estate went to Savanah for "her lifetime so there will be no division of land, as some of them thought would be."[61] If bitterness or despondency over his lack of an inheritance did not drive Mallard to drink or drugs, mere boredom could have; operating a crossroads store could be a maddeningly dreary occupation.

Mallard probably sold Kodak cameras and photograph albums in his store and could have taken pictures of his family to demonstrate home photography to his customers. Picture albums complemented Bibles as archives of family history with the middle-class mother typically responsible for adding to both. It was common in the early twentieth century for middle-class girls to compile scrapbooks of photographs, mementoes, and notes that were, in effect, ongoing efforts at autobiography or self-portraiture. Many girls titled their scrapbooks "Me," explicitly telling future readers to see or remember them as they appeared in the pages. Some women and girls even made albums known as "scrapbook houses," clipping images of furniture and decorative objects from magazines and pasting them on individual pages or two-page spreads to make collages that represented their fantasies of domestic interiors.[62] No scrapbooks survive from Earline's childhood, but she passed down two photograph albums that are the greatest evidence of her adolescence and young adult life. Some of the photographs in the first album include the Moore siblings as children and their Christopher cousins as teenagers, indicating that Annie made the early additions, probably after Mallard purchased the albums and a camera from his store's inventory. Someone, probably Annie, drew an arrow to Earline in one photograph and wrote "Erline," without an "a," beneath it. Earline later labeled other pictures "Auntie Velma" and "Earline," with the "a." In a school picture taken when she was about twelve years old, her brother Alva, sister Velma, other children, and even the three teachers looked at the camera with expressions that hinted at their personalities—timid, earnest, shy, mischievous, placid, confident, happy, amused, or bold. Earline, however, gazed impassively at the photographer as she sat on a bench that had been brought outside the schoolhouse, her back straight, hands clasped in her lap, and feet crossed properly at the ankles. The small, unpainted school building behind her was typical of rural Alabama schoolhouses, "barn-like structures made of logs or planks," some flea-ridden, with "hogs, goats, and even sheep [huddled beneath the floorboards] in inclement weather[,] stiflingly hot in summer[,] freezing in winter. . . . rarely [with] facilities such as privies; children 'went in the woods.'"[63] In other pictures, snapshots taken beside a fence or an eroded roadside bank, or on a dock, sometimes with classmates, other times with cousins, Earline wore pretty, fashionable dresses—dresses that her mother, an excellent seamstress, probably made for her—but she usually sat or stood at one edge of the group as if she entered the picture reluctantly and at the last minute. Asked as a teenager to pose with her Aunt Bettie for a snapshot, Earline did not bother to smile and her expression implied contempt for her surroundings. Photographed on another visit to Will and Bettie, she sat on a stump in the yard, a kerchief around her hair, and looked down instead of at the camera, as if to deny she was even present.

She may have felt hostile toward impromptu photographers; her daughter did in her adult life. Clearly, being photographed was a frustrating experience for Earline. Like her grandmothers and mother before her, she lived in a world that expected white women to be beautiful, well coiffed, fashionable, and, above all, slender; the contemporary ideal of the beautiful woman was the thin, flat-chested "flapper."[64] Although her maternal grandmother and mother, Ann Elizabeth and Annie, were naturally slender, Earline was plump and large-busted like her paternal grandmother, Savanah. Nor was Earline as pretty as her Christopher grandmother. In a photograph taken in her late seventies, seated outside with a child on her lap, Ann Elizabeth was thin and elegant with wavy white hair arranged loosely around her face. Wearing an ankle-length black skirt with flounces and a white blouse with lace-edged sleeves, she gazed at the child with a slight smile.[65] A similar snapshot portrait of Earline's other grandmother, also posing on a chair brought outside, makes plain the contrast between the Christopher and Moore women. Savanah stared stoically ahead, with her husband, Lanier, noticeably smaller than his wife, in a chair beside her and their youngest son, Will, standing behind them, holding a guitar as if about to strum a tune, the instrument meant to convey the family's musical affinity. A very stout woman with small eyes and a round face, her hair parted in the middle and pulled tightly into a bun, Savanah looked much less comfortable being photographed than did Ann Elizabeth.[66]

The snapshots in the Isney album appear in no apparent order, without any of the supplementary materials that teenage girls tended to assemble—no commencement or party invitations, no notes from girlfriends, no clippings, no ribbons, no locks of hair. Earline's albums seem evidence of disavowal more than of identification with her past, hints that she did not *want* to remember her early life. They suggest that, from childhood, she felt detached from the people around her and endured their company only as long as necessary to get somewhere else. Life must have seemed unfair. Why, Earline wondered, considering the important men in her background, had her mother married Mallard Moore, who provided such a meager lifestyle for them and whose family had no particular distinction? Earline even considered "Mamma," the family's appellation for her mother, too common and strongly resented her mother for naming her Annie Erline, feeling it simply did not convey the proud lineage that ancestral names signified.[67] Earline believed, mistakenly, that the first daughter in each generation of the Fitch family was named "Anne Elizabeth" and bemoaned that, when naming her first daughter, Annie chose her own diminutive nickname instead of "Anne-with-an-E," which Earline considered more patrician, and paired it with "Erline," a name of no family significance, instead of her own middle name, Elizabeth.[68] As her copy of *A Wonder Book for Girls and Boys* reveals, Earline began using "Earline," with the "a," as her name while she was still a girl. When Annie ordered a Bible to give her daughter as a Christmas gift in 1913, she had the cover stamped "Annie Erline Moore" in gold leaf, but once it arrived she inscribed the inside "From Mamma to Earline," conceding her seventeen-year-old daughter's preference.[69] Changing her mother's spelling could not, by itself, however, change the truth that Earline was, as she ruefully joked later in life, "half planter and half redneck."[70]

Two

Marriage

A RING SET WITH THREE SPARKLING OPALS that my mother gave me is the only tangible evidence of Earline's first romance. Earline received the ring from an early suitor and wore it when she posed, tan and thinner than usual, for a picture with three other young women, the fingers of her left hand splayed on her skirt. The formality of that scene and Earline's fixed expression suggest this photograph was more significant than her album's other casual group shots of teenagers clowning for the camera. The glossy, full foliage on the trees in the background indicates it was taken early in the summer, so the occasion could have been her graduation from Isney High, possibly in May 1914 when she was eighteen years old.[1] Her dress that day was ankle-length and white linen, the hem with an open-work border, the bodice and two asymmetrical overskirts trimmed with eyelet and lace, the elbow-length sleeves shirred, the entire frothy costume belted with an enormous satin bow in a medium, contrasting color, probably pink or light blue. The high school romance ended, but Earline saved the ring and passed it on to her daughter in ceremonial fashion on her daughter's sixteenth birthday, Anne repeating the ritual on my sixteenth birthday.[2]

With no marital prospects after graduation, Earline may have consulted her aunt Susie Watkins Christopher, who had been an artist and teacher after going to Tuscaloosa Female College in the old river port town that was the original state capital. Susie's son Edward planned to enter the University of Alabama there. Perhaps Susie encouraged Earline to earn a teaching credential; teaching jobs were plentiful and the surest way for a single young woman to support herself.[3] A move to the state's training program for schoolteachers, Alabama Normal School in Livingston, was less daunting than a move to Tuscaloosa: the depot at Silas was a short drive away, and from there Earline could take one train as far as York and another for the short ride to Livingston. Furthermore, her family had roots in the Sumter County seat: her great-grandfather had established the Methodist church there.[4] To earn money for the tuition, Earline probably taught in or near Isney in a rural school that employed non-credentialed teachers.[5] Finally, when she was twenty years old, she took the entrance examination and enrolled in the state normal school, which she called "S.N.S.," for the summer term of 1916, moving into Webb Hall, an imposing three-story brick dormitory with three parlors and a dining room on the first floor.[6] She saved photographs from her years at Livingston in a new album but in no apparent order and with few captions, as with the album of Isney scenes. In most of the shots, groups of young people posed outdoors, the girls wearing loose tunics over long skirts, or "middy" blouses in honor of the troops (the United States had entered World War I), or "lingerie dresses" made of light, transparent fabric and worn over a colored slip or under dress—all styles that were flattering to Earline.[7]

Black servants, some looking and sounding almost like antebellum slaves, waited on the young women. In a scrapbook marketed to female college students, another student at Livingston preserved a photograph of an elderly house servant who wore a long skirt and bonnet.[8] One servant reportedly praised the school's president, George W. Brock, as her ruler: "'De man at de head uv dis school ought to have de prize, and a good prize, too,'" she said, according to a newspaper writer. "'Yas'm he jest stands up and rules like a gentleman.'"[9] Brock's white moustache, white hat, and light-colored jacket gave him an antebellum air when he posed with Earline's new friend Grace Shields, an assistant instructor of history, and other deferential faculty members for a photograph outside Webb Hall.[10]

The school's two-year curriculum for teachers included education courses; a foundation of academic courses; and mandatory classes in cooking and sewing, thus preparing young women to go immediately to work as classroom teachers, continue at the college and earn baccalaureate degrees, or marry and begin careers as homemakers.[11] When Earline completed her first term, her seventeen-year-old brother J. C. gave her an anthology of works by William Wordsworth, inscribing it "From J. C. to Earline, Aug. 25, 1916."[12] Perhaps when he gave Earline the book, J. C. hoped to join her at the college. Not yet old enough to register for the draft, he enrolled at the normal school in 1919 along with their twenty-year-old sister Velma. Mallard visited the three on the campus that winter, his eye more bulging, possibly the effect of the eye disease strabismus, and an unsmiling Earline posed with him for a photograph that Velma probably took. Mallard died a few months later "of smoking," possibly a respiratory condition, according to family legend.[13] The Moores carried his remains to Annie's family cemetery at Christopher Chapel and buried him beside his infant son, Mallard Lester.[14]

Within two weeks of her father's death, Earline prevailed upon Brock to write a recommendation for her; his letter and her state teaching certificate became part of the small assortment of letters, documents, and newspaper clippings that the family preserved. The president did not suggest that Earline was passionate about teaching, but he implied that a school superintendent would not regret hiring her. "Miss Moore is a young lady of excellent character and is a promising teacher," he wrote. "I commend her to any community needing her services."[15] With her friend Grace, Earline found a job at the elementary school in Holt, an unincorporated village surrounding a foundry and blast furnace plant on the outskirts of Tuscaloosa. They shared a rented house with four other teachers, all of them young, single, white women.[16] It was a bleak landscape of denuded ravines, bare dirt streets, horse-drawn wagons, and raw picket fences. Steam billowed from the foundry as barges lined up along the bank of the Black Warrior River to receive loads of coal that train operators dumped from the end of a tall trestle. Earline's pupils, children of the foundry workers, lived in company houses, identical small, frame structures with hipped roofs that perched along Main Street, at the edge of a treeless, terraced hillside, and on the steep short streets that connected Main to the Holt Road.[17]

The terrifying pandemic of "Spanish flu," which killed millions around the world, was underway. About 50 percent of people who were exposed to the virus became ill and there were no effective treatments for the symptoms. Most victims suffered very high fevers, fluid and hemorrhaging in the lungs, and delirium before sinking into unconsciousness. Thousands died in Alabama. So many died in Holt, the memoirist Nancy Dean Blackman recalled, "there were scarcely enough well persons to bury the dead." Susie Powers Tompkins, a woman from Grace's home county, wrote, "Whole families would succumb to the disease. . . . I . . . watched the continuous funeral processions pass by on the way to the nearby cemetery."[18] On Saturdays, if they were brave enough to risk contagion, Earline and her housemates could ride the electrified streetcars on the four-mile "dummy line" that ran from Holt to the heart of Tuscaloosa. There they could see the new dishes and knickknacks at Allen and Jemison Hardware or stroll through the park at Stallworth Lake, where they might take a boat ride or a spin on the merry-go-round.[19] They might run into Earline's cousin Edward, a popular, good-natured young man who went by "Chris" and planned to practice medicine in Isney. As a member of the Student Army Training Corps, Edward probably participated in the Armistice Day parade in Tuscaloosa on November 11, 1918. Church bells rang across Holt that day and many residents took the dummy line to see the parade and listen to the joyous speeches outside the courthouse.[20]

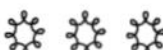

The jazz number "Margie" was a hit in 1920 and Earline bought a copy of the sheet music; it became part of a large collection of music for piano that she and her daughter, Anne, eventually amassed. Since Earline wrote her maiden name on the cover, she acquired "Margie" while she lived in Holt.[21] We can imagine her and other teachers playing the piece on the school piano after hours and talking about the young men who also were teachers in Holt. One of the housemates, Eliza Jane Dansey, gave Earline a copy of *Pollyanna Grows Up* that year. This was one of only two popular novels belonging to Earline that survived in the Findley family's home library. That Earline carried the book with her from the shared house in Holt to her married home and saved it throughout her life, investing in it enough significance that her daughter also kept it to the end of her life, makes it important evidence about the cultural ideas to which Earline was exposed. The book was the sequel to Eleanor H. Porter's novel *Pollyanna,* itself the subject in 1920 of a popular film. The character of Pollyanna was a cheerful orphan who finds a beautiful and loving home;[22] Eliza may have liked the book because she was an orphan herself.[23] The author was a New Englander who spent a year, in the same period as Earline's early childhood, in Chattanooga, Tennessee, where she could have seen firsthand the phenomenon of actual southern belles and the concomitant expectation that young women should attract suitors.[24] Resolutely cheerful, Pollyanna fit the stereotype for twentieth-century southern daughters who were dutiful and pleasant regardless of life's adversity. "'I shall never marry,' she said blithely. . . . 'I'm not pretty you know.'" Her fondest dream was "to cook and keep house," although not, of course, as a servant, yet by the book's happy ending, Pollyanna found true love even though she was not beautiful: her suitor, Jimmy, "swept Pollyanna into his arms and [she] lay unresisting in the fiercely tender embrace." In a classic plot twist that Porter could have taken from popular chivalric literature of the South, Pollyanna's aunt objected to the romance because Jimmy's ancestry was a mystery—"We know nothing whatever about his people, and his pedigree"—but in the end, the truth about his respectable ancestors surfaced and the aunt relented.[25] Porter's book offered hope to young women like Earline and Eliza.

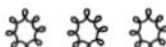

From more of Earline's photographs, we know she went out strolling around Holt one sunny winter day with another housemate, Bessie Massey, and two young men. Bessie was from Livingston and, like Earline and Eliza, fatherless; she had lost no time in preparing herself to earn a living, receiving a certificate from the normal school at the age of nineteen.[26] The four took snapshots of each other leaning against trees and sitting on fence railings. One of the men leaned toward Earline, appearing to say, "Won't you smile for the camera?" Wearing an elegant Empire-waist cloak that had a wide collar embellished with three stripes of grosgrain ribbon, Earline gazed resolutely to the side, hands clasped on a crossed knee, but a small smile belied her aloof posture. In a few photographs taken at the height of summer, she and another young man stood in a bare-swept yard. He seems to have paid a surprise visit, as her hair was in disarray, pulled loosely up and back. He held her wrist firmly as she tried to twirl away from him and again a smile revealed her pleasure in the moment.[27] In another picture the same friend posed on a bridge with three other young men who wore jackets and hats and stood in a row, carefully clasping the railing. Earline's friend had climbed to a lower section and sat at the very edge, jacket off and sleeves rolled to mid-forearms, one arm loosely around a support, the opposite knee bent, gazing boldly at the photographer. Earline wrote no captions for these pictures, so his name, like that of the young man who gave her the opal ring, is lost.

Earline's mother, Annie, had purchased a one-story frame bungalow near her brother Charles Christopher's grocery store in a working-class neighborhood of Meridian, Mississippi, probably using her husband's inheritance after her mother-in-law died. With no income, aged, stooped, and gray, and losing her teeth, as a photograph captured, Annie found work, with Charles's help, as a seamstress at the East Mississippi Insane Asylum. Charles also helped Earline's brothers find jobs: Alva as a mill hand; J. C. at the grocery; and Otis as a runner for Western Union.[28] Earline probably visited her family on vacations and some weekends, riding the Alabama Great Southern Railroad from Tuscaloosa to Meridian. She could help with cooking, cleaning, and gardening, and she and her mother probably sometimes worked together on a new dress or suit for her teaching job. Returning to Holt, Earline took the streetcar from the train station in Tuscaloosa, riding north along Greensboro Avenue and east on University,[29] passing the grand homes wealthy families built in the decades before and after the Civil War.[30] The Jemison-Van de Graaff mansion was festooned with wisteria and frilly with jigsaw work, its front porch in shadow. Lace-like iron trim supported the porch of the Hester-deGraffenried house. The Dearing mansion looked toward the river, its massive colonnade framing a grand entrance. White matrons supervised black maids in uniform who swept the expansive porticos. Black yardmen in overalls and straw hats tended the flowerbeds. Some houses had small servants' quarters, even former slave quarters, in the backyards. Signs of the southern fantasy surrounded Earline, constant reminders that while her antebellum relatives in the extended Christopher family were part of the ruling class, she belonged to a lower class because her mother married into the Moore family.[31]

For a young woman like Earline, the only route to a life more like those of the women who lived in the mansions on Greensboro Avenue was marriage to someone with a profession or property. Her sister Velma married a police officer in Meridian and worked into old age as a seamstress and shop clerk; her housemates Grace and Bessie married tradesmen and worked as schoolteachers for decades, spending their lives in the lower-middle class.[32] Earline wanted more. She wanted a different kind of life, as different as possible from her mother's, from the endless chores and the impossibility of making a beautiful home, from the bitter knowledge that by marrying "down," Annie squandered the only social capital she had.[33] If Earline could not be a belle, pampered and adored, free to flirt and break men's hearts, with no responsibility or work to do, she would, at least, marry well and become a distinguished lady, in effect a former belle, "idolized," as a young Alabama lawyer put it in 1860, "and almost worshipped by her dependents, and beloved by her children, to whom no word ever sounds half so sweet as *mother* and for whom no place possesses one half the charms of *home*."[34]

When she met Herbert Lyman Findley, he was a young lawyer and military officer, hardly dashing, considering that he was not quite five feet, six inches tall, but fairly handsome with a confident expression. Friendly and courteous, he enjoyed joking around and cheerfully went by "Skeeter" to close friends, but he did not seek to be the center of attention. In short, he was a gentleman. Herbert had entered the University of Alabama after his graduation from Tuscaloosa High in 1912, focusing on law while his brothers Hargrove and Preston studied engineering as their father had done. Adventurous, he went with Preston to New York in the summer following his freshman year. He completed the requirements for baccalaureate and law degrees in five years. The three brothers registered for the draft on June 5, 1917, the first of three federal draft days, Herbert and Preston having gorged on bananas to reach the minimum weight requirement, according to a family story. Herbert was commissioned as a second lieutenant of field artillery but missed combat duty; when armistice was declared, he later recalled, he was on a transport ship in New York Harbor. Returning to Tuscaloosa, he began practicing law and served the remainder of his military duty as a judge in the Alabama National Guard. The three bachelor brothers lived with their father in the family home on University Avenue.[35] Several small, oval, steel luggage tags stamped with Herbert's name, the date July 20, 1920, and the symbol of the Masons indicate when he joined the fraternal order and hint that he already had political inclinations.

Like Earline, Herbert possessed few volumes of fiction, so those he read before meeting her are important sources of information about his ideas on courtship and marriage. There were a few works by Sir Walter Scott, including the narrative poem "The Lady of the Lake" and the novel *Ivanhoe,* which glorified hunters, Scottish Highlanders such as the Findley ancestors, and chivalrous young noblemen. Scott's work had long been popular in Tuscaloosa: a literary journal established there in 1839 was called *Southron,* an archaic Scottish word that Scott used for "Southerner," and a merchant in Tuscaloosa had fifty-four copies of Scott's novels in his inventory in 1843. Henry W. Hilliard, an English professor at the university who was a former congressman, wrote a novel, *De Vane: A Story of Plebeians and Patricians,* which followed an aristocratic Ivanhoe-like character who lived on a university campus and fell in love with a plebian Methodist minister's daughter. Before and after the Civil War, during Herbert's adolescence, and for decades to come, Scott's works reinforced the self-image of southern farmers and their descendants as standard-bearers for an aristocratic tradition, a code of behavior for wholesome, virile men and fragile women. John Massey, a memoirist who grew up in Choctaw County, expressed this idea of the pioneer: "Our ancestors came from a virile race holding the value of liberty above all other blessings. . . . They . . . braved the dangers of the ocean and the fury of savage men." In an erotic scene in *Ivanhoe,* Scott's hero came to the defense of the maiden Rebecca, whose "profusion of sable tresses . . . fell down upon . . . a lovely neck and bosom." He rode into the tiltyard, much as a lawyer might stride into court in the twentieth century, saying "readily and boldly, 'I am a good knight and noble, come hither to sustain with lance and sword the just and lawful quarrel of this damsel.'"[36]

Another of Herbert's books, *The Little Shepherd of Kingdom Come* by John Fox Jr., was derivative of Scott's dramas and a best seller in 1903. Its young Kentucky hero, Chad, idolized white southern pioneers, "hunters, adventurers, emigrants, fine ladies and fine gentlemen who had stained [the road] with their blood [until] that road had broadened into the mighty way for a great civilization." For Chad, and for real young men such as Herbert, pioneer ancestry was a significant form of status with brave pioneers merging with brave soldiers as heroic figures. Like Herbert's great-grandfather, Chad's father served in the War of 1812. Like Herbert, Chad lost his mother when he was a boy: She "'jes' kind o' got tired' . . . and soon to her worn hands and feet came the well-earned rest." Chad attended college in a town that sounded like Tuscaloosa, with "the gentlest courtesies [and] the finest chivalry, that the State had ever known." Just as the memory of Herbert's mother lingered in his family's house, memories of the "beaux and belles" of older generations hung about Fox's fictional town, peopling it with "phantom shapes, and [giving] an individual or a family here and there a subtle distinction." Chad moved among the slaves "with a . . . lordly, righteous air of authority." In Fox's world, the slave-based economy that made possible the planter lifestyle of balls and hunts was simply part of the perfect order. When the Civil War began, Chad suffered a crisis of conscience before enlisting in the Union Army, not out of opposition to slavery but from devotion to the nation. His great-uncle, his friends, and the girl he loved were grieved and angry, but, most strikingly, an enslaved man called "Old Tom" politely disapproved, asking, "'You foolin' this ole nigger, Mars Chad, ain't you?'" When Chad shook his head, Tom responded, "'I'se sorry to heah it, suh,' . . . with dignity, and . . . turned to his work." *The Little Shepherd* could have been a manual for how Herbert, as a patriotic American in the twentieth century, should understand and reenact the chivalric ideal. Showing a new generation of Southern boys that they could serve the United States while not dishonoring their heritage, Chad went to heroic lengths as a Union officer to aid and rescue individuals in three southern families. He survived the war and won the heart of the beautiful Margaret, who, "dressed in white, flowers in her hand," forgave him for rejecting the Confederacy. At this point, Fox gave his impressionable readers an entire page of suggestive prose: "That any man could ever dare even to dream of touching her sacred lips had been beyond [Chad's] imaginings—such was the reverence of his love for her—and his very soul shook when, at the gate, Margaret's eyes dropped . . . and [then] she suddenly lifted her face."[37]

The Harvester by Gene Stratton-Porter was published in 1911 when Herbert was sixteen and by the next year was the best-selling work of fiction in the country. The hero of the title was a brave and skilled woodsman who lived in his ancestral home and revered the memory of his mother. He learned, like Herbert, "to be frugal, economical, and to work. [']All I've earned either has gone back into land, into the bank, or into books.'" Living alone with his dog, Belshazzar, whose name meant "to protect," he was lonely but not sure that he wanted to give up the freedom of bachelorhood for domestic life. Then his "Dream Girl" appeared in an erotic vision, like Scott's lady of the lake, as "a misty, moving shimmer of white" coming across the water on a "bridge of gold." This "wonderful, alluring, lovely" figure came closer, "warm with a pink glow," and "the fountains of twenty-six years' repression overflowed in the breast of the man and all his being ran toward her in a wave of desire." The Harvester "could scent the flower-like odour of her body and wrapping, even her hair." The heavenly being "leaned closer . . . and softly but firmly laid lips of pulsing sweetness on his." She vanished, and "reverently" the Harvester wondered, "my gracious Heavenly Father . . . would it be like that?"[38]

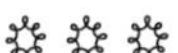

Preston Findley was married in September 1920.[39] A few months later Herbert turned twenty-six years old, the same age as the protagonist in *The Harvester* when he married. One family story is that Herbert's friend Archie Hamby, who later married Earline's housemate Grace Shields, introduced him to Earline.[40] Another possible link was Herbert's maternal aunt Lula May Hargrove, who was the assistant principal of Holt Public School by 1924.[41] Separated from her family and working to support herself in an ugly environment, the smoky foundry village of Holt, Earline was rather like the girl in *The Harvester*: she needed a serene home and a chivalrous man in order to blossom into a happy and beautiful helpmate. In a photographic portrait made around this time, Earline was plump but had heavy, glossy, dark hair and large, expressive eyes. She was short enough that Herbert could look down into those eyes. Her teacher's salary also was attractive, as Herbert was still developing his law practice. All in all, Earline looked like a good catch, but Herbert believed lineage was of fundamental importance; years later he mused in a letter to his daughter, "If each has perfect respect for the other, two people of similar heritage, if intelligent, [can] find a happy place in life together."[42]

It is not clear whether Earline told Herbert any of the stories of her heritage: that her ancestor Walter Chiles was speaker of the Virginia House of Burgesses in the mid-seventeenth century; or that a more recent ancestor, William Chiles, was a private in the Fifth Virginia Regiment during the American Revolution; or that William's son Thomas White Chiles migrated from North Carolina to Greensboro, Alabama, became a planter, and represented Greene County in the state House of Representatives. Earline may have been unaware that her great-grandfather Ralph Griffin Christopher was a minister and physician, or that in Greensboro he was a friend of the future governor John Gayle and his wife, or that Griffin was one of the founding elders of the Alabama Conference of the Methodist Church. However, she certainly mentioned that several of her maternal uncles were physicians and her first cousin Oliver B. Christopher was the sheriff of Choctaw County and a lawyer and former prosecutor.[43] Unfortunately, there was little to tell about the Moore line except that her late father was a Mason. An amusing element of the family story of Herbert and Earline's courtship is that before proposing, he contacted a judge in Choctaw County to ask whether Earline's family had any embarrassing secrets. Whatever the judge said must have been satisfactory. Herbert proposed, perhaps following Stratton-Porter's advice that "there [were] a number of things a man deeply in love can . . . do with a woman's white hand[; h]e can stroke it, press it tenderly, and lay it against his lips and heart."[44] He gave Earline an engagement ring with a two-thirds-carat diamond in an illusion setting that made the stone appear larger than it actually was.

They were married in Meridian on June 29, 1921. Earline had a home wedding, a small afternoon affair in Annie's parlor, which they decorated with ferns, palm fronds, and flowers. Home weddings were a respectable upper-class antebellum custom—Griffin Christopher officiated at a home wedding in Greensboro in 1827—and a good choice for a widow with little income. In fact, some southern families of great as well as modest means held home weddings. Later, the society editor for the *Tuscaloosa News* explicitly associated home weddings with plantation culture: "The lavish, beautiful old fashioned southern wedding of 'Sis' Partlow and Harry Pritchett brought to mind much of the old South [when] faithful servants worked for weeks . . . and all was as merry as a wedding bell."[45] Earline wore a tailored suit "fashioned of midnight blue tricotine with grey accessories" and carried "bride's roses." The only guests from the groom's side were Herbert's father, Kenneth Murchison "Murk" Findley Jr., and, in place of Herbert's late mother, his aunt Lula. The newspaper mentioned no members of the extended Moore family. A classmate of Earline, who worked in Meridian as a stenographer, sang and then Earline and Herbert approached an improvised altar. A local Methodist minister officiated and Herbert slipped a 14-carat carved gold wedding band on Earline's finger. The newspaper noted the couple departed on a three-week honeymoon, divulging only that their destination was "to the east,"[46] but there are clues that Herbert and Earline went to Kentucky to visit her cousin Edward, who by then was enrolled in the University of Louisville School of Medicine: Earline saved two snapshots of Churchill Downs, the racetrack near Louisville, but no pictures of other recognizable cities. Herbert had traveled by train to Louisville before, on the way to officer training at Camp Zachary Taylor.[47] Her photograph album contained one other hint that Earline and Edward were close: undated photographs of Isney Cemetery. As usual, Earline wrote no captions beneath the snapshots, but she could have taken them while attending Edward's burial or visiting his grave. He died of pneumonia in 1922, shortly after receiving his medical degree, and was the first member of the Christopher family to be buried in the Isney Cemetery.[48]

Returning from their honeymoon, Earline and Herbert settled into Murk's house. Tall willow oaks shaded the broad unpaved road and a straight sidewalk led to Murk's two-sided front porch.[49] The house was simple but stately enough thanks to the generous porch, high-ceilinged rooms, and property occupying one-half of a city block. It stood on the corner of the intersection with Fourth Avenue, roughly between two landmarks on the other side of the road: the large brick home of Eugene Allen Smith, a socially prominent university geologist, and the entrance to the grounds of Bryce Hospital, the state mental asylum.[50] Murk rented a small building on the northeast corner of his property to a grocer and his wife, who operated a store on the first floor and lived upstairs.[51] Across Third Avenue, there was an enclave of modest rental houses called Daly Bottom; Herbert sometimes called it Frogbottom. Smith had observed a few years earlier that half-wild dogs roamed the neighborhood, some of them fed by African American residents of Daly Bottom, and speculated they were responsible for killing his family's pet dog. If feral dogs were still a problem there on the eastern edge of town that summer, Earline could hear them at night, barking and howling, through the screen on the open window of her new bedroom. Just beyond Daly Bottom, University Avenue became a gentle incline and skirted another African American neighborhood with the ironic name of Castle Hill, where the houses were what a Bryce patient called "tumble-down cabins." Frogbottom and Castle Hill made up a community of houses, churches, and a school where many domestic servants and university employees had lived for decades.[52]

The interior of Murk's house was a man's world, with rooms that probably were rather bare.[53] Although his unmarried sister Mollie and his unmarried sister-in-law Lula may have helped Murk run his household after his wife, youngest son, and mother all died in 1908, providing some maternal attention to Murk's three surviving sons, Mollie died in 1911 and Lula was a working schoolteacher so she could not have helped full-time.[54] Murk probably paid an African American woman, perhaps Mary Collins, a private cook who lived in a rented house very nearby, to keep house and prepare meals for him.[55] He enjoyed having friends over on a Saturday night for drinks and a game of cards around a tilt-top tea table known in the family as "Father's card table," which had an oval top constructed of a single piece of walnut.[56] Like rural farmers, he shaved on the back porch, his washstand a simple fall-front secretary known in the family as "the plantation desk," the water from the basin sloshing on the plank top so often that over time it warped,[57] and he liked to have sorghum three times a day. An inexpensive, strongly flavored syrup made from cane, the lowest and cheapest grade of molasses, sorghum was marketed to African Americans but Preston's wife, Ila Blackman, kept it at the ready for times when Murk dined with them. Whereas the writer James Agee observed that impoverished families in Hale County poured their sorghum from a Mason jar, Ila served it in a silver-plated pitcher and saucer that had been part of Preston and Herbert's mother's tableware. Ila's daughter Ida Louise later recalled that the family "used it on all the breads with real butter. It was very strong tasting but good."[58] Once she joined the family, Earline probably kept a pitcher of sorghum on her table, too.

Portraits of ancestors were de rigueur in the homes of aristocratic southern families, and the Findleys had large framed photographic portraits of Murk and of Herbert's late mother, Ida Belle Hargrove Findley. They were "crayon portraits," images first printed faintly on large sheets of paper and then colored by commercial studio artists.[59] In hers, Ida appeared serene and confident. According to a family story, the dark, high-collared dress she wore was her "second-day" dress. The custom of choosing a special dress for the day after one's wedding, to wear for receiving visitors and then for a portrait, was a southern practice that spanned the antebellum and postbellum periods.[60] A few of Ida's other garments remained in the house. One was a two-piece dress, made by a very skilled seamstress, which Ida probably wore for formal afternoon events. Of deep red, silky broadcloth with narrow fabric-encased bone stays, it had gray ribbon and buckles embellishing its long sleeves and cuirasse, a close-fitting bodice with a high neck, pointed waist, and two long tabs in the back. The skirt was floor-length with one deep, pleated ruffle.[61] From the size of these garments, Earline could see that Ida possessed, in addition to the pretty eyes and distinguished forehead visible in the portrait, the small waist that was one of the most important qualities, indeed accomplishments, of the southern belle. Murk also had saved Ida's writing caddy, a small wooden box with a curved handle, recessed spaces for ink bottles and pens, and a drawer for paper and stamps. Ida had used a fountain pen to embellish the inside of the small drawer with the inscription "Remember thy correspondence in the days of thy youth! Ida B. Hargrove, 1885," drawing decorative flourishes and writing with a fine hand. As a young single woman in a household with servants, Ida had plenty of leisure time to perfect her penmanship and write letters.[62] Earline, whose own handwriting was sloppy and who rarely wrote letters, would have noticed Ida's penmanship upon discovering the box.

Two small photographs hinted at the tender care Ida gave her children. Like the portraits of Earline and her siblings, the earlier picture probably was taken by a traveling photographer. Murk and Ida's two oldest children posed before a large gardenia. Hargrove wore a calf-length pleated coatdress and boots and had a solemn expression, his left hand on the arm of the chair in which his infant brother was propped. Baby Preston wore a light-colored gown and a sweater or cape edged in lace; someone had tucked a blanket around his legs. He gazed placidly ahead while an adult stood barely outside the frame of the photograph, one shoe visible, ready to catch him if he tipped forward. The other picture was taken at a photography studio when Murk and Ida's third child was about eighteen months old. The older boys wore short suits, large silk bows, and boots. Herbert perched on a wicker chair between them, dressed in a dark jacket and pleated skirt. Blond and bright-eyed, all three boys appeared secure, Hargrove with a thoughtful expression and the younger boys with happy smiles. Except for these relics of Ida, the house had so few feminine touches that Herbert knew no more than to select bedroom furniture for his bride, like the protagonist of *The Harvester* who surprised his "Dream Girl" with furniture that he designed and made himself. That Herbert bought dark, heavy pieces that came as a set, probably from a local store, without consulting Earline became the basis of another gentle joke in family lore. Never again, it was said, was Earline left out of a decision about their house and its furnishings.[63]

As a newlywed, Earline had family landmarks to see and relatives to meet. The Findleys' second-oldest antebellum home, Riverview, was a short drive past Bryce Hospital in a neighborhood overlooking the Black Warrior River. Earline may not have seen the interior of the house on her first visit since Murk probably was renting it. Herbert's paternal aunt Tranquilla Cherokee Findley Stone and her family lived across the river in Northport in the original Findley home, one of the oldest houses in the vicinity. Sitting well back from Main Avenue (known earlier as Byler Road), its hewn logs encased in clapboard that probably was painted white by 1921, the Northport house was quite modest in comparison to some century-old Tuscaloosa houses, but the central hall and double doors with a transom and sidelights were vestiges of the original dogtrot—concrete evidence of the family's pioneer status.[64] Herbert's cousin Otis Paschal Stone, who lived with his mother, was a student of family history; years later, he spread his collection of genealogical records across the family's square piano for Earline's daughter-in-law to see. Otis and Herbert could have taken Earline to Robertson-Stone Cemetery nearby to show her their pioneer ancestors' graves.[65] Another of Earline's early social calls must have been to Herbert's aunt Lula, whom she met at the wedding if not at Holt Elementary. Aunt Lula and her mother, Minerva Eugenia Thomas Hargrove—"Grandmother Hargrove," as Earline would have called her, in the antebellum manner—lived together in a house on the other side of the university campus, supported by Lula's income as a schoolteacher and

Minerva's small quarterly Confederate widow's pension. To visit the ladies, Earline boarded the streetcar at Lawn Station, a block from Murk's house, and rode west, just as she did on trips from Holt to downtown, alighting at the corner of Twelfth Street. Minerva's house was on the corner of University and Hargrove Alley.[66] Listening to the Stones in Northport, and the Hargrove ladies, and Murk as he told old tales of pioneers and military men, Earline heard rich stories about her new family. Telling stories, listening to them, and passing them on comprised the Findleys' fundamental ritual, linking their rural, feudal origin to urban contemporary life, continually polishing their sense of themselves and their kin as brave, honorable, humble, and humorous, steeped in history but without pretension.

Three

Legends

To be descended from the very earliest pioneers was a special distinction in southern commemorative culture. Herbert's great-great-grandfather John Findley was a Scottish Highlander who immigrated to South Carolina around 1767 to obtain a colonial land grant. His oldest son served in the Revolutionary Army; his youngest son was Herbert's great-grandfather Kenneth. One story about Kenneth was that he was a spy for the United States in the War of 1812, the idea lingering in Tuscaloosa lore, carved with seeming authority on his grave marker, passed on by Findley descendants, and repeated by newspaper feature writers and amateur historians despite a lack of documentation.[1] Another story that Herbert's grandfather Murchison Findley told, and other Findleys repeated, was that their family was among Alabama's earliest pioneers, arriving in 1816 at a spot on the Black Warrior River fall line, the village known as Canetuck or Kentuck because of the thick stands of cane in the river bottoms and eventually called Northport. (A story that Davey Crockett told of a near-death experience in the Tuscaloosa County canebrake in 1816 was an enduring legend.)[2] Thus Kenneth may have enlisted because of the promise of a land grant in Alabama. During the same period, the United States waged a vicious war with Creeks in the Alabama Territory, forcing them to give up twenty-three million acres for white settlement. This land grab inspired "Alabama Fever" in thousands of eastern farmers who moved to the territory with visions of rich new plantations.[3] Kenneth could have made a reconnaissance trip to Canetuck in 1816—a local story recalls that a man named Findley visited the village in

1817 and commented on the thick canebrakes—but public records show that he was in Georgia in 1818. The earliest clear evidence of the family's residence in Tuscaloosa County is from August 1819.[4]

Kenneth's youngest son, Murchison, was a small boy when the family moved. He remembered their new home on the north side of the river as "a wild forest, the haunt of the Indian and game." There were almost no roads or paths, and Kenneth acquired land on both sides of the wagon trail later known as Byler Road and still later as Main Street, which led over and down Robertson Hill to the riverbank. He eventually built the dogtrot cabin that Herbert's aunt occupied when Earline married into the family.[5] He and his wife, Catherine Murchison, probably planned their migration with the Robertsons who settled nearby; Kenneth had lived near a family named Robertson in Pendleton, South Carolina,[6] and the most famous of the Pendleton Robertsons, the Revolutionary veteran James "Horse Shoe" Robertson, settled near Tuscaloosa by 1822.[7] (Horse Shoe was a sly old storyteller whose tales of the war became the basis for *Horse Shoe Robinson*, a popular novel by John Pendleton Kennedy. When a Tuscaloosa newspaper reporter interviewed Horse Shoe about the book in 1838, he said it was "all true and right—in its right place excepting about them women, which I disremember.")[8] When Catherine died in 1821, Kenneth buried her remains in the Robertson-Stone Cemetery across the road from his cabin.[9]

Literate, musical, prosperous, and public-minded, Kenneth and Catherine's children valued neighborhood and kinship. They tended to live close to each other after marrying and to name their offspring for each other. The oldest, John, married a Robertson daughter. Mary moved to neighboring Jefferson County, marrying David Crockett Hawkins, a namesake of the frontier hero. William owned a violin and numerous books, married into a nearby political family, and was elected sheriff in 1834 at the age of twenty-six.[10] Their youngest, Kenneth Murchison, served in the Second Seminole War, a series of battles between 1835 and 1842 in which thousands of southern troops floundered through Florida swamps in an effort to suppress the Seminoles and recapture the escaped former slaves whom they harbored. When the governor called for volunteers early in 1836, offering land grants as an inducement, a compelling local politician, Dennis Dent, organized a militia unit of Tuscaloosa County men.[11] About twenty-three years old, Murchison signed up for a three-month stint. The community staged a send-off where a young woman presented a flag to the men and one of the volunteers, Alexander Beaufort Meek, gave a rousing acceptance speech.[12] Here a coincidence with Earline's family history emerges. Alexander's father was Samuel Mills Meek, a minister-physician-pharmacist who mentored Earline's great-grandfather Griffin Christopher in North Carolina and migrated to Alabama shortly before Griffin.[13] A journal that Alexander kept suggests the stories that Murchison could have told about his short military career in Florida. Trudging over hills and through dense forests, they fended off ambushes by Seminoles who fired on them from dense hammocks. Their fight on Thonotosassa Creek, where Seminoles led by the famed warrior Osceola shot at them from close range, was one of the most memorable engagements of the war, but the swamp campaign was, overall, an undeniable failure. Murchison, Meek, Dent, and the other Tuscaloosa volunteers were back home by June.[14]

More coincidences: The following year, three enslaved men, two held by Samuel Meek and one by Dent, were accused of conspiring to murder Dent. Although Dent survived, at least two of the accused men were convicted and hung.[15] Then in 1838 Murchison was reunited with Dent on a jury that acquitted a white man of murder in a duel on a downtown street.[16] Finally, in 1841, Murchison followed his late brother the sheriff into the Cook family by marrying a younger sister of William's widow—and Samuel Meek officiated at their wedding. Rebecca Mahala Cook Findley died in childbirth two years later, leaving Murchison with a daughter also named Mahala. Busy with nine slaves and three hundred acres of farmland, he apparently entrusted the girl to the Cooks during part of her childhood. He remarried in 1851, soon after exchanging his military warrant for forty acres of bottomland.[17] This time he chose seventeen-year-old Lucy Virginia Keene.

Lucy's middle name was a tribute to her father's home state.[18] Oliver Towles Keene was the son of a Revolutionary War veteran, slaveholder, and prosperous miller in Fairfax County, Virginia. He migrated to Tuscaloosa County around 1827, buying land, establishing a mill for lumber and corn on Hurricane Creek, and naming a road Keene's Mill Road, just as his father had in Virginia. One story that adhered to Oliver involved his becoming rich by inventing or patenting an innovative waterwheel. In one version, his invention was a turbine-style wheel that he placed on its side in his large mill. However, turbines were in wide use in Virginia and Tennessee during Oliver's lifetime, so this probably was not the real basis of the invention legend. In another version, he invented a "treadmill" for use in rice fields. His machine could have been a treadwheel for pumping water from one field to another. Farmers in Asia had operated treadwheel pumps for centuries, but the machines may not have been in use in the Carolinas. Perhaps on a journey through Charleston, South Carolina, Oliver saw the large treadwheel or "everlasting staircase" that was used to torture slaves at the notorious commercial prison known as "Sugar-House,"[19] and had the brainstorm to use human foot-power to pump water into rice fields. Oliver's arrival in Tuscaloosa was another family story. In 1986, two of his grandsons, Oliver Maxwelton Keene (whose middle name hearkened to the Scottish town in the song "Annie Laurie") and Wiley Lewis Keene, told a newspaper reporter that Oliver rode to Alabama on horseback and met his future wife on the Huntsville Road. Oliver "came through here riding a horse," Max said. Wiley, who went by "Petie," picked up the story, saying, "My grandma was young, working for a fellow running a hamburger joint." Petie's nephew corrected his leg pulling: "It was a stagecoach stand." Petie went on, "'It was a stagecoach stand and it was on the Huntsville Road. . . . He was a hobo, but she married him,' he declared with a grin."[20]

As Earline learned, Petie was himself a favorite subject of family stories. He was "gassed," it was said, while serving in France in World War I. When a public health official insisted he install screens on his windows as protection from disease-bearing mosquitoes, he complied by installing chicken wire. He was best known for keeping goats: the memoirist Emily Hiestand recalled that "the shack where Wiley Keene lived with his goats" was a landmark on the road to Holt. Askance at his scruffy appearance when she first encountered Petie, Herbert and Earline's daughter-in-law asked, "Who is *that*?" and Earline giggled as she responded, "He's *kinfolk*!" When Herbert took my five-year-old brother, Jimbo, to meet Petie, the old scamp put Jimbo on a goat in a humorous reenactment of a Masonic ritual; the animal ran across the yard and into a fence, knocking Jimbo off.[21]

Lucy bore three daughters, Tranquilla Cherokee ("Trannie"), Mary Sophia ("Mollie"), and Sydnia, by the time she was twenty-five. Perhaps to help with the children, Mahala came to live with them, possibly bringing one or more enslaved servants; in 1855, Mahala reported owning personal property worth two thousand dollars.[22] In 1858, with Lucy soon to bear a fourth child, Murchison began construction of a house on the bluff overlooking White's Landing on the Black Warrior River, about a mile to the east of the state mental hospital that was under construction at the same time.[23] The house on River Road, which the family came to call Riverview, eponymous for the neighborhood that developed around it, was unlike the typical "plantation plain" homes of nineteenth-century farmers in Alabama because it had a two-story central section with two one-story perpendicular wings. Just as odd, it was decorated with a cutout, above the upper-story front windows, of the playing card symbol for clubs. Riverview was the subject and setting for several family stories that Earline must have heard. Lucy's brother Taylor Keene, who was about thirteen years old when the house was built, had told his daughter Sydnia Keene Smyth that Lucy designed the Riverview house.[24] Perhaps Lucy gathered ideas as she rode about town. The millwork on the front porch and the pair of tall lancet windows with pointed arches resembled those of another local house that was built in 1844, and the temple-with-wings design resembled the staggered wings of the Alabama Insane Hospital.[25]

Several elements of the stories about the house could explain the resemblance of Riverview to the hospital. Taylor Keene said a contractor named Robinson built the house in compensation for cornmeal that Murchison provided for enslaved carpenters, bricklayers, and other workmen on the asylum project. In an article about the Riverview house in 1966, the *Tuscaloosa News* also referred to an indebted contractor.[26] A brick mason named William B. Robinson did work on the hospital for Robert Jemison Jr., a powerful local legislator who sponsored the bill to create the hospital and was the lead contractor for its construction.[27] Of course, the contractor who owed Murchison for the cornmeal could have been Jemison himself. The name that Murchison and Lucy gave their first daughter is a hint that they were close to the older man; Jemison's daughter was the first Tuscaloosa girl to be named Cherokee and the Findleys' daughter apparently was the third.[28] Moreover, Jemison "rented," to use the term of the time, some of his enslaved workers to Murchison for construction of the house during the same time that he rented slaves for construction of the asylum. Hiring out slaves to perform skilled and semiskilled labor was typical in antebellum cities and towns, and Jemison practiced this type of business extensively, recording the transactions in an account book. Between October 1858 and January 1859, he rented twenty-two different men to Murchison, sometimes dispatching them to the Findley site for part of the day and to the asylum for the rest, but there is no surviving record of the payments he received for the slaves' labor. He could have provided the enslaved workers to Murchison at no charge.[29]

A third possibility is that another construction contractor, John Drish, actually paid Jemison for the slave labor on Murchison's house. Drish was a prominent planter, physician, and former legislator whose estate was one of the most imposing in Tuscaloosa. His daughter Katherine was the young woman who presented the flag to Murchison and the rest of Dent's volunteers back in 1836. According to local speculation, Drish was an alcoholic, incompetent doctor and unlucky gambler who was financially ruined by Emancipation while Katherine eventually lost her mind and was kept in a third-floor bedroom of the Drish house and tended around the clock by slaves.[30] A different Findley legend holds that Murchison won Drish's mansion in a game of cards. If the tales of the indebted contractor and the card game are true, it follows that Drish could have built Riverview in exchange for his own house. A coincidence supports this theory: When Drish had his house remodeled earlier in the 1850s, he added a three-story central tower similar to Riverview's center section.[31] Further, while the patrician and fun-loving planter who won or lost an entire plantation in a single game of chance was a stock figure in legends of Old South life, Murchison could in truth have been a sharp card player. He came of age when the frontier village of Northport was notorious as "a gambling den," and Taylor Keene said Murchison enjoyed the popular card game called Euchre and that the cutout of the ace of clubs commemorated a particular game with a friend who was a regular opponent.[32] In one version of the Findley family's gambling tale, Murchison returned the deed to Drish's house soon after their game. In another, he allowed the Drish family to continue living in the house and returned the deed to the widow after Drish died. Of Drish's death, one of Tuscaloosa's most prolific chroniclers, Matthew William Clinton, wrote that Drish "drank so much that he had delirium tremens. . . . One day [he] broke away from his servant, ran for the stairs, plunged down the steps and, with a cry of despair, fell dead midway of the hall." Kathryn Tucker Windham, a folklorist beloved in Alabama, added another thrilling element to this legend: "After his death Negroes on the plantation . . . claimed they heard Dr. Drish's stumbling footsteps followed by his agonized cry." And there was more: the ghost of Drish's widow also haunted the house, burning candles in the "tower room." In any event, the Drishes occupied their house in November 1860, two years after Riverview was completed.[33] Regardless of its accuracy, the legend of Murchison winning the Drish house in a card game and returning it demonstrates that the Findleys cast Murchison in the role of a benevolent planter who was the social equal of the wealthy physician.

❊ ❊ ❊

After a month-long lull in work on the house, there was a push up to December 23, perhaps so the family could move in by Christmas. The workers finished the job in January. For the most part, the interior of the completed house is a mystery, although a comparison of memory drawings by Taylor Keene and Preston Findley reveals that a kitchen was added behind the original "library or school room," with the library subsequently used as a dining room and the original dining room converted to a bedroom.[34] One piece of furniture, a massive chaise longue, is specifically linked in family stories to the Riverview house. The piece is seven feet in length, its front and back constructed of single pieces of walnut with simple curves in the fashionable American Empire style, its short eight-sided legs ending in bun feet. Part of the story of the chaise is that when Murk rented out the house after the death of his sister Mollie, he left the chaise in place—a detail that is believable since the piece is extremely heavy and not particularly comfortable. Another element is that the Riverview tenants kept the chaise on the front porch, although someone could have been thinking of Sydnia Smyth's 1929 photograph of the house, which showed a sofa of another style on the porch. Eventually the tenants left Riverview, taking the chaise with them, and Earline's later retrieval of the piece became another family story.[35]

By the time Lucy was preparing for the family's third Christmas at Riverview, Alabama was on the brink of secession. Tuscaloosa County voted on Christmas Eve in 1860 to elect delegates to the state secession convention, choosing the slave-renting contractor Jemison and William R. Smith, who both, like the hero in *The Little Shepherd of Kingdom Come,* opposed secession out of loyalty to the United States. Jemison was so passionate about preserving the Union that when the vote at the convention went against them, he broke down. Smith cried, too, but vowed that although he "regretted the necessity of the separation, now that the Single Star was unfurled he would always be found the advocate of Alabama's rights."[36] Lucy's father also opposed secession, according to Max and Petie Keene, and didn't want his sons to enlist but two did anyway, Lewis Bourbon in an Arkansas regiment and Taylor in the University of Alabama cadets.[37] Murchison, however, was almost fifty years old and had his military service in 1836 to his credit. He and Lucy had four or five children (their first son, born in 1860, could have died by this time; he did not live to the age of ten) and fourteen enslaved workers to support and supervise, most of them women, children, or the elderly.

Lucy also became pregnant again around the time the war began. There is no evidence that Murchison even joined the Home Guard, a militia unit for the town.[38] Maybe he helped the cause by delivering fresh fish to wives who were struggling to feed their families. Shortages of meat were severe, as Jemison warned the Confederate Congress, and Murchison caught huge quantities of fish using traps in the shoals below his house.[39]

The Findleys' main experience of the war took place shortly before its end, during the raid on Tuscaloosa by Union general John T. Croxton, a dramatic and devastating episode that became the town's best-known legend. In the spring of 1865, rumors that Union troops were about to invade flew through Tuscaloosa. The university cadets were guarding the Huntsville Road east of town and the Home Guard was on duty at the Northport bridge when Croxton marched his troops into Northport via Watermelon Road on the night of April 3. Residents rang the big bell at Northport's Methodist church to warn everyone in earshot and the guard tried to dismantle the bridge, but the Union brigade managed to cross it. The cadets, including Taylor, hurried downtown and skirmished briefly with the Union soldiers until the university president, realizing defense was hopeless, ordered them to retreat. Croxton's men soon seized control of the town and burned most of the campus, which the Union considered a military facility. The rapid events that night were terrifying. Did Murchison or Lucy hear the church bell, across the river and two to three miles to the west, or see the flames of a burning factory in Northport, or hear the shooting at the downtown bridge? They undoubtedly heard the explosion when the Federals torched a powder magazine, remembered as "the loudest noise ever heard around Tuscaloosa." A Federal platoon confiscated mules and horses at the mental hospital, and the asylum superintendent, Peter Bryce, sent an employee riding east on horseback to warn others. Did he also send someone down River Road to warn the Findleys?[40]

When they retreated, the cadets marched east along the south bank of the Black Warrior to White's Landing and up the bluff to the Huntsville Road, passing the Findleys' house. Taylor's arrival before dawn, shouting, "The Yankees are here!" certainly would have motivated Murchison and Lucy to hide or flee.[41] In notes accompanying her memory painting of Riverview and Preston's memory drawing of the floor plan, Ila Findley included a fragmentary story about the raid, recording that Murchison hid his wife, children, and female slaves in "secret closets." Hiding people was a variation of the story of hiding valuables from the thieving Yankees, itself a standard part of

Southern Civil War lore. A local memoirist, James Robert Maxwell, recalled that while Croxton's troops were in Tuscaloosa, his father and the family's plantation overseer hid "all the darkies and the mules and the horses" in a swamp. However, Murchison and Lucy would not hide their children in the house if they knew that Croxton burned buildings in town, since the children would be trapped in a fire. It is more likely that Murchison hid possessions in the closets but only considered hiding Lucy, Mahala, Tranquilla, Mollie, Sydnia, little "Murk," and slave women and that Mollie told some version of the closet story when Ila came to Riverview for piano lessons as a small child. In retelling the story, Ila cast Murchison as chivalric protector.[42]

Murchison and Lucy had named the son born in 1862 Kenneth Murchison Jr. but called him "Murk," the same nickname Murchison used.[43] In 1875, when young Murk was thirteen, he received a copy of *The King Bee's Dream,* a book-length poem about the war. Inscribing the book, he wrote "Mirk Findley, Tuskalosa [*sic*]." Later he changed the spelling, adding "Murk Findley, Tuscaloosa, Ala., December 25th, 1875." The author of the poem, Thomas Maxwell, was the local planter who hid slaves and livestock together in a swamp. He excoriated Croxton for burning the campus and in a passage clearly derived from Scott's "Lady of the Lake" even alluded to the shoals of the Black Warrior: "Resting near the Warrior's falls," his narrator prayed that an Indian spirit might appear, "her footsteps on the wave or stream."[44]

With the emancipation of his workers, Murchison's assets plummeted from fifty thousand dollars in 1860 to four thousand in 1870. The Keene fortune also eroded and Lucy's brother Taylor became a laborer for another farmer in the county while her sisters remained unmarried.[45] "Nearly all of [the] state's aristocracy were 'uncomfortably embarrassed,'" one Alabamian observed. "Poverty was . . . quite literally making planters into red necks."[46] Jemison told his former workers they could remain only if they continued to behave like slaves, working in a crop-sharing arrangement and never "gadding abroad without a pass."[47] Whether the Findleys' and Keenes' former slaves stayed on their farms is unknown, but an elderly black gardener, Elijah Webster, and his middle-aged wife or daughter were the Findleys' closest neighbors to the west. Like his father-in-law and his grandfather John Findley in South Carolina, Murchison operated a gristmill. Lucy sometimes volunteered at the hospital, helping Peter Bryce's wife, Ellen, by teaching

Sunday school for the patients. The Findleys owned a piano,[48] so Lucy could have given music lessons as their daughter Mollie later did; that could be why Taylor called one of the public rooms of the house the "school room." Three of the children attended school while seventeen-year-old Tranquilla helped care for Flora, born in 1866 and named for Flora MacDonald, a Scottish heroine whose legend was associated with the Findleys' ancestral home, the Isle of Skye.[49] To the east, the neighborhood bustled with professionals and tradesmen who were finding ways to survive financially in the post-slavery world.[50] Murchison must have surmised that his son would need a profession to supplement income from farming.[51] Engineering was a field with opportunity; railroads were expanding and the US Army Corps of Engineers planned a series of locks and dams on the Black Warrior, some to be near the Findley house.[52] When the university established a degree program in civil engineering in 1881, young Murk enrolled.[53] That year, the engineering professor sat with four of his students for a studio portrait, their pose like a "conversation picture," an eighteenth-century style of painting that conveyed the conviviality of social peers. Three of the young men wore cadet uniforms and posed with tools as if they were shortly to embark on a surveying mission, their attitude suggesting their boldness and military, as well as intellectual, strength. Their names are missing but one of the young men resembles later portraits of Murk.[54] After receiving a bachelor's degree in engineering in 1885, Murk worked as a railway engineer and helped his father manage the family farms. The university identified him as a "planter and engineer," the social meaning of "planter" being elastic enough to encompass relatively small-scale farmers like Murk and his father, whose families had status as pioneers or antebellum planters.[55]

Pretty, petite Ida Belle Hargrove could have known the young engineer her entire life, or perhaps they met at a Sunday afternoon orchestra concert at Lake Lorraine, a popular park near the Findley home.[56] Ida was part of a large and well-known family in Tuscaloosa County, her great-grandfather Dudley Hargrove a minor legend in Alabama Methodism for his stand, two generations before the Civil War, in defense of slavery. Born in Virginia, Dudley was a lay minister and related to William McKendree, one of the denomination's founding bishops. He migrated to Alabama with his family and slaves in 1818, settling near Big Sandy Creek, a few miles southeast of the small village of Tuscaloosa. Anson West, the first chronicler of Methodist pioneers in Alabama, recorded that Dudley led worship in a brush arbor and founded a church. The historian James Sellers perpetuated this story of

Dudley's founding role in county Methodism, elevating him to "Reverend" status.[57] In 1819 Dudley's fellow Methodists nominated him to be a deacon on the Tuscaloosa circuit, a lay position that would allow him to assist presiding elders in administering the sacraments. However, the Tennessee Annual Conference, which governed Methodist churches in Alabama, strictly prohibited deacons and ministers from holding slaves, so the question "Shall Hargrove be elected and ordained a deacon?" turned upon Dudley's refusal to emancipate his slaves. Peter Cartwright, a circuit-riding preacher well known for his opposition to slavery, recalled that the debate was "vehement and vigorous" and the ministers decided narrowly against Dudley. The votes against Dudley and another candidate for ministry precipitated the denomination's governing board adopting a policy in 1820 that *permitted* slaveholding by church officials and ministers—a shift Anson West considered God's rebuke of abolitionists.[58] (This meant that when Earline's great-grandfather Griffin Christopher married into a slaveholding family in South Carolina in 1822, there was no impediment to his continuing his ministerial career.)

Dudley's daughter Martha married the Hargroves' wealthy neighbor Hardy Clements; one of their sons went to the Harvard University School of Law. Dudley's son John Harris, who went by "Jack," developed one of the largest plantations in the neighborhood, somehow acquired the title "Colonel," and became a justice of the peace; one of his sons, Andrew Coleman "Cole" Hargrove, also studied law at Harvard. Another of Dudley's sons, Hope Hull, bought land, married, and had seven sons, naming the first Tenedus Allen.[59] Jack and Hope became justices of the peace, so trusted in the community that William R. Smith, the delegate to the secession convention, remembered them as "highly esteemed." When questions arose in 1837 about the disposition of enslaved workers in a local man's estate, the probate court appointed Jack, Hope, and a third man as "commissioners" to determine how the workers should be divided.[60]

Tenedus married Minerva Thomas in 1854. Like Murchison and Lucy Findley, the couple had young children and a farm to run when the Civil War began. Although some Hargrove men quickly enlisted in the Confederate Army, Tenedus refrained until the Confederate Congress passed an unpopular conscription act in 1862. He served a short time in a unit with some of his brothers, but around the time his brother James was captured by Federal troops at Vicksburg he provided a substitute in order to obtain a discharge.[61] Reenlisting a few months later, Tenedus joined his other brothers and cousin Cole in Lumsden's Battery, which engaged in horrifying battles, but received a medical furlough and was at home with the family at the end of the war; his children recalled that he was "broken in health." During his absence, Minerva had, like many Confederate wives, managed the farm. Now she "rallied his courage, and strength."[62] Beginning with Ida, who was born in 1865, Minerva and Tenedus had five more children, two of whom died in childhood.[63] By 1870, their farm was one of the largest agricultural employers in their census precinct and Minerva had two former slaves as live-in house servants. A decade later, six servants, including a mulatto man, four black teenagers, and a black nine-year-old boy, lived in a separate house on their property. Their son William Hope gradually took over running their farm, and when Tenedus died in 1882, Minerva and the younger children, Ida, Thomas, and Lula, moved to the house on University Avenue.[64]

The family story about Murk and Ida's courtship was that in 1891 she attended a church conference in Knoxville, Tennessee. The conference probably was a meeting of the new Epworth League, an organization for Methodist young adults; the minister at First Methodist Episcopal in Knoxville, Lyman E. Prentiss, had organized the league's first southern chapter, and Ida's distant cousin Bishop Robert Kennon Hargrove later was a president of the league. Murk followed Ida to Knoxville to persuade her to marry him. She accepted his proposal and Prentiss officiated at their wedding.[65]

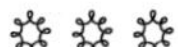

Murk and Ida had four sons. For their first baby, born the year after they married, they combined three surnames: Murchison Hargrove Findley; he went by his middle name throughout his life. They named their second son Preston Sydney Findley, possibly in honor of William Preston, an important Scottish figure in the history of Freemasonry, and Murk's closest sibling, Sydnia.[66] Their third son was Herbert Lyman Findley, his middle name in memory of the Knoxville minister who had died the year before.[67] Naming sons for important ministers was an old Methodist custom. Ida's grandfather was one of many namesakes of Hope Hull, a charismatic founder of the Methodist church in Georgia, and her cousin the bishop was a namesake of Robert L. Kennon, a Methodist minister in Tuscaloosa in the 1820s.[68] Finally there was John Emmett Findley, born in 1898. The significance of his name is unknown, but the Findleys' immigrant Scottish ancestor was John Findley and the United Daughters of the Confederacy had established its first chapter in Tuscaloosa two years earlier, naming it for Robert Emmett Rodes, a local Civil War hero.[69]

The year after Hargrove was born, Ida provided the money, perhaps a gift from her mother, to purchase a farm of two or three hundred acres near Keene's Mill Road. In a nineteenth-century practice, the property was then known for its original owners as the Old Snow Place, but in a subtle change that had the effect of redefining the property as original Findley land, the Findleys came to call it the Old Place; the local chronicler Temo Callahan remembered it as "the Findley place."[70] Much later Preston carefully drew, from memory, a floor plan of the one-story house at the farm, noting it was built of twelve-foot logs. It had a central hall and two rooms of almost equal dimensions, which probably comprised an original two-room dogtrot cabin. Two wings appear to have been gradual additions for a total of five bedrooms, two kitchens separated by a screened porch on the back of the house, and a six-foot-deep porch that wrapped one side and the front. Preston's wife, Ila, an enthusiastic amateur artist, painted a picture of the Old Place as she remembered it, the front and side porches enormous, the yard of swept dirt enclosed by a picket fence, like the yard and fence in the early photograph of Hargrove and Preston posing in front of a gardenia bush.[71]

Herbert enjoyed relating how the family rode from the Old Place to town and back, laughing about how his brothers gobbled the candy their parents purchased for them while he slowly savored his, but when I heard that story he did not mention whether little Sam got to go on the trips to town or if anyone brought candy back to him. Sam Long was a four-year-old African American child who lived in Murk and Ida's home as a servant in 1900. This was not unusual. Other white households in the family had black children as live-in servants, and Ida's mother had a seven-year-old black girl named Ada Long living in her house. Sam and Ada were siblings whose parents worked as farm laborers in south Alabama. They probably were "apprenticed" or "bound," by probate court ruling or informally, to the Findley and Hargrove families. Perhaps their parents asked the Hargroves to temporarily take in their older children when they moved to Butler County.[72] Apprenticeships were a post-Emancipation invention to enable former slaveholders to indenture children, a variation on the practice whereby slaveholders rented or "hired out" slave children to other whites. On the grounds that the children's parents could not care for them, probate judges awarded custody of many African American children to white families that used them as laborers.[73] Earline was familiar with this type of arrangement when she married Herbert. Her uncle and aunt Frank and Susie Christopher had an eleven-year-old black servant named Edward who lived with the family and worked as a "nurse," supervising Earline's cousins, in 1900. Her cousin Oliver Christopher, a lawyer and future sheriff, took in a nine-year-old white boy as an "apprentice" in 1917. As recently as 1920, Oliver's parents had nine African American servants including two "bound boys" living in their house or on their property. The practice was so common that the terms "bound boy" and "bound girl" were official designations of the US Census.[74] In a sense, little Sam Long was not the only person "bound" to Murk when Herbert was a child. Murk became the road supervisor for the county in 1901 and eventually held the position of county engineer during a period when Alabama counties put some jail inmates to work on road projects and "leased" many others to private individuals. Like a planter directing his overseer, Murk directed a foreman who supervised inmates wearing black and white stripes as they did roadwork.[75]

But what jobs could four-year-old Sam do as a servant in Murk and Ida's home? His duty may have been simply to play with Herbert and John when their brothers went to school. For black children to serve as companions to white children was a custom that persisted from the antebellum period into the twentieth century. Ida's future across-the-road neighbor Mrs. Eugene Smith arranged for "little black chums" to go with her young son and his cousins when they went swimming in a pond.[76] Sam probably performed simple chores such as feeding the chickens at the same time he watched over Herbert and John.[77] And what if Sam missed his own family, or sometimes cried himself to sleep? Did Herbert ask his mother how this was fair?[78] Ida might have answered as Victoria Clayton of Tuscaloosa did, by quoting Leviticus 25:44 and 25:46: "Both thy bond-men, and thy bond-maids . . . shall be of the heathen that are round about you. . . . And ye shall take them as an inheritance for your children after you."[79]

Murk and Ida bought the property that became Earline's married home from a real estate development company in 1906 and completed construction of their two-story house the following year, perhaps using a mail-order house plan.[80] School could have been Murk and Ida's primary reason for moving into town. Hargrove was fifteen and a student at the university. Preston was about fourteen and Herbert and John about twelve and nine.[81] Though smaller by half than block-sized antebellum properties nearby, their town property resembled the homes of Tuscaloosa's wealthiest families, which typically had "flower and vegetable gardens, stables, and outhouses for . . . an abundance of servants."[82] The move brought the Findleys closer to the new county courthouse that was under construction, where Murk was to have an office, and to important friends and associates such as the circuit judge Henry Bacon Foster. Now Ida could participate in more of the lively social events at the Methodist church and could accept invitations to gatherings such as the "at home" party that their friends Norfleet Harris and his wife, Anna, "a delightful character," gave in September 1907. Ida was closer to her Hargrove family, too. If Ida invited her mother and siblings to her new house for Christmas dinner that year, she probably gave some thought to the centerpiece for the table. When Mrs. Smith across the road entertained the Daughters of the American Revolution a few years later, her centerpiece was "a pyramid of winter fruits with clusters of grapes and crimson ribbons giving another bright touch." Ida was not able to enjoy entertaining in her new house for long, however. Just as spring began in 1908, she and ten-year-old John became seriously ill. They died within two hours of each other, she of pneumonia and he of pneumonia and measles, both highly contagious diseases. With one of the surviving boys lying ill with pneumonia, Murk called the Methodist minister to conduct the funeral and had Ida and John buried in Evergreen Cemetery.[83]

✲ ✲ ✲

When Earline moved into Ida's last home thirteen years later, a brilliant red and green woolen coverlet, the initial "I" embroidered in one corner marking it as Ida's, was in pristine condition, carefully stored to protect it from moths. Known in the family as the New Albany Coverlet, the double-faced Jacquard piece had an image of the 1851 Alabama capitol, a background of alternating crimson and green triangles in the Birds in Air pattern, a central Wreath and Star pattern of grapes, roses, leaves, and a sunburst, and a border of grapes and urns. This lightweight blanket was the subject of a story that Lula Hargrove carefully documented in a letter to Herbert on the occasion of his passing the coverlet on to Anne, the details coming from stories Lula had heard and her own early memories. In 1874 or 1875 Tenedus and Minerva Hargrove commissioned a mill in New York to make a woven coverlet, with wool from the family farm, for each of their children. One of the family's former slaves, "Aunt" Jane, prepared the wool for shipment, in "home-woven" bags, to the mill. "When the Civil War was over and the

Negroes all free[,] 'Aunt Jane' did not want to leave her 'white folks,'" Lula wrote, echoing the fantastical interpretation of James Sellers, her fellow Methodist and the local historian. "She was given a house and all the land around it that she wanted, for a garden, cotton patch, chicken yard etc., free of rent, near the 'Big House' as long as she lived. . . . Each week Aunt Jane got a supply of groceries, and each day a meal if she wanted it at Marster and Mistress kitchen. She lived many years; always loyal to the family of Hargrove father and sons." Referring to Tenedus's brother James, Lula added Aunt Jane "grieved for 'Mars Jimmie' who had died in a Federal prison at Vicksburg." She ended her story, "When Aunt Jane died she was buried by the white folks she had loved, and served and who had served her."[84]

Some of Lula's statements are verifiable. Tenedus produced forty pounds of wool from thirty head of sheep in 1870. Carding wool was a routine chore for black and white women on small farms. The bags in which the Hargroves shipped the wool could have been "home-woven."[85] Lula's approximate date of 1875 for the coverlets makes sense because textile manufacturers marketed a selection of commemorative designs for coverlets directly to wool-producing farm families, so it is plausible that the mill that purchased wool from the Hargroves also offered designs such as the Alabama capitol. (The centennial of the American Revolution in 1876 was one of the historic events that such coverlets typically commemorated, thus the common reference to "Centennial coverlets.") "New Albany" could have referred to Albany County, New York, where the Harmony Manufacturing Company established the largest textile mill in the world in 1872, and Lula could have confused the New York county with the town of New Albany, Mississippi.[86] In addition to the details about the provenance of the coverlet, Lula's background description of the Hargrove households is credible. The second and third generations of Hargroves in Tuscaloosa were slaveholders. Tenedus's brother James did die of typhoid fever while he was a prisoner of war, although he was in Alton Federal Military Prison in Illinois, not Vicksburg.[87]

Jane's identity is a mystery, however. Lula glossed over the servant's surname by referring to her simply as "Aunt Jane" in quotation marks, which implied an affectionate relationship between the Hargroves and the elderly woman.[88] She could have wanted to obscure the fact that she and Jane had the same last name; a sixty-year-old black woman named Jane Hargrove lived in the vicinity of the Hargrove farms in 1870. Since that Jane was born in Virginia about 1810, she could have been in one of the "droves" of enslaved workers and children that Amy Chapman told Ruby Tartt were herded "like cattle" to Alabama.[89] Lula's characterization of Jane as a loyal and contented former slave who chose to remain dependent on the Hargroves is questionable. Many emancipated African Americans wanted to leave home to test their freedom. Charlie Johnson told Tartt "atter de S'rrender," what freedpeople tended to call the defeat of the Confederacy, "Papa took us chillen en moved over 'bout a mile from Livingston, en us stayed dere 'bout a year. Den we come back hyar, en ain't never lef' no mo.'" Another former slave in Sumter County remembered, "'Mos' all de niggers dat had good owners stayed wid 'em, but de others lef'. Some of 'em come back an' some didn'.'"[90]

Did Jane stay on the Hargrove farm because the Hargroves were "good owners," as James Sellers would have believed, or because she had relatives nearby, or because she was isolated with no means of transportation or contacts who could help her get settled elsewhere? Did the Hargroves threaten Jane as Robert Jemison Jr. did his employees, warning that if they left his land, they could not return?[91] Did the Hargroves provide housing for old and infirm freedpeople because federal authorities compelled them to do so, and did Lula's parents neglect to mention this detail to her?[92] Did the Hargroves actually pay Jane for her labor or, like some former slaveholders in Alabama, merely provide shelter and food, just as in slavery days? Perhaps the Hargroves promised Jane a coffin and a burial spot in the family cemetery as an inducement to stay on the farm; a planter down in Marengo County did exactly that. Some white people considered black deaths opportunities, like black weddings, to exhibit noblesse oblige by contributing to burial arrangements, arranging for a newspaper report, or even attending funeral services.[93] (Herbert and Earline's friend Roland Harper took their son Lyman to the funeral, in Castle Hill, of a black janitor in 1943.)[94] Despite Lula's claim about Jane's final resting place, there is no evidence of Jane in the Hargrove family cemetery located near Duncanville. There seems to be no record at all of when the freedwoman Jane Hargrove died or where she was buried.[95]

Past middle age at war's end, Jane could have chosen the predictability and security of working for the Hargroves over starting a new life elsewhere. She could have been grateful that the Hargroves supported her instead of evicting her.[96] She may even have considered herself a faithful member of the Hargrove family, as Lula believed,[97] but the essence of Lula's story, that the coverlet was material evidence of the gratitude of a dependent black servant, is impossible to confirm. Lula's letter about the coverlet reflected the prevailing white view of slavery.[98] Although she did not call Jane a "mammy," in other regards she expressed the attitude that was typical of postbellum upper-class white families, that "Mammy" belonged to them. Lula's story of "Aunt" Jane was part of the fantasy of the Old South, the set of ideas that dominated wishful thinking about African Americans at the time Earline became a Findley.[99]

Four

The Bungalow

EARLINE CONTINUED TO WORK FOR TWO YEARS after her wedding, her income helping to furnish the house that she and Herbert built in 1922.[1] The young couple could have continued living in Murk's house in town. Although its design was ordinary (one might say characterless), the house on University Avenue had enough elements of planter style—a processional sidewalk and central front entrance, the second story—that Earline could have envisioned making it a home something like the historic houses in Livingston. There was plenty of space on the property to build a separate small house for Murk, allowing Earline and Herbert privacy in the main house. Alternatively, she and Herbert might have moved into the old house at Riverview, just as Preston and Ila lived in the house on The Old Place. For a woman of sufficient imagination, Riverview could have been the stage for an Old South lifestyle and a lifelong role as a gracious matron,[2] but Earline evidently wanted a new house. Maybe she did not feel free to improve and decorate Murk's town house as she would have liked, and the Riverview house probably was not a highly desirable home for a young couple; the photograph by Sydnia Smyth shows half-dead shrubs and bare dirt in the front yard as well as a sagging sofa on the porch.[3] Worse, it was on the far side of the mental hospital in a neighborhood of small, working-class homes. Developers were rapidly creating dozens of new subdivisions in Tuscaloosa, such as Alberta City, where the Hambys bought a house,[4] but Murk encouraged Herbert to build on the University Avenue property by selling it to him for one dollar. Making gifts of land to children at the time of their marriages was an old custom; Murk's parents had given him part of the Riverview property soon after his and Ida's marriage.[5]

Although Murk and Herbert determined the location of the new house, Earline probably had the deciding vote on the architectural style.[6] In planning her home, she referred to a large cloth-bound catalog of architectural trim titled *Building with Assurance.* One of its full-page, full-color illustrations showed a woman greeting a guest on the front steps of a Colonial Revival house that was painted pale pink with green shutters and a gleaming white portico. Earline could have chosen the same fashionable style.[7] She could also have chosen what we might call a "Dogtrot Revival," a one-story house with a center hall, to evoke a gradually expanded pioneer cabin like the Findley houses in Northport and on The Old Place. During the two years she spent in Livingston, she was surrounded by examples of that vernacular style. Many small houses on the blocks around the town square had been gradually expanded with enclosed center hallways and gracious front porches. Some had been expanded upward into two-story houses with impressive double porticos.[8] Earline, however, wanted a house in the fashionable Craftsman style. Craftsman plans promised the woman of the house that she could add her own "artistic" touches to express, as Emily Post encouraged homemakers, "*your* old-fashioned conventions [or] your emancipated modernism—whichever characteristics are typically yours," decorating the interior to meet "a desire for . . . psychic comfort." The style's creator, Gustave Stickley, called Craftsman bungalows "honest homes"; they were a reaction to "picturesque" residential architecture with extreme ornamentation in a variety of styles, so it must have appealed to Herbert's practical side. Earline's choice, considering the bungalow's location on a main thoroughfare, was a visible, even prominent, expression of modernity and of a national, rather than regional, aesthetic. By choosing to build a Craftsman house, she identified herself in her new community as a modern matron rather than one devoted to perpetuating antebellum culture.[9]

To conserve some of his new property for other uses, Herbert positioned the bungalow, which the family usually referred to as "329" for its street number, so close to Murk's house that the older building loomed over the west side. The driveway and "car barn" were on the east side. A chicken yard and a smokehouse abutted or straddled the line dividing the backyards, probably serving both households.[10] With formal living and dining rooms, a small den, three bedrooms, a kitchen with a butler's pantry and breakfast bay, and three porches, the bungalow was spacious, similar to designs such as the “York” and “Walton” in catalogs of bungalow plans.[11] It had front-facing gables and Italianate brackets beneath the eaves, hallmark elements of Craftsman style.[12] Many of the town’s prominent new residences were brick, but Herbert and Earline chose a plain wood exterior, painting the front and sides of the house white and leaving the back of the house unpainted for at least a decade, as a photograph taken in the early 1930s shows.[13] Some companies offered kits of ready-cut lumber with their house plans, but Herbert had lumber cut on the Old Place, using longleaf pine for the frame and plank siding, American black cherry for the flooring and possibly the paneling in the dining room, and walnut for the mantel, which one of Herbert’s cousins, a carpenter, made.[14] As with Herbert’s selection of the honeymoon bed, there is a parallel in these construction materials with the chivalric literature he read as a youth: “I don’t say that I could afford to buy burl maple, walnut, and cherry for wood-work,” said Stratton-Porter’s hero in *The Harvester,* “but since I have it, you can stake your life I won’t sell it and build my home of cheap, rapidly decaying wood. The best I have goes into this cabin.”[15]

Brick piers and painted columns supported a large two-sided front porch. Porches were another hallmark of Craftsman style, promoted for allowing air and light to easily enter the home.[16] Like dogtrots in pioneer cabins and spacious porticoes on columned antebellum houses, porches welcomed the interplay of breezes, the scent of flowers, and the greetings of passersby. Earline’s porch wrapped the northeast corner as if to mirror the porch that wrapped the northwest corner of Murk’s house. Although mail-order designs for bungalows did not typically include screens, she and Herbert added screens to their porch, making it habitable, despite the mosquitoes, for sitting, visiting, and regarding the view across the wide avenue to the asylum grounds. Earline loved flowers and established conventional plantings around the house as quickly as she could, with a foundation of camellias, or “japonicas” as folks were likely to call them, azaleas, and daffodils and narcissi across the front; a banana bush—a shrub in the same family as magnolias—on the east side of the porch like one on the east side of Murk’s porch, where the family could enjoy its fragrance in the spring; and a fast-growing pecan tree for shade and nuts.[17] Along the outer edges of the driveway and backyard, she planted rows of cherry laurel, a traditional shrub in patrician southern gardens that evoked long residence because it grew slowly.[18] A black servant, possibly the yardman she later referred to as Sam, probably assisted her in the planting.[19] The novelist and essayist Sara

Haardt described Tuscaloosa in 1925 as "one of the loveliest havens this side of paradise," its "wide streets and . . . luxurious shrubbery [giving] it an air of culture, dignity and leisure; above all, a charm that is like the faintly tarnished but romantic beauty of a distinguished lady."[20] The writer Clarence Cason formed a similar impression of the town. When he and his wife and child moved to Tuscaloosa in 1929, the Findleys' bungalow on the eastern outskirts of town probably was one of the first houses they saw. "Behind the japonicas," Cason wrote a few years later, "the houses are not pretentious, but they are rightly designed." Front porches, he thought, were part of the "conception of aristocracy . . . sitting quietly . . . throughout long summer evenings 'one after another.' In everything one senses the lack of the contemporaneous."[21]

The interior of Earline's house also had many common Craftsman elements including the generous scale of the rooms and hallway, built-in storage spaces, and an absence of dead ends, with every room leading to at least one other.[22] Two of the bedrooms connected to a sleeping porch, a Craftsman feature that promised the protection of fresh air against contagions.[23] There was a bookcase in a corner of the living room and another in the hallway; a china cabinet with glass doors in the dining room; the butler's pantry with more glass-door cabinets; and a convenient linen cupboard flanking a passage between the den and front bedroom.[24] In the butler's pantry there was a long counter with tools affixed for grinding meat and cracking pecans and lower cabinets for storing canned goods and serving pieces. A Dutch door in the kitchen, uncommon in the mosquito-ridden South but a feature of some antebellum houses, enabled Earline to open the upper half of the door to exchange words with servants and peddlers who came to the back porch while leaving the lower half closed and bolted to block their entrance.[25] She also could lean through the upper opening and ring her cowbell to call the children or the hired man or washerwoman; beckoning servants with a bell was a centuries-old ritual of the master class.[26] The bungalow movement encouraged using the kitchen as a living area, instead of solely as a workspace,[27] so Herbert and Earline probably shared most morning and evening meals at the table in the breakfast alcove, which had large windows on three sides, unlike the cramped, dark, booth-style nooks of many bungalows.

A formal dining room for special occasions was an essential element of a genteel home.[28] For her dining table, Earline chose silver flatware in the Chantilly pattern that had been introduced in 1895 but crystal and china patterns that were brand-new in 1922. The Woodland stemware by Fostoria was elaborately etched with twining vines and flowers; the Theodore Haviland Eden china was feminine and lushly decorated yet distinctly modern thanks to the dramatic shapes of its serving pieces. Of the china pattern, Haviland advised that "nothing could be more appropriate for Christmas, or more permanently beautiful and useful in table decoration."[29] Earline probably purchased pieces of silver, crystal, and china a few at a time, expanding her dinner service for special meals with members of the extended family. Herbert's brothers and their families may have joined Earline, Herbert, and Murk for the first Christmas dinner at the bungalow. Preston was a surveyor for the US Corps of Engineers; he and Ila had a six-month-old baby named Ida Louise for their mothers.[30] Hargrove and his wife, Olive Knighten, lived in Ashland (Clay County), where Hargrove probably was working in the graphite mining industry. They had a son, Murchison Hargrove Jr., but the child died the day after Christmas that year, when he was not even two years old, and was buried in Evergreen Cemetery in a sad echo of Ida's and little John's deaths soon after their first Christmas in the first Findley house on University Avenue.[31]

While Clarence Cason wrote gently nostalgic descriptions of front porches as seen from the road, another professor at the university vividly described a view that Earline could see from the bungalow. A member of the university's English department for six years, Carl Carmer wrote a blurry mélange of memoir and fiction about the living conditions and social customs of white and black people in Alabama, the title, *Stars Fell on Alabama*, a reference to a meteor shower that had occurred a century earlier. The reading public was horrified yet fascinated by Carmer's stories of lynchings and race-baiting and the book became a best seller.[32] In one dramatic section, he described a nighttime parade in Tuscaloosa by members of the Ku Klux Klan. Although Carmer did not say whether the story was true, and referred to the century-old oaks on downtown streets as elms, his description of how the moonlit Klansmen appeared seems real: "Beneath the tall elms on Queen City Avenue rode three horsemen robed in white. . . . One of them raised a bugle and . . . the minor four-note call sounded. Behind the mounted trio stretched a long column of marching white figures, two by two, like an army of coupled ghosts." In his story, Carmer and a friend followed the parade in a car, turning left at Bryce Hospital "toward a glow that was growing in the sky to the north of us," then right on River Road, passing the old Findley place at Riverview, which Carmer called "Riverside[,] and suddenly [they] were in a wide cleared area beside the river." A "great arc" of "white-robed men" stood in the clearing and hundreds more people listened to a speaker rail against Negroes, Catholics, college students, and the federal government.[33]

If Carmer's Klan parade really took place, the marchers passed the Findleys' houses on University Avenue. His dark tableau of masked men on the shadowy riverbank was typical of public performances staged by the Klan in the 1920s, when social discontent helped it attract thousands of new members in Georgia and Alabama. While Hargrove and Olive lived in Ashland, a dentist from the town, Hiram Wesley Evans, became the Imperial Wizard of the Klan. Evans is remembered for leading a group of Klan members in kidnapping a black bellhop from a Dallas hotel and using acid to write "KKK" on his forehead. White men could join the Klan for ten dollars and acquire a greater sense of identity, a feeling that they were important parts of their world instead of existing on its margins. The Klan typically rustled supporters from Protestant churches, and one night in 1924 three thousand Klan followers in Tuscaloosa attended a weeknight sermon where a Methodist evangelist from Birmingham, James Oscar Hanes, spoke on the topic "The State, the Klan and the Church."[34] The same year, a photographer named Raynor perched in a boat and shot frames for a wide-format picture of a Klan rally beside a wide creek or the Black Warrior River in Tuscaloosa. The panorama shows about two hundred men posing in white robes, the holes in their hoods like deep eye sockets, the upside-down reflections of their bedsheets like faint chalk smears on the dark water.[35] Raynor probably sold copies of the panorama as mementoes of the rally. Huge gatherings like the Tuscaloosa rally were ritualistic spectacles, like lynchings or official hangings, and souvenir photographs helped spread and perpetuate knowledge of the events.[36] The rally that he photographed could have been the event Carmer described. There was a landing below the Findleys' old house so someone could have carried Raynor in a boat from the bank to the middle of the river for him to take the shots for the panorama.[37]

If the Findleys watched Carmer's Klan march from the bungalow's front porch or from safely inside the darkened living room, the scene could have prompted Murk and Herbert to tell Earline the story about the fatal involvement in the Klan of Murk's cousin Murchison Findley, whom we will call Murchison the Second to distinguish him from Murchison Findley Sr. and Murchison Findley Jr. The story of Murchison the Second came down through the family as a bare fragment that Herbert mentioned to correct a local acquaintance's misconception that Herbert's grandfather died in a Klan raid. It was not his grandfather, Herbert said, but a cousin with the same name.[38] Two years after the incident, a congressional subcommittee, the same one that interviewed witnesses about the murder of Abe Lyon in Earline's grandparents' neighborhood, collected information about this episode. As witnesses told the story, it began in April 1869 when two young white men driving a wagon on Byler Road in Northport slowed down to tease a small black boy, threatening to take him with them so that he would never see his family again. When the terrified child ran crying into his home, his father emerged, furious and brandishing a gun, and followed the white men up the road, warning them not to frighten his child. After dark the white men, now with several reinforcements including twenty-one-year-old Murchison the Second, returned, apparently bent on whipping the father, if not worse, as punishment for his insolence. A short gun battle took place in front of the man's house and he shot Murchison. The other white men carried young Murchison to the Findley cabin where he soon died; in the turmoil the shooter escaped to Hale County. Murchison's death caused "quite a panic in the city and country," one witness testified, and there was "a terrible excitement, growing out of that disorder"; men in Klan garb seized and lynched two African American men and whipped others.

Acting like antebellum "paterollers" and slave hunters, wreaking "lynch justice," Ku Klux Klan members had committed more than one hundred murders in Alabama since the Confederate surrender four years earlier.[39] Dressed up like "ghosts of the Confederate dead who had arisen from their graves," they wore white hoods, had guns prominently holstered on belts over their robes, and terrorized freedpeople in Tuscaloosa. A local newspaper publisher, Ryland Randolph, was the leader or Exalted Cyclops of the Tuscaloosa chapter of the Klan. He printed and distributed posters with nonsense such as "Shrouded Brotherhood! Murdered Heroes! Fling the bloody dirt that covers you to the four winds! . . . Beware! Beware! Beware!" A cartoon that he published, depicting a lynching of carpetbaggers, or Northern interlopers, became particularly notorious. It showed two white men, one holding a carpetbag labeled "Ohio," hanging from a tree while a mule labeled "KKK" ambled away.[40] Now Randolph warned readers that "punishing Negroes indiscriminately" for Murchison the Second's death could move the federal government to declare martial law,[41] but this could simply have been a veiled call for vigilantes to make sure they murdered the right black men. In desperation, a group of African American citizens wrote to Governor William H. Smith on April 22: "A band of Ruffians known as KuKluks snuck an attack on a colored man night before last he being aware of them was prepared and succeeded in killing one of the Clan. . . . Yesterday . . . about forty came through town . . . in pursuit of the man[,] . . . mounted on horses with Double barrel shotguns loaded with buck shot. . . . We look to be murdered any moment."[42] Despite their plea, the terrorism continued and by late May some white residents grew tired of Randolph's rabble-rousing. A group of "Loyal Leaguers" went to the editor's office, threatening to tar and feather him, and Robert Jemison Jr. wrote to his son-in-law Cole Hargrove that Randolph's editorials were as much to blame as the "Radical" Republicans for the "Tuscaloosa troubles."[43]

Whether or not Murk and Herbert told Earline about the ignominious end of Murchison the Second, she must have recognized the malignant influence of the Klan. Two years after the riverside rally that Raynor photographed, one of her contemporaries from Choctaw County, Charles Campbell "Charlie" McCall, ran for state attorney general on a Klan ticket. Charlie's father was the probate judge during Earline's childhood; his grandfather was Daniel McCall, the neighbor who alerted Squire Christopher to the lynching of Abe Lyon. McCall won the 1926 race, but the Klan's tactics became so controversial he resigned from the organization the following year, calling the Klan "the greatest menace." One hundred and fifty Tuscaloosa Klan members resigned in agreement with him.[44]

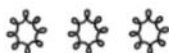

Wanting the option to continue teaching, Earline took a summer course at the university in 1924 to earn a lifetime teaching credential. Plans changed, however. In December, about six months pregnant, she resigned from her teaching job.[45] She was finally free to devote herself to the role she wanted, that of the beloved mother. Earline knew that pregnancy and childbirth still threatened every woman with possible death and that some babies died at birth (the wife of one of her cousins delivered a baby girl in 1919 who died the same day), but advances in obstetrical care made delivery in hospitals safer, with new anesthetics offering a painless experience, and Druid City Hospital had opened in 1923 just a block away and across University Avenue from the bungalow.[46] Earline delivered both of her children there, naming their first Herbert Lyman Jr. and a daughter, born in 1928, Anne "with-an-e" Elizabeth.

The early photographic portraits of Lyman and Anne that survive among the family's artifacts were typical of those of upper-middle-class families at the time.[47] In the first, Lyman, about twelve months old, wore a long infant gown and leaned against the cushioned side of a sofa, looking attentively at someone outside the camera's range. When Anne was about eighteen months old, Earline took her to the J. Virgil Jones photography studio. Anne posed, chubby hands clasped and her hair cut in crooked bangs, on a chaise longue or sofa. Earline bought at least two copies of this picture, which the studio packaged in sturdy cardboard folders, and gave one to Velma and her husband. Earline had another portrait taken when Anne was about three years old, just after having Anne's honey-blonde hair cut in a perfect pageboy. She costumed her in an underdress or slip and a short, sheer, dotted Swiss dress trimmed with double rows of ruffles at the round collar and hem, pinning a large silk bow at Anne's shoulder like a corsage. She "completed the costume," as the society writer for the *Tuscaloosa News* often wrote in describing local women's ensembles, with a golden bangle bracelet, white ankle socks, and white patent leather shoes.[48] Anne posed for that picture on the woven cane seat of a low bench, feet crossed at her ankles, smiling demurely. The photographer tinted her lips a rosy pink and her cheeks and dress a paler pink so she looked like she was glowing in the dimly illuminated scene. Then, when Lyman was about seven and Anne about five years old, Earline had a portrait shot of them together, Lyman in a white suit and striped necktie, Anne in a sleeveless dress elaborately trimmed with turquoise ribbon and braid, a large turquoise bow precariously clipped to her fine blonde hair. Those prints also were tinted, the children's cheeks pink and the sprigs of flowers on Anne's dress pink and green. Earline made another elaborate costume for Lyman when he appeared as George Washington in an historical pageant in 1932. The jacket and pantaloons were satin and the sleeves ended in deep lace. The costume became a treasured heirloom that Lyman's grandsons wore for large photographic portraits.[49]

Like portraits and a good wardrobe, good manners were an essential indication of upper-middle-class status, and Earline taught Lyman and Anne proper etiquette for every situation, from saying "yes, ma'am" and "no, sir" to writing thank-you notes to passing serving dishes at the table (always to the right). Ladies, Anne learned, did not eat (or smoke) while walking. Herbert reinforced Earline's lessons, particularly in the matter of how gentlemen deferred to ladies, and repeated them for my brother, reminding him to remain standing until Anne sat at the table.[50] A small book in the family's library, *Essentials of Etiquette: Complete Rules of the Social Game* by Ellen Dryden, probably was Earline's frequent reference on all of these points. It was common among elite families for a young woman's mother to give her such a book, but *Essentials of Etiquette* was published in 1924, suggesting that Earline purchased it herself, perhaps feeling she did not possess all of the etiquette skills she needed despite being an adult, a college graduate, and a married woman.[51] The manual was a foolscap octavo, a compact volume with maroon leatherette binding and gilt on the top edges of the pages. A stamped image of a gentleman bowing low to kiss a lady's hand decorated the front. It contained pen-and-ink illustrations of prosperous, attractive white people at weddings, dinner parties, and dances and a two-page spread of line drawings of a young boy, napkin around his neck as a bib, practicing the proper ways to handle a fork, knife, and spoon. "Whenever in doubt as to the proper implement to use for conveying food to the mouth," the handbook advised, "remember that where one can use the fork, one never uses fingers, knife or spoon."[52] This became the subject of a joke, Herbert writing to Anne that he did "not even have a piece of pie to eat with a spoon."[53]

In spite of Earline's rigorous etiquette training, Lyman and Anne had pampered childhoods. Lyman had a set of toy soldiers; Anne had a china-headed doll. Both children had hollow wooden figures, fashioned with removable heads, which held their crayons. There was a nine-volume set of children's books called the University Bookshelf, published when Lyman was a year old, in the bookcase in the hallway. Volume 1, *Fun and Thought for Little Folks,* had many detailed drawings, full-color paintings, cartoons, photographs, finger play and counting games, poems, and folktales. Anne learned to chant one of its nursery rhymes, perhaps from Earline while she baked in the kitchen:

> This is the way we bake our cake,
> bake our cake,
> bake our cake;
> This is the way we bake our cake,
> so early Saturday morning.[54]

Annie pieced and quilted a coverlet and quilt, in Earline's favorite combination of pink and green, for Anne's doll bed, the tiny quilt pieces and perfect stitches evidence of her skill as a seamstress.[55] Murk often played with the children. Noticeably taller than Herbert, with a distinctive moustache and a mischievous manner, he lived with Herbert and Earline in the bungalow for several years and spent a good deal of time with Lyman and Anne even though he worked as the engineer for the county.[56] He built a playhouse for Anne in the backyard and hid his whiskey bottle in it—a secret that Anne mirthfully helped him keep from Earline.[57] In their old age, Anne and her childhood playmate Margaret Robb "Robbie" Shook both took pleasure in sharing happy stories about times with Murk. Robbie wrote that Father Findley sometimes walked with Anne, Lyman, and their neighborhood friends to the drugstore on University Avenue and bought licorice for them. He let the children accompany him when he inspected the fruit trees on the town property, picking apples for them to eat, and went with them into the barn to visit the family's cow. When Herbert and his brothers were children, they went with Murk and Ida on trips to town; now Herbert's children and their playmates went with Murk on outings to the Old Place.[58]

Herbert also was playful with the children, as a letter that Lyman saved in a childhood scrapbook confirms. When Lyman was four years old and visiting the Meridian relatives with Earline and Anne, Herbert typed this letter on his law office letterhead. A vivid account of a visit by an opossum, the letter had many familiar details so the little boy could envision his father's escapade when Earline read it to him: "Last night while I was reading I heard OLD MAGGIE just a barking and barking" at the big house, Herbert wrote. "Then the telephone rang and Mr. Shook called me and said that old Maggie was after an O'possum and to come over there. . . . I got my flash light . . . and went [out] in the chicken yard and climbed over the fence at the fig tree." Then the real excitement began! "I shined my flash light in the corner of the fence and saw a great big O'possum. While Mr. Shook held old Maggie I walked up close to the O'possum and caught him by the tail." Wrapping up the story, Herbert wrote, "We put him in a box and I think that Mr. Shook is going to give him to one of his negroes that works for him. If [Mr.] Shook keeps the O'possum until you come home I will show him to you."[59] During my own childhood, Herbert leaned down on a summer day, eyes twinkling, to show me how to insert a broom straw in the small holes in the sandy soil of the driveway, chanting, "Doodlebug, doodlebug, come out of your hole." He sang snatches of the antebellum minstrel song "Dixie"—"I wish I was in the land of cotton; old times there are not forgotten"—and the World War I song "Over There!"[60] He taught my brother and me to ride our bicycles, pushing us in a circle around the backyard until we were pedaling steadily and then letting us go. Once Lyman and Anne learned to ride their bicycles,

Earline allowed them to venture beyond the house and yard, their world extending as far as the range of the cowbell that she rang to call them home.[61]

By August 1929, when Herbert wrote to Lyman about the opossum, Murk had rented his large house and garage to Robbie's father, Robert S. Shook, who was the superintendent of a nearby coal mine. Murk may have temporarily occupied the bungalow's back bedroom—where he could have his own entrance to the house via the sleeping porch—but the family eventually built a small guesthouse for Murk, known as The Little House, behind the car barn. This allowed Herbert and Earline to reoccupy the spacious back bedroom and rent the den and front bedroom to "roomers." The Great Depression was underway and many households in Tuscaloosa took in relatives or rented bedrooms to roomers or, if they were particularly desperate, to "boarders," the latter paying to take meals with the family.[62] Earline and Herbert first took in her twenty-five-year-old brother Otis, who found a job as the manager of a café in town. At other times they rented the den at the front of the house to a young woman who worked in a laundry and the master bedroom, more desirable because it had a direct entrance to the main bathroom, to Roland Harper, a quirky botanist at the university who was kind of like Professor Zamo, a humorous character in a cartoon called "Our Boarding House" that anchored the comics page in the *Tuscaloosa News*.[63] The Findleys' roomers used the front door as their entrance while the family used the kitchen door.

For Earline, sacrificing so much of her beautiful home to strangers was hard. Roomers meant more housework. Having Otis in their home must have been stressful; when he eventually moved back to Meridian, his drinking problem drove Earline's mother "crazy."[64] The family probably spent most of its time around the kitchen table and in the back bedroom, so Earline rarely had a private moment.[65] Worst of all, having lodgers demonstrated that the family was financially needy. She emphasized that their lodgers were *roomers*, not boarders,[66] meaning she did not serve meals to them, and when some of their tenants were slow to pay the rent, the Findleys did not press them.[67] For Herbert, however, the arrangement meant more income; for Murk, The Little House was a private place for him to relax, entertain, and perhaps enjoy a drink with friends. For Lyman and Anne, the roomers meant more adults to play with them. The laundry worker befriended little Anne, sometimes letting her sleep with her,[68] and Harper treated the children as surrogate grandchildren; he once drew a cartoon of them racing up a mountainside to greet Santa Claus.[69]

If my childhood Christmases in the 1960s are any indication, each Christmas season at the bungalow was a ritualistic reenactment of various family customs, some of antebellum origin. Earline made toffee cookies using an old Alabama recipe and pecans the children helped gather and crack.[70] Around December 20, Herbert took the children to the downtown farmers' market to select a cedar for their Christmas tree, and Earline supervised decorating it with strands of colored electric bulbs, ornaments, and thin strips of metallic "icicles."[71] As the twenty-fifth drew near, the adults pretended to spot Santa's elves hiding here and there in the house.[72] On Christmas Eve, Herbert supervised the children while they played on the lawn with sparklers, a safe version of the South's traditional Christmas fireworks.[73] They held the slender, sizzling wires at arm's length, stretching and waving to draw twinkling white arcs on the night's dark backdrop. At the end of the evening, the adults permitted each child to open one present before tucking them into bed, listening as they recited their bedtime prayer, the same one that genteel children in the Old South had said:

> Now I lay me down to sleep;
> I pray the Lord my soul to keep.
> If I should die before I wake,
> I pray the Lord my soul to take.[74]

As the children drifted off to sleep, the twenty-seven bells of Denny Chimes, the university carillon in a towering brick campanile four blocks away, chimed every quarter hour.[75]

My brother and I learned to race down the bungalow's hallway on Christmas morning and shout "Christmas gift!" to Herbert and Anne. This custom originated as a ritual form of begging by slaves. For slaveholders to hand out ceremonial Christmas gifts to enslaved workers linked generosity with gentility, implied a familial relationship, and perpetuated the idea that any monetary compensation to slaves was a gift rather than something that whites owed them. The ritual became a gentle jest in many elite white families. When Earline's great-grandparents Griffin and Nancy Ann Christopher were visiting their neighbor Sarah Gayle at her home in Greensboro in 1827, Sarah's husband, John Gayle, the future governor of Alabama, arrived home unexpectedly. The Gayles' seven-year-old son Matt jumped up to greet his father, exclaiming, "*Christmas gift*, Pah!"[76] There was a predictable form to the rest of Christmas morning, too: Jimbo and I waited for everyone to assemble in the hall. We entered the living room together and found that Santa had left us notes, filled our stockings with oranges, apples, and almonds (customary southern Christmas treats)[77] and small gifts, and arranged books and toys in two displays, one for each of us.

By examining newspaper advertisements and articles and by considering the physical layout of the bungalow property and its location in relation to the streetcar line, we can speculate on Earline's routine as she performed her most continuous and burdensome duty, purchasing food for the family and providing three meals per day, over the thirty-two years of her married life.[78] Groceries were available at many stores in town.[79] For last-minute purchases, she might send a servant or one of the children to the store on the northeast corner of the block, which Murk rented to different grocers over the years, or to Anders Grocery on the southeast corner.[80] However, the Tuscaloosa Curb Market, which took place on the sidewalk beside the courthouse, was the vibrant economic heart of Tuscaloosa County.[81] Farmers offered a huge variety of produce and handmade products; shoppers came from around the countryside; romances budded between vendors; and guitarists and banjo players strummed from tailgates while itinerant preachers proclaimed under the shade trees and inmates called down from the windows of the nearby jail. Beginning in 1935, Herbert's cousin Kate Keene Seay, a sister of Max and Petie Keene, officiated as the prominent and powerful "market master," so greeting her was probably part of Earline's shopping routine.[82] At the curb market on a typical Saturday in the early summer, spring crops were still available—in Cason's lovely pastel language, "little bundles of fragrant sassafras, mustard greens flecked with drops of water, butter beans of pale green, prickly okra, buttermilk in green fruit jars, [and] golden honey"—and there were early onions and potatoes. At other times of the year, the curb market had muscadines, poultry, snap beans, pole beans, turnip greens, peaches, watermelons, and fresh sorghum syrup. If Earline resisted buying the pretty roses, petunias, phlox, and sweet peas that farmers' wives cut before dawn, it was because she had her own flowers at home to cut and arrange.[83]

Returning from her shopping trip, stepping off the streetcar at Lawn Station, Earline would feel gritty and unpleasantly damp. The heavy Saturday traffic stirred up a lot of dust that blew in the open windows. The car would have been crowded, too, with African Americans standing in the back.

Shifting her bags from the crook of one arm to the other, Earline crossed the road and the bungalow's side lawn. Entering the house through the kitchen door, she carried her bags to the pantry and then sat at the table. Through the windows of the breakfast bay, she could see people and vehicles on University Avenue, visitors who pulled into the driveway, and their yardman, who would knock at the back door because for a black man to approach the front door of a white home was a grave violation of the caste system.[84] To refer to a recipe, Earline might open her copy of *Holland's Cook Book*. She used this cookbook extensively, copying recipes on the inside covers and affixing handwritten notes, recipes clipped from newspapers, and can labels to some pages. The materials she used to alter her cookbook are important evidence about her favorite dishes and about her friends.[85] For example, the recipe that she wrote inside the front cover was for a rich, sweet, fluffy concoction called apricot cheese salad. She noted in parentheses that it was from Eugenia, probably Eugenia Latimer, an unmarried teacher and longtime family friend. Eugenia also gave Earline recipes for coffee cake, icebox rolls, and applesauce cookies and Eugenia's mother gave Earline a recipe for lemon cheese filling.[86] The preponderance of sweet dishes among Earline's handwritten recipes indicates that, like elite white women in the antebellum South, she left preparation of routine meals to a cook when possible and devoted much of her time in the kitchen to making complicated or even fantastical treats such as the congealed apricot salad, these specialties part of her identity as a privileged woman.[87] Assuming the dishes that Anne prepared for Herbert after Earline's death were the same ones that Earline made for him, Earline often assembled a salad plate by topping a leaf of iceberg lettuce with a square of congealed salad or a slice of tomato and a dollop of cottage cheese, half of a canned pear with some grated cheddar cheese, a scoop of Waldorf salad featuring chopped pecans, or a small mound of canned fruit cocktail. These were typical salads that women learned in early twentieth-century home economics classes.[88]

On a routine summer weekday, Earline prepared a congealed salad early so it could "set up" in the icebox. While she cooked, the children's nurse, Annie Mary, might take Lyman and Anne to visit Auntie Lula and Grandmother Hargrove.[89] It was nine blocks from 329 to the ladies' house, and Lyman and Anne were slow going, being so small. Earline might instruct the nurse to depart on their walk just a short time before Earline would return from shopping so that she would have plenty of time to herself in the kitchen. The nurse probably also worked as a cook, laundress, and maid.

On their return, she could shell peas, kill and pluck a chicken, or start a roast, all the while watching the children. The Findleys employed Annie Mary, whose last name Anne recalled was Peoples, as early as the summer of 1929.[90] She lived in a small house in the backyard, probably the converted smokehouse, so, unlike servants who went home once or twice a day, she was almost always available to work.[91] Having at least one black woman at her beck and call was the minimum necessary for the elite woman's way of life in Tuscaloosa. Practically everyone Earline knew hired servants to handle laundry and many middle- and upper-class women had a nurse or maid in addition, but the most luxurious arrangement was to have "live-in" help.[92] The idea that the loyal black "mammy" should do the hard work of caring for white children was pervasive, and the archetype of the happy (or grouchy) and everlastingly loyal old black woman who cared for generations of a white family's children reached the height of popularity during the decade when Earline's children were born. This mythical servant personified the white fantasy that African Americans were so content with their deprived and oppressed lifestyle that black women could be trusted with white people's children.[93]

Thanks to Annie Mary, Earline could cook as she pleased, enjoy the domestic arts of sewing and flower arranging, and participate in her church circle's weekly social meetings, but life in the bungalow was not entirely rational. Commenting on Tuscaloosa customs from his office at the university, Clarence Cason pointed out that "there is no logical explanation of a southern woman's refusal to ride on street cars unless they have separate seats reserved for Negro passengers, while she has left her child at home to be cared for and influenced during its formative years by a Negro nursemaid."[94] The memoirist Emily Hiestand captured the fantastical mentality, describing Ila Findley's paternal kin in Holt: "Firmly embedded in the culture of segregation . . . they and their African-American neighbors had lived on adjacent lands for a long time and their connection was real: collard greens, peanuts, tools, and sick-bed courtesies were exchanged."[95] The Findleys lived like nobility. Herbert associated with the most powerful men in the community; low-paid servants enabled Earline to choose the domestic chores she would perform herself. Father Findley sometimes seemed to merge into the figure of Santa Claus, both of them looming, loving, laughing, white-haired men bearing gifts.

❋ ❋ ❋

Murk entered politics in the spring of 1932, running for the county revenue board that formerly employed him. Earline went to Meridian during the final week of the campaign, probably because her mother, Annie, asked her to come help with Otis, whose drinking was so unmanageable, Annie was "living in . . . dread all the time."[96] Murk lost his campaign but his relations with prominent older men in the community probably helped Herbert receive an appointment two months later as a part-time instructor in the School of Commerce and Business Administration at the university. The salary was a valuable supplement to Herbert's income from practicing law.[97] That summer, he and Murk took the family, including Earline's beleaguered mother, to Florida. They traveled by train to Boca Grande, a resort town promoted as "an island colony of quaintly old distinction."[98] Back home, Anne declared she was saving her pennies so they could make another trip.[99] Earline placed about a dozen snapshots from the vacation in her photo album, labeling the group "Bogregrande, Florida." In one picture, Anne and Lyman stood outside a one-story stucco building, possibly a tourist court. Two black men whom Earline identified as cooks posed at attention in the background. Tall palms shaded the building and clumps of blooming lantana, coleus, and vinca edged a small lawn; Earline eventually grew lantana in one of her flowerbeds. She appeared in a few of the pictures, standing at the edge of the frame and gazing without smiling at the children. She must have taken the snapshot of Herbert, the children, and Murk and Annie together, Herbert seated and relaxed, straw hat in hand, with Lyman by his side and Anne on his lap, Murk tall and erect, and Annie tiny and stooped in a long, old-fashioned dark dress.

The children's nurse disappeared at some point during these early years of the Depression. Annie Mary was not like Jane, the woman in Lula Hargrove's story, who kept working for the Hargroves after the Surrender, her devotion earning her the honorific "Aunt" Jane. Nor was she like "Aunt" Sally Tucker, a "widely known negro nurse" who "faithfully" served another Tuscaloosa family from the age of fifteen until she died in 1933 at age forty-five.[100] Annie Mary not only did not stay forever on the Findley place, she left without saying good-bye.[101] It was not unusual for domestic workers to simply not show up for work. "Living in" was too much like slavery—some domestic workers felt they were not free if they were required to sleep where they worked—and the work was hard and wages low.[102] Moreover, after a massive departure of African Americans to northern cities during the period between 1916 and 1930, a shortage of maids, cooks, and nursemaids in southern towns meant a skilled domestic worker usually could find another job.[103] It also was not unusual for white employers to suspect African Americans of stealing[104] and another part of the family story about Annie Mary's departure—a story so dramatic that Earline's daughter-in-law, who did not marry into the family until approximately fifteen years later, clearly remembered it in her mid-eighties—was that a ring belonging to Earline disappeared at the same time that Annie Mary left.[105]

Annie Mary probably acted the role of the contented servant until the day she left, making her disappearance a shock to Earline.[106] To have black domestic servants contributed to white women's sense of security and order as well as to their leisure time and social status. It was reassuring to believe the black underclass was content with its lot, disinclined to walk off the job or, worse, rebel in a violent manner.[107] Thus Annie Mary's disappearance was more than a personal betrayal of Earline, who had entrusted her children to her; more than a theft; more even than the refutation of the idea of the "loyal darkie."[108] As Jennie Smith, who lived across the avenue in a large house surrounded by expansive flowerbeds, wrote, having live-in help enabled one "to think and take interest in other things[,] especially my flowers[, so that] everything is looking very beautiful."[109] Annie Mary's departure was a reminder that without willing servants Earline could not maintain the beautiful world she had created in and around the bungalow.

Five

Distant Bells

IF THEY SAW EACH OTHER AFTER CHURCH on September 17, 1933, Earline and her close friend Hatchett may have paused to chat. Tabitha Hatchett Hinton, whose friends called her by her maiden name, and her husband, William Newton "Newt" Hinton, had several ties with Earline and Herbert: Newt's sister was married to Herbert's first cousin once removed, and the Hintons' children were close to the Findleys' children in age. The two women belonged to the Laurel Class, an adult class at First Methodist that had recently held a picnic at the Riverview landing. On September 17, the women could have discussed projects of the Verner School Parent Teacher Association—Earline was secretary—or the upcoming Blue Eagle parade, a celebration of new federal wage and hour standards.[1] While they talked, Herbert might have visited with Newt about hunting; predictions were good for doves, squirrels, turkey, and deer.[2] For anyone who grew up around Alabama adults, it is easy to imagine the idiom of the next turn in the men's conversation. Herbert would have asked Newt about "that business in the newspaper," referring to a front-page report that Dennis Cross, an African American employee of the dairy farm that Newt operated with his brothers Claude and George, was accused of attacking a white woman. Newt would have replied, "I'll tell you what Claude already told them. There is no way Old Cross did what that girl said."[3]

Virtually every weekday afternoon and Sunday morning since the spring, the *Tuscaloosa News* had delivered frightening front-page news, not just about the ongoing world economic crisis but about outbreaks of disease, crimes, manhunts with bloodhounds, and racial terrorism. Updates on the appeals by the nine black men known as the "Scottsboro boys," who had been convicted of raping two white women on a boxcar in north Alabama, often appeared. The circuit judge, Henry B. Foster, blamed local crime on "widespread unemployment [and] resulting business stagnation."[4] Fear of black men became an epidemic, like the annual summer fears of polio and rabid dogs. The newspaper's anonymous gossip columnist described how two little white girls wandered away from home during the night and became frightened of some African Americans: "Alice started calling . . . 'hurry up, daddy is calling for us,' thinking that this ruse would keep the negroes from bothering them." In a separate incident, white men pulled alongside a black motorist on Ninth Street and shot him through the window of his car, hitting his left arm with so much buckshot that it had to be amputated.[5] There also had been the murder earlier in the summer of a young white woman named Vaudine Maddox.

Beginning on June 15, the newspaper frequently published reports on the front page, often beneath banner headlines, about the Maddox case. After police and deputy sheriffs rounded up two young African American suspects, Dan Pippen Jr. and A. T. Harden, a mob of several hundred men gathered outside the jail and Foster transferred the prisoners to Birmingham for protection. Police arrested a third suspect, Elmore "Honey" Clark, who was known in the black community as a "mean nigger" despite having a withered arm, and a grand jury indicted all three men.[6] When the families of Pippen and Clark hired two young local lawyers to represent them, Foster drafted three more experienced criminal defense attorneys to help the families' lawyers without compensation. One of the new lawyers, Reuben H. Wright, was admired as "the best all around lawyer at the Bar." To Temo Callahan, he "exuded strength and confidence" and "treated all his clients alike, whether rich or poor, educated or ignorant"; he "did hundreds of little favors for people that no one ever heard about."[7] The Maddox case became vastly more incendiary when a left-wing New York organization, International Labor Defense (ILD), sent three more lawyers to Tuscaloosa to try to take over representation of the defendants. When the ILD called the defense lawyers whom Foster appointed "lynch lawyers," local indignation escalated; the newspaper described the mood in the courthouse as "deep resentment." An estimated two thousand people, many from outside the county, drove into town in caravans of cars and trucks for the opening of Pippen's trial, some rolling down University Avenue past the Findleys' bungalow. They congregated outside the courthouse where city police, deputy sheriffs, and National Guardsmen pushed them back from the steps. After Pippen told Foster that he had not retained the ILD lawyers, Foster asked the National Guard to escort the outside lawyers to safety. Other guardsmen patrolled downtown, using tear gas to break up a fight among protesters.[8]

Concerned about security for the three defendants, Foster had given the sheriff an undated order to transfer them to another jail again if necessary. After hearing rumors a few days later that a group planned to abduct Pippen, Harden, and Clark from the county jail on a Saturday night, the sheriff reportedly directed several deputies to move the men back to the Jefferson County jail in Birmingham. The convoy included Robert Murray Pate, a deputy known as "a nigger-killer."[9] The deputies later claimed that they expected to be pursued by would-be lynchers if they drove directly east out University Avenue, so they drove "a circuitous route," leaving town by Hargrove Road, cutting north to Keene's Mill Road, and following more dirt roads before turning east on US Highway 11. The next events were a replay of an episode so common that the Association of Southern Women for the Prevention of Lynching had specifically called for sheriffs to do more "to guard their prisoners at all costs," blaming law enforcement officers for failing to protect black defendants and for helping mobs abduct and murder suspects.[10] Soon after crossing the county line, the deputies said, they encountered a gang of about ten armed, masked men who stopped them, saying, "We want those niggers." The deputies relinquished the prisoners and the kidnappers drove Pippen, Harden, and Clark to another location where they shot all three, killing two.[11]

With three gunshot wounds and a broken arm, Clark pretended to be dead until the murderers left. He wandered through woods and fields for more than twenty-four hours before seeing an African American woman and asking her for help. She called upon a neighbor, Pearl Hargrove, who probably was descended from workers held by Herbert's maternal ancestors.[12] As the *Tuscaloosa News* reported, Hargrove "went to Tuscaloosa for medical aid, walking the entire distance of twenty-five miles." He found a doctor and together they notified the sheriff. Deputies went to the woman's house to pick up Clark and bring him back to the jail, where he eventually received medical attention.[13]

The *Tuscaloosa News* reproduced the contents of a telegram from the ILD that accused Foster and the sheriff of being "directly responsible" for the murders and demanded that the governor see to the "immediate arrest" of the judge, sheriff, and "all deputies and private persons concerned, and immediate prosecution and enforcement [of the] death penalty." At the same time, Foster convened a grand jury investigation of the abduction and condemned the murders. Considering the ILD's criticism of Foster and the suggestion by a sociologist at the University of North Carolina, Arthur Raper, that some southern judges were "apologists" for lynching, Foster's statement to the grand jury was deserving of the lengthy excerpt the newspaper provided: "Mob violence . . . represents not the orderly will of the majority as expressed through the mandates of law, but the inflamed and irrational hatreds of the few," he said. "Lynching disrupts the harmonious relationships of the community and results in hatreds that lead to further disrespect of the law." Foster urged the grand jury to "take all the time" it needed to "summon before you all the witnesses who know anything" about the murders.[14] But the grand jury issued no indictments. Some citizens had information about the murders, according to the sheriff, but were "so terrorized . . . they will not testify in court." Raper came to Tuscaloosa in the fall to interview citizens and surmised that the deputies who drove Pippen, Harden, and Clark actually delivered them to the killers. He all but accused Pate of the murders. Pate's guilt, Raper hinted, was an open secret in the town, these lines seemingly worded to avoid a libel charge: "A number of Tuscaloosa citizens" felt the "deputies knew about the plans of the mob and . . . actually participated in the lynching. R. M. Pate . . . has the reputation of being quick on the trigger, where Negroes are involved." Temo Callahan also thought "just about everybody seemed to know who had done it," but no one volunteered enough information for charges and no arrests were ever made.[15] As the trial of Clark, the remaining defendant in the Maddox murder, began, the horror of both Vaudine Maddox's death and the highway murders of Pippen and Harden were subsumed under resentment of northern outsiders' assassination of the characters of the defense lawyers and judge.

Burglaries and robberies, accidental deaths, police shootings, and murders continued throughout the brutally hot summer. One of the older women of First Methodist, whose son-in-law was Herbert's good friend Toombs Lawrence, died in July after a black driver speeding east on University Avenue struck her.[16] Each incident that involved a black suspect added to whites' fears. Subscribers to the *Tuscaloosa News* read about at least two lynchings in Mississippi, two in Georgia, one in Louisiana, and one in North Carolina. In one of the Mississippi cases, the victim was accused of insulting a white woman. In Louisiana, where the body of a fifteen-year-old white girl was found in a cane field, the Associated Press reported "police had not even identified the suspect by name" when he "was seized quietly by [a] mob and hanged."[17] The accusations and attacks against black men had a ritualistic quality, with details sometimes resembling those of earlier incidents.[18] For example, the railroad setting of the Scottsboro accusations recurred when a black man jumped from a freight train car near Moundville, south of Tuscaloosa, in June and a railroad employee shot him in the face, destroying his left eye. After a scuffle between a railroad conductor and a black man in Deatsville, Alabama, in August, the local prosecuting attorney chased the man down and held off a mob of about fifty men who tried to seize the "hobo," shouting, "We don't like the Scottsboro . . . justice."[19]

Front-page reports of racial violence could even serve as scripts for impromptu performances. A week before the accusation against Dennis Cross, the *Tuscaloosa News* reported that in Montgomery a young woman and her escort were abducted from a parked car and dragged to a cornfield, where the woman was assaulted and murdered.[20] Within a day or so, eighteen-year-old Alice (or Allis) Johnson began spinning a story, apparently in an attempt to get a new dress. She approached the staff of the Tuscaloosa Emergency Relief Committee and a woman at a private residence, asking both for a dress to replace one that was old and torn and saying a black man tore the dress while attacking her. She told the same story at the police station in Tuscaloosa, possibly at the urging of her husband, who later went to the police to press for an arrest in the case, but the police did not take her claim seriously because Alice Johnson was known for telling implausible stories. Then the newspaper reported that a white woman in New York City said "a huge negro," naked to the waist and barefoot, attacked her in an empty restroom in a subway. "The negro jumped to the tracks and fled toward the next station with a crowd of men . . . at his heels," and police officers "with drawn pistols" had to hold off a mob of people shouting "Lynch him!" and "Shoot him!" The next day, Johnson noticed Cross, who was forty-nine years old and in poor health, at the relief center. Pointing at him, she cried out that it was he who attacked her. Someone called the police and she elaborated for them: She was walking alone along a wooded road between the river and some railroad tracks, during the heat wave of the week before, and Cross grabbed her and tore her clothes. When she screamed, he ran off. The police immediately arrested Cross and the *Tuscaloosa News* reported the accusation and charge against him on the front page the next day. Newt Hinton's brother Claude, a widely known and well-liked local figure, told police that he didn't think Cross had done anything. Cross had been partially paralyzed for years so he could not have "run off" like the young woman said, which meant he had not attacked her either. However, a white man named Jim Brown came forward to contradict Claude, saying he had been in the area at the time of the attack and saw Cross run into the woods. Someone, probably the Hinton brothers, posted bond for Cross a week after his arrest. Cross spent four days at home with his family before a group of about seven white men came to his door early on Sunday morning, claiming to be law officers, and abducted him. A few hours later, he was dead, struck forcefully on the forehead with a blunt weapon and shot four times. Jim Brown reported finding his corpse.[21]

Over the next few days, Foster instructed a grand jury to investigate the crime and implored citizens to come forward if they had any information. The governor offered a reward of four hundred dollars for leads. The newspaper called Cross's death a "stupid murder" and launched a crusade to stop mob violence and lynchings in Tuscaloosa County. A group of black and white ministers, led by the Findleys' and Hintons' minister, issued a joint statement in favor of law and order, denouncing "the 'lawless element' that has been active under cover of darkness, terrifying negroes and stirring up racial discord." Reaching out to whites who enjoyed black music, St. Mark African Methodist Episcopal Church announced a special service with "negro folk songs, spirituals and plantation melodies" with reserved seats so white visitors would not have to sit beside black worshippers. Many white residents attended meetings, joined committees, and generally agreed that the murder of Dennis Cross was a terrible injustice.[22]

The former English professor Carl Carmer no longer lived in Tuscaloosa but followed the events of 1933 and speculated about the public's angry mood. "I can picture them milling about," he mused in the afterword he was preparing for *Stars Fell on Alabama*. "The old irresistible urge is upon the shifting crowd. No ties will hold them when that madness lowers."[23] Black fear mounted as the city commissioners discussed getting the police department its own pair of bloodhounds to be "kept ready for instant use."[24] After three white men stabbed an elderly African American man as he pushed a wheelbarrow of corn along Fifteenth Street, an elderly white woman spoke out. Emily Estes Snedecor was the widow of a former superintendent of Stillman Institute, a Presbyterian college for African Americans. She couched the situation in terms middle-class whites might appreciate, warning in a letter to the newspaper that good black workers were likely to move away. "They are quiet law-abiding people . . . in a community that will lynch people without a trial—that will lure a man from his home and shoot him," she wrote. "The best of our negro friends will go—leaving the rabble, untrained and uneducated without good leaders of their own race."[25] Despite the furor that fall, however, other local news soon overshadowed the murders of Vaudine Maddox, Dan Pippen, A. T. Harden, and Dennis Cross. Foster eventually dismissed the charge against Elmore Clark in Maddox's death.[26] No one was ever charged in Cross's murder and his death disappeared from the pages of the newspaper.[27]

Judging from the society columns on page five of the *Tuscaloosa News* on weekdays and the society section on Sunday, the paper provided constant distractions from murders and mobs, particularly for mothers focused on training the next privileged generation. Hattie Porter Collier, a junior high school principal and the wife of a pharmacist, was the newspaper's society editor, one of the social arbiters of Tuscaloosa. Collier's descriptions of local parties could be so "grandiose," Earline's daughter-in-law, Margaret Findley, later drawled, "You didn't even know it was yo' pah-ty." It was not unusual for an elite white woman to hold the job of society editor for the newspaper in a southern city. In fact, Earline's close friend Grace Hamby wrote the weekly column "Alberta City News" for the *Tuscaloosa News* in 1941 and 1942.[28] Cason, a journalism professor at the university, ridiculed the flowery writing of "gushy small-town society editors,"[29] but for the female readers of the *Tuscaloosa News*, its society reports were important views of private social events. As the circuit court prepared to try Harden, Pippen, and Clark, the paper advised that an eleven-year-old boy's mother had invited "twenty-five youthful belles and beaux" to his birthday party. When a member of the American Legion Auxiliary had a reception in her "beautiful colonial home" for "about two hundred matrons," she recruited "popular sub-debs," girls in their early teens who were future debutantes, to pass "delicious ices, assorted cakes, and mints" at twilight. For children, for young people of marrying age, and for mature adults, antebellum themes were always popular. Guests came to a birthday party for five-year-old Lylla Jean Kirk dressed as clowns, cowboys, ballet dancers, and "southern darkies"; a young gentleman threw a "real old fashioned Southern barbecue" in honor of his sister and her fiancé; the Auxiliary held an "old plantation luncheon."[30] Pink had been a favored color for party decorations since "pink teas" were popular when Earline was a little girl, and the newspaper's details of a party for "a pretty little blonde" validated Earline's favorite color scheme of pink and green while conveying the dramatic processional nature of formal parties. The birthday girl "received her friends" in "a perky frock of sea green satin." Candles flickered as the children "were ushered into the dining room." "Ribbons extended from the centerpiece [to] individual fortunes and good luck pieces. Tiny French baskets in pink and green held mints for each guest," information that could have inspired the large cardboard model of a structure resembling a castle, with many small windows from which guests could extract tiny gifts, that Roland Harper made for Anne's birthday party one year.[31]

In another form of entertainment that middle-class mothers staged, Anne made her debut in December 1933, at the age of five, when Earline entered her in a pageant called a "Tom Thumb Wedding." The newspaper estimated that more than a thousand people attended the performance at the Tuscaloosa High School Auditorium. Anne posed as a bridesmaid while her two-year-old third cousin, Sydnia Smyth's granddaughter, was one of a "coterie of flower girls." These pageants were a custom that began after the wedding in 1863 of a circus celebrity with the stage name General Tom Thumb.[32] Weddings were always material for fantasy and drama; two years earlier, a small girl made a surprise appearance at a local bridal shower "dressed in a bride's costume [with] her lovely blonde hair . . . caught with a wreath of orange blossoms."[33] In fact, mock weddings were integral to white fascination with black life. Some slaveholders, such as the prominent Drish family, had staged weddings for slaves. The Tuscaloosa memoirist James Robert Maxwell said after his father "had gotten his negroes home from Virginia, he . . . wanted the grown men and women to pair off" so he held "a big wedding frolic." Telling the story to demonstrate his father's generosity, Maxwell wrote, "One day our family all went down to the plantation, and ten couples all were married on the porch of the overseer's [dogtrot] house by a preacher of their own color."[34] The historian James Sellers, Earline's church acquaintance, interpreted faux weddings of enslaved workers as evidence of "a common spirit of friendship and gayety," but they could be sources of racist amusement as well as kindly largesse.[35] Weddings were frequently the centerpiece of minstrel acts, an antebellum theatrical genre originally performed by whites in blackface and eventually by black performers. Like concerts of spirituals, minstrelsy contributed to the myth of the happy servant class and became increasingly popular after Emancipation.[36] Commercial publishers released wedding-themed "blackface talking acts" such as

Scrambled Courtship, Whar's de Groom? and *Coon Creek Courtship,* and by the 1930s blackface weddings were popular material for amateur theatrics in Tuscaloosa. Temo Callahan played the fiddle and a young white woman played the part of the minister in a skit that was a school fund-raiser.[37] In a twist of the mock wedding, Jack McGuire performed in a mock divorce at the monthly courthouse talent show shortly before Foster appointed him a volunteer defense lawyer for Dan Pippen and Elmore Clark.[38] In another twist, Herbert played a groom named Samuel Large in "Womanless Wedding" at Grace's school while Callahan and Bob Kyle performed as the "Fiddlin' Mirage."[39] Kyle, a reporter for the *Tuscaloosa News,* later combined minstrelsy and courthouse hijinks with a condescending article about a black couple that came to the police station on Christmas night to inquire about obtaining a marriage license. An officer performed the marriage ceremony and Kyle wrote that "the witnesses had sixshooters on their hips and stars on their chests[;] even the preacher who performed the rites had a blackjack in his hip pocket."[40]

"Negro" spirituals also were popular material for white amateur theatrics.[41] Herbert's cousin Smyth played the guitar and sang as "an old negro mammy" at club meetings and pageants. In October 1933, two local matrons sang "Massa's in the Cold Ground," an 1852 song by Stephen Foster, for the Twentieth Century Club. The song expressed the fond belief that many blacks mourned the loss of the benevolent institution of slavery: "Massa made de darkeys love him [because] he was so kind."[42] When Earline planned the program for a meeting of the American Legion Auxiliary in 1941, she asked the Presbyterian choir director, Herbert Caldwell, to sing a mournful African American spiritual, "Ain't Dis a Hard Trial," and "Short'nin' Bread," the latter with the popular refrain, "Mammy's little baby loves short'nin, short'nin." "Short'nin' Bread" had been one of Caldwell's standards during his brief career as an opera singer in New York. The lyrics were by a Tuscaloosa native, Clement Wood, the author who made the sound of baying bloodhounds the first impression in his sympathetic 1922 novel, *Nigger.*[43]

The genteel matrons who sang Stephen Foster's sentimental song exemplified one of the fundamental ideas in the fantastical canon: the southern lady had artistic ability that she gladly used to entertain her family and friends.[44] Sheet music that Earline labeled with her married name indicates that she continued to play the piano. She knew Herbert's late aunt Mollie Findley gave piano lessons at Riverview, and his aunt Collette Barnes Hargrove, who studied music and voice at the university and abroad, sometimes sang at ladies' gatherings; the newspaper recalled that Collette's "beautiful voice . . . charmed, soothed and inspired this community for more than three decades."[45] Earline began giving piano lessons to Anne when Anne was four years old, writing exercises for her in a series of three blank music booklets. At some point after Anne's fifth birthday, Earline took her next door for lessons from their tenant Louise Shook. Quite a few women in Tuscaloosa, and at least one man, gave private music lessons during the Depression; some even held recitals that were social events.[46] Mrs. Shook was a somewhat sad figure, in that her first two children had died, one as an infant and the other at the age of eight of pneumonia. Her mother and unmarried sister lived with her, her husband, and their two daughters. They may have had financial troubles even though Robert Shook was employed.[47] Louise Shook set Anne to working through short pieces with titles such as "A Pleasant Morning" and "Distant Bells." Then, in 1934, Earline walked Anne across Fourth Avenue to the house on the corner opposite from the Shooks to begin lessons with Virginia Killingsworth Moore, who was a relative by marriage of the Keenes.[48] She was the granddaughter of a judge and there was an aristocratic cast to her family.[49] Like Louise Shook, "Miss Jennie" became a close friend of Earline and a significant adjunct to the Findley family.

The legend in the Findley family was that from 1907 to 1914 Jennie studied in Vienna under a teacher who had been a student of Franz Liszt, one of the greatest composers of the nineteenth century.[50] It was a romantic tale—Miss Jennie resembled Victoria Beaumont De Leon, a character in the Montgomery writer Sara Haardt's story "Each in Her Own Day," who, "it was said . . . studied music in Vienna as a girl"[51]—and at least partly true. Jennie moved to Leipzig, Germany, the location of the Royal Conservatory of Music where about three hundred foreigners were enrolled, in 1907.[52] A book copyrighted in 1908 that she marked "Jennie K. Moore, Vienna, Austria," and eventually bequeathed to Anne, indicates that she moved the next year or later to Vienna, the location of the Imperial Academy of Music and the Performing Arts. As for Jennie's musical lineage descending from Liszt, the Findley family story did not go so far as to reveal who her teacher was; Liszt taught hundreds of pianists in his lifetime and many claimed, on the basis of a single encounter, to have studied under him.[53] When Jennie's mother died in 1921, she returned to Tuscaloosa to care for her father and mentally ill brother.[54] After her father died thirteen years later, Jennie and Edward lived on in the rented green house at 407 University Avenue among the remaining relics of the family's past good fortune: the piano; her sheet music and books; the French furniture, a chaise méridienne and a Louis XV bergère that belonged to "Ma Moore," as Miss Jennie referred to her grandmother Anna Mariah Forney Moore; and the portrait of "Judge Moore," as her grandfather Samuel Dalton John Moore was forever known following his brief tenure as probate judge. Unmarried, Jennie earned a living by giving piano lessons in the room she called her studio while Edward sometimes banged on the walls of his locked bedroom or escaped to run about the neighborhood naked.[55] Jennie's stories of European lineage, military heroism, the judiciary, and musicality were so important to Anne's own identity that she recorded them in notes, stories that were tinged by the slow demise of prominent families, a reminder that beauty and artistic ability were means to the end, which was a fortuitous marriage.

The sheet music that Anne saved throughout her life reveals the conventional course of the training that Earline arranged for her. Miss Jennie soon led her through the first book of Theodor Kullak's *Method of Octave Playing for the Piano*, noting on one page that Anne should practice on a Saturday afternoon from three to five-thirty. Anne worked her way through *Fifteen Studies for the Pianoforte* by Jean-Baptiste Duvernoy, in a heavily used 1895 edition repaired more than once with tape, and seven volumes of exercises by Carl Czerny, who had his own important musical lineage as a pupil of Beethoven and one of Liszt's teachers.[56] Anne was a quick learner and Earline encouraged her to practice for longer and longer periods. She progressed to Chopin's *Twelve Etudes, Opus 10*, in a heavily used book that also was repaired with tape, and his "Minute Waltz" (*Waltz in D-flat, Opus 64, No. 1*), which Anne, like many piano pupils, played as rapidly as she could, prompting Miss Jennie to note "Slow down" on the music. Anne came to regard the works of Liszt as the highest plane of piano virtuosity and eventually played for four hours per day. Because of this schedule, her friend Elna Fairy Bolding considered Anne's parents "rigid." Another family legend is that the baby grand piano Herbert and Earline bought for Anne was the only purchase he made on credit in his lifetime. The piano not only was a finer instrument for Anne's use, it was a new symbol in the Findley living room of the family's gentility.[57]

☼ ☼ ☼

In November 1933, a few weeks after the grand jury reported that it could find no one to accuse in the murder of Dennis Cross, Earline set up a small table and chairs in the front yard so that five-year-old Anne and a playmate could pretend to have a tea party. It was an unusually warm day. The Findleys' roomer, Dr. Harper, recorded the event in a cartoon, depicting Anne holding a bone behind her back for a small white dog. Standing on the front porch, Earline called, "Hurry up and eat your soup and I'll give you-all some spinach"; a bird sang "Tweet! Tweet!" from the top branch of a tall tree.[58] At the same time, children at Lyman's school were receiving inoculations for diphtheria and smallpox.[59] The town was recovering from a dangerous typhoid season that summer and fall. One of several outbreaks came to light when a black family living in a one-room shack on Hargrove Road was stricken with typhoid from contaminated drinking water. Word reached the local public health officer, Dr. Arthur A. Kirk, whose granddaughter Lylla Jean Kirk had the costume party where some children dressed as "southern darkies." He dispatched a nurse, who found "the mother dangerously ill . . . and an 11-year-old child dead on the floor." Kirk immediately ordered typhoid inoculations for the black and white families in the crowded neighborhood. His health department inoculated more than thirteen thousand people by the time of Earline's mock tea party for Anne.[60] Then, much worse news: Hatchett Hinton's children, nine-year-old Jane and five-year-old Bill Newt, were stricken with polio, possibly because the high temperatures encouraged circulation of the poliomyelitis virus.

Earline dreaded polio and the unpredictability of the disease contributed to her fears. Even if she kept the children away from water fountains and crowded theaters and public pools, they might not be safe. Worse, if children contracted polio, parents were nearly powerless to treat them. Doctors isolated children in polio wards where parents could rarely visit. Many children died and many others survived with lifelong paralysis or other complications. The Hintons took Jane and Bill Newt to the Roosevelt Warm Springs Institute for Rehabilitation, President Franklin Delano Roosevelt's clinic in Georgia, probably paying high fees. Jane recovered enough to come home by April, but little Bill Newt spent over a year at Warm Springs where, the society writer for the *Tuscaloosa News* reported, he swam "every day" with the president. Bill Newt never fully recovered and sometimes was bedridden.[61]

The weather took another odd turn in March when more than an inch of snow fell. Dr. Harper became ill; perhaps to keep the children quiet so they would not disturb him, Earline gave them the task of practicing their letter-writing skills by writing to "Mamma," their grandmother in Meridian.[62] Within ten days, however, the temperature reached the mid-sixties, the wisteria that covered porches and porticoes in Tuscaloosa was blooming, and the children could play outside again.[63] Then, in mid-July, the cry "He attacked me!" created a new stir in the Findleys' neighborhood. A young white woman, a summer student at the university, claimed a black man attempted to rape her as she was walking to a bus stop about a half-mile east of the bungalow. Unlike Alice Johnson, she reported her attack to police immediately and in detail. He was carrying a hammer. He approached her a few minutes after twelve o'clock. He spoke to her, tackled her, and threw her to the ground. She screamed and fought him before running to a nearby house. Word spread quickly and scores of white men searched Alberta City, Grace Hamby's neighborhood, seizing several black men and taking them to the courthouse where the woman "dismissed each as the wrong man." Soon a witness reported seeing Robert Michael acting suspiciously in the vicinity. Michael was a thirty-two-year-old black ex-convict who had moved to Tuscaloosa two weeks earlier after serving five years in prison for assaulting a white woman. The witness led the prosecutor and two deputies to Michael's home, a rough cabin on Castle Hill. The officers arrested Michael and took him to the jail, and a large crowd gathered to wait for news about the case. Michael confessed; a grand jury indicted him; Michael waived a jury trial; and Foster gave him the maximum sentence, nineteen to twenty years, all within twenty-four hours of the woman's claim. At the conclusion of the trial, Foster commended the citizenry for, as the *Tuscaloosa News* reporter put it, "determining that the court proceed in an orderly manner."[64] The same ritualistic drama unfolded again ten days later. A white farmer on Hargrove Road told the sheriff's department that an eighteen-year-old black man, Matthew Washington, chased the farmer's ten-year-old daughter along a wooded path until they came into sight of the farmer, and then turned and ran in a different direction. Two deputies found and arrested him. They were Hal M. Curry, one of the officers who had arrested Michael earlier in the month, and Robert Pate, one of the men implicated in the kidnapping of Harden, Pippen, and Clark. The teenage suspect reportedly first said he thought the girl "was a Negro" but under continued interrogation said he knew she was white and had planned to attack her for some time.

The same grand jury indicted him; like Michael, Washington waived a jury trial; and again the circuit judge issued the maximum sentence.[65] Reporting this second whirlwind conviction, the *Tuscaloosa News* was silent on whether Foster praised the public for not lynching Washington. For the second summer in a row, accusations against black men, angry white crowds, and nearly constant violence dominated conversations and news reports in Tuscaloosa, competing with the emerging story of Adolf Hitler's police state in Germany.[66]

Pondering the season of lynchings in Tuscaloosa, Clarence Cason reflected in 1934 that "any person who might have come to Tuscaloosa during the late summer and early fall of 1933 would have received an impression of horror." Cason clung to a pretty vision of the old town. "Ordinarily Tuscaloosa is a town of serene and comfortable beauty," he wrote, "where one may look forward with happiness to spending the rest of his days. It has fine old houses, great oak trees, and people whose warm friendliness makes it easy and agreeable to live with them." However, he accused the ruling class of doing too little to prevent or punish racial terrorism and murder. "The 'best' people of the town," he acknowledged, "wished to support the cause of justice," but "popular indifference," he warned, would lead to "future lynchings."[67] Here Cason echoed the sociologist Arthur Raper, who observed that "in practically every community with a lynching . . . there were some people who were heartily opposed to what took place; but after a time, even the 'best citizens' usually came to feel that 'it is all over now, and the sooner it is forgotten, the better for the community.'"[68] Cason made his observation in a collection of essays, *90 Degrees in the Shade*, and sent the manuscript to the University of North Carolina Press, where a group of social scientists had been attempting to raise public awareness about the epidemic of lynchings in the Deep South.[69] The editors at the press found Cason's book "well balanced [and] humane" and scheduled its release for May 1935.[70] In a brief foreword that he completed in December 1934, Cason thanked his wife, Louise Rickeman, "for patient assistance which far exceeded the bounds of the marriage vows" and their six-year-old daughter Jane "for the tender consideration which persuaded her to play quietly in her own room while her incomprehensible father sat long at his desk."[71]

A few months later, on May 7, 1935, Cason again sat long at his desk, contemplating how his family's neighbors and friends would react upon the release of his book, fearing their fury would be so great he and his family would have to move away. A history professor in Florida had been pressured to resign in 1911 simply for writing in an article that "the North was relatively right, while the South was relatively wrong." The Scottsboro case had become a cause célèbre among liberals and scholars; to be perceived in that camp might destroy Cason's standing in Tuscaloosa's small upper-middle class. The southern reluctance to directly address racial murders was as entrenched as ever.[72] That very afternoon, the *Tuscaloosa News* carried a report on a filibuster in the US Senate over an anti-lynching bill. Alabama senator Hugo Black, in many regards progressive, had created a dramatic scene in the Senate chamber, criticizing the bill's sponsor merely for collaborating on the legislation with a black man.[73] Although Carmer's book *Stars Fell on Alabama* was hugely popular outside the South, it had met local scorn (some southerners thought Carmer had abused their hospitality), but Carmer was long gone from Tuscaloosa when his book was released in 1934.[74] In contrast to Carmer, the Casons lived in Tuscaloosa. The stakes for them were higher. With the Depression more severe than ever, Cason's job at the university provided unusual security. Jane was in elementary school. The family went to Christ Episcopal Church.[75] To challenge the status quo in any manner was a grave breach of etiquette, one the community might forgive in an elderly white lady like Mrs. Snedecor, who decried Dennis Cross's murder in a letter to the newspaper, but might not forgive in a white man writing for a national audience. Cason's editor had assured him that no one in Tuscaloosa would criticize the book, but in fact Cason had gone further than other contemporary critics of southern race relations.[76] Worst of all, he blamed the white power structure for allowing lynchings to occur. Facing the rejection that was likely to come, thinking Louise and Jane would be better-off without him, Cason shot himself. The news of his suicide shocked the community, which read the grisly details on the front page of the *Tuscaloosa News*.[77]

A few days later, Lustig's Book Store advertised first editions of *90 Degrees in the Shade*.[78] The paper published a review of the book by Hamner Cobbs, a white-supremacist editorial writer whom the Casons probably knew through their church. By emphasizing that Cason blamed the ILD for the murders of Pippen, Harden, and Cross, Cobbs perpetuated the very distortion and denial that Cason had wanted to stop.[79] Cason had acknowledged the possibility that "none of the lynchings would have taken place had it not been for the resentment directly created by the three Communist lawyers" but in the same sentence wrote that his "loyalty to our town" might "color my judgment in this particular." More significantly, Cason made the point that "the lynching problem in the South involves far more than sporadic eruptions of mob violence. . . . The real menace to legal justice is the tolerance . . . towards cases of extra-legal procedure." Good people would have to speak up, Cason wrote. They would have to "be more unrelenting in their demands for a civilized attitude, and . . . willing to take personal and commercial risks in making these demands known."[80]

Although Cason was just a year behind Herbert at the university, Earline and Herbert evidently were not friends with the Casons—or Carl Carmer, for that matter. Carmer left the university before Herbert became an instructor in the business school and Herbert had had little reason to interact with Cason on campus. The Findleys and Casons belonged to different churches. Although Anne and Jane were the same age, they apparently attended different schools at the time Cason died. No copies of Carmer's or Cason's books were preserved in the bungalow library, even though Herbert had a lifelong interest in local history, and no one remembers any discussion by the Findleys of either writer.[81] Whatever ideas or feelings Earline and Herbert had about the 1933 lynchings or Cason's challenge to "good people" to stand up to racial terrorism died with them.

Figure 1. The lock of hair that Annie Moore clipped and saved when her first child died in 1894. (Collection of the author.)

Figure 2. A portrait, circa 1905, of the Moore children with a detail from an earlier portrait (circa 1901) showing that Earline had blonde hair as a young child and was a brunette by the age of nine. (Collection of the author.)

Figure 3. Earline Moore (right) with her aunt Bettie Moore. (Collection of the author.)

Figure 4. The Jemison-Van de Graaff house on Greensboro Avenue, 1934. (Historic American Buildings Survey, Library of Congress.)

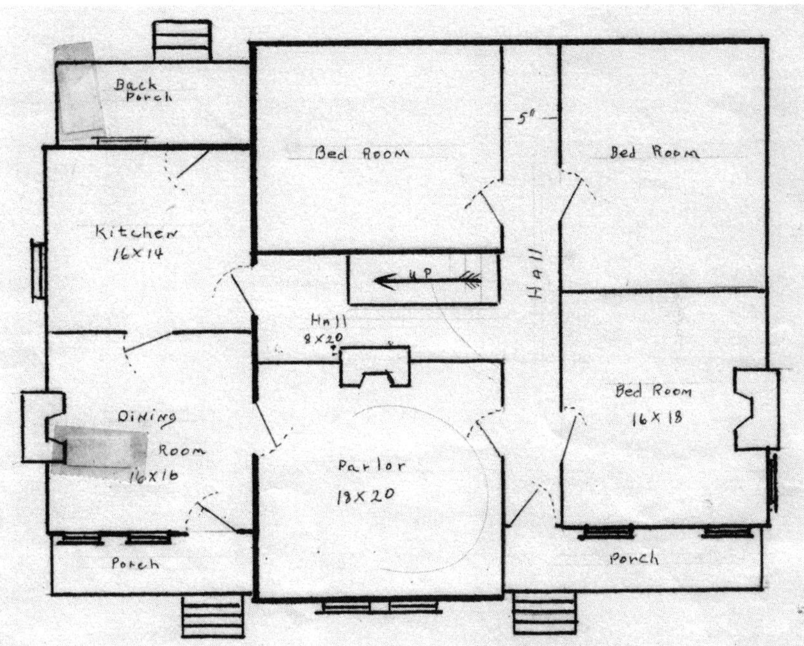

Figure 5. Remembered views of Riverview: Ila Findley's painting and Preston Findley's floor plan. (Collection of the author.)

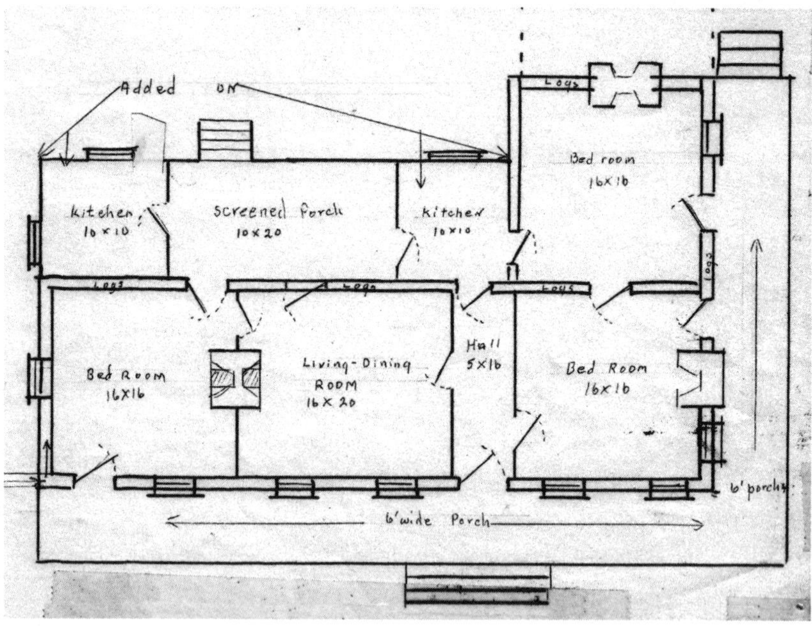

Figure 6. Remembered views of The Old Place: Ila Findley's painting and Preston Findley's floor plan (detail). (Collection of the author.)

Figure 7. Detail of a photographic panorama of a Ku Klux Klan rally in Tuscaloosa, 1924. (Courtesy of Alabama Department of Archives and History.)

Figure 8. Portrait, circa 1932, of Lyman and Anne Findley. (Collection of the author.)

Figure 9. Herbert Lyman Findley Sr. (right) with Blondie and Dagwood at a foxhound competition. (Collection of the author.)

Figure 10. The Tuscaloosa Curb Market. (Roland Harper Photo Collection, courtesy of University of Alabama Special Collections.)

Figure 11. Anne Findley (left) in the tableau vivant. (Collection of the author.)

Figure 12. The 1946 portrait of Anne Findley by Nina Struss. (Anne Findley Shores Collection, courtesy of University of Alabama Special Collections.)

Figure 13. The Findley bungalow as it appeared circa 1934 and following renovations. (Photograph by Roland McMillan Harper from the collection of the author; copy of line drawing by James J. Andrews courtesy of Margaret Koster Findley.)

Figure 14. The final portrait of Earline Moore Findley, for which she wore the floral brooch. (Collection of the author.)

Figure 15. Woman walking home in the afternoon of December 23, 1951, in an alley of African American residences, probably Oak Alley, in Tuscaloosa. (Roland Harper Photo Collection, courtesy of University of Alabama Special Collections.)

Figure 16. A staged photograph of the wedding of Burmiss Barnett Lewis and Robert L. Gunn Jr. at the University Club in 1952, with Anne Findley second from left. (Collection of the author.)

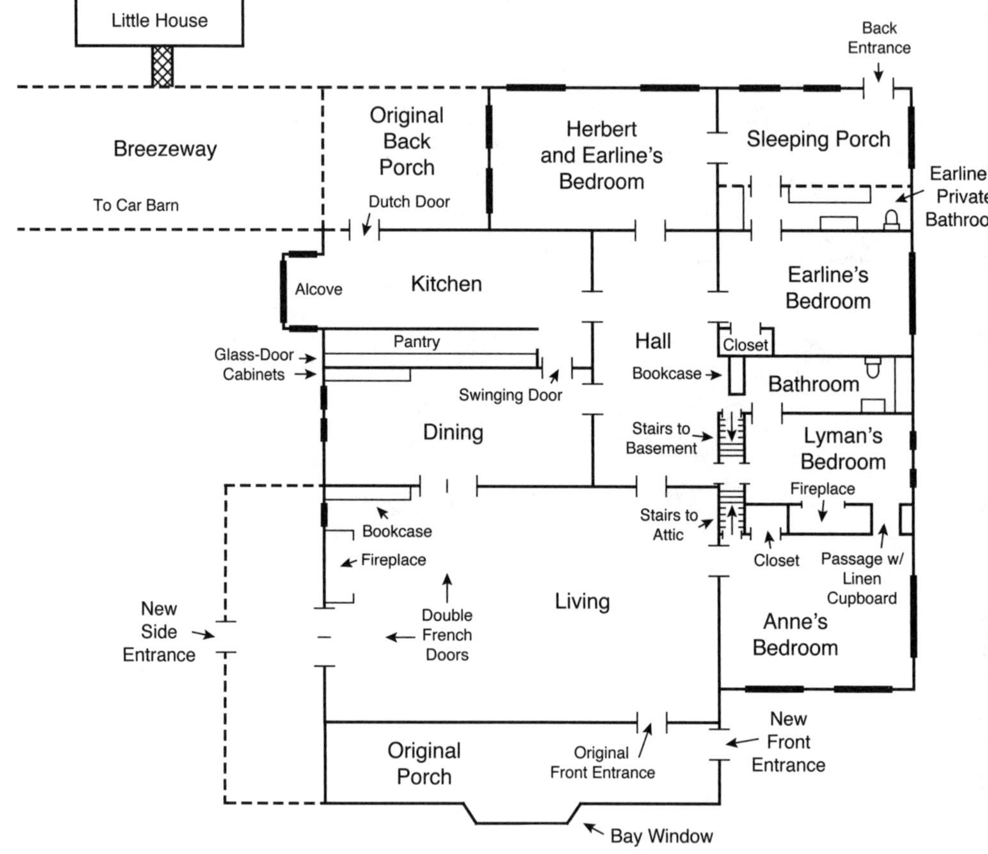

Figure 17. The author's memory of the floor plan of the bungalow, with Earline's renovations indicated by dotted lines. (Design by Layet Johnson)

Figure 18. Earline's scrapbook photograph of a pink house. (Collection of the author.)

Figure 19. A 1961 Christmas snapshot of the author's brother, James Layet Shores III, with the fireside chair (moved to the center of the room to make space for the Christmas tree), the portrait of Anne, the chaise longue, and one of Earline's hooked rugs visible. (Collection of the author.)

Six

The Judge's Wife

Two of the books that I found on the bungalow's hall shelves as a child, *Those Plummer Children* and its sequel, *Narcissus an' de Chillun*, were charming, lighthearted treatments of bourgeois life in the twentieth-century South. The author, Christine Noble Govan, drew many of her scenes from her childhood in Franklin and Chattanooga, Tennessee, and based her white characters, the middle-class Ellery and Plummer families, on her own family and that of Judge Josiah Carr Eggleston of Franklin, calling him "the best friend any child ever had." Ida Longley, the sister of the music teacher Jennie Moore, lived in Chattanooga, like Govan, and may have given Anne the Govan books. A high school English teacher, Ida was fond of little Anne and gave her several books including two novels by Louisa May Alcott, both of which she inscribed "To Anne from Mrs. Longley, 1938."[1] For Anne's copy of *Those Plummer Children*, Ida may have skipped an inscription because the frontispiece already bore one by the author. Above a drawing of a small black boy in overalls, Govan had added a speech balloon: "Howdy Miss Ann—Ise come ter play wif yer!" For readers like Earline, who probably read *Those Plummer Children* to Anne, Govan's vision was a pleasurable immersion in the life of the southern gentry, reinforcing the archetypes of the kindly judge who ruled over home and the barely glimpsed exterior world; the gracious lady of the house; the daughter who more or less gladly took up the role of belle; and the young master who reveled in country life but exhibited perfect manners, all portrayed in beautiful drawing rooms, kitchens, and bedrooms and attended by dim-witted and loyal black servants.

Govan believed the devotion of her cartoonish black characters was realistic: "Their patience and service will never be forgotten by those who knew them, and I wanted my own children to see them as we did." Narcissus was a maid and nurse who lived in an African American neighborhood that Govan called Hardbargain. Her children were twin boys named Sears and Roebuck who "moved along slowly, as all their people moved," easily distracted by "the soft pattern that the sunlight and shade made through the leaves."[2] The white children in Govan's fictional world played with the black children and were very fond of their families' adult black servants. Her autobiographical protagonist, Chris Ellery, was particularly affectionate toward a servant they called Mom Jinny who lived in a "familiar gray unpainted shack," told whites she remembered having "plenty o' time ter play" as a child slave, and demonstrated "with childish eagerness" her gratitude for visits and gifts from white folks.[3] Although no hint of racial discord clouded Govan's humorous stories for young readers, Jinny did resist handing over her treasured blue-glass lamp, turning down "white ladies [who] offered [her] all sorts of money." Govan described the lamp in such detail that it could have been a real fixture in the home of a servant to the Noble family. To Jinny, the lamp was too special to ever sell. Hinting at the grief and hope of black mothers whose children fled the South following the Surrender, Govan wrote that Jinny "had it lit every night and set in the window for her boy, Henry, who had run away from home some forty years before."[4] Mom Jinny deeply hoped that when she died her survivors would give her a "pink funeral." She wanted a coffin that "was to be pink if possible, and if not, then it must have a pink lining [and] she wanted all the flowers sent to the funeral to be pink." The white children fulfilled her wishes, arranging for a mule-drawn hearse to carry her to the cemetery and making sure "all the white folks [furnished] pink roses and phlox, and old-fashioned spicy pinks from their gardens."[5]

Chris's family was poorer than before the Civil War but her mother persevered at the necessary social rituals, aided by Mom Jinny and a cook named Hattie. Twice a month, Mrs. Ellery was "at home," meaning she invited visits by ladies "who all flocked to the old brick house, to sip tea or chocolate, nibble at sandwiches, and chatter." Wearing a gingham apron, "her eyes shining happily" like a grown-up Pollyanna, Mrs. Ellery "mixed cup-cakes or cut out sandwiches." Chris and her friend Judy Plummer helped Hattie polish the silver. When Mrs. Ellery attended a tea or cultural meeting, "the late summer afternoon sunshine fell softly on the group of ladies with their full, soft-colored frocks, their beflowered, wide-brimmed hats, and their tilted parasols." These aristocrats' homes were places of "dim awesomeness" with "soft-carpeted floors, filmy white curtains, and beds with draped canopies"; "lovely drawing-rooms [were] hung with portraits and filled with strange and wonderful furniture." Judge Plummer's portrait, a symbol of southern aristocracy, hung in an upstairs bedroom.[6] Some novelists used lawyers and judges as symbols of southern injustice, men dedicated to preserving racial inequality, "faded inheritor[s] of the southern past," but Govan's Judge Plummer entered her stories only as a genteel figure who provided his wife and children with a secure and comfortable life in a house that was the scene of many entertainments and happy private moments, a fair and generous white man like Henry Foster, the venerated circuit judge in Tuscaloosa.[7]

For the bourgeois class of Tuscaloosa, Foster personified civility and the rule of law. He had had an illustrious career as a captain of the revered Warrior Guards, at the front in the Spanish-American War, and as county prosecutor, mayor, and legislator. His courthouse was the site for community events as well as trials and the center, more than any single school or church, more than the university, of county life. That his campaign in 1890 used the courthouse auditorium to commit election fraud cast no shadow on his reputation. At that time, hundreds of African American men in Tuscaloosa were registered voters. Foster, or his allies, invited about two hundred black voters to come into the courthouse for free barbecue on the eve of the election and then held them there until they could be led to the poll to vote for Foster. Vote buying of this kind seemed appropriate because "treating" voters with barbecues was a traditional part of political campaigns in Alabama. Someone was bound to buy the black vote, Foster's supporters reasoned, so it was for the best that his campaign did so because he subsequently became one of "Alabama's greatest, most distinguished and beloved jurists."[8] Herbert revered Foster, who helped carry Ida's coffin to her grave as an active pallbearer when Herbert was thirteen years old, and grew up wanting to enter the legal profession rather than his father's field of engineering.[9]

At another family funeral, in 1932, Foster was an honorary pallbearer and Herbert was an active pallbearer.[10] Mingling that day with the judge and another honorary pallbearer, the former governor and current county probate judge, William W. "Plain Bill" Brandon, could have given Herbert the idea that he, too, might become a judge. Some courthouse observers thought he was not aggressive in a courtroom despite having a "smart, quick mind," and Herbert had endured years of teasing for being short, but Brandon was even shorter, barely five feet in height, yet had enjoyed a long political career.[11] Over a period of four months in 1933, after the ILD attacked his hero, Herbert aggressively climbed to a higher political position in the county. The week that Foster appointed the three prominent local lawyers to help represent Pippen and Clark, Herbert obtained his own appointment as defense counsel in a municipal case. His clients were four hotel guests who began celebrating the end of Prohibition before the repeal of the federal law had taken effect, prompting three crusading ministers, including A. M. Freeman of First Methodist Church, to alert the police. Liquor cases dominated courtrooms in Alabama at the time and many citizens in Tuscaloosa strongly opposed drinking. In fact, the previous fall the formerly popular legislator Temo Callahan had been driven to resign from Holt Baptist Church, where he was a deacon and song leader, because he voted for a "near-beer" law which would allow the sale of beer with very low alcohol content.[12] Around the same time, the local bar association appointed Herbert to a committee to deal with the National Recovery Act, a law that promoted shorter working hours and increases in minimum wages. Three days after the heavily attended trial of the hotel beer drinkers, Herbert and his fellow committee members, including Richard C. Foster, a cousin of Henry Foster, announced the bar association's pledge that law firms in the county would comply with the wage-and-hour law.[13] Herbert had several things in common with Richard Foster. They were the same age and both had attended the university and become lawyers, although Richard had gone to Harvard Law School. Both had been in the artillery during World War I; Herbert became a second lieutenant and Richard a captain, two ranks higher. Herbert received another appointment with Richard Foster a few weeks later, this one to the legislation committee of the local American Legion post. Finally, in January 1934, when Richard Foster was elected president of the Tuscaloosa County Democratic Party, Herbert was elected secretary.[14]

Now Herbert had an official position among the Democrats. The timing was excellent. His former law partner, John R. Bealle, the county inferior court judge, decided that year to run against the county prosecuting attorney who was politically vulnerable because some ministers and the editor of the *Tuscaloosa News* blamed him for not prosecuting anyone in the murders of Pippen, Harden, and Cross. Herbert entered the race for the open seat. His opponent was a state senator, W. Charles Warren. With a full slate of contested county offices and a three-way race for Congress, the primary season in Tuscaloosa that year was exceptionally exciting. Herbert's circles of friends and potential supporters were large and overlapping. In addition to the bar, the American Legion, and the Democratic Party, there was Rising Virtue Lodge No. 4, the local Masonic chapter that had about six hundred members who were civic-minded and likely voters.[15] To meet even more voters, Herbert attended square dances, fiddlers' conventions, political rallies, and foxhunts.[16]

For more than a century, square dances had been excellent opportunities for political meeting and greeting in Alabama. Sarah Gayle enjoyed dancing at a wedding in 1827 when "the sound of the fiddle drew a set of young people to the floor," even though her minister, Griffin Christopher, warned "an awful day of reckoning would come" for the dancers. Fiddle music was part of life in Tuscaloosa County as early as 1836, when the sheriff William Findley (Herbert's great-uncle) owned a "fine violin and case."[17] Newt Hinton's brother, Clarence, known as "Boss," was frequently the caller at square dances that were fund-raisers for school projects and other local causes.[18] The fiddlers' convention was an exhibition by virtuosos who played fast-paced pieces, even imitating "the howling of wolves, the whistle of locomotives, the singing of birds, the cackling of hens and the crowing of roosters." A favorite number was the minstrel hit "Pop Goes the Weasel," which Herbert enjoyed singing. Upon reaching the word "Pop," the fiddler dramatically moved his violin to a different position, continuing to play to his audience's amusement. Temo Callahan was a highly skilled fiddler and often presided at conventions including one at Holt High School in 1933 that was a rally for the repeal of Prohibition.[19]

Temo's daughter Nancy Callahan later reminisced about the huge popularity of political rallies in the county, speculating that they grew out of fiddlers' conventions as fund-raisers for small schools. In some campaign seasons, rallies took place every night. "Traditionally, the first rally [was] in Cottondale on the day after the March 1st qualifying deadline," she recalled. "The last one, on election eve, [was] in the Tuscaloosa County High School football stadium, where as many as 2000 attendees would fill the bleachers." Some candidates' wives attended the rallies with their husbands, standing in receiving lines to greet voters. During the final week of Herbert's first campaign, the rallies included a plate supper at a mill on Keene's Mill Road;

a box supper and forum for candidates in Tuscaloosa and Pickens counties; another box supper at the Sterling church; and "an entertainment" put on by the Ladies Home Demonstration Club of Duncanville where there was to be music, stunts, refreshments, and even dominoes, as well as speeches.[20] In 1940, when Herbert ran against Warren again, the *Tuscaloosa News* estimated that five hundred citizens attended a rally at Etteca School in Northport, where a free meal, a midcentury example of "treating," was part of the program. Other rallies took place at the Barbee, Bethel, Brandon, and Brownville schools, in Cottondale, Coker, and Coaling, and at the county courthouse.[21]

Herbert went on foxhunts to mingle with older, powerful men in the Tuscaloosa establishment.[22] Through hunting, men earned and reinforced reputations for integrity and reliability. Because its point was purely the pursuit, rather than catching game for food, foxhunting was the most aristocratic type of hunt, with the horns and baying dogs, the crackling firelight, and the smell of barbecue all reminders of antebellum plantation life. It was a tradition that southern fathers taught their sons, a sign of gentility as well as virility. Alluding to hunting as a coming-of-age ritual in which wealthy young men were accompanied by enslaved men, Ruby Tartt wrote, "up that hill, [Charlie Johnson] and his young masters had ridden on many a starlit night, coming home from the hunt."[23] In *The Little Shepherd of Kingdom Come,* the hero "never forgot the first starlit night when he was awakened by the near winding of a horn" for a foxhunt. At "the kill[,] the General gave Chad the brush with his own hand,"[24] the gesture of bestowing the fox's tail on a favored disciple conveying the entire trans-Emancipation tradition of archetypal white, aristocratic planter-officers passing down responsibility for the southern world.

W. R. Smith, later one of the county's delegates to the secession convention, captured the importance of hunts in early Tuscaloosa County politics. Seth Barton was running for the legislature in 1824 and asked a friend to arrange a hunting expedition with local opinion-makers so Barton could meet them. Afterward, Barton wrote "The Hunting Song," mentioning Herbert's great-grandfather Hope Hargrove; Hope's brother Jack; and their wealthy brother-in-law, Hardy Clements:

> From far and near the gentry came,
> Jack Hargrove in the van;
> Came Hope, the charmer, with his horn,

And Blocker with his can;
Even Hardy Clements left his mint
To join the jolly crew;
And when his trusty rifle blazed,
He had a center view.

Barton won the election.[25] In twentieth-century Tuscaloosa powerful politicians still came together in exclusive hunts. The guest list for one that Parker Patton gave in 1917 shows the intergenerational social and political ties among foxhunters: there was George Little, a former secretary of the county Board of Trade and one of the veterans who recorded Cole Hargrove's Civil War heroics; Norfleet Harris, a city commissioner and one of the pallbearers for Ida; Bernard Harwood, a prominent lawyer and past circuit judge; and Harwood's son, Bob, who later was elected to the state supreme court. Glenn Foster was a banker and city treasurer. Fleetwood Rice was a lawyer and later the county probate judge. Hardin D. Billingsley became chief of police.[26] For three generations, men of means in Alabama had hunted, gathering to release their trained dogs and bringing along black men to prepare barbecue feasts and tend the hounds.[27] Herbert took Lyman on hunts and raised two hounds with him. They named the dogs Dagwood and Blondie for the comic strip characters and boarded them at a private kennel on the grounds of Bryce Hospital, where the asylum superintendent, William Dempsey Partlow, and William Mark Faulk, a former mayor of Tuscaloosa and Partlow's assistant, operated the kennel with a "faithful attendant" who cared for the dogs.[28]

Although some men rode to the hounds, Herbert and his friends usually engaged in a plebian form of foxhunting, driving their vehicles to one of their favorite spots at night, releasing a caged fox and then their dogs, and listening to the ensuing chase while standing around a campfire, the distant baying of the hounds like an echo of manhunts during slavery time. Lyman's wife recalled that the hunters "just got together and ate and stood around and listened to the dogs. . . . I think Dr. Partlow would bring a cook from the hospital." As the *Tuscaloosa News* put it in a humorous editorial, foxhunters in Tuscaloosa County liked to "toast their pants before a hilltop fire, and jaw back and forth as to whether it was George's thin-voiced Sally or John's fast-stepping Blue which toted that fox across that skirt of pines." The white men debated the merits of wily foxes and the attributes of each other's hounds, such as a dog's "mouth," or its willingness to gently carry and return prey. Herbert described these times in a letter: "When a new dog [was] brought into the pack we all discussed the new dog, examined him and commented on his breeding and appearance."[29] When it was time to go home, they called the dogs back by blowing their horns. Herbert's horn, made of an actual cow horn, later hung in the bungalow attic.

Field trials, where owners entered their dogs in competitions, were more occasions for renewing friendships and discussing politics. In an undated photograph, Herbert and a friend held the leashes to Dagwood and Blondie at a nighttime show on the grounds of the asylum, both men in suits, neckties, and fedoras, Herbert with a white ribbon in his hand; the camera flash illuminated two African American men in work clothes gazing toward the photographer from the background. At the Tuscaloosa County Fox Hunters Association's annual barbecue in 1934, Faulk was master of ceremonies and Parker Patton, by then a member of the Board of Trade, known as the "father of foxhunting" in the county, was a special guest. Before the hunt, members feasted on "barbecued mutton, pork and lamb, [and] gumbo stew." Plain Bill Brandon and Herbert's Democratic Party ally Richard Foster gave speeches.[30]

Herbert's entry into local party activity and his friendly personal campaigning were successful. He defeated Warren easily and won the general election with no Republican opponent. On the fall ballot, yellow-dog Democratic voters could simply draw a single large "X" beneath the Democratic Party's emblem, but Herbert had become so popular in the county that he tied for the highest number of complimentary votes in the form of checked names.[31] (Bealle was less successful. He also led on May 1 but lost in the June 12 run-off, his defeat becoming a humorous part of local political lore. Some voters told him, "We know you've done a good job and if it was anybody else running against you, we would certainly vote for you but your opponent has promised to marry my niece if he is elected.")[32] Herbert took office in January 1935, succeeding Bealle in the court that heard family, civil, and misdemeanor criminal matters, with wide powers over families in his jurisdiction, now a modern version of the archetypal southern ruler.

Like campaigning beside their husbands, volunteering for worthy causes was a cultural expectation for middle- and upper-class women, but when her children were younger Earline confined her volunteer work to small jobs such as being secretary of the PTA at Lyman's school. Now she occasionally hosted the monthly social meetings of her Sunday school group with Hatchett Hinton sometimes helping as a cohostess. After Herbert took office in 1935, Earline joined the American Legion Auxiliary, supervising schoolgirls who sold lapel decorations on Poppy Day and serving as a cohostess at an Auxiliary meeting. She volunteered with the local chapter of the Junior Red Cross and joined a literary organization, the Qui Vive Club, serving on its program committee with Neva Foley, whose daughter, Mary Luella, was one of Anne's close friends. The club's theme in 1936 was "The American Home." Gradually venturing into even more civic activities, in 1937 Earline worked with Herbert on a community fair.[33]

She also became pregnant that year. There is no way to be sure how Earline felt about another pregnancy but she was forty-one years old, Herbert's career was well underway, and with Lyman and Anne in school she enjoyed the leisure time to participate with friends in clubs, make fine clothes, and visit relatives. The death of her brother Alva, just a year and a half older than Earline, that May was a reminder of her own mortality[34] so she must have been terrified when it developed that her pregnancy was ectopic. Ectopic pregnancies could be fatal. If the tiny misplaced fetus was lodged in one of her fallopian tubes and the tube ruptured, the hemorrhaging was internal and the first signs of trouble were pain and lightheadedness; Earline could have lost consciousness. She may also have experienced heavy external bleeding.[35] When she was stricken on a day in October, the family physician, Joseph Emil Shirley, came to the house. Part of a well-known Northport family, Shirley had attended Earline at the births of Lyman and Anne and was the physician for Hatchett's children. Now he and Herbert carefully carried Earline out of the bungalow, probably on a stretcher. Frightened, Lyman asked the doctor, "Are you going to bring my mother back home?" and Shirley replied, "I'm going to do my best." Earline had surgery immediately. Afterward, the newspaper reported that she was recovering from "a major operation" and hoped "to be able to be removed to her home on University Avenue within a few days."[36]

Two months after Earline's near death, the Findleys probably listened to the Rose Bowl game on January 1. Radios were popular and common in southern homes by this time and Herbert was a devoted Alabama fan who listened to football broadcasts on the radio in the kitchen during my childhood. Excitement had mounted in town since a local radio station announced Alabama's fourth invitation to the Rose Bowl.[37] The school had tied in one bowl and won in two, but this year the traditional New Year's Day good-luck meal of black-eyed peas, turnip greens, hog jowl, and cornbread was not enough for a win. The beloved Crimson Tide lost to the University of California, 13–0.[38] More bad news came that evening or the next morning as word spread of the death of a past Crimson Tide hero, Herbert's cousin Hargrove "Hog" Van de Graaff.[39]

Hog's family was well known in town for having two lawyers, three football stars, and an atom-smasher. His grandfather, the lawyer and Civil War hero Cole Hargrove, was a first cousin of Herbert's grandfather Tenedus Hargrove. Hog's mother, Minnie Cherokee Hargrove, had married a graduate of Yale University and the Alabama law school, Adrian Sebastian Van de Graaff of Gainesville (Sumter County), whom we shall call Adrian Sr. Five years after marrying into the Hargrove family, Adrian Sr. bought an enormous plantation known as Gee's Bend in Wilcox County with a vague plan to evict the one hundred black tenant families who lived there and re-create the estate as a landscape of small independent farms for white yeomen. His dream, he wrote, was "that the salvation of this section lay in breaking up the Negro majorities in the Black Belt, and breaking up the large plantations into small farms to be tilled by white men."[40] He never implemented his idea, however, and struggled to make the plantation and other properties he bought break even. He served in an appointed capacity as circuit judge in 1916–17 and for one term in the Alabama House of Representatives. Minnie and Adrian Sr.'s children, Hog, his sister, and three brothers, grew up in the imposing Jemison mansion on Greensboro Avenue.

When Herbert was in high school, Hog's older brother, Adrian Van Vinceler Van de Graaff, whom we shall call Adrian Jr., was a star guard on the university football team and known as "Moose" and "Big Vandy"; he became a lawyer like his father. By the time Herbert was at the university, Hog was captain of the team. The next brother, William Travis ("Bully"), was in Herbert's class. He became a tackle for the Tide and the first Alabama football player to receive an All-American award.[41] The fourth brother, Robert Jemison ("Tee"), was legendary for a different reason, going north to the Massachusetts Institute of Technology and inventing the electrostatic generator.[42] After Adrian Sr. died in 1922, Adrian Jr. moved home from Birmingham to practice law, frequently advising other lawyers and even judges but rarely or never trying a case himself. Temo Callahan saw him as "an unmarried man" who was "the end of a long line of wealthy, southern aristocrats, who had about run out of money and prestige."[43] The Van de Graaffs' sister, also named Cherokee, married and had a child but died in 1934, and Minnie, still living in the old mansion, intermittently took in her only grandchild, Asa Rountree III. The three generations—grandmother, bachelor uncles, and little Asa, who was Lyman and Anne's fourth cousin—had summer meals in the dining room but spent most of the winter near the fireplace in the library where Cole Hargrove, as we will see later, had shot himself, with three black servants to cook and perform the household chores.[44]

Hog managed the family's properties including coal mines and Gee's Bend, an example of the absentee landlord whose management, a researcher for the WPA observed, tended to be "the final stage in the decline of a plantation."[45] As cotton prices fluctuated, the plantations became a financial drain on the family. Hog did not evict farmers at Gee's Bend who could not pay their rent, but the family of a local merchant who had extended them credit was less generous; in 1932 he seized practically all of the portable possessions of sixty black families who lived on Van de Graaff land. The raid, which the tenants remembered as "the break up," was cataclysmic, the families surviving on wild fruit and game until the American Red Cross delivered provisions.[46] The next year, a federal jobs program employed some of the Van de Graaffs' tenants on road-building projects for fifty cents a day while Hog focused on activities in Tuscaloosa, helping develop a municipal airport, obtaining a contract to operate Riverview Park, and participating in the American Legion post along with Herbert.[47] In 1934, the Federal Emergency Relief Administration began lending the black farmers money. Government and magazine photographers documented the wretched conditions of southern tenant farmers and a minister described life at Gee's Bend in an article for the magazine *Christian Century*. The plight of the people on what was known as "the Van de Graaff place" had become a national scandal.[48]

Adrian Jr. died suddenly in 1936, suffering a massive heart attack a few minutes after discussing some matter with Hog in his office in the Alston Building, the same building where Herbert once had a law office. There were three public events in honor of Adrian Jr.: the funeral at First Presbyterian, burial in Evergreen Cemetery, and a courtroom tribute. The family designated all of the members of the county bar association honorary pallbearers, and lawyers conducted the memorial service in the circuit court chamber with Judge Foster presiding and Richard Foster, by then president of the university and a close friend of Adrian Jr., delivering a eulogy.[49]

Minnie Van de Graaff sold the mansion around then. Turned out of the ancestral home, with his older brother and sister dead, his younger brothers living far away, and his mother elderly and interested in little besides visiting with a few friends in afternoon social calls,[50] Hog must have experienced increasing stress over financial losses as well as remorse over his father's tyrannical scheme to remove the people of Gee's Bend from the land and his own failure to compensate them. He was known as a man with "tolerant views" and a "deep interest in his fellow men" who was "popular with all classes, the rich and the poor, the young and the old, and the black and white." A family friend considered him the "beau-ideal of the old-fashioned gentleman-sportsman," and the *Tuscaloosa News* observed that the unfortunate "always lighted in him a flame of sympathy and understanding." On visits to Gee's Bend, Hog saw leaning, mud-daubed cabins papered with newspapers, meat hanging in tow sacks from the branches of trees for lack of a smokehouse, and women toiling over the quilts that eventually made them folk art celebrities.[51] "Hargrove" and "Cherokee" even entered the patchwork of given names at Gee's Bend, suggesting that some tenants hoped that by naming children for Hog's family they would be assured of his ongoing paternalistic protection.[52] It was the government that was their salvation, however, fulfilling Adrian Sr.'s vision of transforming Gee's Bend into small farms by buying the land from the surviving Van de Graaffs in 1936 and selling five-acre tracts to tenant families, but with black, rather than white, farmers now plowing their own fields and gardens. Suffering from what the *Tuscaloosa News* called "a nervous disorder," Hog checked into Gulfport Veterans Hospital in Mississippi in 1937, "his passionate concern for the poor" that "was known everywhere" perhaps having overcome his will to live. Alone on the coast, he stopped eating and slowly wasted away, finally dying in his sleep on the day of the 1938 Rose Bowl with no family members at his side.[53]

Riding a train back to Tuscaloosa, the football team sent a telegram ahead to add its voice to the tributes to the former Crimson Tide captain. An estimated five thousand townspeople and students crowded around the Alabama Great Southern station on Wednesday morning, January 5, to greet the returning team and hear speeches by President Richard Foster, coaches, and players. Herbert, Earline, and Lyman may have been in the crowd; junior and senior high students were excused until ten o'clock so they could participate.[54] At Hog's funeral, Foster was an active pallbearer and Herbert's hunting friend W. M. Faulk an honorary pallbearer.[55] Like the tributes to Adrian Jr. and the welcome rally for the football team, Hog's funeral was the kind of event where Herbert, running for a second term as chancery judge, and Earline needed to be seen.

Earline agreed to host a meeting of the Qui Vive Club that March. The family had stopped renting rooms by this time, thanks to Herbert's steady income, so it was easier to have acquaintances visit in the living room. She probably arranged daffodils and narcissi from the front shrubbery border and put a maid, or the children, to work polishing the sterling flatware,[56] but Earline must have been uneasy. Hatchett was ill and facing major surgery at a hospital in Birmingham, and the filing deadline in the Democratic primary was that day. Since she planned buffet refreshments rather than a seated meal, she could have cut long, erect branches of glossy green cherry laurel leaves to create a dramatically tall centerpiece for the dining table. As for the menu, it was customary at late afternoon meetings and parties to serve a "plate course" with congealed salad, sandwiches made of canned Boston brown bread and cream cheese, crackers or cheese straws, and cake.[57] Later that afternoon, the newspaper carried a picture of Herbert at the top of the front page above the headline "Judge Findley Re-Elected." The photograph was a formal portrait for which he had worn a dark wool suit with a vest and a necktie with wide and narrow stripes in three colors. "He stands only five feet, five and one-half inches high, and weighs only 125 pounds, but Judge Herbert L. Findley, 'littlest' Tuscaloosa County candidate in the May 3 Democratic primary, was 'big' enough to scare off all opposition and come 'home free' for reelection," the newspaper reported.[58]

Henry Foster's health began to fail during the first year of Herbert's second term. At times, a local lawyer, Tom B. Ward, sat in for the circuit judge. Herbert also filled in for Foster in July. The case involved Robert Pate, the former deputy sheriff who relinquished custody of Pippen, Harden, and Clark to the masked gang in 1933. Pate, now in his third week as a municipal police officer, was charged with shooting an unarmed white man through the rear window of the man's car. Pate's explanation was that he was pursuing the man because he saw him enter a transaction with two prostitutes. When Herbert presided over the preliminary hearing, the sweltering courtroom "was packed and jammed" with officers having "to clear people away from the windows in order to let a little fresh air into the steaming building," but the newspaper failed to report whether citizens attended the hearing in support of Pate or on behalf of the victim. The prosecutor charged Pate with homicide and Herbert set the bond at five thousand dollars, which Pate immediately paid.[59]

When Foster died that November, after listening to the radio as the Crimson Tide lost to Tulane University, 13–0, courthouse regulars were surprised because he had seemed to be in better health in recent months. As with the death of Adrian Jr., all of the local lawyers were honorary pallbearers at the judge's funeral. While they mourned his passing, more than a few also considered how they could take his place. Four men, including Herbert and Tom Ward, went to Montgomery to ask Governor Frank M. Dixon for appointment to fill the unexpired term. Herbert's opponent in the 1934 inferior court race, Charles Warren, and several other lawyers also asked for the job. After Ward promised he would not run for the seat in the next election, the governor chose him, explaining that he did not want to give the advantage of incumbency to anyone who might run.[60]

Herbert did run for the circuit court seat the following year, at the midpoint in his second term as inferior court judge. His opponents were Warren and E. L. Dodson. Warren made a blatant appeal for job security, commenting that Herbert and Dodson, an attorney for the county, already had jobs "which they are filling with honor and . . . will retain if I am elected." The political season opened March 1, 1940, with a rally in Cottondale; the next week Earline hosted a meeting of the church missionary society. When the final rally of the primary season took place, the public's interest was so high, six hundred and fifty people packed the auditorium at the county high school and hundreds more listened to the speeches from a loudspeaker in the cafeteria. Probably glad to help in her father's campaign, twelve-year-old Anne skipped a Girl Scout outing to Camp Cherry Austin that weekend. Turnout was very high on May 7 and Herbert lost narrowly, forcing Warren into a run-off that Warren won. Perhaps as consolation, the American Legion Auxiliary made Earline a delegate to the statewide Legion convention; thus Herbert and Earline were able to spend a few days in Birmingham that summer.[61]

✲ ✲ ✲

In early 1940, with war again spreading across Europe, the film *Gone with the Wind* was a huge phenomenon, an opportunity during uncertain times for the reading and moviegoing publics to remember the overarching southern fantasy of the moral goodness of slavery and enduring black loyalty.[62] I believe Earline and Anne saw the movie together because when Anne took me to a screening in Birmingham in the 1970s, the experience had a ceremonial or ritualistic feel. Women in Tuscaloosa had been quite interested in Margaret Mitchell's book as soon as it was published in 1936. Sydnia Smyth's club, the Tuscaloosa chapter of the Business and Professional Women's Club, had a review of the novel on its agenda, and Carrie Hamner Brown, one of the local members of the United Daughters of the Confederacy, "entranced" members of her church class with her review.[63] Lustig's Book Store advertised a "motion picture edition" for sixty-nine cents, with a full-color photograph of the film's stars, Vivien Leigh and Clark Gable, in costume as Scarlett O'Hara and Rhett Butler, on the cover. The first screening in Tuscaloosa, at the Druid Theater in the afternoon on Easter Sunday, March 24, 1940, was the only scheduled show that did not conflict with school or homework, so Earline probably took Anne to the movie after church and the family's usual Easter lunch. Next door to the theater, Lustig's sold tickets for the movie, setting up three separate tables so that the lines would not be too long. The day was unusually cold, but once inside the theater women and girls could shed their coats and admire each other's new Easter dresses.[64]

Wearing the famous green-sprigged dress to receive admirers in the opening scene, the character of Scarlett was, of course, fiction and film's greatest realization of the southern belle. With a wasp waist, pearly complexion, and flirtatious manner that offset her lack of conventional beauty, she was courted by many young aristocrats. She was deeply attached, like belles in Thomas Nelson Page's fantastical fiction, to her father, heroic in her own feminine way, perfect in the vivid color on the movie screen. The climactic episode of book and film, when Melanie nearly died in childbirth as the Yankees set Atlanta afire and the maddening young house servant Prissy failed to find a doctor, touched on every wife's fears. Butterfly McQueen's performance of Prissy as a lying simpleton must have reaffirmed Earline's conviction that black domestic servants were unreliable and dishonest. She probably did *not* recognize that, when Prissy sang "Jes' a few mo' days, ter tote de wee-ry load," dawdling while the city burned, it was the barest acknowledgment by Mitchell, camouflaged in Stephen Foster's minstrel song "My Old Kentucky Home," that as the Yankees invaded Atlanta, African Americans' subservience was an act. They had freedom on their minds.[65]

Several other books that Anne read and deposited in the hall bookcase perpetuated the South's infatuation with the archetypal belle. In Govan's *Narcissus an' de Chillun*, published two years after *Gone with the Wind*, the character of Lucy was like Scarlett, "happy and dewy-eyed" in a flower-sprigged dress. She was in love with a physician, a genteel, fair-minded young man who sometimes hobnobbed "with his not too aristocratic neighbor 'Old Boggs' Gowen," an amusing figure who lived, like Herbert's cousin Petie Keene, "in a disreputable cabin." Arriving at the Plummers' home for a visit, Lucy had two trunks filled with petticoats "whose ruffles, laced through and through with pink or blue ribbon, were like fountains of froth." Lucy's "skin . . . had not a freckle [and] she could play a piano," inspiring Chris to spend "all of twenty minutes the next day picking out a detestable piece called 'The Daffodils.'"[66] Anne also owned Thomas Nelson Page's *In Ole Virginia*, a pretty view of slavery and the beautiful lives that aristocratic men and women enjoyed.[67] In Page's story "Marse Chan," an archetypal loyal former slave, Sam, told the story of Master Channing, who enlisted in the Confederate Army, and of the delicate belle, Miss Anne, who loved him. Sam recalled how, before leading his troops into battle, Chan told him, "'Sam, we'se goin' to win in dis battle, an' den we'll go home an' git married. . . . Ef I'm wounded, kyar me home, yo' hear?'" Channing was killed and loyal Sam indeed carried him home. Another happy former slave, Uncle Edinburg, reminisced about a Christmas party in the washhouse, telling his listener: "Oh, hit sutney wuz beautiful!" The slaves were allowed to use silver candelabra, a punch bowl for eggnog, flowers "out de greenhouse," china, and dining room chairs. "Oh! oh! nuttin warn too good for niggers dem times." In this story, too, the heroic and handsome young white planter died, not in battle but while rescuing Edinburg from drowning. In the words of Page's imaginary black servants, beautiful young white belles existed to be adored by handsome young aristocrats. Anne, grieving for the dead Channing, was "light ez a piece o' peth, an' so white"; Charlotte descended a staircase "wid her dim blue dress trainin' behind her, an' her little blue foots peepin' out so pretty . . . an' her gret dark eyes lightin' up her face."[68]

At the time Anne received her copy of *In Ole Virginia*, she was immersed in an anthology of Mark Twain's work. She read three of his unabridged novels in December 1940 and one in January, noting the dates on the table of contents.[69] Anne had an affinity for Twain's *Huckleberry Finn*: like Huck, she loved rambling outdoors when she visited The Old Place with Murk; she later revealed a desire to go hunting with Herbert; and some of her friends even called her "Fin."[70] However, she was almost thirteen when she read Twain—old enough to recognize the cultural imperative, encoded by Mitchell and Page, for a girl to appear well-dressed and coy, particularly if, like Scarlett, she was not beautiful.[71] It was Lyman, not Anne, whom Earline and Herbert permitted to enact Huck's adventurous outdoor life, spending days camping with friends beside Hurricane Creek at The Old Place, where they could swim, cook over a campfire, and "stay naked."[72]

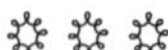

When Murk died in April 1941, Anne cut a tiny picture of him from a snapshot and placed it in a gold-colored locket, a traditional form of mourning jewelry that she passed on to me with Murk's photograph still in place. Two years earlier, the family had held a birthday party for Murk at Ila and Preston's house,[73] but now Earline did not yield her role as mistress or her house as stage. Renwick C. Kennedy, the minister who had written about the Van de Graaffs' plantation at Gee's Bend, had recently described mourning ritual in Alabama towns, his account suggesting the scene at the bungalow following Murk's death: "If the deceased were an important citizen his demise causes as much excitement, and pleasure, as a political rally or a revival meeting. It brings the community together in genial assembly." Concerning the custom of calling on the bereaved, Kennedy explained, "The funeral call . . . is a social gesture, and the caller wants full credit for it. . . . They were greeted at the door by a relative who act[s] as host." Kennedy's version of how friends and neighbors visited the bereaved even captured the layout of the Findleys' bungalow. Visitors passed "through the long hall to the back bed room where the family, appropriately tearful, lolled about in varying stages of sorrow upon beds and chairs." Friends delivered food and "two quart bottles and a half dozen pints of whiskey," taking the latter "quietly to the back door where a Negro servant received them and placed them in the butler's pantry upon a table with glasses."[74]

In the same gesture the Van de Graaff family made at the funeral for Adrian Jr., Herbert designated all of the county lawyers honorary pallbearers for Murk. He and his brothers also named active and additional honorary pallbearers, the list in the newspaper obituary, like Parker Patton's guest list for the 1917 foxhunt, demonstrating the strong filial ties that laced Tuscaloosa's governing class for generations. There was Newt Hinton, Herbert's good friend and Hatchett's husband, and Parker Patton's son Wilson, Herbert's foxhunting friend. Verner Robertson Jr. was a descendant of the

Revolutionary War veteran "Horse Shoe" Robertson. There were Murk's fellow civil engineers Norfleet Harris, a past alderman, and Woolsey Finnell, a past probate judge, both pallbearers for Ida thirty-three years earlier. Joseph Shirley was the family doctor and Robert Shook rented Murk's house. Other pallbearers represented the top layer of political power in Tuscaloosa, such as Fleetwood Rice, who attended Patton's hunt and helped defend Pippen and Clark. The Findley brothers' second cousin Matthew T. Maxwell was the clerk of the county revenue board. Fayette Shamblin, a few years younger than Murk, was the former sheriff whom the sociologist Arthur Raper thought was blameless in the murders of Pippen and Harden. Pelham Deveraux Brown, whose wife reviewed *Gone with the Wind* for the Alathean Class, was a longtime real estate agent and former clerk in the office of the probate judge. Some ties among these people stretched into the future: the descendant of one pallbearer later married a descendant of another.[75]

It was common for funeral services to take place at commercial funeral homes, but this custom was slower to catch on in the South and some Tuscaloosa families persisted in holding genuine home funerals, powerful ceremonies in which the appearance and stature of the deceased and his or her house briefly merged.[76] After the family engaged a mortuary to prepare the body, the remains were returned to the home for a visitation period and the funeral service. The funerals for Murk's old geology professor, Eugene Smith, and Smith's widow, Jennie, were at their house across University Avenue, his in 1927 and hers in 1930.[77] When Murk's sister-in-law Collette Hargrove died in 1930, the funeral was in her home; when his mother-in-law, Minerva, died in 1932, her funeral was at her home.[78] Now the Findleys held a home funeral for Murk at the bungalow with the minister of First Methodist officiating.[79] Next came the procession to the cemetery, another highly visible element of mourning ritual. A caravan of about two hundred vehicles had passed the bungalow on the way to the burial of Plain Bill Brandon in 1934; when Grace Hamby's family held a home funeral for her father, the Marengo County sheriff, in 1937, hundreds of his friends and political supporters departed the Shields home in a procession to the cemetery.[80] Murk's mourners followed his hearse away from the bungalow and the house he built for Ida. With other motorists pulling over to let the caravan pass, they rolled slowly to Evergreen Cemetery, where the family buried Murk beside Ida and John.

Like sympathy visits, home funerals, and processions to cemeteries, news articles were a standard element of death ritual for elite families in

Tuscaloosa. Earline collaborated with Herbert's aunt Lula Hargrove to make notes for an article about Murk that appeared in the university alumni newsletter. The information that Lula recorded indicates what the family considered important: Murk's father was "Murchison Findley Sr.," meaning Murk was his father's namesake. Murchison Sr. came to Tuscaloosa County in 1816, meaning he was a pioneer, and served in the Second Seminole War, meaning he could have been a military hero. Lula and Earline's page of handwritten notes became part of the family's small collection of genealogical documents, demonstrating the care the Findleys took to preserve their history. In the alumni bulletin, the university praised Murk for a "long and useful life in and around Tuscaloosa" and named his sons, noting the graduation years for Hargrove, now a road construction supervisor for the state, and Herbert.[81] The youngest and most diminutive of Murk's sons, Earline's husband had become the most prominent and influential of his generation of Findley men.

Seven

Tableaux Vivants

THE STRONGEST CLUES ABOUT HOW EARLINE experienced the 1940s are in the memorabilia that Lyman and Anne kept, his in a scrapbook and hers in a scrapbook and on a soft satin doll, in the form of a clown, to which she pinned ribbons and insignia. Lyman saved materials from a high school student government convention in Tulsa, his unanimous election as student council president, and his selection as one of twenty boys from the county to attend Boys State, a summer program, in 1941.[1] Anne had kept several mementoes from an NAT Club that spring, including the small card that came with a corsage and a photograph of her with her date. Her dress, of a sheer fabric with an all-over floral pattern, was appropriate for a thirteen-year-old girl, with a full lining, modest heart-shaped neckline, slightly dropped waist, and short puffed sleeves with white satin cuffs.[2] Puffed, cuffed short sleeves show up on two more of Anne's outfits in other photos that she saved, strongly indicating that Earline made all three. One was a simple print dress that Anne wore in the backyard, The Little House behind the bungalow in the background. As someone snapped the picture, she sat in a straight-backed chair and gazed down into another camera in her lap. In a different photograph taken that morning (the scene and shadows are similar), Herbert struck a suave pose beside the car barn, his white, double-breasted suit as bright as the exterior of the garage, a large round button, like a campaign button but marked with a handwritten "'16," on his lapel. The same strange button survived on Anne's doll. A picture in the university alumni bulletin reveals that Herbert was on his way that morning to a large college alumni reunion. No photograph of Earline survives from that day in June 1941, but she probably accompanied him to the reception for the Class of 1916, where all "had a great time greeting each other and their respective wives and husbands."[3]

The puffed sleeves appear next in a photo booth picture taken in April 1942, when Anne wore a bias-cut skirt and matching jacket in a light, striped fabric. She was a bit plump and the suit's narrow stripes complied with the recommendation in Earline's etiquette manual that "the massive woman . . . should affect quiet colors [and] vertical narrow stripes."[4] The striped suit would have been appropriate for the mother-daughter Girl Scout tea that she and Earline attended that month and for the breakfast at a house party that Anne's friend Burmiss Barnett "Bebe" Lewis gave for the NAT Club in early June.[5] Anne was one of "18 outstanding belles" to be invited. Bebe's party suggests a solution for a small mystery: Why did Earline back out of hosting the Laurel Class that month, forcing another woman to open her home for the meeting?[6] Earline could have been pressed to finish making clothes for Anne to wear to the prestigious house party. Although the striped suit could have served for the breakfast on Tuesday, Anne needed outfits for swimming, a picnic supper, and a dance plus a nightgown for overnight.[7] A young woman's wardrobe had always been a sign of status, but in bourgeois, twentieth-century Tuscaloosa, well-made, fashionable clothing was essential for the belle's social prospects.[8] Throughout junior and senior high school, Earline made sure Anne had the right ensembles for special occasions.[9]

Even in a family with a comfortable professional income, a mother was stretched to purchase or make enough outfits for a socially active daughter. Fine sewing was a crucial skill for middle-class women who could not afford ready-made clothes for every event but could, thanks to their low-paid domestic help, spare the time to make many items. The greater one's skill at sewing, the more elaborate and refined a wardrobe a woman, and her daughter, could have. Earline probably learned the basics of dressmaking from her mother and refined her skills at the Alabama Normal School.[10] Because Anne taught me to sew, beginning with simple projects and progressing to cuffs, collars, and linings, I believe that she and Earline made many garments together. Dressmaking tied Earline to her mother, Annie, her sister Velma, and her daughter, Anne—even to her neighbor Louise Shook and Louise's daughter Mary Louise, a home economics student at the university who helped teach public sewing classes for young women.[11] Anne learned to avoid clothing fads and rely on mixing wardrobe pieces in classic styles, accenting them with silk scarves, secrets Anne passed on to me. When Anne and her friends Mary Luella and Bebe attended a youth conference in Montgomery in 1944, she needed clothes for two dinners, a banquet at the Whitley Hotel, meetings, field trips, and a church service. Earline probably helped her daughter pack two skirts and three blouses to be worn with scarves under a single coordinating jacket for travel, the meetings, and the dinners, adding slacks and a light sweater and scarves for the recreation activities and finishing with a dress for church.[12]

In another photograph from Anne's scrapbook, taken in the summer of 1941, she wore a belted, lace-trimmed dress and ankle-strap sandals, making the best of her short figure. She was on a trip to Chattanooga with her piano teacher, Jennie Moore. A sidewalk photographer snapped the picture as they walked past a movie theater, Jennie carrying an umbrella and a paper sack that appeared to contain sheet music, Anne marching, unsmiling, beside her, carrying a hardcover book. Sidewalk photographers typically worked outside camera shops, snapping pictures of passersby and handing out information about how to order and pick up prints.[13] Anne kept the photo as a souvenir, but letters from Earline indicate that her Chattanooga trip was not an exciting grown-up sort of adventure away from home but a painful experience for Jennie and a somber, even frightening, one for Earline and Anne. Earline was nervous when her family members were away from home. At the time Anne and Jennie left, Herbert and Lyman also were gone. Even the Shooks were out of town. Earline wrote to Anne, "I staid [*sic*] here alone Fri. night. Didn't like the idea very much tho [*sic*]."

Jennie's purpose in going to Chattanooga, where they stayed in her sister Ida's house while Ida watched over their brother in Tuscaloosa, was to undergo a series of painful dental procedures. Anne was responsible for tending to Jennie between dentist office visits. Earline repeatedly inserted directions and reminders in her notes to Anne, just as she did when Anne went to Girl Scout camp three years earlier. In 1938, Earline had commanded Anne to write to Jennie Moore "*at once* and put some German in it. Bebe started her [German] lessons this morning. If you did not write Mamma and Auntie Velma *you must*." Now she instructed Anne to "be sure you take care of Miss Jennie," also pressuring her to write to her friends. She wrote, "Suppose you surprise Mary Louella [*sic*] by sending her a card at once" and added the address for Bebe "in case you forgot to write it down." Finally she commanded, "Write us. Love, Mother." Musing, "I think I shall go down to

Meridian tomorrow morning and stay until Saturday," Earline instructed Anne to send her next letter to her "by return mail" and address it to Meridian, *and* send a note to Velma, *and* continue writing to Herbert at home.[14]

Another outbreak of polio in the South that summer of 1941 was the most serious yet. The very word "polio" was terrifying. In July 1936, after two cases of polio were recorded in Tuscaloosa, Dr. Arthur Kirk had warned parents "to keep their children away from public gatherings of every sort, especially swimming places, dances, [and] playgrounds."[15] In 1938, Earline had reported to Anne at camp that Bill Newt Hinton was sick again: "Dr. Shirley says he has an irritation in one lung," adding irrationally, "so you must be very careful and try not to take a cold." Now, a single issue of the *Tuscaloosa News* carried six separate wire service reports about hundreds of new cases of polio in Alabama, Georgia, and Tennessee. In Chattanooga, twenty-eight cases of polio prompted the city to close playgrounds and movie theaters to children under the age of twelve. Earline clipped the article about Chattanooga and mailed it to Anne, commenting, "It's needless for me to tell you that I went to pieces when I read the enclosed. . . . I thought I'd wire you to catch the first train home, but after going up and talking to Mrs. Longley have changed my mind. . . . Please . . . stay away from places where there might be a . . . germ. Ask Miss Moore's dentist what he knows about the situation." Finally, "We shall be anxiously awaiting a reply on the Polio situation. . . . Lovingly, Mother." She wrote again from Meridian, "21 new cases Polio in state today—has gotten me awfully worried." Her fear of contagion was the most common topic in Earline's notes to Anne.

Anne remained in Chattanooga and Earline wondered when she would return, asking, "Let us know when to meet you." Addressing Anne as "Sister," Mary Louise Shook wrote, "I saw your mother this morning and she said she had a letter but you didn't mention coming home. Please don't stay too long 'cause it's awful lonely around here without you." Earline used Herbert to increase the pressure—"I don't think your Daddy will be able to live without you many days longer. He tells me every five minutes what a long week next week will be"—but Herbert tried to amuse and comfort Anne. Writing on letterhead of the inferior court, he thanked her for a "nice little letter" she had sent. He joked, "Mother went to Birmingham Wednesday with the Shook's [*sic*] but I haven't seen anything that she bought except some dough-nuts, and it seems to me that Birmingham is a long way to go to get a piece of bread—and it with a hole in it. Guess I will have to go hunting—to find something to do and some eats." On the news that Alabama schools would delay opening because of the polio outbreak, he commented, "I notice in the paper that school will not begin until September 16th which gives you almost another month." And this: "Have fun and remember that I love you and want to hear you play."[16]

Anne returned safely to Tuscaloosa to enter the eighth grade.[17] There is little evidence of Earline's activities that fall, but the war in Europe was constantly in the news and gradually affected more aspects of her life. There were shortages of dress fabrics and silk stockings. Women gave up metal hair curlers and rolled their hair on old socks. The government used ration coupons to tightly regulate the availability of many foods including sugar, meats, and butter; Earline probably used sorghum, molasses, or cane syrup in place of refined sugar for cookies and cakes.[18] There were blackout drills with National Guard troops patrolling University Avenue. When she hosted a meeting of the American Legion Auxiliary one afternoon in November 1941, the nights were growing darker and the war more frightening. A blackout was in effect and that afternoon the newspaper carried new lists of local men who had enlisted in the US Army, but if the Auxiliary ladies gathered in Earline's living room discussed these frightening developments, the newspaper did not mention it. Readers learned only that the women reviewed a Halloween party they recently gave for patients at the new veterans' hospital in Tuscaloosa. The meeting included several vocal performances with one member's son playing Anne's piano as accompaniment. Earline served sandwiches, cookies, and tea, her good friend Hatchett at her side, and her flower arrangements, "gorgeous white chrysanthemums [in] silver vases [and] bowls of midget chrysanthemums and dahlias," made "a gay background for the guests."[19]

On December 8, 1941, the day after Japan's attack on Pearl Harbor, someone in the family clipped and saved the entire front page of the *Birmingham Age-Herald*. Below the lead article, the newspaper reported "the scream of bombs . . . were . . . an urgent call. . . . The United States Navy . . . expects confidently that Alabama will live up to and surpass its splendid record in sending patriotic manpower to the fleet." By the next day, seventy-five men in Tuscaloosa applied to enlist in the US Navy and Marines.[20] At the annual Citizenship Recognition Day observance at the university two days later, the Tuscaloosa High School band performed, probably with Lyman, now a high school senior, playing the trumpet. Five thousand people were expected to attend the rally.[21] The county defense council planned a network of airplane spotters to watch the sky for bombers. The city had already instituted partial blackouts of streetlights and retail signs, reducing by half the lights along University Avenue, to conserve hydroelectric power for defense manufacturing. Now the council planned an alarm system for air raids and "a blackout of all lights in Tuscaloosa and Northport in case it should be needed."[22]

In many ways, the Findleys and their friends carried on as usual. The PTA at the junior high school met on the Friday after Pearl Harbor. Neva Foley presided and the Glee Club sang Christmas songs. First Methodist held an open house Saturday night for "the young people of the church [and] University students," inviting the English Royal Air Force cadets who were in training at the airport, Hargrove Van de Graaff Field. On Sunday, the university played Christmas carols on Denny Chimes as the YWCA conducted its annual tree lighting in front of Julia Tutwiler Hall, a custom that had been a morale-booster during World War I. The next week, Anne and most of her close friends were inducted into the National Junior Honor Society and Earline's Sunday school class held its annual holiday party, exchanging "white elephant" gifts. On Sunday evening the church school and choir produced a pageant where Anne's friend Joy Pearson performed as an angel. Lyman took a date to a Christmas dance and Herbert joined other elected officials in placing an advertisement in the newspaper to "extend to the people best wishes for a Merry Christmas and a prosperous new year."[23] Continuing his rounds of low-key political activities, he participated in Masonic rites for a longtime member of their lodge (since the man also was a steward of First Methodist, Earline may have accompanied Herbert to that funeral) and played the groom in the "Womanless Wedding" skit at Alberta City School. Once again, no one filed to run against Herbert in the primary.[24]

Despite all of this busyness, it was impossible to sustain any sense of safety or normalcy once the director of the state defense council announced that all "communities within 300 miles of any coast 'should expect to be bombed.'" Adding to the tension, Earline's friend Grace was connected to two disturbing events in the days leading up to Christmas. A black man allegedly shot and killed a storekeeper and his wife in Marengo County, and Grace's brother, who had succeeded their father as sheriff, was in charge of a manhunt by "a posse of more than 100 men" with bloodhounds. The *Tuscaloosa News* reported that the dogs "trailed the killer" and the sheriff said "the posse sighted the negro on two occasions Saturday night," exchanging shots. At the same time, a young cousin of Grace was killed "by a Jap bomb" that sank "a U.S. battleship." Probably using details that Grace, who was still the newspaper's Alberta City correspondent, called in, the *Tuscaloosa News* reported that when word of the young man's death reached his family, his twenty-year-old brother went to "the navy recruiting station in Mobile and enlisted with the avowed purpose of getting revenge."[25]

Clippings in Anne's scrapbook show that the war effort became part of Herbert's civic role in the community. He chaired the county War Savings Committee and went to the Tutwiler Hotel in Birmingham for a meeting of bond drive chairmen. In May 1943, Congressman Pete Jarman commended Herbert and Herbert's cochair, and "all of the fine people of Tuscaloosa," for their service in the war bond campaign. The success of the county bond drives meant that local people could choose a name for a military plane or ship, and Herbert went back to Birmingham to christen the *Tuscaloosan*, a Liberator airplane bomber, at a factory.[26] Anne herself was recognized as a "champion bond seller" at Tuscaloosa High.[27] A small pin on the toy clown reveals she also participated in the Junior Red Cross, which conducted scrap drives and performed other activities in support of the war effort. Earline's friend Neva was chairman and Earline vice chairman of the chapter.[28] However, Earline apparently performed less "war work" as Anne rose through high school and the job of guiding her and dressing her for school, extracurricular, and social activities took more time. During Anne's senior year, 1944–45, Earline's only volunteer role seems to have been on the board of the high school PTA, a fact that surfaces in a photograph in the student yearbook. Short and plump, wearing a hat, gloves, and a coat with a wide fur collar, Earline stood with a smile beside three other women, wives of a high-ranking physician at the veterans' hospital, a prominent music professor at the university, and the respected local lawyer Devane King Jones.[29]

Around the same time, Anne posed with eight other girls for a strange, unlabeled snapshot. They were arranged at the base of a large wooden cross, one girl prone and partly covered with leaves, Anne frowning a bit. From a comparison of the photograph with school portraits, it appears Anne and her friends were seniors in high school. Their plaid shirts and long sleeves indicate it was autumn, as plaids would not be in style in the spring. Anne's friend Elna Bolding later speculated that the photograph was taken at Camp Cherry Austin in Cottondale, which Anne had attended as a reluctant ten-year-old camper back in 1938, when her Aunt Ila was on the camp staff. Ila's sister-in-law Nancy Dean Callahan Blackman (Temo's sister) was known for organizing "*tableaux* in which . . . campers got themselves up as scenes from silent movies." Together, these clues suggest the girls volunteered at the Girl Scout camp in the fall of 1944 and were persuaded to gather beneath the cross for a tableau vivant or "living picture," perhaps the climactic scene in the modern opera *Erwartung* (*Expectation*) by Arnold Schoenberg, in which a young woman searches a wood for her lost lover, finding him dead and half buried by leaves.[30] Kneeling beside Mary Luella, Anne appeared reluctant to join the fun.

Tableaux vivants were an old theatrical custom. Costumed as figures in history or literature, young women produced tableaux as parlor entertainments or fund-raisers. They assembled on a stage, sometimes before a backdrop or on a set furnished in a period manner, to strike their poses. Then the curtain would rise. A tableau vivant in Tuscaloosa in 1864 was so crowded hundreds of people were turned away at the door. "Staged photographs," an extension of costumed tableaux, also originated in the 1860s. Elite white women in Tuscaloosa continued to produce tableaux in the twentieth century, sometimes alternating the silent poses with skits or musical interludes. The "Tom Thumb Wedding," in which Anne appeared as a bridesmaid, was a tableau vivant; so too were "Plantation" or "Darkey Parties" at which guests wore blackface and had their pictures taken. The local president of the UDC starred in a tableau vivant produced by the Tuscaloosa Study Club in 1937, wearing "an old fashioned costume of the Sixties and [holding] the Flag of the Confederacy." The language of tableaux vivants spilled into the language of weddings, with the *Tuscaloosa News* describing one particular wedding as "the beautiful bridal *tableau*."[31]

Belonging to the UDC was prestigious. During Earline's girlhood, many southern women in the expanding urban middle class sought membership in the UDC as a way of strengthening their identity as elite white women. When Earline was a teacher, the organization had campaigned for years to use school history lessons to promulgate the fantastical version of southern history, so she almost certainly was aware of the organization by the time she was an adult. Some historians have suggested that Confederate commemorations waned in social importance beginning in the 1920s,[32] but for a young matron such as Earline, new to Tuscaloosa society in 1921, the value of membership in the UDC was easy to see. Cherokee Jemison Hargrove, Herbert's distant cousin by marriage, was the founding vice president of R. E. Rodes Chapter No. 64 in Tuscaloosa. Cherokee's husband, Cole, had been the most glorified veteran in the Hargrove family and one of the most prominent Civil War heroes in Tuscaloosa, idolized by some of the men who served under him. After suffering excruciating headaches since being shot in the head in the battle of Spanish Fort, he committed suicide a year before the local ladies started the Rodes chapter. Membership was a link to other prominent women such as Josephine Maxwell (the wife of one of the pallbearers for Ida Findley), who was president of the Rodes chapter the year after Earline married Herbert. Herbert's great-aunt Alice Keene and her daughters Belle Keene Ward and Kate Keene Seay—the latter notable as master of the Tuscaloosa Curb Market—also were active in the Rodes chapter. The *Tuscaloosa News* called UDC members "the most cultured matrons in the city."[33] Acceptance by the UDC was proof of the elite white woman's lineage as a daughter of the antebellum South and her commitment to preserving the fantastical vision of noble white men, beautiful white women, and loyal black servants.[34]

Earline was eligible for admission on the basis of the military service of her maternal grandfather John Chiles Christopher, and she had a 1923 letter from a Choctaw County judge who attested to his service. One of the most intriguing questions about Earline's life, therefore, is why she waited so long to join the UDC. Not until 1940 did she make the overture that led the Rodes chapter to write for federal confirmation of John's record. Earline saved a copy of the letter the chapter obtained from the US War Office. It revealed that John enlisted a year after the start of the war and was discharged seven months later "upon furnishing a substitute."[35] John could have stalled because he was ambivalent about secession or even about slavery, but it is more likely that, like Murchison Findley and Tenedus Hargrove, he could not abandon his responsibilities at home.[36] In 1860, he and his wife, Laura; his hearing-impaired brother, Thomas Henry, who worked as a schoolteacher; his widowed mother; his widowed sisters, Mary, also a schoolteacher, and Cornelia; and his widowed mother-in-law all lived in adjacent houses with a total of twelve minor children and sixty-four enslaved workers. John farmed the land belonging to his mother, mother-in-law, and widowed sisters.[37] He would have been loath to leave Laura and the other women in the family for fear the slaves would rebel. He finally enlisted when the Confederate Congress enacted the draft in 1862, going to Butler to sign up and joining Company A of the Fortieth Regiment, Alabama Infantry, as a private, probably so he could serve with other men from the area. The regiment joined the Army of Mobile, its responsibility to protect the port for Confederate commerce.[38]

Letters that Grant Taylor, another serviceman in the Fortieth, wrote to his wife reveal the scenes that John Christopher experienced in Mobile. Taylor suffered a bout of typhoid fever. When an officer's body servant "sauced" a soldier, several men in the Fortieth whipped the slave to death. Taylor was disgusted by the Confederacy's plan to draft slaves as troops and repeatedly asked his wife to negotiate with an older man in their neighborhood to sign up as a substitute for Taylor, offering "the land, houses, and all if he would go," but Taylor's captain stopped accepting substitutes.[39] Earline's grandfather John also wanted to hire a substitute, probably because Laura was pregnant again, and unlike Taylor, he managed to do so. His discharge came through three weeks before Laura's third confinement, but their reunion was brief. As the Christopher family Bible shows, neither she nor the infant lived long after the birth. In January 1864, with forces seriously depleted, the Confederate Congress ordered men who had hired substitutes to reenlist. John evidently complied since Earline's grandmother eventually was found eligible for a pension, but details about his second military stint are lost.[40]

The discovery by the UDC that John hired a replacement to avoid fulfilling his military duty, without the information that he reenlisted, may have embarrassed Earline or even dampened the enthusiasm of the women in the Rodes unit for her membership.[41] Moreover, the year 1940, when the fact of John's hiring a substitute came to light, was a busy time for Earline. She was involved in the American Legion Auxiliary; Anne's wardrobe needs were increasing; and Herbert's father, Murk, who lived in The Little House, was in declining health. It may have been easiest for Earline to put aside her application. Then Murk died in April 1941, presumably freeing her to enjoy a wider social life. Reminders of the social value of Confederate credentials were everywhere: three of Murk's pallbearers were married to women who were active in the Rodes chapter: Matt Maxwell's wife, Nan, was president; Woolsey Finnell's wife, Margaret, was a former president; and Pelham Brown's wife, Carrie, was a member. When Mary Louise Shook was a model in a campus fashion show the next month, delegates to the state meeting of the UDC, going on in town at the same time, were in the audience. When Minnie Van de Graaff died later that year, someone in the Findley family clipped and saved a *Tuscaloosa News* editorial that referred to her father, Cole Hargrove, as a "heroic figure in Alabama history."[42] Still Earline delayed. She did not complete her application to the Rodes chapter for another four years, until April 1945.[43]

There are other possible reasons for her delay. Chapter meetings sometimes coincided with the Friday afternoon social meetings of her Sunday school class. There was a new spin-off UDC chapter in Tuscaloosa; maybe she could not decide which chapter to join. Perhaps after Murk died Earline still had to care for her mother, who spent some periods of time living with the Findleys. Earline could have been reluctant to participate in the UDC with Annie at her side, despite the fact that Annie was the link to Earline's Confederate ancestor; relations between the two women were strained until the end of Annie's life.[44] We could wonder why Earline joined the UDC at all. Herbert probably was confident enough about holding his judicial seat that he didn't need her to expand her social network to help him politically; as the newspaper observed, "Findley has never had opposition for the inferior judgeship since he was first elected in 1935."[45] Like many men of his generation, he did not seem to care about commemorating his ancestors' Confederate service, even though he was keenly interested in local and Confederate history. His closest female relatives, his mother and grandmothers, apparently did not participate in the UDC, and while he was active in the American Legion for years, chairing the local unit's Sons of Legion Committee in 1943, he did not participate in the UDC's counterpart organization for men, the Sons of Confederate Veterans.[46]

All in all, the timing of Earline's application, more than a year before Annie died but just a month before Anne's graduation from high school, suggests why she finally joined the group. "Serenely sedate" and "a fine musician" in the words of her classmates, Anne had matured into the archetypal belle Earline envisioned: attractive, slender, and, in the terminology of the day, "well developed," a pleasing figure at the piano in the Findleys' living room, prepared to entertain guests at a moment's notice. During high school, Anne often played at meetings of her student music club, another pin on the clown doll revealing she was club president. When Earline had the opera singer perform minstrel songs for an Auxiliary program, she had Anne play the scherzo from Felix Mendelssohn's "Mid Summer Night's Dream." Unlike many piano instructors in town, Jennie Moore did not hold recitals in her home, probably fearing that her mentally ill brother might disrupt them, so these events had been valuable exposure for Anne. Other Rodes ladies used the UDC meetings as venues for their daughters: Nan Maxwell's daughter sang "Annie Laurie" at a meeting when she was twenty-one and Carrie Brown's daughter gave a talk on the Civil War at another.[47]

UDC meetings could be new opportunities for Anne to occasionally perform for audiences of socially connected women.

Six days after Earline was accepted by the UDC, the gravest crisis of the war for the Findley family began, and as with John Christopher's military record, enlistment was the issue. Lyman's lifelong friend Nelson Bolling Jones was killed in action in Europe. The oldest of three sons, considered the standard-bearer for the family, Nelson had enlisted in the army after his graduation from high school in 1944.[48] Lyman knew Nelson from Verner Elementary. The boys were frequent playmates and their parents allowed them to camp by themselves when they were as young as ten. Devastated by Nelson's death, Lyman declared he would immediately enlist to avenge the loss of his friend, just as Grace Hamby's young cousin did shortly after Pearl Harbor. Having chosen the profession of his great-uncles in the Christopher family, Lyman was completing the University of Alabama's two-year premedical program, where Neva Foley's husband was one of his professors. Lyman planned to complete a medical degree at the University of Virginia Department of Medicine, which was training physicians for the US Army, and had received an appointment in the Reserve Officers' Training Corps with recommendations from Herbert's hunting friends Dr. Partlow and Probate Judge Walker.[49] Earline knew Neva through the PTA and Junior Red Cross, and Mary Luella Foley was one of Anne's closest friends. In a tense and dramatic episode that demonstrates how terrified Earline was at the thought of losing Lyman, the Findleys prevailed on Dr. James Foley to intervene. He met with Lyman and convinced him that continuing with his plan to become a doctor was a better tribute to Nelson. To everyone's great relief, Lyman accepted Foley's advice,[50] perhaps anticipating that he would still get the chance to serve. The end of the war in Europe came a month later, on May 8. Ten days after that, Anne clipped a small article about premedical students at the university; Lyman was the only student from Tuscaloosa who was going to Virginia. By the time the war in Asia ended on August 1, he was safely in Charlottesville and wrote to Anne, "There is no news, am just going to school and studying. See you in Sept. Lots of Love, Lyman."[51]

Herbert won the Democratic nomination for a fourth term on the inferior court in 1946, again without an opponent, but he resigned before the general election when the university offered him a position as chairman of the Department of Business Law in the School of Commerce and Business

Administration. The *Tuscaloosa News* reported his resignation at the top of the front page, using the same photographic portrait it ran after his second election in 1938, and praised him as "a sympathetic and extremely capable jurist." The governor appointed a temporary judge, and the Democratic Party's county executive committee (presumably with Herbert, its secretary, abstaining) chose a nominee for a special election to replace him, naming a relatively young local lawyer, Eugene V. Bailey.[52] On a Saturday in September, Earline went to the courthouse—where for decades citizens had performed in community sings and minstrel shows and staged mock weddings and divorces—for a mock trial of Herbert. "Three stalwart state highway patrolmen marched Judge Findley" into the courthouse. As the *Tuscaloosa News* reported on the front page, the circuit solicitor read the charge of "wrongfully, unlawfully and with malice aforethought desert[ing] the courthouse." Bailey, Herbert's de facto successor, acted as his defense attorney and other lawyers performed as jurors. Circuit Judge Charles Warren, who had defeated Herbert in the 1940 race, presided and two "witnesses" testified "that among other things, Judge Findley had absented himself from the courthouse to help sell war bonds [and] was 'too hard on bootleg lawyers.'" It was "all in fun," the newspaper explained. Playing the jury foreman, Tom Ward, the lawyer who had won the governor's appointment as interim circuit judge over Herbert and others in 1939, presented him with a ten-volume edition of the state code. Rising at the conclusion of his "trial," Herbert "was noticeably touched," telling the crowd, "I . . . hate to leave . . . but I am glad of one thing: to know that I am leaving such kindly feelings among those with whom I have been so closely associated."[53] Later that fall, Herbert joined some of those courthouse associates in an attempt to thwart voting rights for African Americans. Registration by black voters had increased in the South since the US Supreme Court ruled in 1944 that all-white Democratic primaries were unconstitutional. In reaction, the Alabama legislature referred to the voters an amendment to the state constitution that would require local voter registration boards to determine that applicants could read and "understand and explain" the US Constitution. The proposal, known as the Boswell Amendment, was on the ballot in November 1946, and Herbert signed a large newspaper advertisement endorsing it. The amendment passed.[54]

The county hung a large print of Herbert's campaign portrait, in a wide gold-painted frame, in the courthouse as a lasting tribute to him,[55] but the Findleys did not place a copy of the portrait in the bungalow, unlike Jennie

Moore, who hung a portrait of her grandfather, the probate judge, in her music studio. They did, however, commission a formal portrait of Anne, now a student at the university, in 1946. Photographic portraits were affordable and accessible (in fact, a chain of photographic portrait studios, called Olan Mills Studios after its owner, began in Tuscaloosa in 1932, and Mills himself was so well known he was chosen a convocation speaker in the university's business school that year), but their very accessibility made photographic portraits less prestigious than oil paintings. An oil portrait of Anne would evoke the historic character of the Findley family at the same that it announced Anne's maturation into a beautiful, and thus marriageable, young woman worthy of the upper-middle- and upper-class gentlemen of Tuscaloosa.[56] In choosing the artist to paint Anne's portrait, Earline could have asked Herbert's sister-in-law Ila. The daughter of a newspaper cartoonist and a self-taught artist, Ila at some time painted copies of the large photographic portraits of Murk and Ida. Her work had been in several art shows including one at the university in 1945.[57] However, Earline gave the commission to Nina Ross Searcy Struss, whose father, Joseph A. Searcy, was a family friend, one of the pallbearers for little John Findley at the double funeral for him and Ida in 1908. Searcy had died suddenly in December so Earline may have explained her snub of Ila as a gesture of sympathy to the Searcy family. Nina was prominent in the community, "descended on both sides from men and women noted for their broad culture and mental achievements." She studied art at the university and, as *Tuscaloosa News* readers knew, was devoted to fashion. For a dinner party on the eve of her wedding, she wore "an import of bisque crepe, the short jacket opening over a bodice of chiffon and having sleeves of beige fur" and a hat "topped with a cluster of tiny ostrich tips." At her wedding in the Searcy home, she descended a winding staircase in "a handsome costume suit of woodland brown wool, the bodice of matching lace being enveloped in a coat elaborately trimmed in red fox fur," her "small off-the-face turban . . . adorned with a bright green ornament" that matched the dress of "frosted green crepe with gold ornaments" that her matron of honor wore. After Nina's husband was deployed on a US Navy destroyer escort ship in 1944, she returned with her two small children to Tuscaloosa to live with her parents, giving the *Tuscaloosa News* the opportunity to report on a birthday party she and her mother gave for her six-year-old son: he "welcomed his friends in a play suit of pink linen." In 1945, her husband participated in the dramatic rescue of US seamen on three ships that were caught in a typhoon. Thus a portrait by Nina Struss conveyed even more than the obvious prestige of an expensive painting. It suggested an association with an aristocratic local family and with a belle who had married a true military hero.[58]

The painting that Struss delivered was three feet by two feet, a half-length, full-face image of Anne wearing an evening dress of forest green taffeta, perhaps one she wore to a sorority dance at the university.[59] Whereas Anne's dress for the NAT Club dance in 1941 had a decorous heart-shaped neckline and puffed sleeves, this portrait dress was sleeveless with a plunging sweetheart neckline, large bows attached to the dropped shoulders, and a fitted bodice and gathered waist. A cameo pendant with a gold setting, on a thin gold chain, drew the eye to Anne's décolletage. Struss made Anne's eyes an unnaturally bright blue; her lips clearly outlined, red, and closed, obscuring the space between her front teeth; her cleft chin and the mole beneath her left eye less prominent than in reality. In the fashion of the time, Anne's hair was shoulder length, parted on one side, and styled in heavy waves. It was not the deep brown it actually became by adolescence, as the 1941 dance photograph and 1942 photo booth picture make clear, but blonde, in fact lighter and brighter than the pale blonde of her hair in her childhood portraits. Struss transformed Anne into the archetypal blonde belle of the southern imagination.[60] Anne strongly disliked the portrait, but Earline hung it in the living room of the bungalow, just inside the front door, positioning Anne almost like the scholar Kathryn Lee Seidel's characterization of the iconic belle of Thomas Nelson Page's fiction, "standing in her immaculate gown before her father's plantation portico."[61] However unrealistic the Struss portrait was as a likeness of Anne, it was material evidence of her standing as a belle.

Eight

The Pink Party

EARLINE HOSTED THE UDC CHAPTER AT THE bungalow about two weeks after Anne's nineteenth birthday in 1947, but there is no evidence that Anne, now a sophomore at the university and contemplating a biology major and medical school, attended. She definitely did not perform. Instead, another member's daughter, Emmett Lewis, gave a piano lecture-recital on the topic of "Negro composers," playing "Dance Juba," which alluded to an African American dance form in nineteenth-century minstrel shows. In this choice Emmett echoed her mother, Rovilla Lewis, an amateur minstrel performer herself. Confusing minstrel songs by white composers with works by black artists, Emmett also played "Harmonica Player," a tune that actually was by David Guion, the white composer best known for his arrangement of "Home on the Range." Like "Short'nin' Bread," Emmett's material reflected elite white women's fascination with music that seemed to echo happy, humorous days of the Old South.[1] Earline probably was too busy overseeing the final preparations in the kitchen, however, to pay much attention to Emmett's performance in the living room. For her first UDC affair, she served a charlotte russe, a popular nineteenth-century dessert composed of layers of cake, custard, and fruit that typically were pressed into a deep bowl and then chilled.[2] Earline's friends Hatchett Hinton and Johnnie Farabee (whose son Ray was one of Lyman's friends) served the same dish "from silver trays [on] a perfectly appointed table" at a party in 1941.[3] For the most impressive presentation, Earline had to remove the bowl or bowls from the refrigerator and overturn them on platters or trays; then one or more women carried the platters into the dining room and placed them on the table just as Miss Lewis reached the conclusion of her performance. When the ladies rose from their seats to circle the buffet, a hostess spooned servings of the charlotte russe onto dessert plates.

From the cookbook *Fascinating Foods from the Deep South*, which has three chapters on desserts, we know that Earline's version of charlotte russe, topped with cherries, was popular with Tuscaloosa's elite.[4] The author of the cookbook was the director of the University Club, a private restaurant and reception hall for members of the university faculty, housed in an antebellum mansion. The club held a grand opening just two days after Earline's UDC meeting. Hundreds of guests ascended the steps, crossed the veranda, and passed through the double front doors into the center hall. They explored the drawing room; the main dining room, where prominent local women served coffee and tea at another "perfectly appointed table"; a sun porch that was a 1922 addition; and the other public rooms, admiring lavish flower arrangements and the period and reproduction furnishings.[5] No clipping of the newspaper's expansive article about the opening was among the papers that descended through the family, but it is a safe guess that Herbert and Earline were present since Herbert was one of the club's original members.[6] Seeing the mansion's spacious rooms and tasteful sun porch could have triggered Earline and Herbert's decision to expand the bungalow living room, particularly if the UDC meeting had been crowded.

Enlarging one's family home, rather than packing up and moving to a new, larger house, was common in Alabama from the days when pioneers expanded their original dogtrot log cabins.[7] In fact, houses that looked "brand-new" were no mark of distinction for they were not manifestations, in bricks and timbers, of the occupants' long standing in a particular place. A newspaper feature writer in Alabama, Varian Feare, crystallized this point of view: "The trouble with most houses is that they are of overnight creation." It took time and a series of changes to create a home that fully reflected the owner's history and character. "Houses must be worked over and over again in scheme and plan," Feare wrote. Her articles were part of a series about antebellum homes in Alabama that she and her husband, E. Walter Burkhardt, a professor of architecture at Auburn University, wrote for the *Birmingham News-Age-Herald* while they worked for the Historic American Buildings Survey. From June 1934 to December 1936, the Burkhardt-Feare articles appeared occasionally in the paper's Sunday magazine section and typically included several photographs. Each article was a fawning description of exteriors, interiors, furnishings, and the real or imagined lifestyles of the occupants, derivative, in tone and substance, of the romantic memoirs and fiction of the fantastical Old South, Feare sometimes adopting a conversational first-person style, incorporating dialogue with her husband, a friend, or a black maid who could have been real or fictional.[8] Burkhardt described the Dearing place that became the University Club, "with its majestic colonnade," in their first article.[9] In a second article about Tuscaloosa, Feare commented on the deterioration of the Drish house, by that time in use as a car repair shop: to one "who beholds it in its present use must come a pang of remorse."[10] She and Burkhardt referred to the Dearing and Drish houses again in a third article, noting that "there were no architects available" when the mansions were built. "Instead these masters became their own delineators and supervisors. . . . Often the capitals of the columns and occasionally important Italian marble mantels were brought by boat from the North Atlantic states and Europe and then up the Mobile River into its tributaries. . . . However, the balance of the structure was of local manufacture, largely done by slaves." Like the Findleys' bungalow, "the construction [of the Tuscaloosa mansions] made use of local materials practically entirely. The timbers were cut from the heart of pine, poplar and occasionally oak and walnut."[11] It is easy to imagine Earline and her friends sharing copies of the Burkhardt-Feare articles and speculating on what else was inside those old Tuscaloosa houses.[12] The series foreshadowed many of the changes that Earline made to the Findley bungalow in the later 1940s.

By 1947, decorating and remodeling projects of which Earline could only dream for most of her life finally were possible. The Depression years, when the Findleys gave Earline's brother Otis a home and rented two of their bedrooms to roomers, were over. The war years, when everything was in short supply and civilians felt they were under siege, were over. The family had more income than ever; Herbert and Earline began renting The Little House to university students after Murk's death, creating a new source of rental income, and the Shooks continued to rent the large house next door. Herbert's annual salary as inferior court judge increased in 1945 from $3,600 to $4,200 while he continued to hold a part-time job as a university instructor.[13] Then his faculty appointment in 1946 was a permanent job, unlike his elected position, so his future income was more reliable. Finally, Annie's death in 1946 released Earline from her last responsibility as a caregiver. Now she could devote more money and as much time as she wished to her house. The exact dates of the bungalow makeover are unknown, but it probably took place after the University Club's grand opening since it would have been difficult to finish the work between Herbert's university appointment in September 1946 and the UDC meeting in February 1947.

If Earline wanted to remind passersby of the family's pioneer ancestry, or just demonstrate classical good taste, she could have replaced the wraparound porch with a symmetrical Greek Revival porch to evoke an expanded dogtrot cabin.[14] However, she designed from the interior outward, primarily seeking to make more space in the living room but limiting the new layout to the foundation of the original front porch. The result of her choices for the makeover was an asymmetrical exterior, in the picturesque or Cottage Orné style,[15] that obliterated the bungalow's Craftsman style. The Findleys incorporated the north section of the two-sided front porch into the living room, adding a bay window and a new west-facing front door beneath a small portico. This change gave Earline enough space to accommodate the baby grand piano and seating for about twenty people. The east section of the porch became a sunroom with large windows, paneling, and an exterior door, beneath its own small portico, to the side lawn.[16] The sunroom was not air-conditioned—the surge in popularity of enclosing porches at the same time air conditioners were installed in southern homes was a few years away—so opening the French doors to the sunroom to entertain large groups was more practical in the cooler months.[17]

For a new outdoor lounging area, the Findleys built a deep, covered breezeway to connect the garage and kitchen entrance.[18] Brick-edged beds and a short brick walkway linked the side lawn to the north side of the breezeway; on the other side of the breezeway, one reached The Little House through another small brick parterre. The breezeway and bricks were fixtures of the Burkhardt-Feare articles; Burkhardt explained that a breezeway was a "customary" link between house and kitchen and Feare commented in a dramatized conversation with "Professor Burkhardt" that "the various types of brick amaze one."[19] Earline ordered panels and canopy brackets made of iron trim to support and decorate the new porticoes and breezeway. She was familiar with the use of iron trim as an architectural element, having seen examples of this while a student in the antebellum town of Livingston. From her dormitory there, she could glimpse Lakewood, a large raised cottage that had been the residence of the school's founder, Julia Strudwick Tutwiler, its most striking feature an exterior pair of curving, wrought-iron staircases that led to the main entrance and formal rooms on the second floor. In the Burkhardt-Feare articles, "typical iron lacery" was ubiquitous and "again coming into significance." If neither Lakewood nor the Burkhardt-Feare series was the inspiration for Earline's use of iron trim, there was the university president's mansion, a few blocks away, with iron balustrades on its second-floor portico and small iron balconies on the third. In the old neighborhoods of Tuscaloosa, many private homes also had iron trim. A small house on Greensboro Avenue, in particular, could have inspired Earline. A one-story structure with a central entrance, it had two bay windows and white cast-iron trim supporting a dramatic pitched eave above the front door. Finally, there was the example of a small house elaborately decorated with frilly ironwork on Highway 11 in York, Alabama, which the Findleys passed on trips to Meridian.[20] The design Earline chose, "Bird of Paradise," was a double-faced floral pattern of C-scrolls with acanthus leaves. The trim was cast, rather than wrought, and assembled by welding small sections to steel frames, alternating the orientation of the sections to create a spiral effect. To a connoisseur of southern architecture it was recognizable as cast and new, but it was much less expensive than wrought iron.[21] The family story is that the trim was delivered to Tuscaloosa on a flatboat, just like the marble mantels that Burkhardt wrote were shipped before the Civil War.[22] If so, the bungalow trim probably was from a manufacturer in Mobile, where cast iron had been an important industry for decades. A Tuscaloosa manufacturer advertised ornamental ironwork by 1950, so the flatboat story is not necessarily true.[23]

Picturing the remodeled bungalow, we can imagine the scene as guests arrived. A curving walkway from the sidewalk to the new front entrance encouraged visitors to slow their pace as they approached the Findleys' house, adding to the drama of arrival. Performing the ritual actions of a ladies' tea, Earline's guests entered; stood about to greet each other; walked across the living room and through the opened French doors to the dining room, circling the table to partake of coffee, tea, or other refreshments; and passed into the hallway and by that route back into the living room. They departed by passing through the second set of French doors to the sun porch, through its exterior door, and hence to the side lawn and back to the sidewalk. When Earline received guests in her transformed house, each piece of furniture and every decorative object contributed to the overall effect of a genteel, artistic home, and many items promised stories for anyone who asked about their provenance.[24] The first impressions were of Anne. From the front door, one immediately saw her piano, placed at an angle in the opposite corner beneath a large gilt-framed mirror. Turning to walk further into the room, guests saw the portrait of Anne, her dress matching the forest green of the walls. To the left of the portrait, the doorway to the den, now in use as Anne's bedroom, might be open so that ladies could leave their purses and coats on her bed. Billowy white organza covered the windows and skirted the dressing table and bed, which was covered with a white cotton spread with loop construction, probably one of the common George Washington or Martha Washington spreads sold nationwide.[25] Earline referred to the bed, which was in the Eastlake style that was popular in the 1870s and 1880s, as "Grandma's Bed." Since she had called her own mother "Mamma" and would have referred to her late mother-in-law as "Mother Findley," the bed probably originally belonged to her maternal grandmother, Ann Elizabeth Christopher, who could have purchased it through Mallard's store.[26] Lingering in Anne's pretty bedroom for a moment, women might check their hairstyles in one of the two mirrors, the tilt mirror of a marble-top chest of drawers that Earline had purchased and refinished or the mirror over the dressing table. On the dressing table sat a round metal music box, with an upper chamber for a powder puff and face powder, that played "I Could Have Danced All Night," its forest green finish hinting that it was a gift from Earline to Anne.[27] Small women and girls could sit in the oak rocking chair, a type with no arms made for women to use while sewing or holding an infant. Earline purchased the chair for Anne after the household's last roomer moved out and the family reclaimed the room for Anne.[28]

Back in the living room, visitors might next notice the massive chaise longue beneath the portrait of Anne. Positioned beside the front door, it was a substitute for the customary Victorian hall stand and companion chair or bench, a place where Earline or Herbert could invite a young man, arriving to escort Anne to a dance, to sit. Like imposing Victorian hall chairs, the chaise was stunning to behold but uncomfortable for one's behind.[29] Earline might tell the family story that the chaise originally belonged to Murchison and Lucy Findley and remained at Riverview after the last family member moved out, and how she reacquired it from former tenants by trading a more modern sofa for it. Varian Feare told a similar story, quoting a woman in Montgomery whose sister tried to reacquire a family heirloom: "The conditions of . . . the war scattered family keepsakes," the woman said. "My sister one day called at one of our Negro cabins," she went on, displaying the sense of ownership that extended to black employees as well as to worker housing. "There she noted . . . a very fine four-poster bed. 'That was yoall's [*sic*] mamma's,' old auntie told her." Unwittingly revealing "Auntie's" shrewdness, the woman concluded, "My sister wanted the bed back and told auntie she would buy it later. A delay intervened and lo, one day she returned to find it gone. Auntie could not resist an offer [of] $8 and a new bed for it."[30] Earline had been more successful in retrieving the Findley chaise and had it reupholstered, using a velvet fabric in her favorite shade of green.

To the left of the chaise, a Victorian table supported a lamp in the style of an old oil lamp, its white glass font and shade decorated with hand-painted pink and blue pansies and green leaves. Such fixtures were popular thanks to the lamp-lit scene in the film *Gone with the Wind*, when Melanie Wilkes, huddling with other white women in a sewing circle, sedately but resolutely stood up to Federal soldiers,[31] but the pink and green color scheme was softer than that of typical "Gone with the Wind lamps." Whether Earline selected and placed the lamp in such a prominent position as a reference to the film or merely because it was beautiful, it was the type of artifact that evoked the constant social performance of the refined southern matron.[32]

Another painting by Nina Struss, an arrangement of roses and other flowers that she completed in 1948, hung over the fireplace mantel.[33] Beside the fireplace, a sofa and table formed one side of a symmetrical sitting area. The sofa, a Duncan Phyfe style with rose-colored upholstery, and the coffee table, a Chippendale style with two removable glass trays, probably came from local furniture stores.[34] A large rocking chair with scrolled arms, a fashionable and mass-produced item known as a Grecian rocker, occupied one of this grouping's opposite corners. As with many of the bungalow's furnishings, a small story descended with the rocker. It was made in 1860 and belonged to Earline's uncle Will, who until his death in 1945 kept it on the porch of his dogtrot house in Choctaw County. Similar chairs were available from the Oswego Chair Factory as early as 1857. Providing the fourth corner of the fireplace sitting area, a carved chair, known as a gentleman's library or fireside chair, had a spoon back, padded sides, serpentine front skirt, and cabriole front legs. It was upholstered in a French or French-style tapestry fabric in pink, mint green, and brown on a taupe background. The finely drawn, dense forest scene was typical of French tapestries except that it was devoid of animal or human figures. The absence of tufting indicates that Earline covered the chair herself, carefully measuring and cutting the sections so that the opening in the middle distance of the tapestry scene, which provided a view of distant trees, was in the center of the chair's inside back. Then she folded the edges under and hammered them to the frame with tacks, gluing upholstery trim over the edges. One more piece, a low Victorian chest of drawers, which Earline purchased sometime after 1945 and refinished, adding a marble top, stood between the doorways to the hall and dining room.

In the dining room, the most dramatic furnishings were the eight Black Belt chairs, their backs and arms a continuous graceful line, with vase-shaped splats, cabriole front legs, and saber back legs, the design an elegant interpretation of Empire style by an antebellum French furniture maker, Francois Seignoret of New Orleans. One Burkhardt-Feare article had provided a brief lesson on the history of the Seignoret chair: "Between 1825 and 1860 New Orleans became a great center for making" Empire furniture. "The workmanship was excellent [and] certain furniture makers became quite famous. Francois Seignoret became so for his French type chairs."[35] Genuine Seignoret pieces are difficult to authenticate, but antebellum planters often purchased furniture and other luxury goods through brokers who handled their cotton sales in the ports of New Orleans and Mobile.[36] The original chair in Earline's dining set was, in her daughter-in-law's hazy memory, a bequest by Minerva Hargrove, who could have inherited or purchased a set of the chairs and then divided them among her heirs.[37] A researcher for the Historic American Buildings Survey documented a similar chair, with a slightly different splat, in the foyer of another house in Tuscaloosa.[38] Certain facts suggest the Hargroves could have ordered original chairs by Seignoret, or reproductions of his work, from a New Orleans shop: Andrew Jackson purchased items from Seignoret's warehouse and had them shipped to Tennessee in 1821 and the president of the University of Alabama ordered furniture from Mobile and New Orleans for the president's mansion in 1842.[39] On the other hand, the workmanship and style of the chairs, particularly the curves and lack of ornamentation, match the curves of the chaise longue from Riverview as well as the walnut tilt-top tea table known as Father's card table, meaning a single local furniture maker with the skill and tools to produce one could have produced all. Perhaps Augustin Lynch made the pieces. He manufactured fine furniture in a shop on the Greensboro Road at the time Murchison and Lucy were furnishing the Riverview house, and the legs of Murk's plantation desk resemble those of a secretary that Lynch made around 1850.[40]

As Anne and Margaret both more clearly recalled, the other seven chairs in Earline's set were copies that she commissioned from a Montgomery factory, having the seats covered in a deep blue-green velvet.[41] The maker of Earline's chairs probably was Carlton McLendon, a popular Montgomery manufacturer whose furniture was available in Tuscaloosa. McLendon's primary business was making and selling reproductions of Victorian furniture,[42] but eighteenth- and early nineteenth-century-style pieces were more prestigious than Victorian reproductions. Replicas of high-style antique furniture, if they referred to authentic pieces in the family's history such as Minerva's chairs, bolstered a family's status as gentility because they demonstrated the family's dedication to ancestry. Feare alluded to this phenomenon in describing "two sisters who dwell in the Bird's Nest," an ancestral home near Eufaula: in the past a "solid rosewood piano" stood in their front parlor and "today Miss Augusta has a near replica of the original instrument."[43]

Earline had at least three additional dining chairs that she usually used in the kitchen but could bring into the living or dining room as necessary, two made of tiger maple with bird's eye maple veneer on the splats and one of walnut. The original seats were woven cane but had been replaced with cushions comprised of leather, horsehair, and needlepoint covers in floral patterns on a pink background, the covers probably made by her mother.[44] Her falling-leaf dining table was a reproduction in the Federal style with six tapered legs, two of them swinging out to support the leaves. She routinely kept a low, boat-shaped crystal bowl on the table, and for special occasions she covered the table with an ecru openwork crocheted cloth that she probably made herself. She enjoyed needlecraft projects, and patterns for similar tablecloths were available from a mail-order company that advertised in the *Tuscaloosa News*: "A few squares a week soon add up to the accessory you long for!" The bowl and cloth were standard tabletop decorations in Tuscaloosa. Allen and Jemison, the local hardware and variety store, advertised oblong, round, and flat crystal bowls in 1942 and in 1947 a woman dressed her dining table for a wedding rehearsal party "with a hand crocheted table cloth and . . . low crystal bowl."[45] Anne saved the tablecloth in pristine condition, a laundry tag marked "FIN" still pinned to it after her death indicating she never used it after removing it from the bungalow.

The glass-door, built-in cabinet in the dining room held Earline's collection of china dinnerware and assorted other pieces. For afternoon club meetings, she had at least thirteen china cups and saucers plus a coffee pitcher, sugar bowl, and cream pitcher in the Eden pattern and twelve crystal water goblets in the Woodland pattern. Her silver flatware included teaspoons and dessert forks in classic Chantilly as well as six teaspoons with an "F" monogram, presumably Herbert's share of Ida's silver, and six with an "E" for Earline. Three of her serving pieces were unmarked spoons made of coin silver, possibly antebellum and passed down from Murk's or Ida's parents.[46] A set of dessert plates was hand-painted with delicate purple violets and slender, trailing green stems. A decanter, possibly a prize from a bridge party, was amusingly embellished in gold leaf with the symbols for the four houses of cards. Earline had two pairs of silver candlesticks and a crystal bell to use in calling a servant to the dining room.

She furnished the sun porch with large potted plants; a magazine holder; another tray table, this one a metal tole piece painted with pink and green roses, one of many manufactured by Nashco Products from the 1920s through the 1950s; and a rattan chair.[47] This last was low-slung and eye-catching with a cushion covered in pieced sections of pink, green, yellow, and natural canvas. The chair's form was that of a planter or Campeche chair, a style that was a recognizable symbol of plantation society, but expressed in rattan it was highly fashionable in the 1940s.[48] In this single piece, Earline combined her favorite color combination, a nod to antebellum style, and contemporary fashion. Considered together, her renovation of the bungalow and her interior arrangements of furniture and objects—combinations that were antebellum, postbellum, and modern; original and reproduction; American, British, and European; inherited, reclaimed, and purchased; preserved and refinished—suggest that Earline made decorative choices according to no standard but her own taste. Most, if not all, of these furnishings were in place in 1948.

Anne sometimes appeared in friends' weddings as a bridesmaid or pianist. The sheet music in her collection included "Oh Promise Me" and the "Wedding March" by Richard Wagner, and a photograph from this period shows her posing on a piano stool and holding a plate with what appears to be cake and punch, wearing a hat and corsage and a short-sleeved dress of eyelet. After one wedding, an admirer wrote, "Did you catch the bouquet?" and added, "Mrs. Weatherford . . . says you play 'beautifully.'"[49] (Earline delighted in hearing such secondhand compliments of her daughter, writing to tell Anne of a friend who ran into mutual acquaintances at the Memphis airport. They had declared Anne was "'the most charming girl' they had ever seen . . . so graceful, so poised, such beautiful manners. She always raves about you.")[50] One of Anne's performances was for her friend Lylla Jean Kirk, with whom she had taken dance lessons, participated in the music club, and attended house parties. Lylla Jean was married in September 1948 in a small home wedding. Before the ceremony, their mutual friend Joy Pearson sang "a group of love lyrics" and Anne played one of Liszt's three *Liebesträume*, or "Dreams of Love," probably No. 3, which was the most popular and required considerable technical skill. She also played Claude Debussy's "Clair de Lune," which Joy had played at a 1944 meeting of the music club.[51] Then Lylla Jean stood with her groom before "an improvised altar . . . garlanded with fronds of smilax and plumosa fern," much as Earline did a generation earlier. During the reception, Anne and several other young women greeted guests at the entrance to the dining room while Mary Luella Foley, Bebe Lewis, and still more young women, most of them friends since high school or longer, walked about offering the guests "embossed cakes" from silver trays. Earline presided in the "gift room," where the guests admired gifts that had been delivered in advance and placed on display, receiving "informally."[52]

Earline had known Joy's mother, Madel Pearson, for years. Madel was the choir director at First Methodist. Anne and Joy had been in the NAT Club, National Junior Honor Society, and Junior Music Study Club together. They attended some of the same parties and dances.[53] Just as Earline promoted Anne as a pianist, Madel encouraged her daughter to sing, casting her as a soloist as early as 1944. As a university student, Joy sang in local opera productions and was the town representative on the board of the Women's Student Government Association. She even won second place in the 1948 Miss Tuscaloosa pageant the month before Lylla's wedding—the *Tuscaloosa News* called her a "Tuscaloosa songbird." When Joy, Lylla Jean, and other local young women were volunteer swimming instructors in 1947, they posed in bathing suits for a photograph on the front page of the paper.[54] In summary, not only did Joy play the piano, she sang, participated in student government, and looked good in a bathing suit.

Joy announced her engagement around the time that Lylla Jean was married and asked Anne, Mary Luella, and four other young women to be bridesmaids. Her friends and her mother's friends planned a crowded schedule of parties, called "courtesies" by the newspaper, in the week leading up to the wedding in December. Most of the events were to be small or casual affairs: a shower where guests presented Joy with kitchen items, a bridge party, a buffet dinner, a get-together for members of the church choir. Mary Luella, who recently placed in the top tier in a different beauty pageant, and her sister Patricia planned a luncheon for twenty-four guests. Earline decided that Anne, now twenty years old, should give a party too. If Anne would not play the piano for clubwomen, she could demonstrate her charm and style at a bridal courtesy. In thinking about what kind of party to have, Earline probably turned to her copy of *Essentials of Etiquette*, which advised that "a tea is a favorite method of introducing a debutante daughter or honoring a house guest, a bride, or some other person." Earline offered to hold a large, formal tea and the Pearsons accepted. The *Tuscaloosa News* reported that Marion Parker would be Anne's cohostess. The newspaper also published a follow-up article of four short paragraphs about the tea. Those scant lines, other newspaper articles, and Earline's etiquette guide and cookbook reveal the likely details of her preparations and the events of the party, which Anne recalled on one of the last days of her life, exclaiming "the Pink Party!" with delight and amusement.

In chapter 3 of *Essentials of Etiquette*, "Hospitality and Entertainment," Ellen Dryden confidently explained that "one may be liberal in the distribution of invitations to a tea, for the full number invited will never come."[55] Earline invited more people to the tea for Joy than she did to any other event in family lore. The only comparable events on Joy's wedding schedule were a reception on Christmas Day that was held in honor of Joy and another young bride-elect and the wedding reception itself. Earline planned to serve finger foods—morsels a lady could eat in a single bite or place on a saucer beside her coffee cup—with assistant hostesses to circulate, offering the refreshments from trays. This way, she only needed space on the dining table for the coffee service and could drop the leaves. She would not need plates or forks although she undoubtedly borrowed extra china cups and saucers and silver teaspoons from some of her friends. Considering how many people she invited, Earline may have purchased some of the refreshments, but in the week before the party only one local bakery advertised typical party finger foods in the *Tuscaloosa News*.[56] She probably made many delicacies herself. From the newspaper account, we know she served "pink canapes [and] assorted sweets." By "canapes" the newspaper writer probably meant tiny finger sandwiches filled with savory mixtures of butter or cream cheese and other flavorings. One might spread butter thinly on slices of white bread, form sandwiches, use a cookie cutter to cut them into circles, and decorate them with roses fashioned of cream cheese tinted pink. A variation was to spread beaten cream cheese between slices of rye bread and trim them with strips of pimiento and pickled cucumber in the form of poinsettias—another idea that complemented Earline's floral decorations. The Pastel Sandwich had a layer of "chopped pimiento blended with butter" or "well-seasoned hard-cooked egg yolk blended with butter and paprika."[57] A cookbook by Marion Flexner, a Montgomery native, provides more clues as to what Earline served. Flexner included cheese straws and Alabama cheese balls that were seasoned and tinted with cayenne and paprika. Earline could have used her friend Anna H. Little's recipe for cheese rings, one of the handwritten recipes she saved in her cookbook, and tinted them with paprika.

For the pink "sweets" she served, Earline's copy of *Holland's Cook Book* is the most obvious source of information. Icebox cookies were basic vanilla-flavored cookies made from dough that could be tinted with food coloring. Their advantage was that the dough could be prepared in advance and refrigerated until time for baking, a boon in preparing for a large party. Once the dough was rolled out, it could be cut into shapes such as hearts and Christmas trees. After baking, the cookies could be glazed with a tinted icing or sprinkled with colored sugar. Valentine Teacakes also were simple cookies; they were cut into heart shapes and decorated with pink icing. Under "Fillings and Frostings" there was a recipe for cooked cream filling made with pink sugar that could go into tiny cream tarts.[58] Although Alline Van Duzor's collection of recipes from the University Club was not published until 1962, it is another important source of information about the desserts that women in Earline's social circle considered appropriate for special occasions. In addition to charlotte russe, Van Duzor served tarts, some with fillings such as red raspberry cream that was colored pink with the addition of frozen fruit, and peppermint chiffon, a custard flavored with peppermint oil and tinted light pink.[59] Flexner's recipe for Toffee Squares, which she called "an Alabama cookie with a delightfully 'different' flavor," resembled Earline's recipe for toffee cookies, and as Flexner noted, "they will keep fresh for two weeks," making it practical to prepare batches in advance of a party.[60] As these cookies were one of Earline's Christmas traditions, she may have included them in the "assorted sweets" for the Pink Party, substituting pink crystal sugar for the usual topping of chopped pecans.

Earline purchased roses and poinsettia from a florist, but the pièce de résistance of the tea was a pink Christmas tree. This sort of decorating, according to a color scheme, was typical of upper-middle-class women's parties in the South.[61] Despite Dryden's recommendation that "flowers should appear on the tea-table, but no [other] floral decoration of the room is necessary,"[62]

Earline sent Herbert to the curb market, or went with him, to get a cedar. If they followed the same procedure that Herbert did in later years, they placed the tree in a bucket of water or damp sand, so it would not dry out, and left it on the breezeway for a few days. Next, Earline made pink artificial snow, called flocking, by combining soap flakes, cornstarch, water, and red food coloring. If she had flocked a tree before and knew the material could crumble when the tree was moved, she probably had Herbert erect the tree in the bay window of the living room before she applied the mixture. To create the effect of snow, she scooped some of the mixture with one hand, reached into the tree with the other to grasp a branch, and deposited the flocking on the feathery green needles. Cedars will scratch and sting, so she needed to wear long sleeves or a coat during this project. She had to complete the flocking at least a day before the tea to allow it to dry, so adding the ornaments could have been one of her last tasks early on the day of the party.

It is impossible to know how many servants Earline hired to help during the party. She undoubtedly had her regular maid work extra hours beforehand to wash the china, polish the silver, iron napkins, vacuum and dust the house, and perhaps help prepare the food. She could have hired additional maids to serve; it was not uncommon for women to hire each other's maids, and even their maids' daughters, for temporary work serving at parties, and of course the presence of black servants added to the white hostess's appearance of leisure and privilege.[63] However, Earline could have gotten through the actual party without any domestic staff if Hatchett, Johnnie, and Bertha Parker, Marion's mother, were stationed at the dining table and took turns carrying coffee and tea pots to the kitchen to refill and the younger women who circulated with refreshments refilled the trays of finger foods themselves. Perhaps Herbert was on hand, secluded in the back bedroom, just in case Earline needed help with an unexpected problem. If she did hire one or more maids to work during the party, they ideally were seen but not heard when entering the dining room to replenish the coffee and tea.

Earline must have opened the interior doors to the sun porch a few hours early on the day of the party to allow the central heating system to adequately warm it. Showers were in the forecast,[64] so even though Dryden advised that "guests need not lay aside their wraps [because] there is a certain briskness of circulation at a tea," Earline probably also opened the doors to Anne's and Lyman's bedrooms so women could leave damp coats on the beds. Following Dryden's instructions that "for even a very small tea one draws the blinds (unless it is summer-time) and illuminates with candles (supplemented by other lighting if necessary)," Earline tilted up the Venetian blinds. Shortly before three o'clock, she lit pink candles in the family's old silver candlesticks. At an "important affair," according to Dryden, the hostess waited "near the drawing-room door, with the honor guest . . . beside her, to shake hands with arriving guests," but the bay window was the only space for a receiving line so Earline, Anne, Marion, and Joy had to "greet informally," spotting each arriving guest and welcoming her. The tea was a test of Earline's etiquette lessons, proof that the years of children's parties and musical recitals had fully prepared Anne to perform spontaneously, welcoming every guest, making the perfect brief remark to each mother, daughter, or spinster friend, and leaving all with the sense that they had been recognized and appreciated—in the words of the newspaper society editor fifteen years earlier, "the personification of gracious charm."[65] Befitting a belle at center stage, Anne's dress was pink; Joy's was a complementary green. Earline's canary yellow dress matched the border of her Eden cups and saucers.

According to the *Tuscaloosa News*, two hundred guests showed up, proving Dryden's caveat that "one should be careful not to overcrowd the house." Marion's sister and another of Joy's bridesmaids edged through the guests with trays of party foods and Mrs. John Crowder helped greet, the paper reported. Posting Alta Crowder at the front door could have been a last-minute arrangement. Earline was acquainted with Alta through the Qui Vive Club, the Laurel Class, and the Auxiliary, and Alta's husband, a dentist, was a colleague of Herbert's hunting friend Wilson Patton. However, Alta's name does not appear elsewhere in Earline's or Anne's papers as a friend. Moreover, John Crowder was a Republican who ran for governor a little more than a year later, calling Democrats, and by implication Herbert, "totalitarian,"[66] so Alta does not seem a natural choice for Earline to enlist in advance as a helper on such an important day. Rather, one can imagine Earline feeling almost overwhelmed by the crush of people in the house and Alta, who gave a buffet dinner for Joy the night before, arriving and asking, "How can I help?" to which Earline responded, "The front door is becoming a bottleneck! Please see if you can keep the crowd moving toward the dining room." If the scene unfolded as Dryden prescribed, "each arriving guest, after shaking hands with the hostess and the honor guest, passe[d] on to greet and chat with other guests whom she [knew], and thence to the tea-table." They departed quickly, adhering "to Dr. Oliver Wendell Holmes' witty summarization of an afternoon tea: 'Giggle, gabble, gobble, git.'"[67]

Earline's tea was the kind of ritual that an elite white woman used to relate to her peers in the community.[68] Like other social rituals, it had standard visual elements and a predictable sequence of actions. Innumerable articles in the society columns of the *Tuscaloosa News* established and reinforced the form for these parties. There were cut flowers, openwork tablecloths, candles, crystal, and silver. The guests arrived; hostesses greeted them in a receiving line or informally; everyone sampled dainty refreshments; there was an uplifting component such as a musical performance or talk, or a common reason to celebrate, such as a belle's engagement; and afterward the *Tuscaloosa News* reported on the event, describing certain women's costumes if the function was part of the "courtesies" surrounding a wedding, sometimes characterizing hostesses as performers and other times as artists. Joy's mother, Madel, for example, "played the role of hostess" in 1946 "with a beautiful luncheon" at her "handsome home." When Wilson Patton's wife gave a party for her sister-in-law on the night before her wedding, the paper noted "the chosen tones of pink, orchid and silver" and enthused, "Seldom has a home been more artistic."[69]

Grace Hamby may have contributed the article about Earline's tea that appeared in the *Tuscaloosa News*, or Earline could have called the newspaper's society editor herself to provide details.[70] Thumbing through the paper two days later, Earline probably noticed the article on page six about a luncheon for Joy that Hatchett's sister-in-law gave before coming to the report of her tea. At Earline's party, the anonymous society writer shared, "a pink motif prevailed throughout the apartments. . . . Silver bowls of pink Radiance roses, pink poinsettia and a pink Christmas tree accentuated the scheme in the living room which was lighted with pink art candles in silver candelabra." The dining table was "spread with lace and centered with pink roses. . . . Miss Rachel Parker and Miss Ann Ramsdell passed silver trays of pink canapes [and] assorted sweets in pink shades." The bride-elect "was attired in a reception toilette of pale green crepe" and Anne's dress was "a fancy frock of blush pink crepe."[71] For Earline, the Pink Party in the remodeled bungalow was the culmination of all of her efforts, an exhibition of her creativity, taste, and refinement, and the social debut of her daughter, launching Anne as a belle who would carry on the beautiful traditions of southern white aristocracy.

Nine

Haven

Earline and Anne went to Meridian in June 1949 for a short visit with Earline's relatives. Her folks lived near each other in the same neighborhood as Earline's late mother. Uncle Charles Christopher and his wife lived across from the grocery store he owned and operated with his three sons. Annie Moore, Alva's widow and Earline's sister-in-law, lived with her son, Alva's namesake, and was a seamstress at Loeb's Department Store. Velma worked at Loeb's, too. Velma's husband, Gene, was a municipal police officer until his health got too bad; then he worked part-time at a stockyard until the doctor told him he had to quit that, too. Earline's brother J. C. and his wife and daughter eventually moved into the house next to Velma and Gene.[1] Here my brief memories of Meridian in the 1960s intrude, like scenes in Kodachrome snapshots taken by someone with a shaky hand, the garish oranges on juice glasses and the blue of a backyard gazing ball vivid in blurry pictures. I remember drinking juice on Auntie Velma's back porch. I remember the gazing ball glinting in harsh summer light. Photographs that Earline saved supplement these glimpses: Velma's irises and zinnias; Gene, whom I never knew, in his police uniform, the whistle Anne eventually inherited dangling from a ring on his belt.

On a hot summer day, the back porch was the place for the Moore relatives to sip iced tea or Cokes and catch up. Helping Velma pour drinks that weekend, Earline could have mentioned that she was eyeing a set of aluminum tumblers in "gorgeous hues" that a shop in Tuscaloosa was advertising; each time Herbert opened a small bottle of icy Coke in the 1960s for my brother and me to share, he divided it in two of the tumblers. Perhaps Earline told Velma how she recently had been an assistant hostess for the Laurel Class. An undated snapshot shows Velma posing beneath large palm trees somewhere on the Gulf; perhaps Velma and Gene were planning a little trip to the coast. Their brother Otis's widow, Margaret, who went by "Snookie," had remarried after Otis died in 1942 and lived down in Biloxi, Mississippi, with her sons, Buddy and Butch. J. C. owned a music store and several jukeboxes in Meridian and sometimes told stories about conventions he attended; a few years later he described seeing a new young recording artist named Elvis Presley perform and predicted the boy would become a star.[2] Jukeboxes might remind Earline of Jim's Place, a café and gambling den that now operated at the northeast corner of the bungalow block. It was open day and night with crowds on holidays. Back in the fall of 1948 the police had seized two pinball machines and a slot machine, she might have said, and in the winter there was a break-in![3] J. C. and Gene probably wanted to know about Lyman, who was an officer in the US Navy.[4] He planned to reenlist in August and was corresponding with a Northport girl, Margaret Louise Koster. Their romance must have been a relief to Earline. When she and Herbert went to Lyman's graduation from the University of Virginia medical school two years earlier, Lyman was dating a young nurse whose father was a coal miner. Earline had been so upset that Lyman had to reassure her that he would not marry the nurse. This episode gained in drama and humor over the years. When one relative told me Earline "was so upset she took to her bed," another relative gently chastised her: "Now, that's an exaggeration."

Anne probably had known Margaret since high school. When Anne was a rushee of a sorority called the LOL Club, Margaret was a member, possibly one of the hostesses who wore "exquisite party frocks" and stood about "the spacious gardens" to welcome the new girls. One year behind Lyman, Margaret and her twin sister, Gene, were members of the Honor Society and elected "Best Dressed" by their classmates. Margaret had earned a degree in home economics at the university and gone to New York to secretarial school. Earline met her when the Findleys' family doctor, Joseph Shirley, died. She and Hatchett went to Northport to pay their respects to his family, and Margaret, one of Shirley's granddaughters, was among the family members receiving callers.[5] An attractive, tasteful, local belle, the granddaughter of the very physician who saved Earline's life during her ectopic pregnancy, Margaret was the kind of wife any mother would want for her son.

The biggest news that weekend in Meridian, however, was that Anne had graduated from the university earlier in the week. There was an elegant tea at the president's mansion for graduates and their families with Governor and Mrs. James Folsom in the receiving party. The president's wife, Lua V. Gallalee, wore "a white lace gown with a corsage of camellias[.] Garlands of gardenias, blue hydrangeas and pink dahlias" decorated the "punch tables on the lawn."[6] Now Anne was about to enter a one-year certificate program for medical technicians at the medical school in Birmingham. She was nervous about leaving home, but it helped that Mary Luella Foley was going, too. In fact, Mary Luella's father, who helped talk Lyman out of enlisting during World War II, now was on the medical school faculty in Birmingham[7] and probably encouraged Anne to join his daughter in the technician program.

The folks in Meridian undoubtedly talked about recent events in Tuscaloosa. A gang of costumed Klan members had marched around downtown, apparently as an insult to the *Tuscaloosa News*. With a spate of terroristic Ku Klux Klan actions occurring around the state in May 1949, the paper had published four front-page articles and an editorial about the local chapter of the Klan. It packaged the articles as a groundbreaking series but actually only described details of a few Klan meetings, quoting, without attribution, a single source. At one meeting, Klan members seemed to threaten local legislators Temo Callahan and Henry H. Mize for opposing Klan activity. The paper hinted it would identify local Klan members by name but in the grand finale of the series refrained from doing so. Nonetheless, the series was the talk of the county. The Klan, the newspaper concluded, was a "gullible" and embarrassing organization that was not even necessary for maintaining racial order. "Reliable negro citizens . . . will see that their fellows keep within the confines of generally accepted Southern custom," an anonymous editorial writer confidently declared on May 31. "Policing by the Klan," he sniffed, "will not be of assistance."[8] This elitist effrontery did not deter the Klan in Alabama. While Earline and Anne were in Meridian, sixty hooded men burned a cross on the lawn of a white woman at her home west of Birmingham, threatening to kill her because she had been selling whiskey. Another "robed mob" stormed into a café northwest of the city, threatening the owner because he served black customers.[9] Despite this violence, Earline and Anne went on to Birmingham and Anne moved into the medical school dormitory. Writing to her one evening later in the week, Earline made no comment on the Klan events. "How I miss my baby! Before I realize it each night I put the third cup and saucer down. Coffee time!" She closed, "Remember me to all the Foleys." The next day "a hooded gang" gave a white man in Birmingham a flogging because the man's wife held a job. As terrorism continued around the state through June, Henry Mize introduced legislation to ban masked activities. With Governor Folsom's support, the bill passed.[10]

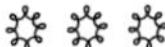

When Lyman and Margaret became engaged in August 1949, Earline began planning the rehearsal dinner—customarily given by the groom's parents—and Margaret asked Anne to be one of her bridesmaids. Anne worried that she would look fat at the wedding, but Lyman assured her that "there's such a little bit of you I don't see how you could look fat. . . . I'm sure that it is just your imagination. There's no doubt about it, you will be the prettiest of the bridesmaids."[11] As usual, the *Tuscaloosa News* described the food, flowers, dresses, and guests at the events surrounding the November wedding: Earline wore a black crepe dress for a dinner party at the Linger Longer Lodge. Velma and Gene, and J. C. and his wife, Virginia, and daughter Velma Ruth, came over from Meridian and Aunt Snookie came up from Biloxi with her second husband and sons. Velma stood in for Margaret in the wedding rehearsal. A photograph reveals Anne was, as Lyman predicted, very thin and attractive with her hair cut in a new style, shorter than when she enrolled in the medical technician program in June. Earline and Herbert's rehearsal dinner was in an 1827 tavern that Herbert's friend Wilson Patton and his wife had rented for a bridal party two years earlier. The evening wedding at First Methodist had a pink color scheme that Earline probably admired. Herbert was Lyman's best man and Earline wore "an aqua crepe gown featuring a collar of silver beadwork" with "long white kid gloves," adhering to the advice in her etiquette manual that "full evening dress calls for long gloves, of white or light colored suede or glazed kid." Her corsage, like Lua Gallalee's at the university reception in June, was a white camellia.[12] Lyman and Margaret soon moved to Camp Pendleton, the Marine Corps training facility at Oceanside, California, every turn of their lives reported in the newspaper's "Personal Mention" column,[13] presumably thanks to the newspaper's one-time Alberta City correspondent, who was such a close friend of the family that Anne always referred to her as "Aunt" Grace Hamby.

Anne saved a brochure about the Tuscaloosa garden pilgrimage the following spring so Earline probably asked her daughter to come home and go on the tour with her. The pilgrimage was similar to an annual event in Natchez, Mississippi, where white women dressed in antebellum costumes to greet visitors touring homes and gardens.[14] This year the University Club was a stop on the route and the festival coincided with National Hospital Day so the hospitals in town also held open houses.[15] Festivalgoers driving from the University Club to Bryce, or vice versa, passed the bungalow. For elite white women in Tuscaloosa, the front garden was a crucial creative outlet that was literally always on exhibit and Alta Crowder, who was chairing the pilgrimage, had encouraged women to plant May-blooming flowers for passersby to see.[16] By May, Earline's azaleas, daffodils, and narcissi were spent and her Festiva Maxima peonies—a variety common in old southern gardens, white with flecks of scarlet, like drops of blood, at the center—were shriveled and brown, but her daylilies probably were blooming: the lemon daylilies an heirloom species that could have come from Riverview or The Old Place and Caballero, a tall daylily cultivar with red and yellow flowers that was introduced in 1941, her lantana echoing the daylilies' colors. From early spring through the fall, there was always something fragrant and beautiful in Earline's yard. Tidy mounds of evergreen candytuft grew beside the small front portico. Her sweet shrub, banana bush, abelia, and snowball were mature shrubs, the first two with intensely fragrant flowers, the abelia with small pinkish flowers that continued until frost, the last with enormous blossoms that she sometimes shared with her friends. Her camellias were so large that they fully screened the breezeway, and the cherry laurel shrubs had become huge hedges,[17] the east hedge blocking the view of the asylum, the rowdy barbecue joint on the corner, and Daly Bottom, the neighborhood of African American laborers, but hospitals still loomed at the edges of Earline's vision. An enormous new municipal hospital was under construction on Castle Hill. Whereas the old Druid City Hospital was a block to the west of the bungalow, the new one would be a short distance to the east.

War with North Korea began the month after the flower pilgrimage. By mid-November, Lyman was a medical officer aboard the escort ship USS *Rupertus*. Margaret returned to Tuscaloosa and sometimes Earline and Herbert invited her to join them on car trips to Meridian. Passing through the small town of York, Earline always spoke up to admire the house with a great deal of cast-iron trim. It was painted a pale pink, and Earline commented that she would like to have the bungalow painted pink but, Margaret recalled with a laugh, "no one seconded that idea." Margaret also went with her in-laws on a summer evening to see Roland and Mary Harper's moonflowers. Although they are members of the same genus as morning glories, the ghostly white moonflowers opened at night, unfurling in a rapid, dramatic fashion if the evening was warm enough.[18]

Lyman came close to battle between May 14 and July 4, 1951, when the *Rupertus* was part of a blockade and escort task force off the west coast of Korea. Concerned that the danger would unnerve Earline, he wrote to Anne, "If Mother worries about me, try to keep her spirits up. Really we are perfectly safe."[19] But how could a mother not worry? Lyman was so dear to Earline; he looked so much like her cousin Edward, who had died as a young man. It was hard to think about him on the dangerous ocean: Nina Struss's husband had been on that escort ship that had to rescue all those men in a typhoon.[20] To distract herself, Earline made hooked rugs, floor coverings that were traditional yet always in fashion. Other local women's hooked rugs had been prominent attractions of the garden pilgrimages in Tuscaloosa at least three times in the 1940s. To make a rug, one purchased a burlap "canvas" with a printed pattern, stretched the canvas on a frame, and used a rug hook to fill in the pattern with wool yarn, rolling the completed portion on one side of the frame just as quilt makers did in quilting. Earline made four rugs using Colonial-style patterns, with central medallions on cream fields and borders of acanthus leaf scrolls and pink roses on burgundy or deep green fields,[21] with a larger rug and a smaller one in each color scheme.

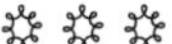

After Lyman was discharged in late July 1951,[22] he and Margaret moved to Birmingham so that he could begin a residency in obstetrics and gynecology at Jefferson-Hillman Hospital. Anne also got a job there as a medical technologist, again probably thanks to Foley.[23] With their children safely settled, Earline and Herbert enjoyed more of the life of the southern gentry. In March 1952, Earline wrote to Anne that Herbert and his friend Toombs Lawrence, a psychiatrist at Bryce Hospital, were anticipating the opening of turkey season.[24] Skeeter and Toombs also went fishing together, sometimes spending the night at Ezell's Fish Camp, a lodge on the Tombigbee River in Choctaw County operated by relatives of Earline's sister-in-law Virginia Ezell Moore. Usually an African American cook was on hand to prepare and serve dinner so the white men could relax and rehash old stories[25] such as the one about the African American man in Tuscaloosa who accidentally struck and killed Toombs's mother-in-law at the corner of University and Fourteenth avenues one night, or the strange tale of Toombs's uncle, who disappeared in Birmingham in 1930 and was found in Jackson, Mississippi, the next year, "dazed and wandering." For eight years no one could determine the man's identity. Then in 1939, a New York radio program told his plight, nicknaming him "Mr. X," and newspapers and magazines picked up the story, running a photograph of him. Relatives who saw the picture recognized Toombs's uncle and Toombs went down to Jackson to bring him to Tuscaloosa.[26] Earline also reported to Anne on the cattle that Herbert and his brothers began raising on The Old Place. "Skeeter and I went up Wed. p.m." to check on some calves, she wrote. "They both are just as sprightly as can be," she reported. "Archie Hamby . . . was quite intrigued with them." Concerning an expectant cow named Brindley, she wrote, "Skeeter . . . is of the opinion that I am going to be more nearly right on 'Brindley's' time than he or Mr. Archie."[27]

While Herbert roamed about the countryside, Earline liked having company at the bungalow. Velma and Gene sometimes came over from Meridian so Gene could attend football games with Herbert; the men liked to walk to the stadium. Anne brought two of her Birmingham classmates home with her for a weekend in March 1950. However, the next year Anne regretted inviting friends to the bungalow for dinner on Thanksgiving weekend, fearing that playing the hostess had been too much for Earline. She told her mother she "looked pretty as a picture and put on a happy face" but was afraid Earline was "dead tired after having such a lovely dinner for that mob." Anne wrote, "I couldn't help wishing all the time that it had never come about since I know you worked yourself down to a nub." She promised she would not soon impose on Earline in that way again. Anne's concern suggests that Earline's health was worrying the family, but Earline remonstrated that she was fine and having the guests was no trouble. "You should know by now, how very much I do enjoy having yours and Lyman's friends around. . . . If you see that that doesn't happen again, you will be depriving me of a very great pleasure," she wrote. "Now don't do me like that."

Six short notes that Anne saved from this period are the only concrete evidence of Earline's interactions with the family's African American servants. In December 1951, Earline reported, "Sam and I are doing yard work tomorrow if it isn't raining." She referred to Sam again when he planted boxwoods beside the front steps.[28] Like the Hargroves' former slave "Aunt" Jane, Sam the yardman appears in family papers without a last name. However, public records show African American laborers named Sam Long, possibly all the same individual, living in Tuscaloosa in 1932 and between 1935 and 1940, so the gardener could have been Herbert's childhood housemate. If so, Sam was a living representative of the archetypal faithful family servant.[29] Perhaps this connection protected him from Earline's displeasure. Concerning a maid named Bessie, Earline confided to Anne in February 1952 that she was waiting to fire her until after a UDC meeting at the bungalow "for she does clean very nicely." Later the same month Earline hired a woman she called "Shep's maid" for one day but was not sure she would hire her again: "She's a snuff dipper."[30] Regarding "old Ollie," another domestic servant whom she hired on a trial basis, Earline was harsh: "You know I think she will steal nickels off of [a] dead man's eyes." Ollie also appears in Earline's notes with no last name, but in 1940 the federal census found at least nine African American women in Tuscaloosa whose given names were Ollie, two employed as laundresses and three as maids. Like Jane, Earline's maid could have had the surname Hargrove; in 1950 Mrs. Ollie Hargrove, a black woman, lived in Alberta City, about two-and-a-half miles from the bungalow.[31] Earline was so suspicious that Ollie would pocket household items that she declined an invitation to accompany two friends to Meridian on a day when Ollie was scheduled to work. "Gosh, I'm going to fire her," she wrote to Anne in March 1952. "I can't let a stealing nigger interfere with my gadding around."[32]

Earline's use of "nigger" in writing is startling. Herbert spoke the word (in the 1960s, I heard him chant "Eeny, meeny, miny, mo / catch a nigger by the toe," lines of a song that was popular during his boyhood),[33] but when he wrote a letter to little Lyman in 1929 he used "negroes" to refer to Robert Shook's employees. That Earline used the word "nigger" in a letter to Anne suggests she routinely spoke the word aloud in conversation and no one in the family rebuked her. Some upper-middle-class whites referred to "good" servants as "darkeys"; some used "nigra" as a compromise between "Negro" and "nigger."[34] White southerners who wanted to demonstrate the greatest civility used "Negro," as Herbert did in the letter. Perhaps Earline refrained from using "nigger" in public, or maybe she used the word everywhere, having never aspired to the aristocratic image that the use of "nigra" supported. Her hostility toward African American servants could have simmered ever since the disappearance of Annie Mary Peoples, the nurse who quit without giving notice when Lyman and Anne were small, and boiled over by 1952 such that she lost any self-control she previously practiced concerning the racial slur. Despite her suspicions, she mentioned Ollie again on April 4 so she apparently did not fire her. Ollie probably knew Earline suspected her of stealing and wore a carefully composed mask of quiet subordination in order to keep her job, her self-aware performance reflecting a fuller understanding of their relationship than Earline herself had.[35]

Racism was as ugly and omnipresent as ever. For example, on the same page as a "Tuscaloosa Town Topics" item about one of Anne's suitors, the *Tuscaloosa News* ran an article with a photograph of a Klan leader, arms folded across his chest. The accompanying article reported that eight white men in North Carolina were charged with kidnapping and assaulting a young black woman.[36] Yet only once in her notes to Anne did Earline refer to the outside world and that was not in the context of race relations per se but of politics, when she wrote in September 1952 that she did not watch a television appearance by Richard Nixon, who was the Republican nominee for vice president and the opponent of Adlai Stevenson's running mate, Senator John Sparkman of Alabama. The state Democratic Party was rallying traditional Democratic voters behind the Stevenson-Sparkman ticket, but many in the party deeply resented the federal civil rights program that Democratic president Harry S. Truman had begun. From his office in the Commerce Building at the university, which had recently been named Bidgood Hall, Herbert followed political and legal news closely and had to recognize that racial segregation was coming to an end.[37] In March 1949, just before Klan activity escalated in Alabama, the US Supreme Court had sided with the National Association for the Advancement of Colored People and struck down the Boswell Amendment, the Alabama strategy for limiting black voter registration that Herbert endorsed. Two more high court decisions in 1950 brought integration of higher education closer, but the Alabama legislature fought back, referring another Boswell-type amendment to the voters, who narrowly approved it in 1951.[38] Then, in September 1952, Pollie Anne Myers and Autherine Lucy attempted to enter the University of Alabama. They had received acceptance letters, but when they arrived on campus officials saw their ethnicity and refused to enroll them. The *Tuscaloosa News* and the *Birmingham News* both reported the incident on the front page on a Sunday morning, so Earline and Herbert must have been keenly aware of the situation. George LeMaistre, an instructor at the law school, sensed a "growing uneasiness [about race relations] in the community."[39] Finally, in December 1952 the US Supreme Court heard arguments in the group of cases known as *Brown v. Board of Education of Topeka*.[40] The three-day hearing on the matter began December 9. Out at Wilson Patton's place on Crabbe Road that night, the chief of the state supreme court, a former Tuscaloosa lawyer, gave a speech at the annual barbecue and hunt of the Tuscaloosa County Fox Hunters Association. He kept his remarks light, recalling "the old-time fox-hunts in the Tuscaloosa County hills," but some of the hunters undoubtedly asked him what he thought about the *Brown* case. As an Associated Press reporter put it in an article the *Tuscaloosa News* published the next afternoon, "segregation as practiced primarily in the South was under attack."[41]

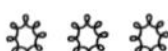

Earline had severe coronary disease, the same condition that killed her mother. She suffered from angina—pain in her chest and possibly her shoulders, arms, neck, and jaw—and was sick enough in the fall of 1952 that friends began calling on her unbidden. She wrote to Anne on a September morning, "back in bed after that bitter coffee, whole wheat toast and egg." She apologized for not writing the day before, but "Ollie cleaned in the morning and I thought I'd write you a line after the afternoon nap but before I got dressed and the note written, Hazel Jones and Julie Leatherwood came and staid [*sic*] too long." Writing to Anne in the evening apparently was too difficult; "you know I don't do much stirring around after 6 o'clock." Hoping that losing twenty pounds would restore her to health, Earline reassured Anne: "I'm ok—have reached my half-way goal—125—10 more to go. Love Honey, Mummy."[42] When Velma's husband, Gene, who was two years younger than Earline, died in October, Earline's fear must have intensified,[43] but she managed to dress and go out the next month to play her part as an assistant hostess at the lavish late afternoon wedding of Anne's childhood friend Bebe Lewis.

Combining the elegance of an antebellum home wedding with contemporary local cachet, the event at the University Club included all of the ritual elements of Tuscaloosa weddings—with Anne as one of the bridesmaids. Emmett Lewis, the piano teacher who played "Dance Juba" at the UDC meeting at the bungalow, and Joy Pearson Dendy, the honoree at Earline's Pink Party, provided the musical program. The bridesmaids wore identical gowns "of ruby velveteen, made with deep V-necklines, three-quarter length sleeves, and full skirts with matching slippers" and carried large "cascade bouquets of white Fuji chrysanthemums tied with white satin ribbons." The dramatic high point came when Bebe descended the beautiful staircase and her father, the chairman of the university's mathematics department, escorted her to the "improvised altar in front of the imposing mantel of the formal living room." After the ceremony, the bride and groom, their parents, and their attendants continued standing before the altar in a receiving line, Bebe's mother in "sea foam green chiffon over taffeta trimmed with rhinestones." Earline's friend Neva Foley and Anne's contemporary Elna Bolding helped serve at the reception. Louise Cason, the widow of the late journalist Clarence Cason, was one of the out-of-town guests.[44] Anne saved a glossy black-and-white print of a posed photograph of the wedding party, proof that, if not yet a bride, she was the perfect belle, tiny, slender, and lovely.

Since Herbert was the chairman of the university's business law department and he and Earline were members of the University Club, Earline probably gave some thought to having Anne's wedding at the beautiful old mansion, assuming Anne ever said "yes" to one of her beaux. In spite of her fatigue and bouts of severe chest pain, Earline invited Anne's friend Dave, a graduate student in biochemistry at the medical school, to the bungalow for New Year's Eve that winter.[45] Again, the suppers that Anne prepared for Herbert during my childhood suggest what Earline served to Dave. There might have been pot roast seasoned with catsup and raisins and Earline's special asparagus casserole, which involved a white sauce made of butter, flour, and milk. There could have been meatloaf stuffed into cored green bell peppers. For lunch, Earline and Anne might have prepared salmon croquettes or chipped beef on toast, also with the white sauce. These dishes reflected the "scientific cooking," typical at normal schools when Earline was a student, that called for disguising virtually any meat or vegetable beneath a plain white sauce, or in breaded patties, or by stuffing it into something.[46] Always, there was a side salad presented on the ubiquitous lettuce leaf. During the Christmas season, it might be Earline's Cranberry Salad, a tart, congealed dish. Velma Ruth Moore Kynerd inherited recipes from Earline's sister Velma, the instructions written on worn and splattered pieces of notepaper, and passed them on to me for safekeeping, noting, "As you can see [Velma] really used Aunt Earline's Cranberry Salad."[47] Another of Earline's holiday traditions, along with the toffee cookies, congealed salad, and asparagus casserole, was ambrosia, a combination of oranges and coconut, lightly sweetened with sugar. In her footed green glass bowl, it was a pretty part of a holiday buffet. Recipes for muscadine and blackberry wine, passed from Earline to Velma, then to Velma Ruth, and then to me, show that at some time Earline relented on the matter of alcoholic beverages. One of Anne's suitors had speculated in 1950 that Anne had "a generous supply of eggnog on hand" for Christmas in Tuscaloosa, so the Findleys almost certainly served eggnog to Dave.[48] Earline dictated her instructions for eggnog to Velma, who noted in parentheses that the recipe came from "Erline," using the original spelling of Earline's name. The eggnog recipe began, "to each egg yolk add 1 tbs sugar [and] 2 [tbs] whiskey."[49] Margaret laughingly recalled the "whiskey wardrobe" in the hallway where the family usually hid a bottle and how they were surprised once, when preparing to make eggnog, to find the bottle empty, speculating that a servant had been taking surreptitious nips.[50]

If Earline was exhausted by the time Anne and Dave left, she could have made another familiar family dish for supper by simply crumbling some leftover New Year's Day cornbread in milk and then gone to bed early. Herbert and Earline had completed some final renovations to the bungalow earlier in December, creating a bedroom suite for Earline by remodeling the small bedroom opposite the kitchen. They added a closet and a window air conditioner (the latter recently became affordable) and took in part of the adjacent sleeping porch to create a bathroom with green ceramic fixtures and a large mirror over a built-in dressing table.[51] Dave joked to Anne, "I hope that you can now find your way around the house and are not sidetracked by the new closet which would result in your mother thinking you are lost again."[52] This new room was a sanctuary for Earline and a new opportunity to indulge in creative decorating.[53] She had the room papered with glittery pink wallpaper and furnished it with a diminutive four-poster bed and a highboy chest of drawers. Opposite the bed sat a graceful small chaise known as a méridienne. Forced by her own poor health to move to Chattanooga to live with her sister,[54] Jennie Moore had given Earline and Herbert the méridienne, which she told them belonged to "Ma Moore," Jennie's paternal grandmother, Anna Moore. She also gave them a small upholstered recliner she called "Pa's chair."[55] Earline placed the recliner in the large back room that served as Herbert's bedroom as well as the family den. She had the chaise recovered in chintz with pink roses on a green background. Now she could retire as early as 6:00 P.M., if she wished, while Herbert watched television in the back room.

☼ ☼ ☼

When her uncle Charles died in Meridian in January 1953, attending his funeral may have been difficult for Earline. A few weeks later she was too weak to send a birthday gift to Anne, managing only to write her a note. The angina was worse and now her doctor required her to wear a heart monitor for an hour at a time, which indicates she suffered from the unstable form of the disease and was at risk of a heart attack.[56] After Anne paid a visit to the Moore sisters in Chattanooga in April, Ida wrote, "You looked grand, so lovely in your coat suit, and that lovely blouse," and asked, "How are Judge and Mrs. Findley? Better, I hope your mother is." Ida speculated that Earline "overdid herself in remodeling her home" and concluded "rest and quietude are two important assets for her recovery."[57] Earline did spend more time resting in her new dimly lit bedroom. From her bed, she could admire the méridienne and glimpse the Shook house through the single window. If Anne played the baby grand piano in the living room on her visits home, Earline could hear the music. Anne considered Chopin's *Fantasie-Impromptu in C-sharp Minor, Op. 66*, her greatest accomplishment as a pianist.[58] Chopin's piece required memorization and dexterity that were possible only with extensive practice; it was a typical part of a bourgeois virtuoso's repertoire. The *Fantasie* filled the bungalow with the thrilling rising trills at the beginning, the sweet melody evoking grief as much as beauty, the pounding descending chords resounding through the rooms and hallway, the introduction of a new melodic phrase hinting at hope, and, last, the slow quiet death of the music.

Two lamps, adapted from kerosene lamps, illuminated the bedroom. The smaller lamp was ordinary, with a flared pedestal and undecorated font. The larger had an unusual shape with a dramatically wide pedestal and a massive font with a flat, rather than rounded, shoulder and a pressed Greek key pattern of decoration at the top and base.[59] The glass of both lamps had turned lavender from exposure to the sun, indicating they were manufactured between the 1860s and 1915, when glassmakers substituted manganese for lead because lead was in demand for manufacturing bullets.[60] The provenance of Earline's lavender lamps is lost, but Anne always referred to them as "the cemetery lamps." To place glass objects and crockery atop graves was an old southern custom, sometimes intended as simple decoration and sometimes as symbolic illumination for the dead's passage to the next life.[61] Describing grave decoration by poor families in Hale County, James Agee wrote that "offers are set in the clay[:] a horse shoe; or a dead electric bulb; or a pretty piece of glass or china."[62] Earline's lamps could have been from a cemetery in Brookwood or Kellerman, small communities strung along County Road 59 in the coalfields east of Tuscaloosa. The Findleys' tenant

Robert Shook engaged in mining in that vicinity in the 1930s and 1940s. As he and his partners leased more land to expand their mines, they may have had to relocate the remains in a cemetery. If the cemetery had many unmarked graves, as genealogists discovered that Brookwood Cemetery did in 2000, the mining company workers would have had trouble determining how to reposition any associated grave decorations.[63] We can imagine Shook salvaging the lavender lamps and bringing them to his wife, Louise, and that Louise at some time gave them to Earline.

Oil lamps captivated Agee. In *Let Us Now Praise Famous Men*, a brilliant, challenging book, he described families lighting lamps in their cabins as darkness fell: "It is late in a summer night, in a room of a house set deep and solitary in the country. . . . I am looking at a lighted coal-oil lamp." The lamplight so moved Agee, he described it again in a passage about African American farm workers: "The negroes down beyond the spring have drawn their shutters tight, the lamplight pulsing like wounded honey through the seams into the soft night." This illumination, this instinct to resist darkness and sleep and death having triggered one of Agee's most powerful passages, he went on: "All over the whole round earth . . . people are drawn inward within their little shells of rooms, and are to be seen in their wondrous and pitiful actions." Agee envisioned the occupants of shuttered houses "in chairs, reading, setting tables, sewing, playing cards, not talking, talking, laughing inaudibly, mixing drinks, at radio dials." They were "eating, in shirtsleeves, [or] carefully dressed"; they were "courting, teasing, loving, seducing, undressing"; or they were "alone and writing a letter urgently, . . . in family parties, in gay parties, preparing for bed, preparing for sleep."[64] Agee's collaborator on the book, the photographer Walker Evans, made a lamp much like Earline's Greek key lamp the central image in a photograph that became one of the icons of American documentary photography. His view into the Burroughs family's rough dogtrot home has been carefully studied. The historian James Curtis deduced that Evans removed the clutter of other objects on the kitchen table so that the lamp became the focal point of his picture. The biographer James R. Mellow found Evans's photograph "almost Vermeerlike [with] a sense of time stopped." The Memphis painter Carroll Cloar referred to Evans's picture for the painting *Dicey and Icyphine, Dressed Up* (1979), reproducing the table and lamp, a hutch in the background, and a dishcloth hanging from a nail as they appear in the photograph. Cloar's painting, in which two small African American children pose in special clothes, emphasizes the tension between the hopelessness of making domestic interiors beautiful and the hope implicit in providing nice clothes for children, as if to echo the tearful comment of Allie Mae Burroughs, "Oh, I do *hate* this house *so bad!* Seems like they ain't nothing in the whole world I can do to make it pretty."[65]

Two other objects in Earline's bedroom echoed the lavender of her sun-tinted lamps. The first was a small, unmarked porcelain vase with a ruffled neck, hand-painted with a repeating pattern of violets and green leaves and embellished with gold leaf and moriage in the form of a trellis-like diagonal grid of dots, the type of object that was common in department stores and gift shops when a young Earline and her teacher housemates could have strolled through Tuscaloosa's downtown on a Saturday. The final lavender object was an old-fashioned whole-cloth quilted coverlet, each side constructed of two pieces of satin. The satin on one side is pink, on the other lavender. The quilting consists of a round center medallion in the form of a flower, corners of roses and stylized fern fronds, and an overall diamond pattern like the moriage on the violet vase. The quilt maker carefully folded the lavender edges twice and then over the pink edge to form the hem. It is possible that Earline's mother, Annie, made the satin coverlet as a gift for Earline, since she made two quilted pieces for Anne's doll cradle and pieced a set of Sunbonnet Sue squares for Anne, all with pink as a primary color. However, an unfinished top for a Victorian-style "crazy quilt" suggests Earline could have made the coverlet herself.

A fad that originated in the postbellum period, crazy quilts lacked the aristocratic tradition of whole-cloth quilts but had the potential, like other pieced quilts, for encoding one's stories.[66] A family storyteller could spread out a crazy quilt and talk over the individual pieces, just as they might reminisce about the ancestors in entries in a family Bible or scenes in a photograph album. Earline's crazy quilt has several pieces that appear to be fabrics she used in upholstery and dressmaking projects. Narrow strips of forest green velvet could be scraps from the Findley chaise longue. The deep-blue cut velvet with a floral pattern could have been left over from the Seignoret-style dining chairs. The large, irregularly shaped pieces of navy and white striped sateen appear to be the material in the spring suit Anne wore in the 1942 photo booth picture; the green taffeta could be a scrap from her 1946 portrait dress. Although the newspaper report of the Pink Party said Earline's canary-colored dress was chiffon, the vivid gold silk in the crazy quilt certainly could be characterized as "canary." Finally, two pink rectangles in the crazy quilt probably are scraps from the "fancy frock of blush pink crepe" that Anne wore on that momentous day. If so, it is not possible that Annie made the crazy quilt since the Pink Party took place two years after she died. We can imagine that Earline made the pink-and-lavender coverlet and then, wanting another stitchery project, undertook the crazy quilt because the scraps from upholstery and dresses were at hand. But she did not add the batting and a back to complete the quilt. Perhaps by then she was bedridden and could not work at a quilting frame, or maybe she was not satisfied with the quilt. It is embellished with the type of embroidery in vivid colors that was typical for crazy quilts, but the images of flowers, dogs, a sunburst, and other objects are very amateurish in comparison to her meticulous dressmaking projects.[67] Anne eventually put the crazy quilt top away in a chest but she placed all of the lavender objects in her own bedroom, always keeping the coverlet folded across the foot of her bed even though it often slipped to the floor because of the smooth finish of the fabric. If Earline likewise kept the coverlet at the foot of her bed, and it sometimes fell, she could ring her crystal bell to summon Ollie to her bedside to retrieve it.

Ten

Shrine

HERBERT TOOK EARLINE TO JEFFERSON-HILLMAN Hospital in Birmingham in April 1953. Her angina was worse and although the new Druid City Hospital had recently opened a few blocks from the bungalow, Lyman thought his mother could get more advanced care at the medical center.[1] Anne lived just across Twentieth Street South from Jefferson-Hillman and Lyman and Margaret lived nearby,[2] so Herbert returned to Tuscaloosa for the night on Monday, April 20, confident that his children could be at Earline's side quickly if she needed them. Her death sometime after midnight was sudden. Lyman was the first to receive word that she was gone. He called Anne and then Herbert's friend Toombs Lawrence, asking Lawrence to go to the bungalow and stay with Herbert until Lyman, Margaret, and Anne could get there. Margaret called her mother, who alerted Earline's close friend Hatchett Hinton; they both also went to Herbert's side. Someone called the Foleys.[3] These contacts were the first in a rapidly expanding circle of communication as the people in Earline's world began the ritual response to death.[4] Anne's apartment mate, Gloria Goode, helped spread the word, probably calling Elna Bolding and Alice Murphy, friends of Anne from high school who shared an apartment in Birmingham.[5] Alice called Rachel Parker, who had helped serve refreshments at the Pink Party, and Rachel called her sister Marion, who was Anne's cohostess that day. Gloria wrote to her sister and to medical center friends who lived around or outside the state and were not likely to attend the funeral. Their classmate Carolyn Baker Loy responded by writing to Anne, "Please convey my most sincere sympathy to Skeeter." She went on, "I wish . . . I could be there with you," addressing Anne as "Findley." Some friends' parents joined the wave of feminine sympathy that washed over Anne. Gloria's mother sent a telegram with "heartfelt sympathy" and her father wrote, "Gloria is heartbroken over the passing of your Mother." Loy's mother wrote, "Carolyn was so fond of your mother. She said she was a wonderful person."[6]

The family immediately arranged for the funeral to be at the bungalow the following day.[7] Both the *Tuscaloosa News* and *Birmingham News* reported the death that afternoon, probably because Alice, a reporter for the Birmingham paper, wrote its brief article; it noted that Earline was the "wife of Judge Herbert L. Findley, University of Alabama law professor."[8] In a follow-up article, the *Tuscaloosa News* provided a list of active pallbearers but nothing regarding honorary pallbearers, perhaps because the time was too short for Herbert to prepare a suitable list. If they were uncertain of the protocol for funerals, Herbert, Lyman, and Anne could consult Earline's copy of *Essentials of Etiquette*, which advised that six was the customary number for pallbearers.[9] Herbert did choose six, each one a reminder of the history and primary associations of the Findley family: Newt Hinton and Toombs Lawrence were perhaps his closest friends, Newt the dairy farmer and husband of Earline's best friend, Hatchett, Toombs the psychiatrist and Herbert's hunting and fishing partner. Tom Koster was Lyman's father-in-law. George Johnston was the longtime county tax assessor and one of the honorary pallbearers for Murk Findley in 1941, now among Murk's last surviving friends.[10] Walter B. Jones, a geologist at the university, was the father of Lyman's close friend Nelson and husband to Hazel, who had visited Earline at the bungalow. James Foley, of course, was the physician who persuaded Lyman to enter medical school instead of joining the fight in Europe to avenge Nelson's death.

A Tuscaloosa mortuary handled the preparation of the body and delivered the casket to the bungalow, placing it in the dining room before the windows. With the dining table removed, Earline's eight Seignoret-style dining chairs would have accommodated Herbert, Lyman, Anne, Margaret, Earline's sister Velma, and her brother J. C., sister-in-law Virginia, and niece Velma Ruth in two rows. Other close family members, such as Herbert's brothers Hargrove and Preston and their wives, could sit on the maple and walnut back-up chairs or stand behind them. The pallbearers may have stood, ready to lift the casket at the conclusion. The rest of the mourners probably sat in improvised rows in the living room and sun room, both pairs of French doors wide open to allow people to move through the house and hear the Methodist minister officiate.[11] Afterward, they waited in their cars, parked on both sides of the avenue, for the hearse and other lead vehicles to depart from in front of the house. Forming a caravan, they proceeded east toward Tuscaloosa Memorial Park, a fairly new cemetery that was within a mile of Herbert's birthplace, the family farm known as The Old Place. The old highway ascended Castle Hill, following a slight curve and passing Druid City Hospital. A police escort probably led the procession for Earline with the funeral home vehicles, one bearing the casket and another her family, next, and then the long line of private vehicles, their headlights on in the customary practice for signaling oncoming drivers to pull to the side of the road. The weather was clear and warm. After the graveside ceremony, Anne struggled to speak with the mourners and accept their expressions of sympathy (a year earlier she confided to Earline, "I never know what to say to sorrowing people"), but she performed her role so well that her friends Glo, Alice, and Elna complimented her later, Alice writing, "Glo, Elna and I all agreed . . . your mother would have been exceedingly proud."[12]

Anne remained at the bungalow to keep Herbert company and begin the task of responding to the enormous volume of cards, notes, and gifts the family had received. Following Dryden's advice, they could use engraved cards to acknowledge the printed sympathy cards,[13] but they had to write at least eighty-two personal notes to thank friends and relatives for handwritten notes and for gifts of flowers and food.[14] Some of the sympathy notes recalled periods in Earline's life. Totsie Jones, the clerk of the probate office, mentioned the day in 1922 when Earline and Herbert signed the deed for the property on University Avenue that Murk gave them. "I can just see you both as you were," she remembered. "You both seemed so happy and Mrs. Findley looked so pretty and sweet." A clubwoman wrote, "I always thought so much of Earline and we always had so many happy hours at our club and other parties—I shall miss her. . . . She lived her life well. Always so kind and thoughtful of others." The Shooks' daughter Margaret wrote first to Herbert—"Mr. Findley, . . . your loss has been a real blow to me"—and later to Anne, addressing her affectionately as "Sister": "Your Mother will always remain in my mind a sweet and wonderful woman." Ida Longley, whose sister succeeded Louise Shook as Anne's piano teacher, wrote, "Your dear lovely mother was a friend to all besides her family. Tuscaloosa will hardly find her like again. . . . We mingle our tears with yours."[15]

Among the many messages the family received, one was a brief letter to

Herbert from another local lawyer, Devane Jones. Four years behind Jones at Stafford School, Herbert probably had known him most of his life. Jones had been a close friend of Herbert's cousins the Van de Graaffs, serving as an honorary pallbearer for Hog and an active pallbearer for Hog's mother, Minnie. Descended, like Jennie Moore, from the Revolutionary veteran and member of Congress Peter Forney of North Carolina, related to the thirteenth vice president, William Rufus King of Cahaba, Alabama, Jones had been "admired for his . . . gallantry" since he was in high school.[16] His letter was a model of the sympathy note, with an opening that came straight to the point, a middle section of comments that demonstrated the writer's awareness of the dead person's accomplishments and character, and a closing that focused on the future and the writer's commitment to ongoing friendship. Jones wrote:

> Dear Herbert, I sympathize with you deeply in your great loss. You have had a beautiful home life and have been fortunate in that and in the beautiful home which you provided for Earline and which she kept for you, and I hope that your family and home and your spiritual resources will help you in your time of need. Hoping to see you soon, and with best wishes for yourself and each member of your family, in which my family and partners join, I am—Sincerely your friend, Devane K. Jones.

In sympathizing "deeply" with Herbert's "great loss," Jones alluded, without indulging in self-pity, to the sad early death of his own first wife, in effect establishing that he and Herbert had a powerful bond.[17]

Anne replied on Herbert's behalf to some of the notes he received. The unusual trouble she had spelling common words hints at the trauma she felt: on the back of one card, she wrote "thoughtfullness" and "thoughtfulness" to compare their spellings. She also tested a spelling of the word delicious: "delisci." Similarly, Herbert took one of the family's Bibles, the one Earline's mother gave to her in 1913, from a bookcase or Earline's bedside. Finding no section of blanks for a family record, he turned to the back of the book. On the last page, a blank page facing a map of Palestine, he wrote "Marriages," underlined the heading, and noted "Herbert L. Findley and Earline," here using the spelling she preferred. Pausing, he crossed out "Earline," as if the act of writing her name was too hard. Making another attempt, he wrote

"Earline Moore Findley" but crossed out that attempt, too. Wanting to follow the protocol for genealogical records, Herbert next wrote "Annie Earline Moore" and the date of their wedding, "June 29, 1921." Turning the page, he added and underlined another section heading, "Births," and beneath it wrote "Herbert Lyman Findley, Jr." and "Anne Elizabeth Findley," but without dates, too grief-stricken, perhaps, to recall his children's birthdays at that moment. On the blank inside of the Bible's back cover, he created a third section, "Deaths," underlining that heading, too, and wrote "Earline Moore Findley April 21, 1953."[18]

After Anne returned to Birmingham, Ollie, the maid whom Earline believed was a thief, took care of the house, training her daughter Melody to do the same. The women maintained all of the rooms as Earline left them. At some time, Herbert began mowing the front and back lawns himself, perhaps after the laborer named Sam Long died in 1956. He frequently went to the University Club for supper, sitting alone in the main dining room, with his back to the wall, and chatting with friends who stopped at his table to greet him. He declined to go through the buffet line, however, and the waiters knew that he expected to be served a tossed salad in a bowl.[19] After decades of dealing with the slippery lettuce leaves on Earline's salad plates, he found that easier.

Roland Harper and his wife went to the bungalow in November to cut some of Earline's flowers (considering the time of year, probably the camellias in front of the breezeway) for a memorial arrangement in the sanctuary of Methodist Campus Church, noting for the printed order of service that the flowers "were taken from the garden which she planted" and giving a copy of the program to Anne. Two days before the first anniversary of Earline's death, they visited Herbert again and posed for a photograph standing before Earline's rose bed, Mary holding three long-stemmed pink roses.[20] The US Supreme Court released its long-awaited decision in *Brown v. the Board of Education* the next month, ruling on May 17, 1954, as many observers had expected, that the *Plessy* "separate but equal" doctrine was unconstitutional. Alabama's Hugo Black and two other southerners on the court voted with the majority to make the decision unanimous. The *Tuscaloosa News* called for "a calm and deliberate" reaction to the ruling and expressed hope that actual integration could be avoided if southern school districts redrew their boundaries to establish single-race zones and then funded the zones for white and black children equally, but the "growing uneasiness" of segregationists that the Tuscaloosa lawyer George LeMaistre sensed in 1952 must have been even greater. Near the end of 1955, the Montgomery bus boycott began, with African American domestic workers walking to their jobs. The civil rights supporter and memoirist Virginia Foster Durr recalled the boycotters were like "black tides [that] would come up out of the black section of town and go to work and then sweep back again." Over the next three years, terrorists bombed more black churches and homes in Alabama than in any other state.[21]

Autherine Lucy returned to the university campus in February 1956, driving the segregationists among the students and in the community insane with fury. On the night of February 4, a mob took over University Avenue, burning a cross in the middle of the street a few blocks to the west of the bungalow. Neither Herbert nor Anne ever mentioned the riot to me, but Wayne Greenhaw, at the time a teenage sportswriter for the *Tuscaloosa News*, witnessed it and described it in an essay. He was returning from covering a game when he came upon the riot. "A mob was filling the broad street[,] screaming 'Hey, hey, ho, ho, Autherine's got to go!' When a car approached, the mob surrounded it. They beat the roof and hood with sticks. They climbed onto the bumpers and jumped up and down." Scanning the whole fire-lit tumultuous scene, Greenhaw noticed the terrified face "of a small black boy in the back window" of the car. "His frightened face stayed with me," he wrote a half century later. The next morning, a crowd estimated at a thousand waited on campus for Lucy to appear. A reporter for the *Tuscaloosa News* speculated that "if they could have gotten their hands on her, they would have killed her." The university suspended Lucy, ostensibly to protect her, and now the *Tuscaloosa News* publisher, Buford Boone, took a stand alongside African Americans who were demanding equality. "The University administration and trustees have knuckled under to the pressures and desires of a mob," he wrote in a front-page editorial. "We have a breakdown of law and order, an abject surrender to what is expedient rather than a courageous stand for what is right."[22]

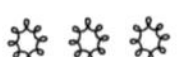

With Anne's help, Herbert gave an eggnog party that December. Festive spirits had been a complement to humor among the elite in Tuscaloosa since pioneer days.[23] W. R. Smith, the poet-lawyer-legislator who recorded "The Hunting Song" in 1824, apparently was an eggnog enthusiast. He noted in his memoir that "the *first* egg-nog in Tuskaloosa" was served in 1816 or 1817 at "a little shanty of a tavern."[24] In 1841 the legislature convened in Tuscaloosa on Christmas Day, but so many members had enjoyed "the usual Christmas festivities" it was "generally conceded that the House was not in a condition to transact business." Some members wanted a recess in order to partake of more refreshments and Smith drafted a resolution concerning the problem. "Be it enacted," he wrote, "that the two Houses assemble in the Hall of the House of Representatives, this day at 11 o'clock, for the purpose of singing the following JOINT SONG!":

Now Christmas comes, and merry
The Senators are dozing—
The thing is evident;
They all feel like reposing—
Some are at least half bent. . . .
Adjourn the House of Asses,
And let them bray no more. . . .
Fresh bowls, they say, are foaming,
More eggs are coming in,
Another boat is coming
With oysters, wine and gin.[25]

For the party at the bungalow, Herbert and Anne bought an enormous crystal punch bowl and cups that they placed on the dining room table. Herbert probably helped make the eggnog; two years later he grinned as he operated an electric mixer in a photograph that Anne labeled "Xmas, '58—Eggnog." As Earline had described the process to Velma, one beat the egg yolks, added sugar, and continued beating until they were fluffy. "Then add whiskey and beat 'til stiff." They whipped cream separately, whipped egg whites separately, and folded both into the yolk mixture. Before serving the eggnog, they grated nutmeg on top.[26] A large crowd of friends and relatives in Tuscaloosa attended the party.[27]

After Herbert retired from the university in 1965, my brother and I sometimes stayed at the bungalow while Anne worked at the medical center in Birmingham.[28] Herbert prepared our breakfasts and occasionally took us on errands, but we were under the maid Ollie's supervision much of the time. Once, after passage of the Voting Rights Act of 1965, an African American man came to the kitchen door to ask Herbert for advice on voting. The man stood at the bottom of the short set of steps to the breezeway, holding open the screened door while Herbert spoke through the open upper half of the Dutch door. I was too young to retain the details of their conversation, but I registered the measured, courteous timbre of Herbert's response. Since Herbert mowed the grass around the house himself, the man at the back door probably was not a gardener. Did Herbert know the man because he worked as a janitor at the courthouse or at the School of Commerce, or was the man there to pick up Ollie at the end of her shift and simply took the opportunity to seek the judge's advice?[29] Was his request sincere or an attempt to ingratiate himself with my grandfather, and considering that Herbert once tried to block Alabama blacks from registering to vote, how did he feel about the man's question? There is no way to know. As always, the problem with memories is that they are incomplete impressions of events.

Conclusion

Self-Portrait

In examining objects in the bungalow, we have glimpsed scenes of Earline's life—births and deaths, weddings and funerals, storytelling, cooking and sewing, reading the newspaper, listening to the radio, hunting, campaigning, holidays, and hospitality. The performative theory provides a handy set of terms for interpreting these events. The elite white woman's house was the stage for scenes in which she, her husband, and their children all played archetypal roles in a theater, as the scholars Inga Bryden and Janet Floyd put it, "where the boundaries between fantasy and reality, performance and 'natural' behaviour were blurred."[1] Most of the Findley family's colorful and dramatic rituals can be interpreted as performative, and many involved some aspect of unequal race relations. Amateur theatrical productions such as "Womanless Wedding" and Herbert's mock trial reinforced the power and self-image of upper-middle-class white men as humorous, fun-loving members of the ruling class. Political rallies, as spectacles of public will, perpetuated the antebellum culture of the courthouse square but were the opposite of extralegal lynchings. Herbert's version of foxhunting was more plebeian than riding to the hounds, which the historian Nicolas W. Proctor suggested "dramatized the unvanquished power of white supremacy," but nonetheless black men handled the dogs as Herbert and his friends collected ribbons. Storytelling sustained the Findleys' sense of being brave and honorable. Although the historian John Bell Henneman Sr. sneered at "the fond memory of maiden aunts,"[2] family stories are deeply revealing about the assumptions or pretenses of the storytellers. Every line of Lula Hargrove's account of "Aunt" Jane, the freedwoman who prepared the wool for the Centennial coverlets, demonstrated Lula's naive belief in loyal servants. Ila Findley's tale of Murchison Findley hiding the family and its female slaves in a secret closet during Croxton's raid supported the archetype of the genteel white father as protective ruler in this small-planter family. The stories of the piano teacher Jennie Moore linked the Findleys to Old World aristocracy.

It would seem that Earline embraced the southern lady's duty to create, as the scholar Lucinda MacKethan put it, "the accoutrements [of] a very highly regulated, subtly ritualized style of life."[3] She played her part as the modern matron, even purchasing an etiquette guide to fill the gaps in the training she received from her mother, and raised Anne and Lyman to play the same roles that she and Herbert played. From Lyman's creekside camping and early political bent and Anne's childhood tea party and music lessons, to teenage dances and recitals, everything led to the climactic ritual, the Pink Party, and the denouement, Earline's home funeral. Merely to reconstruct the scenes at the bungalow does not, however, show us Earline's perspective. Fortunately, the material culture scholar Kenneth Ames suggested that by "knowing the inner house," we can . . . know "the inner person." As the historian Mark Reinberger added, vernacular changes such as Earline's remodeled living room demonstrate "the lives *and thought* of the people who created them" (emphasis added). The rituals of planter-class life, the historian Steven Stowe said, can show us a way to study the planters' consciousness—if we explore further and question our assumptions about the South's privileged white class.[4]

Did Earline believe in the fantasy of the Old South and her part as a pampered, elite woman? She did not. When she gazed out of the bay window, she did not see the fantastical South of heroic white men protecting beautiful women in pastel dresses, their faithful black servants waiting upon them. She saw a frightening exterior world: epidemics, tornadoes, hospitals on three sides, fatal car crashes and masked Klansmen on the avenue, and neighborhoods of working-class black women and men she feared would steal from her, or worse. She remembered the blazing sun and broad fields of Choctaw County and the treeless hillsides of Holt. She was one of the southern women whom the social critic Lillian Smith saw as preoccupied with food, flowers, and old furniture as a means of "turning away from the ugliness which they felt powerless to cope with."[5] Earline was neither actor nor puppet in the continual southern fantasy because she could not have believed in the archetypal happy black servants. Earline did not enjoy the luxury of live-in domestic help as a child. Instead, she and her sister Velma grew up helping their mother perform endless household chores. Whereas some girls and women of Earline's generation created scrapbooks that the design scholar Jessica Helfand found were "visual autobiography, a genre rich in emotional, pictorial, and sensory detail,"[6] Earline's two photograph albums contained no ephemera, suggesting she had no strong desire to remember her childhood and adolescence. Her sister-in-law Ila made nostalgic memory paintings of two of the historic Findley houses but Earline did not even save snapshots of her childhood homes. Her modern taste in architecture and tableware suggests that as a young woman she did not identify herself with the antebellum South; her long delay in joining the United Daughters of the Confederacy is further evidence of this. Rather than doting on archetypal "Mammy" figures such as Lula's "Aunt" Jane or Govan's fictional Mom Jinny, Earline was suspicious of and hostile toward black servants. The story of Annie Mary, told as her abandonment of Earline and the children and her theft of Earline's jewelry, suggests that Earline held this suspicious attitude as a young woman; the notes that she wrote to Anne show it persisted to her last years. Earline did not even pretend to believe her maids were devoted to her, her reference to Ollie as a "stealing nigger" the proof.

Earline was motivated by three related ideas: that she was unlovable, that she was unattractive, and that she was unsafe. The first of these originated in the weak bond with her mother and the consequent unmet need on the infant Earline's part for a strong sense of physical security and protection from a loving caregiver, a sense the developmental psychologist Abraham Maslow ranked as the foundation of social-emotional health. This weak bond could have been part of the pattern, which went back for generations, of loss and grief apparent in the barely legible records of lost babies in the Christopher family Bible. One of the central facts of the family history was that Earline's grandparents John Chiles and Ann Elizabeth Christopher were only married because Earline's great-aunt Laura Louise died after the birth of her third child. Then Ann Elizabeth experienced the death of that child while she, Ann Elizabeth, was pregnant with her own first baby. If Ann Elizabeth resisted forming a close early attachment with her babies for fear of losing them, her daughter Annie then was poorly prepared to demonstrate love to her own children. Next, Annie lost her first child, Mallard Lester, while she was pregnant with her second, which must have deepened her ambivalence about motherhood. Resisting a strong emotional attachment to Earline, Annie would have passed on the negative core assumption that mother and child each was unlovable, ensuring that the cycle the psychologist John Bowlby called "the transgenerational transmission of neurosis" continued.[7]

The second of Earline's negative ideas was that she was unattractive.[8] The importance of physical beauty was constantly impressed on girls in her world, and the few extant photographs show that she had reasons to be unhappy with her appearance: her hair was dark instead of blonde and she resembled her unattractive Moore grandmother in being thick-waisted. The societal belief that a woman must marry well, and to do so she must be beautiful, was deeply entrenched, and the consequence of failure was to be without a protector. Earline's mother had resorted to marrying Mallard, a physically unattractive man and poor provider. From the rough appearance of their unpainted house, their lack of domestic servants and the corresponding domestic toil, the higher professional status and income of the Christopher uncles in comparison to Mallard, and Mallard's probable dependence on the Christopher men for his employment, we can deduce that economic hardship dogged Earline's family. If Mallard was an alcoholic, as the obituary for his father hinted, his drunkenness added to the sense of insecurity as well as social inferiority in Annie and her children. Earline's fear that she would fail, as her mother had failed, to attract a protector fed and reinforced her sense of danger, the third of her core ideas.

Death was an invisible monster that lurked everywhere. Diseases threatened everyone who survived pregnancy and childbirth: Great-aunt Laura had died; baby Lester had died; the mother of one of the few little white girls who lived near Earline died.[9] The influenza epidemic that began in the fall of 1918 killed thousands of Alabamians just as Earline faced having to find a job and live on her own. The next summer, dozens of people, many from Holt, drowned or disappeared in the Black Warrior River when a tour boat capsized while carrying sightseers to and from Tuscaloosa. Two months before she married Herbert, a tornado killed four people in a nearby community. There were the deaths of Ida and little John Findley and her cousin Edward Christopher, all from pneumonia. A few weeks after the stock market crash in 1929, the Black Warrior flooded large areas of Tuscaloosa County. When another tornado killed thirty-eight people in Northport in 1932, rescue workers deposited gravely injured victims, "some moaning, some screaming, some unconscious . . . all over the floor" at Druid City Hospital, a block from the bungalow.[10] During World War II, volunteers watched Tuscaloosa's sky for bombers and Lyman almost enlisted. There was her brother Otis's alcoholism; the death of Hargrove and Olive's infant son; outbreaks of typhoid; the polio that attacked Hatchett's children; Earline's terrifying ectopic pregnancy; and another outbreak of polio when she "went to pieces." While Lyman was at sea during the Korean War, news of casualties was constant on the pages of the *Tuscaloosa News*.

Crossing under and over all of these experiences, there was racial fear. It was the warp of Alabama life. The perceived threat of rape by animalistic black men, what W. J. Cash called the "rape complex," was a societal fever that peaked when Earline was a young girl, promoted in large part by powerful white men who found that the idea encouraged poor white men to remain compliant in an economic system that did not benefit them.[11] Earline lived, among hundreds of individuals who clearly remembered slavery, in a milieu where manhunts with bloodhounds and lynchings were still accepted. Her black neighbors knew the southern fantasy of the benevolent white ruler was a lie and some of them even spoke that truth aloud to Ruby Tartt, stepping out of their culturally imposed roles as happy servants. Their knowledge and knowing looks, if the masks of contentedness slipped, were reminders for Earline's generation that a retaliatory black bogeyman might materialize from the shadows.

Even though she found love, beauty, and safety by marrying Herbert and creating their bungalow home, we know from the notes that she wrote to Anne that Earline was afraid of contagion and of being alone. She still occupied what the philosopher and humanist geographer Yi-fu Tuan called a "landscape of fear," and events in the exterior world could always trigger her core anxieties. The Findleys' bungalow was situated on a major road, like Kenneth Findley's cabin on Byler Road—the scene of the terroristic threatening of a small black boy and the death of Murchison the Second—and like young Daniel Herd Brown's home near DeSotoville, where forged documents were planted to incriminate the doomed Jack Turner. The forces of the past kept passing by: marching, robed, and hooded Klan members going east, caravans of would-be lynchers going west. From the vicinity of the Greensboro Road and Big Sandy Creek, where Vaudine Maddox died, and from Hargrove Road, where a white farmer claimed a young black man accosted his daughter, even from a nearby bus stop, came frightening reports of marauding black rapists. In the end, cardiovascular disease gripped Earline's heart, slowly killing her. "Haunted by fear," as Tuan put it, she could never feel safe for long.[12] Her fundamental motivation, then, was not to commemorate a fantasy but, in the nature of all emotionally insecure individuals, to attain a sense of safety, so she turned away from the window to enjoy the beautiful interior of her house: the green walls, the burgundy and pinks of the rugs, the gleaming finish of the baby grand piano, the fireside chair upholstered with a tapestry depicting a magical forest with roses as large as trees.

Earline felt what Maslow called "a truly basic," albeit not universal, "aesthetic need" that could only be satisfied by beauty.[13] For a proper southern matron, home decoration was an appropriate outlet for this urge. The ways in which twentieth-century homemakers experienced their houses as ongoing art projects are well established: Clifford E. Clark Jr. called the middle-class home "an instrument for creative display" and its decoration the "major task for the housewife." Elizabeth Pleck referred to a middle-class woman's efforts to set "a beautiful . . . table" as "an artistic performance" and called formal affairs such as the Pink Party "a female art form." Marilyn Motz characterized party decorations as "a continuous display of . . . creative skill" that women's peers judged "according to local artistic standards." Catherine Howett observed that for Katharine Reynolds, the estate called Reynolda was "at once her mission and her masterpiece—analogous, in its human and temporal dimensions, to performance art rather than a material object." The bungalow property was modest in comparison to Reynolda, but it was a genteel house, strikingly different, as the cultural historian Richard Bushman put it, from "the unpainted frame and log houses of commoners."[14] A story that the renowned interior decorator Elsie de Wolfe told suggests a way of understanding Earline's deep need for a beautiful interior. Wolfe said she "became sensitive" to house interiors "through an experience of revulsion," when she felt severe distress as a child by the sight of ugly wallpaper and cried, "It's ugly! It's so ugly!" The wallpaper incident pushed Wolfe to feel "she was 'an ugly child' living 'in an ugly age. . . . From the moment I was conscious of ugliness and its relation to myself and my surroundings,' she wrote, 'my one preoccupation was to find my way out of it. In my escape I came to the meaning of beauty.'" The scholars Jean Gordon and Jan McArthur found Wolfe's response "superficial" and "vacuous," but I find it deeply meaningful. Like Wolfe's wallpaper, Earline's memories of the unpainted houses of her childhood were, as the scholar Clare Cooper Marcus put it, "a psychic anchor" and "a mirror of [her] inner psychological self"; to escape them was her driving purpose.[15]

Earline's assemblages of architectural finishes, furniture, textiles, decorative objects, and garden plants were creative acts. The rituals that she planned and produced at the bungalow were performance art pieces. Hardly original, her choices were vernacular, drawn from local styles. She understood that each object offered symbolic meaning; for example, she disliked zinnias and cannas, calling them "gas station plants." The social events she held in the bungalow also involved symbolism: the centerpiece for little Anne's birthday party, with tiny gifts hidden inside the windows of the pasteboard castle; the charlotte russe for the UDC meeting; the array of pink sweets at the Pink Party; the processional nature of each gathering, with guests rising to circle the dining table—all evidence for her peers in Tuscaloosa of Earline's legitimate place among the town's elite women. Her gradual acquisition of the Riverview chaise longue and Seignoret-style chairs reflected a deepening awareness of the cultural expectation to preserve or re-create antebellum homes, "an ambience of enduring aristocracy," but she drew from contemporary fashion in selecting the rattan planter's chair and the George Washington bedspread. The decorative choices that she made, most dramatically in her small private suite—the glittery pink wallpaper, the pink-and-lavender coverlet, and "the cemetery lamps"—were idiosyncratic. She selected only what was beautiful to her—the historian of Alabama architecture Robert Gamble said that the Cottage Orné style was "ornamented by its owners according to individual taste"[16]—because her motive was not to commemorate her ancestors or reinforce her social status but to create a beautiful home where she could feel attractive, loved, and safe.

One of my clearest, if fragmentary, memories of the bungalow is of Anne gazing into the backyard in the early 1970s, contemplating construction on the lot behind the property and observing in a mournful manner, "They cut down the cherry laurel," almost as if the erasure of the south hedge was an erasure of Earline. To conclude that Earline identified with her house, and that the family shared that sense, requires no imaginative leap. By the time Earline reached adulthood, the identification of middle-class women with their houses was very strong. The work of Beverly Gordon and Katherine Grier is seminal here. Gordon found that popular culture treated the middle-class woman "as the embodiment of the home" and the home "as an extension of . . . her corporeal and spiritual self." Gordon credited Grier for connecting the practice of inviting guests by announcing one would be "at home" to the corporeal nature of the house.[17] To the psychologist Mihaly Csikszentmihalyi, objects in the home are "props" that enable the individual to sustain a clear sense of identity or place—in history, in a current network of relationships, and in the future.[18] Thus the home funeral that the Findleys rushed to hold for Earline was both the final opportunity for her to be "at home" for visitors and the event that established her identity for the future.

Portraiture, I have shown, was a crucial source of identity for the privileged class. One displayed portraits of ancestors prominently and responded to those portraits in a predictable way. Describing a cottage in Newbern, Varian Feare mentioned portraits among "keepsake[s]" that "show . . . years of regard." In the drawing room of an antebellum house in Eutaw, she told her readers, there were "family portraits that bring us to a pause." Morton Rubin, the anthropologist who studied race relations and class identity in Wilcox County, observed that "old family portraits . . . on the walls" signaled that a family had maintained its antebellum standard of living, or something approximating it.[19] Powerful men sat for occupational portraits; elite women commissioned portraits to be made the day after their wedding. A good mother dressed and posed her children for portraits over and over, preserving the evidence of her careful attention to their health, training, and wardrobes. If she employed a black nursemaid for her children, she might even compel that woman to pose with the children for a portrait. Some adult wedding parties posed for pictures just as children did in Tom Thumb wedding tableaux. By the time Anne was of marrying age, the oil portrait was one of the most powerful emblems of the Old South.

For her own last photographic portrait, Earline wore a black dress with an illusion bodice of mesh and lace. Her face was smooth, her hair lustrous and dark with only a hint of gray at the temples. Her cheeks and lips were tinted pink, just as in the childhood portraits she commissioned of Anne. Unfortunately for Earline, there was a tension between the cultural expectation that an elite white woman would sit for portraits throughout her life and the largely unattainable standard of feminine beauty. The scholar Elizabeth Eastmond noted this tension regarding the work of the painter Frances Hodgkins, who, like Earline and Anne, disliked being photographed. Hodgkins overcame this dilemma by labeling as self-portraits two paintings of tabletop arrangements of flowers and other objects, conflating, as Eastmond put it, "the genre of self-representation with the genre of still life." The architectural historian Herbert Gottfried and the design scholar Jan Jennings suggested that middle-class homemakers in the twentieth century found the same solution: to create domestic interiors "that looked and functioned like a picture," reflecting the woman's "personality and character," with "color . . . a key element . . . because [of] its power to create a warm or cold emotional atmosphere."[20] Earline also wore a brooch, a piece of costume jewelry that Anne saved throughout her life, in her last portrait. Two inches wide by almost four inches in length, made of gold-tone cast metal in the form of a spray of flowers, it had three rosebuds comprised of enameled petals and glass cabochon centers, one stem of bright blue rhinestones, and one of costume pearls.[21] Her choice to wear the brooch for the portrait reflected the roses in the Struss painting over her living room mantel, what Gordon called "an interpenetration . . . between the adornment and presentation of women and the adornment and presentation of the women's environments."[22]

More than any photograph, the bungalow property itself was, as Devane Jones sensitively perceived, how Earline wanted to be seen and remembered. Even though an ugly and dangerous world surrounded her, her beautiful house made her beautiful and therefore she could be loved and safe. It was her self-portrait, framed by cherry laurel hedges; furnished, like Hodgkins's paintings, with careful tabletop arrangements of decorative objects, the color of an opalescent blue hobnail ruffled vase on the table in the bay window exactly matching the blue morning glories in the floral painting; the rooms forever ready for another pink party. Thanks to Margaret Findley, who commissioned a series of line drawings of the Findley houses by a local artist, Earline's self-portrait survives, the cast-iron trim and curving walk she designed still visible.[23]

Our last question remains. Why didn't Earline change? Some of her contemporaries demonstrated sympathetic interest in African Americans as individuals or as a people. Charlie McCall renounced the Klan. Ruby Tartt spoke out against discrimination in Livingston. The concern that Herbert's cousin Hog Van de Graaff felt for the tenant farmers at Gee's Bend seems to have precipitated a nervous breakdown. Clement Wood called his novel *Nigger*, flinging the word in the faces of racism's white perpetrators. Yet in her extant letters to Anne, Earline mentioned no concern for the victims of racial oppression; she also failed to express any outrage at racial terrorism, unlike Clarence Cason, who risked ostracism to write about Tuscaloosa, or Temo Callahan, who openly opposed the Klan in the 1940s. (Nor did Herbert, of course, but he had more actual reason to believe the fantasy of a benevolent world in which noble whites protected childlike black servants.)[24] Why didn't Earline open her eyes and heart to the suffering of people around her?

Discoveries in neuroscience offer a new way of understanding the moral paralysis that gripped southerners such as Earline. She was literally incapable of empathy, that capacity for imagining the perspective of another, the ability to enter "the private world of the other and [become] thoroughly at home in it," as the psychologist Carl Rogers put it.[25] One must be the beneficiary of empathy in order to learn its practice,[26] and she evidently did not find love or security in her relationships with her parents. Playing with other children could have ameliorated that factor to some extent—play supports the young child's developing ability to understand the perspectives of others—but as a small child, Earline had few playmates.[27] The frightening exterior world of Choctaw County, where hundreds of economically oppressed freedpeople surrounded Earline's home and family, constantly reinforced the idea common among people who lack empathy that the world is a dangerous, even malevolent, place.[28] Finally, there seems to be a link between the failure to tell detailed autobiographical stories and a lack of empathy. Bowlby, the psychologist who introduced attachment theory, proposed that insecure children grow up unable to "tell coherent stories about their lives" and either dismiss their pasts or remain "bogged down" in them.[29] In this regard, Earline seems to be a clear example. She left no record of efforts to document or describe her early life or family history. Despite her ambivalence about her father's "redneck" background, I heard no passed-down stories about her mother's pioneer ancestor, a circuit-riding preacher and doctor ordained by the great Methodist bishop Francis Asbury[30] who migrated to the Alabama frontier and was one of the founding elders of the church there. I heard nothing of Griffin Christopher's aristocratic in-laws, the Chiles family, although Earline was aware of the story that Walter Chiles reached Virginia in 1638, "bringing with him in his own ship his wife, two sons, and four other persons." I did not hear the scrap of a story that Walter actually built the ship he took across the Atlantic.[31] Almost every fact I uncovered about the Christophers' involvement in slavery came from sources other than family stories. Nor did I hear about Abe Lyon, who was lynched in DeSotoville when Annie was a child, or Jack Turner, who was lynched in Butler a few years later, although these omissions are more understandable as the kind of forgetting the art historian Anthony W. Lee calls "collective amnesia."[32] I heard almost nothing of Mallard Moore or his brother Sim, and the only fact I learned about his brother Will concerned the rocking chair that Earline placed in the bungalow living room. There were no stories of Aunt Bettie, although Earline's mother saved a few pictures of her. The shortage of stories of Earline's past and family in Choctaw County suggests she did not develop what Bowlby called "autobiographical competence" because reflecting on her past was too distressing.[33]

Earline *was* like Clarence Cason in one respect: she was driven by fear that her family's tranquil home life would be destroyed. To compensate, she made the bungalow property a haven. When she had the spacious front porch enclosed, she erased the threshold—what the French anthropologist Arnold Van Gennep called a *zone de marge* or liminal space. The house was no longer open in the Craftsman sense of fluid movement between indoor and outdoor spaces. The new breezeway, cool because of its expansive concrete floor and protected from public view by several large camellias, relieved Earline of exposure to passing traffic, people walking to and from Daly Bottom and Castle Hill, and the driveway to the insane asylum. The material culture scholar Sue Bridwell Beckham interpreted porches in terms of Goffman's theory of performativity, with front porches "where performances are staged" and "back places" where "the actor . . . can be herself." More to my point, however, the scholar and interior designer Candace M. Volz attributed the shift from spacious front porches to sheltered patios, which occurred in the twentieth century, to the noise that increasing automobile traffic created at the front of the house. As the geographer Yi-fu Tuan put it, Earline's screens of cherry laurel and camellia were "an attempt to keep inimical forces at bay." Her objective was not to retreat from a public stage but to retreat from the dangers of the exterior world. As her heart gave out, she retreated further to a bedroom sanctuary, an air-conditioned, shadowy space where, in the words of the material culture scholar Beverly Gordon, a woman might achieve "a kind of heightened experience . . . that was aesthetically and sensually charged and full," a "saturated" interior world.[34] In the addition of lavender to Earline's palette, we can see traces of her final dreams.

I have been a participant-observer of a kind, experiencing firsthand the Findley family's preservation of the bungalow as a shrine to Earline; handling and caring for the objects she loved; listening to family stories and passing them on here, but memories are risky sources and none are riskier than my own. Not only are my memories incomplete and possibly inaccurate, my interpretations of them are debatable. For example, I assume that the "Christmas gift!" greeting descended through the Christopher line because I found a passing reference to the ritual taking place in the presence of Griffin and Nancy Ann Christopher, but perhaps the Hargroves or Findleys, or someone else, introduced the custom to the family. In sorting through the possible meanings of the "Christmas gift!" ritual, I am left wondering whether Herbert ever ceremonially placed a candy or coin in little Sam Long's hand on Christmas morning and how the boys each felt about this ritualistic begging. And what about the family stories that only exist because I remember hearing them? In my faulty recollection, Anne mentioned Robert Jemison Jr.'s real antiwar efforts at the secession convention in Montgomery but also said that Jemison freed his slaves upon his return to Tuscaloosa and then enlisted in the Confederate Army, declaring that he would not fight for slavery but would fight for the South. None of these latter statements is true, and it seems impossible that she told such a completely inaccurate tale. What did I hear her say that contributed to such a false memory on my part? Anne also pondered the problem of shaky memories. She wrote to her aunt Ila, "You say the house [at The Old Place] burned 'about 1926'. I was born in 1928. I've always thought I had a vague recollection of going in to breakfast one morning and hearing from Father (Grandfather Murk) that the house at the Old Place had burned the night before. I wonder now if my 'recollection' is real or whether it's something dreamed up to fit my parents' account of it." Anne's memory of The Old Place, the terrain that she repeatedly explored, was firmer. As she wrote to Ila, she remembered "well . . . the pecan orchard, Ole Will's house, where the 'spring house' was, [and] the blueberry bushes on the way down to the swimming hole"[35]—although her scenic reminiscing raises a new question: Who was Ole Will?

Anne later associated Earline's death with Easter, dreaming that her mother, as an angel, visited her and brought her "a new Easter hat." Whether Earline made it to First Methodist on Easter Sunday, April 5, 1953, is lost to history. Because we have examined the objects she left in the bungalow, however, we can imagine that Earline sat at her dressing table that morning to arrange her hair and apply powder to her face, pinned the floral brooch to her dress, and retrieved a new hat from the closet shelf, hoping, to the end, that she would make a beautiful impression as she attended church on her husband's arm.[36] Upon her death, her very self was preserved in the layout and decoration of the bungalow. The house was inseparable from Earline;

her *petit récit*, to answer Jean-François Lyotard's question, was that the bungalow was "the beautiful home," as Devane Jones observed to Herbert, "she kept for you."[37] Considering that the property exists now only in a few individuals' memories, it is understandable that Earline's husband and children preserved her tabletop tableaux for as long as possible, causing my brother to experience the house as a "memorial" to our grandmother (an idea he did not share with me until I began the research for this book, but one that corresponds to my impression of the house as a shrine).

The tragedy of the neurotic personality is that one can never do enough to attain a sense of safety and security. As soon as Anne mastered one difficult piano piece, Earline needed her to learn another. Anne's own final assessment of her brief life as a pianist was that although she mastered Chopin's *Fantasie-Impromptu*, she failed because she did not master the works of Liszt. She confessed to feeling anger at Jennie Moore for using her to prove Jennie's greatness as a piano teacher, but her anger would have been more deservedly directed at Earline.[38] Forever striving to overcome the fears and anxieties of her childhood in the unpainted house, Earline could have died still thinking of ways to make her daughter and home more beautiful. Near the end of my research on Earline's life, I returned to her second photograph album and found, between blank pages near the back, a two-sided leaflet from Chase Nursery Company, a business in north Alabama. On one side of the six-by-nine-inch sheet, the nursery advised, "A planting of shrubs around the foundation of your home serves to 'tie the house to the ground,' to make a house into a home." The other side bore a full-color photograph of abelias and hypericum planted around the front of a house. A curving cement walkway, like the one at the bungalow, led to a recessed entryway framed by two pairs of gleaming white columns. The house was painted a pale pink.[39]

Appendix 1

Postmaster Appointments in the Extended Christopher Family, 1841–1915

Date	Appointee	Post Office	Alabama County
Feb. 2, 1841	Thomas T. Chiles	Eutaw	Greene
Nov. 2, 1846	James Chiles	Eutaw	Greene
Feb. 5, 1878	John J. Chiles	Pleasant Ridge	Greene
May 6, 1893	Walter C. Chiles	Knoxville	Greene
Feb. 3, 1894	Robert M. Moore	Jachin	Choctaw
1899	Robert M. Moore	Jachin	Choctaw
1903	Robert M. Moore	Jachin	Choctaw
March 17, 1904	Walter H. Christopher	DeSotoville	Choctaw
1906	Robert M. Moore	Jachin	Choctaw
March 1, 1906	Charles H. Christopher	Isney	Choctaw
1907	Robert M. Moore	Jachin	Choctaw
Feb. 17, 1909	William M. Watkins	Isney	Choctaw
March 23, 1909	Lula F. Christopher	Jachin	Choctaw
April 16, 1910	William R. Christopher	Naheola	Choctaw
July 12, 1912	William C. Moore	Jachin	Choctaw
Sept. 23, 1912	Lula F. Christopher	Lisman	Choctaw
Feb. 11, 1915	Nora Bennett	Jachin	Choctaw
July 1, 1915	Lula F. Christopher	Lisman	Choctaw

Source: Records of the Post Office Department, Record Group 28, National Archives and Records Administration.

Appendix 2

Enslaved Members of Christopher Chapel Methodist Church (Held by the Extended Christopher Family)

Name	Year(s)*	Slaveholder(s)
Amy	1854, 1857	Captain and Mrs. Fitch
Any	1860	Nelson
Barber	1854	Ann T. Christopher
Betsy	1860	Nelson
Briggs	1854, 1860	B. J. Thompson
Caroline	1857, 1860	DeLoach, Nelson
Chaney	1860	Nelson
Charlotte	1854, 1857	Captain Fitch, Mrs. Fitch
Dave	1857	J. J. Nelson
Davie	1860	Nelson
Dick	1854	Captain Fitch
Elbert	1857	J. J. Nelson
Elizabeth	1857	J. J. Nelson
Ellin	1854	J. Nelson
Emaline	1860	Neson
Hager	1854, 1857	B. J. Thompson
Hardy	1854, 1860	B. J. Thompson
Jacob	1854, 1857	J. M. DeLoach
Jane	1857	J. J. Nelson
June	1854	J. Nelson
Libby	1854, 1857	J. M. DeLoach
Lindy	1857	J. J. Nelson
Margaret	1860	Thompson
Mariah	1860	Nelson
Martha	1854, 1857	J. M. DeLoach
Mary	1854, 1857	B. J. Thompson
Mary Ann	1860	Nelson

Miles	1854, 1857	Captain Fitch, Mrs. Fitch
Minty	1860	Nelson
Phillis	1854, 1857	J. M. DeLoach
Rose	1854, 1860	Ann T. Christopher, Christopher
Sally	1857	Christopher
Wash	1857	Mrs. Fitch

*These are the years of two extant lists of church members.
Source: Rolls of members for the years 1854, 1857, and 1860, Ann H. Gay, comp., Christopher Chapel Methodist Church, "Record Book," ALGenWeb.

Appendix 3

Books in the Findley Home Library, with Inscriptions

*Now in the University of Alabama Special Collections
**Now in the private collection of Margaret Koster Findley
***Now in the Julia Tutwiler Library, University of West Alabama, Livingston

Alcott, Louisa May. *Aunt Jo's Scrap-Bag.* New York: Grosset and Dunlap, 1929. "Please Return—August 10, 1939. Anne Findley."

———. *Eight Cousins.* Philadelphia: John C. Winston, 1931. "To Anne from Mrs. Longley, 1938."

———. *Little Men.* New York: Blue Ribbon Books, n.d.

———. *Little Women.* New York: Garden City Publishing, 1932. "Anne Elizabeth Findley, Christmas, 1938."

———. *Lulu's Library.* New York: Grossett and Dunlap, 1930.

———. *Rose in Bloom.* Philadelphia: John C. Winston, 1933. "To Anne from Mrs. Longley, 1938."

———. *Under the Lilacs.* New York: Grossett and Dunlap, 1928.

Ashmun, Margaret, ed. *Modern Short-Stories.* New York: Macmillan, 1914. "H. L. Findley, Tuscaloosa, Ala., University."

Baruch, Bernard M. *A Philosophy for Our Time.* New York: Simon and Schuster, 1954. "H. L. Findley from Anne Xmas 1954" (in HLF Sr.'s hand).

Bowen, Catherine Drinker. *John Adams and the American Revolution.* Boston: Little, Brown, 1950. "Ida Moore Longley, 1951."

Brown, Calvin S., ed. *Enoch Arden and the Two Locksley Halls by Alfred Tennyson.* Boston: D. C. Heath, 1910. "Erline Moore"; "Dedicated to my husband who so faithfully performed the 'duties of Lise'—Selah" (in a different hand).

Burke, Edmund. *Burke's Speech.* New York: MacMillan, 1907. "Hargrove Finley [*sic*]. M. H. Findley. Burke = Whig." (In the collection of Herbert Lyman Findley Jr. and Margaret Koster Findley.)

*Cooke, James Francis. *Standard History of Music.* Philadelphia: Theodore Presser, 1936.

**Cooper, James Fenimore. *Deerslayer.* Boston: Ginn and Co., 1910. "Earline Moore."

Darwin, Charles, *The Origin of Species.* New York: The Modern Library, n.d. "Lyman Findley, 9–1–44."

**Dickens, Charles. *A Tale of Two Cities.* New York: MacMillan, 1914. "Earline Moore. November 23, 15[,] Isney, Ala."

***Dixon, Thomas. *The Clansman.* New York: Grosset & Dunlap, 1905. "Herbert L. Findley."

Dryden, Ellen. *Essentials of Etiquette: Complete Rules of the Social Game.* New York: Carey Craft Press, 1924.

***Eliot, George. *Silas Marner.* London: Macmillan, 1912. "Erline Moore[,] Jan. 19, 1913."

Fox, John, Jr. *The Little Shepherd of Kingdom Come.* New York: Grossett and Dunlap, 1903. "Herbert L. Findley, Jan. 2nd, 1914, U. of A."

Freeman, Douglas Southall. *Lee's Lieutenants,* vol. 1, *Manassas to Malvern Hill.* New York: Charles Scribner's Sons, 1942. "Herbert Findley from Anne 1952."

———. *Lee's Lieutenants,* vol. 2, *Cedar Mountain to Chancellorsville.* New York: Charles Scribner's Sons, 1943. "Herbert Findley from Anne 1952."

———. *Lee's Lieutenants,* vol. 3, *Gettysburg to Appomattox.* New York: Charles Scribner's Sons, 1951. "Herbert Findley from Anne 1952."

Gardner, Elsie Bell. *Maxi Searching for Her Parents.* New York: Cupples & Leon, 1932.

George, A. J., ed. *Selections from Wordsworth.* Boston: D. C. Heath, n.d. "From J. C. to Earline, August 25, 1916."

Govan, Christine Noble. *Narcissus an' de Chillun.* Boston: Houghton Mifflin, 1938. "For Anne Findley with the good wishes of Christine Noble Govan, November 1, 1938."

———. *Those Plummer Children.* Boston: Houghton Mifflin, 1934. "For Ann Findlay with the best wishes of Christine Noble Govan." (Bubble quote attached to illustration of black child: "Howdy Miss Ann, I'se come to play wif yer!")

***Gulick, Charles Burton. *The Life of the Ancient Greeks.* New York: D. Appleton, 1910. "H. L. Findley."

*Handford, Thomas W. *Boys of the Bible.* Akron, OH: Werner Co., 1898. "Presented to Hargrove, F By Hopewell Sunday School For the best and perfect recitations during the year 1898."

Hawthorne, Nathaniel. *A Wonder Book for Girls and Boys.* Rahway, NJ: Mershon Co., 1903. "Erline Moore, Jachin, Choctaw, Ala." and "Earline Moore, Isney, Ala." (A shopping list in pencil on the inside front cover: "Milk, Ice, sugar, Eggs, Salt.")

The Holy Bible, Containing the Old and New Testaments. London: Eyre and Spottiswoode, n.d. "Herbert Lyman Findley from Mother June 5, 1905."

The Holy Bible, Containing the Old and New Testaments. Philadelphia: John C. Winston, n.d. "From Mamma to Earline Xmas 1913."

The Holy Bible, Containing the Old and New Testaments. New York: American Bible Society, 1864.

Horne, Olive Browne, and Kathrine Lois Scobey. *Stories of Great Artists.* New York: American Book Co., 1907. "Earline Moore."

***Johnston, Harold Whetstone. *The Private Life of the Romans.* Chicago: Scott, Foresman, 1903. "Herbert L. Findley."

Kane, Harnett T. *Spies for the Blue and Gray.* Garden City, NY: Hanover House. "H. L. Findley from Anne. Xmas 1954."

Lancaster, Bruce. *From Lexington to Liberty.* New York: Doubleday, 1955. "H. L. Findley from Anne—June 19, 1955."

*Lawrence, Robert. *Wagner's "Ring of the Nibelung,"* vol. 4, *The Twilight of the Gods.* New York: Grossett and Dunlap, 1939.

*Lawrence, Robert, and Barry Hart, illus. *Wagner's Aida: The Story of Verdi's Greatest Opera*. New York: Grossett and Dunlap, 1938. "August 1940, Anne Elizabeth Moore [*sic*] Findley, Meridian, Mississippi."

*Lawrence, Robert, and Alexandre Serebriakoff, illus. *Wagner's Lohendrin*. New York: Grossett and Dunlap, 1938. "Book Week November, 1938, Poster Prize, Anne Findley."

**Litchfield, Mary E., ed. *Irving's Sketch Book*. Boston: Ginn & Co., 1901. "M. H. Findley."

***———. *The Sir Roger de Coverley Papers*. Boston: Ginn and Co., 1899. "Earline Moore[,] Livingston, Ala.[,] Feb. 7, 1917."

London, Jack. *The Call of the Wild*. New York: Macmillan, 1931. "Herbert Lyman Findley, Jr."

———. *Jack London's Stories for Boys*. New York: Cupples and Leon, 1936. "H. L. Findley, Jr."

———. *White Fang*. New York: Grossett and Dunlap, 1933. "Lyman Findley, Xmas 1938—Please Return!"

Lovett, Robert Morss, ed. *Shakespere's The Merchant of Venice*. Chicago: Scott, Foresman, 1908.

**Maxwell, Thomas. *The King Bee's Dream: A Metrical Address Delivered before the Druid City Literary Club of the City of Tuskaloosa, Alabama, May 12, 1875*. Tuskaloosa: George A. Searcy, 1875. "Mirk Findley, Tusklosa [*sic*]; Murk Findley, Tuscaloosa, Ala., December 25th, 1875; Murk Findley; Murk Findley: 1875."

*McBain, Howard Lee, and Isaac William Hill. *How We Are Governed in Alabama and the Nation*. Richmond, VA: Bell Book and Stationery, 1908. "Herbert Findley, April 22nd 1909."

*Morgan Woodwork Organization. *Building with Assurance*. Cleveland: Author, 1921.

Morrow, Abbie C. *Bible Morning Glories*. Louisville, KY: Pickett Publishing, 1896. "Erline Moore," with a second inscription on the blank page opposite the inside back cover: "Earline Moore—Aug. 28, 1914."

The New Testament of Our Lord and Savior Jesus Christ. New York: Daniel D. Smith, 1823.

Oberdorfer, A. Leo. *Oberdorfer's Alabama Justices' Practice*. Charlottesville, VA: Michie Co., 1905. "Findley."

Page, Thomas Nelson. *In Ole Virginia*. New York: Scribner's Sons, n.d. "Anne Elizabeth Findley, January 24, 1941."

Palmer, Thomas Waverly, comp. *A Register of the Officers and Students of the University of Alabama*. Tuscaloosa: University of Alabama, 1901.

Percy, William Alexander. *Lanterns on the Levee: Recollections of a Planter's Son*. New York: Knopf, 1950. "Anne to Skeeter, Jan[.] 1954."

The Poetical Works of Collins, Gray, and Beattie. Boston: Phillips, Sampson, and Co., 1857.

Porter, Eleanor H. *Pollyanna Grows Up*. Boston: Page Co., 1919. "To Earline from Eliza Jane, Feb. 29, 1920."

Rice, Alice Hegan. *Mrs. Wiggs and the Cabbage Patch*. New York: D. Appleton-Century, 1936. "Anne Findley, 329 University Ave."

Sabatini, Rafael. *Mistress Wilding*. New York: Grossett and Dunlap, 1910. "H. L. Findley, 2/2/33."

Scott, Sir Walter. *The Betrothed and the Highland Widow*. New York: A. L. Burt Co., n.d. "Herbert L. Findley."

———. *Ivanhoe*. Chicago: Scott, Foresman, 1908. "Herbert Findley, March 6th, 1909, Stafford School, Tuscaloosa, Ala."

———. *The Lady of the Lake*. Chicago: Scott, Foresman, 1908. "Herbert L. Findley."

Sellers, James B. *History of the University of Alabama, 1818–1902*. Tuscaloosa: University of Alabama Press, 1953.

**Shakespeare, William. *As You Like It*. Boston: D. C. Heath, n.d. "Earline Moore[,] S. N. S.[,] Sept. 25, 16."

**———. *A Midsummer Night's Dream*. Boston: Ginn and Co., 1910. "Earline Moore[,] Livingston, Ala. 'Hillford.'"

***———. *Twelfth Night or, What You Will*. Chicago: Scott, Foresman, 1906. "Herbert Findley."

Stratton-Porter, Gene. *The Harvester*. New York: Grossett and Dunlap, 1911. "Herbert L. Findley."

***Tarkington, Booth. *The Gentleman from Indiana*. New York: Grossett and Dunlap, 1902.

———. *Penrod and Sam*. New York: Grossett and Dunlap, 1916. "H. L. Findley, Jr."

———. *Penrod Jashber*. New York: Grossett and Dunlap, 1929. "H. L. Findley, Jr."

***Tennyson, Alfred. *The Complete Poetical Works of Alfred Tennyson, Poet Laureate*. New York: Hurst and Co., n.d. "Herbert L. Findley."

Thayer, Tiffany. *The Greek*. New York: Old Wine Press, 1931.

*Turner, Mrs. E. V. *Holland's Cook Book*. 6th ed. Dallas: Texas Farm and Ranch Publishing, 1928.

*Tuscaloosa High School. *The Black Warrior*. Tuscaloosa, 1912.

*———. *The Black Warrior*. Tuscaloosa, 1943.

*———. *The Black Warrior*. Tuscaloosa, 1944.

*———. *The Black Warrior*. Tuscaloosa, 1945.

Twain, Mark. *The Favorite Works of Mark Twain*. New York: Garden City Publishing, 1939. "Anne Findley, 329 University Avenue, Tuscaloosa, Alabama."

———. *The Prince and the Pauper*. New York: Grossett and Dunlap, 1909. "Anne Findley, 329 University Avenue, Tuscaloosa, Alabama."

———. *Tom Sawyer Detective and Other Stories*. New York: Grossett and Dunlap, 1924.

Underwood, Charlotte Whipple, ed. *Shakespeare's The Merchant of Venice*. New York: Macmillan, 1911. "Earline Moore."

University of Alabama. *Corolla*. Tuscaloosa, 1915.

———. *Corolla*. Tuscaloosa, 1946.

———. *Corolla*. Tuscaloosa, 1947.

University Society. *The Bible Story*. New York: 1925.

———. *The Home University Bookshelf*. 9 vols. New York, 1927.

———. *The Manual of Child Development*. New York, 1927.

Warner, Ezra J. *Generals in Gray: Life of the Confederate Commanders.* Baton Rouge: Louisiana State University Press, 1959. "With best wishes for a Merry Christmas [and] Happy New Year. Mrs. Longley. 1959."

***Warren, Henry P., ed. *Stories from English History: From B.C. 55 to A.D. 1901.* Boston: D. C. Heath, 1907. "Herbert L. Findley."

*Wheeler, Opal, and Sybil Deucher. *Mozart the Wonder Boy.* 7th ed. New York: E. P. Dutton, 1937.

Wright, Harold Bell. *When a Man's a Man.* Chicago: Book Supply Co., 1916. "Earline Moore."

*Ziemann, Hugo, and Mrs. F. L. Gilette. *The White House Cook Book.* Akron, OH: Saalfield Publishing, 1905.

Appendix 4

Enslaved Workers Rented by Robert Jemison Jr. to Murchison Findley, October 7, 1858–January 21, 1859

Name	# Shifts	Activity	Same-Day Assignments
Alfred	1	—	—
Allison	29	—	Asylum*
Anderson	3	Carpenter	Asylum
Bill	7	—	Asylum
Brown	25	—	Asylum, T. Prince, Lost**
Charles	1	—	—
Crane	19	—	Asylum
Dan	33	—	—
Dick	2	—	—
Elisha	2	—	Asylum, Lost
George	1	—	—
Jake	3	—	Asylum
Jerry	3	—	Asylum
Jim	2	Meachresly [?]	Sloan***
Lewis	3	—	Asylum
Ned	5	Clear land	xAsylum
Nelson	1	—	—
Scott	4	—	Asylum
Stevens	1	—	—
Thad	4	—	Asylum
Thornton	18	—	Asylum
Walker	10	—	—

*Alabama Insane Hospital

**This indicates the worker was idle for a half day.

***This could have been Fletcher Sloan, the building superintendent for the asylum.

Source: Robert Jemison Jr., Plantation Account Book, Robert Jemison Jr. Papers, University of Alabama Special Collections.

Notes

Abbreviations

ADAH	Alabama Department of Archives and History
AFS	Anne Findley Shores
AP	Associated Press
BNAH	Birmingham News-Age-Herald
CBS	Claude Bowman Slaton
EFS	Elizabeth Findley Shores
EMF	Earline Moore Findley
HABS	Historic American Buildings Survey
HLF	Herbert Lyman Findley
JCM	Joan Christopher Mitchell
MKF	Margaret Koster Findley
TN	*Tuscaloosa News*
UA	University of Alabama
UAB	University of Alabama at Birmingham
USFC	U.S. Federal Census
UWA	University Collection, Julia Tutwiler Library, University of West Alabama, Livingston, Alabama
VRMK	Velma Ruth Moore Kynerd

Introduction

1. Shores, *On Harper's Trail.*

2. Burke, *History of Knowledge II*, 80; Huffer, *Maternal Pasts*, 137.

3. Callahan, "Personnel"; Masello, "I Love My Bed," 42; A. K. Callahan Jr., "Windham's Columns Always Good," letter to the editor, *TN*, Feb. 6, 2003. (All *TN* articles were retrieved from https://news.google.com/ unless indicated otherwise with "clipping.") Concerning the use of "enslaved" versus "slave," I recognize that some scholars object to using "slave" in any context, believing it unnecessarily defines an individual. I use "slave" wherever the point of the passage is the thoughts or view of others because "slave" is the term that Earline and the people around her used. Similarly, I use "freedmen" and the equivalents rather than "freed men" because the former was in use during her life. However, I use "slaveholder" rather than "slave owner" because, of course, it is not possible for one person to own another person.

4. Howett, *World of Her Own Making*, 3, 16, 26; Scott, *Invisible Woman*, 244–45; Stowe, *Intimacy and Power*, ix; Motz, introduction, 3.

5. Most of Earline's photographs, letters, family Bibles, and ephemera are available to researchers in the AFS Collection, UA Special Collections.

6. Cohen, "Embellishing," 261; Hallam and Hockey, *Death, Memory*, 1, 5–6; Bryden and Floyd, *Domestic Space*, 2; Motz, introduction, 4; Hamlett, *Material Relations*, 9–13; Gordon, "Cozy, Charming," 125; Schlereth, "Introduction," 5; Ames, conclusion, 184; Lewis, "Common Landscapes," 117–18; Jones, "Event Analysis," 202–3; Herman, "*Bricoleur*," 38, 43; Burke, *Cultural History*, 71–72; Jones, *Folk Art*, 61–67. See also Sies, "Toward a Performance Theory," 200–201. On the design of a house contributing to "human drama," see Domosh and Seager, *Putting Women in Place*, xxi. On the need to examine "personal dramas of marriage, pregnancy and childbirth," etc., see Theophano, *Eat My Words*, 7. On "objects associated with the private or domestic sphere" as evidence of "emotional connection," see Gordon, *Saturated World*, 201.

7. The cut-out newspaper articles that I found among Anne's papers are denoted "clipping."

8. Baker, "Under the Rope," 320–21; Miller, *Remembering Scottsboro*, 10. For more on newspaper-reading habits, see Dickens, "Time Activities," 8; Rubin, *Plantation County*, 115.

9. "Little Miss King Celebrates Birthday," *TN*, Nov. 23, 1933, 5.

10. On using newspaper reports to analyze social relations, see Davis, Gardner, and Gardner, *Deep South*, 105, 149–70; Palmer, *Domesticity*, 19–20; Cook, "Growing Up," 276.

11. The Alabama Historical Commission reproduced the series by Walter Burkhardt and Varian Feare in a commemorative publication, Burkhardt, Burkhardt, and Alabama Historical Commission, *Ante-Bellum Architecture*, in 1976. All of the Burkhardt-Feare articles appeared originally in the *BNAH* and subsequently in that volume.

12. Swift, "A New Day in Wilcox County," 15; Rubin, *Plantation County*, 116, 118–19, 176–77.

13. Davis, Gardner, and Gardner, *Deep South*, 102, 169.

14. Powdermaker, *After Freedom*; Dollard, *Caste and Class*. See also Johnson, *Shadow of the Plantation*.

15. Agee and Evans, *Famous Men*; Agee, *Cotton Tenants*; Danny Heitman, "Let Us Now Praise James Agee," *Humanities* 33, no. 4 (July/Aug. 2012), National Endowment for the Humanities, www.neh.gov.

16. Kern, *The Jeffersons*, 204; Garvey, *Writing with Scissors*, 209; Johnson, *Shadow of the Plantation*, 17–18.

17. Photocopy of handwritten notes in *The Holy Bible, Old and New Testaments* (New York: American Bible Society, 1864), AFS Collection, UA Special Collections.

18. Christopher, "Autobiography," 1; Application by Percy Larkins DeLoach, Sons of the American Revolution Membership Applications; Laura Jones to EMF, Oct. 30, 1946 (notes from articles in *Virginia Historical Magazine* and other sources), AFS Collection, UA Special Collections. Nancy Ann's father, Thomas Chiles, owned sixteen slaves in 1820 (1820 USFC). For the migration of planters with their slaves, see Tadman, *Speculators and Slaves*, 228.

19. On the small-planter class, see Abernethy, *Formative Period*, 61; Oakes, *Ruling Race*, 76; Hagood, "Rewriting the Frontier," 6.

20. Map, "Choctaw County," UA Alabama Maps. When the community was renamed DeSotoville is unclear. At the time of the Christophers' arrival, the area on the west side of the Tombigbee, where DeSotoville was established, was unmapped; no towns appeared on two maps published in 1833, nor on a map published in 1834 or two published in 1835. Linden, about twenty-six miles to the east, was the closest town. See H. S. Tanner, "A New Map of Alabama," in *Universal Atlas* (Philadelphia: H. S. Tanner, 1833); Anthony Finley, "Alabama" [map] (Philadelphia: A. Finley, 1833); David H. Burr, "A Map of the State of Alabama" (New York: Illman and Pilbrow, 1834); Thomas Gamaliel Bradford, "Alabama" [map] (Boston: T. G. Bradford, 1835); Jeremiah Greenleaf, "Map of the State of Alabama" (Brattleboro, VT: J. Greenleaf, 1835). As late as 1837, no communities in the vicinity of DeSotoville were marked on a map published in New York, although Kinterbish Creek to the north and Tuckabum Creek to the south were labeled, along with "Alligator Ponds" and Brashier's Ferry north of Kinterbish Creek. See John LaTourrette, "An Accurate Map of the State of Alabama and West Florida" (New York: Colton & Co., 1837). In 1840, the state still labeled the entire region "Choctaw Cession of 1830." See James H. Weakley, "A Diagram of the State of Alabama" (Florence, AL: James H. Weakley, Surveyor General of Public Lands in Alabama, 1840). In 1841 a cartographer showed the towns of Moscow, Gaston, and Dansboro nearby but not DeSotoville. See Henry Schenck Tanner, "A New Map of Alabama: With Its Roads & Distances from Place to Place along the Stage and Steam Boat Routes" (Philadelphia: S. A. Mitchell, 1845). All maps mentioned in this note are in UA Alabama Maps.

21. Lanier, "Christopher Chapel," 44; Wiggins and Truss, *Journal of Sarah Haynsworth Gayle*, 3, 7, 22, 24–26, 54, 57, 79, 107. The editors of Gayle's journal identified her minister and neighbor in Greensboro as "William Christopher," but I deduce that they mistakenly interpreted Gayle's handwritten "Griffin" as "William" because Ralph Griffin Christopher is the only adult Christopher male who appears in census records for Greene County for 1820 or 1830, and no William Christopher appears in the Minutes of the Annual Conferences of the Methodist Episcopal Church for the years 1773–1828. Moreover, Gayle made numerous references to members of the Chiles and Crenshaw families in Greensboro who were Griffin Christopher's in-laws.

22. At least two women in Choctaw County died in childbirth during a twelve-month census period two years earlier (USFC Mortality Schedules). On the fear of pregnancy among Confederate women, see Faust, *Mothers of Invention*, 124, 128; Stowe, *Doctoring the South*, 116; Painter, "Introduction," 39; Liddell, *Southern Accent*, 3.

23. Application by Henry Lloyd DeLoach, Sons of the American Revolution Membership Applications; "RE: Morton Christopher of Culpeper Co Va.," Oct. 12, 2007, http://www.ancestry.com.

24. *The Holy Bible, Old and New Testaments* (New York: American Bible Society, 1864), AFS Collection, UA Special Collections.

25. Hall, *Revolt against Chivalry*, 3; Holley, *Medicine in Alabama*, 26–27; Scott, *Invisible Woman*, 194; Wertz and Wertz, *Lying-In*, 110, 118–20; McMillen, *Motherhood*, 32,

54; Faust, *Mothers of Invention*, 123; Stowe, *Doctoring the South*, 5–6.

26. USFC, 1900; CBS, pers. comm.; Find a Grave Index. The grave marker for Simeon and Viola's child at Christopher Chapel Cemetery read "Infant Son of S. W. and Viola Moore." "Christopher Chapel Cemetery," Feb. 1998, Rootsweb.

27. Sisk, "Diseases," 60; Doss, "City Belles," 10–11; McMillen, *Motherhood*, 115, 166–67, 173; Kierner, *Beyond the Household*, 174; Faust, *Republic of Suffering*, 148. Also see Nuwer, *Plague among the Magnolias*. When federal census enumerators in Choctaw County began collecting data about deaths, first for the period from June 1849 to May 1850, 47 percent of the slave deaths and 67 percent of the white deaths were children ten years of age or younger. From June 1859 to May 1860, slightly more than half of the deaths were children ages zero to ten years, with the rates for white and slave children more comparable than during the earlier period. Diarrhea, dysentery, scarlet fever, whooping cough, and "smothering" frequently killed children, but often no one could identify the cause of death (USFC Mortality Schedules). A contemporary of Earline in nearby Gastonburg (Wilcox County), Alabama, Viola Goode Liddell, observed her father's fear that his wife would die in childbirth: "His own mother had lost several children at birth and had herself died at an early age of childbed fever; thus with good reason he had feared this business of having a baby" (Liddell, *Southern Accent*, 3). In 1900, when Earline was four years old, a census enumerator recorded in Rockford, Alabama, that George and Catherine Hatchett's eight-month-old baby, later to be named Tabitha, was known only as "Sister" (1900 USFC).

28. Pleck, *Celebrating the Family*, 25–26.

29. Cardinal, "Memory Painting."

30. Blight, *Race and Reunion*, 283, 286. On the impact of this "legendary material," see Dollard, *Caste and Class*, 365–67, 383–84. "Fantastical," a Middle English variant of "fantastic," is typically used in reference to Arthurian chivalric romances, the material that, in Sir Walter Scott's hands, became the seminal influence on white southern identity. See, for example, Paolini, foreword, vii. The term particularly connotes the distortion of history into fantasy, as works in "the Arthurian canon" describe an "apparently historical medieval past which is in fact fantastical" (Semper, "'My Other World,'" 179).

31. Hague, *Blockaded Family*, 125; Clay-Clopton and Sterling, *Belle of the Fifties*, 6–7; Fry, *Old Cahaba*, 59–60; MacKethan, *Recollections of a Southern Daughter*, xiii. For more on memoirs, see Cook, "Growing Up," 407; Faust, *Mothers of Invention*, 60–61; Hale, *Making Whiteness*, 44, 51; Brundage, "White Women," 126–27.

32. McElya, *Clinging to Mammy*, 54, 56.

33. Blight, *Race and Reunion*, 216–17; Atkins, "The Romantic Ideal," 243–44.

34. Page, *Social Life*; Radford, "Identity and Tradition," 99. On the effect of Old South fiction in teaching lower-class whites "to think correctly," see Bailey, "Patrician Cult," 515.

35. John David Smith, "Ulrich Bonnell Phillips," [April 1, 2003] Aug. 30, 2013, New Georgia Encyclopedia, http://www.georgiaencyclopedia.org.

36. Fleming, "Home Life"; Fleming, *Civil War*, 276–77; W. E. B. Du Bois quoted in Green, "Walter Lynwood Fleming," 498–99, 506–7.

37. James B. Sellers, letter of recommendation, Aug. 18, 1924, collection of Elizabeth Findley Shores (hereafter EFS Collection); *Polk's Tuscaloosa Directory* (1924–25), 240, 273, U.S. Phone and Address Directories; clipping, "Judge Findley Re-Elected," *TN*, March 3, 1938, 1, 2; Doss, introduction, ix–xvi; Sellers, *Slavery in Alabama*, 129, 140, 146–47.

38. Goffman, *Presentation of Self*; Burke, *Cultural History*, 39–40, 93; Gunn, "Analysing Behaviour as Performance."

39. Foster, "Women and Refinement," 201; Brundage, *Southern Past*, 119, 184, 225. See also Wyatt-Brown, *Southern Honor*, 331; Stowe, *Intimacy and Power*, 1; Gulley, "Women and the Lost Cause"; Bailey, "Patrician Cult"; Brundage, "White Women"; Brundage, "'Woman's Hand'"; Cox, *Dixie's Daughters*.

40. Brundage, *Southern Past*, 119.

41. Noe, *Reluctant Rebels*, 46.

42. Fleming, *Civil War*, 276–77.

43. Sterkx, *Partners in Rebellion*, 11.

44. Rubin, *Plantation County*, 25–26.

45. Cash, *Mind of the South*, 4–5.

46. Cleveland, "Social Conditions in Alabama," 20.

47. Fry, *Old Cahaba*, 61–62.

48. Cash, *Mind of the South*, 20–21; Davis, Gardner, and Gardner, *Deep South*, 88.

49. Page, *Social Life*, quoted in Seidel, *Southern Belle*, 129–31.

50. Scott, *Southern Lady*, 4, 23; Cook, "Growing Up," 3–4, 8; Bleser and Heath, "The Clays of Alabama," 135; Roberts, *Confederate Belle*, 32. On beauty as a cultural imperative, see Jabour, *Scarlett's Sisters*; Roberts, *Pageants, Parlors, and Pretty Women*, 16; Wilson, *Judgment and Grace*, 145, 150.

51. Goffman, *Presentation of Self*, 38; Wyatt-Brown, "Mask of Obedience"; Goldfield, *Black, White, and Southern*, 3; Pleck, *Celebrating the Family*, 210; Blight, *Race and Reunion*, 286–87. For broader overviews of the historical scholarship on southern class identity and race relations, see Boucher, "Wealthy Planter Families"; O'Brien, *American South*; Foner, *Reconstruction*; Hall, "Partial Truths"; Doss, introduction.

52. Massey, *Reminiscences*, 28. See also Tompkins, *Cotton-Patch Schoolhouse*, 79–80.

53. Bailey, "Patrician Cult," 513; Egerton, *Speak Now*, 588; McGovern, *Anatomy of a Lynching*, 5; Brundage, "White Women," 115–17, 134.

54. Egerton, *Speak Now*, 38, 606–8.

55. Powdermaker, *After Freedom*, x; Bernstein, *Racial Innocence*, 6–8. Planter aristocrats never spoke the word "slave," according to the fantastical novelist John Fox Jr.: "the negroes were 'our servants' or 'our people'" (*Little Shepherd*, 175). Mary Wallace Kirk, a privileged white woman who was Earline's contemporary, demonstrated this "not-noticing" in her memoir of her family home in Tuscumbia, Alabama, reflecting fondly on the African American servants who worked for her parents and for her without ever acknowledging their ethnicity (Kirk, *Locust Hill*, 26–27).

56. Wilson, *Baptized in Blood*, 16.

57. Clay-Clopton and Sterling, *Belle of the Fifties*, 6.

58. Goffman, *Presentation of Self*, 17.

59. Fox-Genovese, *Plantation Household*, 27.

60. Burke, *Cultural History*, 123.

Chapter 1

1. Burke, *Eyewitnessing*, 23; Tucker, *Telling Memories*, 266.

2. Photographs of the Moore children, circa 1901 and 1905, one courtesy of VRMK, both EFS Collection. The youngest child, Charles Otis Moore, was born around 1904 and appears to be about a year old in the second photograph (1910 USFC).

3. Rand McNally and Company, "Alabama" [map], in *Enlarged Business Atlas and Shipper's Guide* (Chicago: Rand McNally and Company, 1910), UA Alabama Maps; Henderson, *Smith's Alabama*, 64, 142–43. The road that linked York and Butler could "only by the most charitable use of the word . . . be described as a road" (Rogers and Ward, *August Reckoning*, 47).

4. For descriptions and views of the rural countryside, see Yerby and Lawson, *Greensboro*, 25; Hickman, *Mississippi Harvest*, plate vii; Dorothea Lange, "A Note on Transportation: Eden, Alabama," Prints and Photographs Online Catalog, Library of Congress; Natural Resources Conservation Service, *Soil Survey of Choctaw County*, 12; Brundage, *Southern Past*, 185–88.

5. Schlereth, "Country Stores," 346–47; Cromley, *Food Axis*, 111; Agnew, "A House of Fiction," 13; Bryden and Floyd, *Domestic Space*, 7; Graffam, "'They Are Very Handy,'" 231.

6. Photograph, "Aunt Bettie Moore," EFS Collection; Bettie Bennett Moore to Viola Taylor Moore, March 18, 1911, courtesy of CBS.

7. CBS, pers. comm.; photographs, "Viola Taylor Moores [*sic*] home in Petal MS rare north side view" and "Viola Taylor Moores [*sic*] home in Petal MS 2," photographs courtesy of CBS.

8. On the white house as a status symbol, see Bernard, Duke of Saxe-Weimar-Eisenach, *Travels through North America during the Years 1825 and 1826* (Philadelphia: Carey, Lea, and Carey, 1828), 2:26–31, quoted in Benton, *The Very Worst Road*, 33; Cash, *Mind of the South*, 15–16; Sellers, *Slavery in Alabama*, 20; Jordan, *Hugh Davis*, 83; Clark, *Pills*, 34; Le Guin, *Home-Concealed Woman*, 66; Benjamin H. Locke, "The Community Life of a Harlem Group of Negroes" (master's thesis, Columbia University, 1913), 10–16, quoted in Katzman, *Seven Days a Week*, 210; Writers' Program of the Work Projects Administration, *WPA Guide*, 244; Topp, *Smile Please*, 253.

9. Vlach, *Big House*, 163; James E. Breeden, ed., *Advice among Masters: The Ideal of Slave Management in the Old South* (Westport, CT: Greenwood, 1980), 130, quoted in Vlach, "'Snug Li'l House,'" 120.

10. Booker T. Washington, the leading proponent of "Negro uplift," encouraged African Americans to paint their houses, warning that unpainted houses were a "Negro earmark," although the historian Edward L. Ayers speculated it was safer for blacks to leave their houses unpainted because painting them might seem presumptuous. Blight, *Race and Reunion*, 319; "At Home and Afield: Hampton Incidents," *Southern Workman* 43 (1914): 704; Ayers, *New South*, 210. Also see Ritterhouse, *Growing Up Jim*

Crow, 47; John Hayes, "Recovering the Class-Conscious New South," *Journal of Southern Religion* 13 (2011), http://jsreligion.org.

11. Wood, *Nigger*, 87–88.

12. Handwritten notes in *The New Testament* (New York: Daniel D. Smith, 1823), AFS Collection, UA Special Collections.

13. Clear Creek Baptist Church Historical Society Committee, "Clear Creek Baptist Church," 150; Gay, *Choctaw Names*, 22; Wood, "Christopher Family," 83.

14. USFC, 1880; clipping, "In Memoriam" (newspaper unknown); clipping, T. W. Allen, W. H. Christopher, and C. F. Britt, "Tribute of Respect," *Choctaw Advocate*. Annie's father, John Chiles Christopher, must have belonged to DeSotoville Lodge #178, as his grave marker bore the symbol of the Freemasons ("John Childs [*sic*] Son of G. R. [*sic*] & A. T. Christopher"). For the relationships of men in Victorian fraternal organizations, see Campbell-Everden, *Freemasonry*, 12; Dumenil, *Freemasonry*, 19; Bullock, *Revolutionary Brotherhood*, 244–45, 314; Hubbs, *Guarding Greensboro*, 31.

15. Wood, "Christopher Family," 83. Frank Evans Christopher was a physician by 1900 (1900 USFC). Walter Henry Christopher received a medical degree from the Memphis Hospital Medical College in 1901 (Directory of Deceased American Physicians). John Chiles Christopher Jr. was a physician in 1910 (1910 USFC). See also obituary, "Dr. John Childs [*sic*] Christopher," http://www.ancestry.com; Alabama Board of Health, *Transactions*, 558.

16. Several facts point to a longstanding acquaintance of the Christopher and Moore families in DeSotoville. First, Mallard's grandfather helped Annie's uncle James Monroe DeLoach establish the private academy in the town in 1852. Second, Mallard's mother's family, the Jarrells, owned slaves named George and Adaline, who presumably were named for Nancy Ann Chiles Christopher's cousin and cousin-in-law George and Adaline Perrin. Third, someone recorded in the family Bible that Annie's aunt Laura Fitch Christopher delivered her first baby in 1859 "on the Jerrold place," apparently a misspelled reference to the Jarrells' home since there was no family named Jerrold in the vicinity. Ann H. Gay, comp., "Christopher Chapel Methodist Church Record Book," transcript, 1995.

17. Wood, "Christopher Family," 83–84; clipping, Martha Sue Christopher Baker, "Frank Evans Christopher, M.D."

18. *The New Testament* (New York: Daniel D. Smith, 1823), AFS Collection, UA Special Collections. Annie also recorded the facts of her marriage in another Bible, misspelling her husband's middle name as "Malard." Annie Christopher Moore Bible, courtesy of VRMK.

19. Foscue, *Place Names*, 76; Carnes, *Secret Ritual*, 35; Bullock, *Revolutionary Brotherhood*, 244–45, 314.

20. Johnson and Libecap, *The Federal Civil Service System*, 32–34. See appendix 1, this book.

21. Clark, *Pills*, 37–38; Schlereth, "Country Stores," 345; Ownby, *American Dreams*, 8. W. G. Bevill was both a postmaster and merchant in Choctaw County as early as 1878. Berney, *Handbook of Alabama*, 322.

22. Bible and card courtesy of VRMK, EFS Collection. Later a marker engraved

"Infant Son of R. M. and Annie Moore, Nov. 23, 1892–May 9, 1894; 1 Year 5 Months, 16 Days" was added to the grave. "Infant Son of R. M. and Annie Moore," Christopher Chapel Cemetery.

23. U.S. World War I Draft Registration Cards; 1910 USFC.

24. Ann H. Gay, "1907 Courthouse Had No Running Water, No Electricity, No Phones," *Choctaw Sun-Advocate*, Aug. 22, 2007, 6B, ChoctawSun.org; Deutsch, *Housewife's Paradise*, 16, 18.

25. Walter Hines Page, "The Forgotten Man" (typescript of commencement address given at the North Carolina Normal and Industrial Institute, May 19, 1897), quoted in McCandless, "Progressivism," 303. See also Grantham, *Southern Progressivism*, 250.

26. Census records show that William Carl Moore, who only completed the eighth grade, and Bettie Bennett Moore had no live-in help in 1910. Simeon Walton Moore and Viola Taylor Moore had no live-in help in 1900, and by 1910 Sim had died and Viola, still with no live-in servants, had taken in two boarders. Annie's sister-in-law Mary Caroline Moore Lockard had a live-in black cook named Clara. Her sister-in-law Kate Christopher had a live-in cook, Maggie Dunn, and her brother John Christopher's wife, Mollie, had four live-in black servants, three "hired boys," and a twenty-eight-year-old cook, Livy Bryant. *The New Testament* (New York: Daniel D. Smith, 1823), AFS Collection, UA Special Collections; 1900, 1910 USFC.

27. Tucker, *Telling Memories*, 272.

28. Tom Dillard, Glenn Jones, and Bob Ross, Arkansas History Discussion Group (listserv), Jan. 26, 2012.

29. Henderson, *Smith's Alabama*, 49, 120.

30. For examples of white women in families of any means who felt that daily domestic labor was an imposition, see Griffith, *Alabama*, 531; Horton, *Family Quilts*, 110; Le Guin, *Home-Concealed Woman*, 58, 91, 169–70.

31. See appendix 2, this book. Lanier, "Christopher Chapel," 44; 1870 USFC.

32. Doss, "City Belles," 7–8; Fox-Genovese, *Plantation Household*, 111–12, 116, 118, 334; Kierner, *Beyond the Household*, 171–72; Myers, "Black Human Capital," 170, 175; Harris, *Plain Folk and Gentry*, 38; Roberts, *Confederate Belle*, 149.

33. Earline's family lived in Enumeration District 11 of Precinct 2 of Choctaw County. When her uncle Walter H. Christopher was the federal census enumerator in 1900, the district had 300 households. Of these, 217, or 72.3 percent, were African American. Of the African American households, 140 (64.5 percent) were tenant farmers and 47 were farm laborers or day laborers. The other 30 black heads of households owned their farms, but 12 of those had mortgages. The Moores' closest white neighbors, if the 1900 census enumerator visited them in door-to-door order, were Judge Charles Campbell McCall and his wife and their two grandchildren; C. Dave Strickland and his wife and three-year-old daughter; and Dave Flowers and his wife, whose daughters were six, eight, and ten years old. No other whites lived close enough to Mallard and Annie to appear on the same page of census records, and only three other white families appeared on the four pages before and four pages after the entry for Mallard's household (1900 USFC). On census enumerators going door to door, see Owsley, *Plain Folk*, 9. On rural post offices, see Melius, *Postal Service*, 24; Johnson, *Shadow of the Plantation*, 11; Clark, *Pills*, 32, 39, 52, 76; Genovese, "'Rather Be

a Nigger'"; Flynt, *Poor But Proud*, 215–16. On crossroads general stores as centers of community life, see Stover, *Railroads of the South*, 212; Foner, *Reconstruction*, 47; Bull, "The General Merchant." On relations between whites and blacks in country general stores, see Grim, "African American Rural Culture," 119; Walker, "Shifting Boundaries," 85–87; Ritterhouse, *Growing Up Jim Crow*, 43–44. Concerning quotations of the word "nigger," I use them only when the word's use is related to an important point. I use "African American" in most instances but sometimes employ "black" when the dichotomy of blackness and whiteness is central to the meaning of the passage. As the art historian Dora Apel has commented, the terms "white" and "black . . . must be understood as relational terms of identity that depend on each other for meaning" (*Lynching Photographs*, 86n2).

34. Hague, *Blockaded Family*, 153; Fry, *Old Cahaba*, 32; McIlwain, "Harry: Faithful Unto Death," 28. Also see Sellers, *Slavery in Alabama*, 247–48, 253.

35. Brown and Owens, *Toting the Lead Row*, 10. A program of the Works Progress Administration or WPA (renamed the Work Projects Administration in 1939), the Federal Writers Project collected oral histories from hundreds of former slaves during the 1930s (Jackson, introduction, ix–x). Tartt's great-grandfather Hiram Chiles was a cousin of Amanda Chiles, who married into the Crenshaw family just as Earline's great-great-aunt Mary Chiles did. Darby Chiles, "Fifth Generation," Rootsweb; Application by Henry Noland Crenshaw, U.S. Sons of the American Revolution Membership Applications; "Ruby Pickens Tartt Collection" [finding aid], UWA.

36. After construction of Livingston Methodist Church was completed in 1838, Griffin Christopher became its first pastor (Lazenby, *Methodism in Alabama and West Florida*, 206; Card Index of Personal Corporate Names and Subjects; clipping, Frank S. Moseley, "Another Early Alabama Hero"). His widow continued to live in Sumter County after he died the following year (1840 USFC). Of the 217 African American heads of households in Enumeration District 11 in Choctaw County in 1900, 184 were born in or before 1864. Some shared names with relatives of Earline's mother: a day laborer, Ellen Fitch (b. 1850); L. DeLoach (b. 1840); W. Thompson (b. 1853). There was Henry Slay (b. 1843) and the minister, N. Slay, a slaveholder who performed Annie's father's first marriage. Sam McCall (b. 1831), Henry McCall (b. 1852), and Fannie McCall (b. 1857) probably were held by the extended McCall family that lived in DeSotoville. Seven African Americans who were at least ten years old at the end of the Civil War—Ben Ezell (b. 1832), Dan Ezell (b. 1836), Clark Ezell (b. 1845), Nancy Ezell (b. 1845), Ann Ezell (b. 1850), John Ezell (b. 1853), and Tom Ezell (b. 1854)—shared their surname with the family that Earline's brother J. C. married into (1900 USFC).

37. Blassingame, "Testimony of Ex-Slaves"; Escott, *Slavery Remembered*; Fox-Genovese, *Plantation Household*, 32–33; Kammen, *Mystic Chords*, 122; Vlach, *Big House*, xiii.

38. Brown and Taylor, *Gabr'l Blow Sof'*, vii–viii. Regarding Tartt's use of patois, reproduced here, see the cultural anthropologist Zora Neale Hurston's contemporaneous use of patois: "Zora Neale Hurston," *Encyclopedia Britannica*, http://www.britannica.com/biography/Zora-Neale-Hurston; Williams, "Janie's Burden," 99; Alice Walker, "On Refusing to Be Humbled by Second Place in a Contest You Did Not Design," in Bloom, *Zora Neale Hurston*, 103.

39. Brown and Taylor, *Gabr'l Blow Sof'*, 23, 17, 25, 81, 77, 19. In a study of more than

two thousand interviews, the historian Paul D. Escott found that whippings and beatings were "the most universal complaint" in ex-slave narratives (*Slavery Remembered*, 40–42, 54–55).

40. Jordan, *Hugh Davis*, 101. For more on the use of bloodhounds in manhunts, see Campbell, "The Seminoles," 268–70; Franklin and Schweninger, *Runaway Slaves*, 156–64; Harris, *Plain Folk and Gentry*, 176–77; "Recollections of Slavery by a Runaway Slave," *Emancipator*, Sept. 13, 1838, Documenting the American South.

41. Charity Grigsby, interview by Ruby Pickens Tartt, in Born in Slavery: Slave Narratives from the Federal Writers' Project, 1936–1938.

42. Brown and Taylor, *Gabr'l Blow Sof'*, 108. George Young, who apparently was named for his former master, may have felt safe in describing the vicious dog attack because George the slaveholder had died in 1929 (Deaths and Burials Index). Harrison Young apparently survived this treatment and by 1870 lived in the Belmont area of the county and had a son named George (1870 USFC).

43. Franklin and Schweninger, *Runaway Slaves*, 115.

44. Records of the [South Carolina] General Assembly, 1859 #59, and Petition 20184006, Digital Library on American Slavery.

45. Massey, *Reminiscences*, 34; Enna "Big Babe" Mitchell, interview, March 1982, http://www.ancestry.com.

46. USFC Mortality Schedules, 1850–1885; "Burwell Boykin, 1787–1860," http://www.ancestry.com.

47. Sellers, *Slavery in Alabama*, 262–63.

48. Harris, *Plain Folk and Gentry*, 7, 175–76.

49. Roark, *Masters without Slaves*, 15–16, 74–75, 124. See also Faust, *Mothers of Invention*, 51–58; Noe, *Reluctant Rebels*, 55; Eckinger, "Militarization of the University of Alabama," 177.

50. Reid, "The Negro in Alabama," 275; Myers, "Black Human Capital," 40–41; Brundage, *Lynching in the New South*, 5–6.

51. Griffith, *Alabama*, 481; Foner, *Reconstruction*, 271.

52. Brown and Taylor, *Gabr'l Blow Sof'*, 23, 17; USFC Non-Population Schedules; 1850, 1860 USFC. Reuben Chapman "Jr." was the son of the Livingston lawyer Samuel Chapman and a nephew of Reuben Chapman, the thirteenth governor of Alabama. John Mayfield, "Reuben Chapman (1847–49)," *Encyclopedia of Alabama*, http://www.encyclopediaofalabama.org [May 13, 2008] Sept. 30, 2014.

53. Reuben Chapman Jr., testimony, Nov. 4, 1871, in Joint Select Committee, *House Report*, 1940–53. Dozens of African American families, including Amanda Childers, age nine, and her parents and siblings, whom the enumerator categorized as mulatto, lived in Bluff Port in 1870. The planter William Jones owned land worth four times as much as the next-wealthiest landowner in the community. By 1880, Jones had moved to the town of Livingston and claimed to be a civil engineer, while Amanda's father was dead and her mother had moved to Mississippi with her younger sister (1870, 1880 USFC).

54. Justices of the peace could collect fees, keeping a portion to cover their expenses (George F. Moore Esq., "The Justice of the Peace," in Alabama State Bar Association,

Thirteenth Annual Meeting, 161). The only other adult man named Christopher recorded living in the county in 1870 was John's brother Thomas, who was deaf and therefore not likely to have been a justice of the peace (1870 USFC).

55. Daniel McCall, testimony, Nov. 3, 1871, Joint Select Committee, *House Report*, 1899–1916; 1880, 1900 USFC. McCall, his wife, and two of his children were buried at Christopher Chapel. "Christopher Chapel Cemetery," Cemeteries by Sarah Mozingo, Feb. 1998, Rootsweb.

56. Myers, "Black Human Capital," 14; Bruce, *Violence and Culture*, 57–58; Roberts, *Confederate Belle*, 161.

57. Daniel Herd Brown was born Aug. 4, 1870 (Find a Grave Index).

58. Rogers and Ward, *August Reckoning*, 35, 70, 147, 150; 1880 USFC.

59. Mathews, "Lynching," 160; Mathews, "Southern Rite of Human Sacrifice," 44–47; Smith, "Lynching Photographs," 17; Yerby and Lawson, *Greensboro*, 147; Sisk, "Diseases," 54; Tolnay and Beck, *Festival of Violence*, 267; Brantley, *From Cabins to Mansions*, 261; Wood, *Nigger*, 3–5; Raper, *Tragedy of Lynching*, 9; Cash, *Mind of the South*, 115–16, quoted in Cobb, *Away Down South*, 175; Bardaglio, *Reconstructing the Household*, 189; Case, "Historical Ideology," 616; Mathews, "Lynching," 160; Dollard, *Caste and Class*, quoted in Griffin, Clark, and Sandberg, "Narrative and Event," 27; Ritterhouse, *Growing Up Jim Crow*, 25, 50. See Brundage, *Lynching in the New South*, 9–11, for the changing views of scholars on the origin of the sexual predator myth. For examples of manhunts with bloodhounds, see "Fear Lynching in Kentucky," *TN*, Sept. 27, 1910, 1; "May Lynch Indiana Negro," *TN*, Nov. 3, 1910, 1; "Lynching in Alabama," *Sacramento Daily Union*, Nov. 13, 1897, 1, and AP, "Troops Ordered Out to Prevent Lynching," *Los Angeles Herald*, July 17, 1905, both in California Digital Newspaper Collection, http://cdnc.ucr.edu/cgi-bin/cdnc; "The Nigger Dogs," *Montreal Gazette*, reprinted from *New York Sun*, Aug. 19, 1899, 7, Google News.

60. Hawthorne, *A Wonder Book*. See appendix 3, this book. On the analysis of inscriptions in books, see Hayes, *Colonial Woman's Bookshelf*, ix, xii, 8. Simeon Walton Moore gave up farming and moved with his wife, Viola, for a job in a sawmill in Petal, Mississippi; by 1909 he was dead from a workplace injury (1900 USFC; CBS, pers. comm.; "Simeon Walton Moore Sr. headstone," photograph courtesy of CBS). Annie's brothers Frank Evans Christopher and Charles Hamilton Christopher moved to Isney, where Frank practiced medicine and Charles became a postmaster. For the family's postmaster appointments, see appendix 1, this book. The Moore and Frank Christopher residences were separated by six residences in the census records. Later Charles married and moved to Meridian, Mississippi (1900, 1910 USFC). After the Choctaw Lumber Company was established at Bolinger, eight miles from Isney, in 1915, Frank became the company physician (clipping, Martha Sue Christopher Baker, "Frank Evans Christopher, M.D."). In 1915 the nearest railway station to Isney was five miles away at Fail, the northern end of the Choctaw Railway (U.S. General Land Office, *State of Alabama* [map] [Washington, DC: Department of Interior, 1915], UA Alabama Maps). Most of the residents of the family's census precinct in Isney reported their occupations as farmer or farm laborer on a "home farm" or "general farm" (1910 USFC). Walter Henry Christopher also moved to Isney and then to Lisman (Wood, "Christopher

Family," 84). By 1912, Lula was the postmistress in Lisman. Earline's maternal grandparents, John Chiles Christopher and Ann Elizabeth Christopher, also apparently lived in Lisman at the end of their lives. Alabama Board of Health, *Transactions*, 558; Directory of Deceased American Physicians; Application by Annie Elizabeth Fitch Christopher, Confederate Pension and Service Records.

61. Cook, "Growing Up," 314; clipping, T. W. Allen, W. H. Christopher, and C. F. Britt, "Tribute of Respect," *Choctaw Advocate*; Owen, *Statistical Register*, 260; Bettie Moore to Viola Moore, March 18, 1911, and Nov. 19, 1912, and Annie Moore to Viola Moore, April 17, 1932, all courtesy of CBS; Annie Christopher Moore Bible, courtesy of VRMK. A Methodist minister declared "one of the most sacred of a life of pleasant memories is the old family temperance pledge in the family Bible of my father and mother, each of whose children signed the pledge at nine years of age" (Baker, "Practical Methods"). A photograph shows Simeon standing on a street corner in Hattiesburg, Mississippi, in about 1907, "enjoying a glass of beer with friends while holding hands with his wife, Viola. It appears she doesn't want to be in the picture!" "Simeon Walton Moore Sr.," photograph courtesy of CBS.

62. Clark, *Pills*, 30, 43, 137, 237; Schlereth, "Country Stores," 344–45; Trachtenberg, *Reading American Photographs*, xiv–xv, 88; Roth, "Scrapbook Houses," 301, 316; Smith, *American Archives*, 118; Batchen, *Forget Me Not*, 49, 57; Gordon, *Saturated World*, 7, 39; Ott, Tucker, and Buckler, "History of Scrapbooks," 3; Lee, introduction, 4; Helfand, *Scrapbooks*; Ware, "Writing Women's Lives," 427; Garvey, *Writing with Scissors*, 16.

63. Ziegler, *Schools in the Landscape*, 62.

64. Jabour, *Scarlett's Sisters*, 31–33; Howett, *World of Her Own Making*, 309. In 1909, when Earline was fourteen years old and probably highly attuned to society's expectations of white girls, a newspaper in Mobile, Alabama, described a young bride as "one of Tuscaloosa's loveliest girls [who] has hosts of admirers[,] thoroughly charming[,] a perfect blonde [whose] features are delicate and flower-like and [who] is graceful and dainty in her manner and quite bright and attractive." "Engagement of Miss Cribbs and Mr. Mann of Much Interest Here," *Pensacola (FL) Journal*, Aug. 27, 1909, 5, Chronicling America.

65. "Anne Elizabeth Fitch Christopher," photograph courtesy of JCM.

66. "Maranda Savanah Jarrell Moore," photograph courtesy of CBS; Foy, "The Home Set to Music," 66–67.

67. Stowe, *Intimacy and Power*, 170; Glover, *All Our Relations*, 30.

68. AFS to Virginia Ezell Moore and VRMK (carbon), EFS Collection.

69. *The Holy Bible*. See appendix 3, this book.

70. AFS, pers. comm.

Chapter 2

1. The Alabama Normal School reported Earline was a graduate of Isney High School, indicating it was not affiliated with the normal school, but did not give the year of her graduation. *State Normal School Quarterly* (1916), 60, UWA.

2. AFS, pers. comm.

3. Clipping, Martha Sue Christopher Baker, "Frank Evans Christopher, M.D.";

"Bachelor of Science Class, 1919," in University of Alabama, *War Corolla* (1919), 244; Powdermaker, *After Freedom*, 21; Grantham, *Southern Progressivism*, 269; McCandless, "Progressivism," 322.

4. Card Index of Personal Corporate Names and Subjects; clipping, Frank S. Moseley, "Another Early Alabama Hero for the Cross" (Alabama Conference Historical Society, 1958).

5. George W. Brock, the president of Alabama Normal School, noted in 1918 that Earline "has had experience in teaching rural schools." G. W. Brock, letter of recommendation, April 12, 1918, EFS Collection.

6. *State Normal School Quarterly* (1916), 18, 20, 56, 60, UWA. Earline inscribed her copy of Shakespeare's *As You Like It* "Earline Moore[,] S. N. S.[,] Sept. 25, 16." See appendix 3, this book.

7. Darnell, *Victorian to Vamp*, 53, 59.

8. Willie Perry, *The Girl Graduate: Her Own Book*, scrapbook, UWA. On memory books marketed to students, see Helfand, *Scrapbooks*, 113–16.

9. Mrs. Pitt Lamar Matthews, "Livingston Girls of Mobile Return," *Mobile (AL) Register*, June 3, 1917, UWA. The young historian Walter Fleming described African American servants in another Alabama college town, Auburn, in a remarkable essay in the *Sewanee Review*, explaining that old servants, who probably were born into slavery, made "the best and most willing servants" and implying that he was quoting a former slave who did "not approve of the course of 'dese hyeh young niggers' [who] will not stay long enough in one place" to be adequately trained ("The Servant Problem in a Black Belt Village," 11).

10. *State Normal School Quarterly* (1917), 52, UWA; photograph, President G. W. Brock with instructors, UWA; 1920 USFC; Paul Davis, "`Amazing Grace' Ends 47 Years of School Work," *TN*, May 27, 1966, 8. Brock was so conservative that as a state teacher examiner he required every applicant to submit three character references attesting to the fact that the applicant did not drink. Ziegler, *Schools in the Landscape*, 58.

11. *State Normal School Quarterly* (1916), 26, UWA.

12. George, *Selections*. See appendix 3, this book.

13. AFS, pers. comm.

14. Grave marker, "Robert Mallard Moore," Christopher Chapel Cemetery.

15. G. W. Brock, letter of recommendation, April 12, 1918, EFS Collection. As a graduate of the state teacher training program, Earline was "entitled to a first grade state certificate in addition to a standard normal diploma." *State Normal School Quarterly* (1916), 24, UWA.

16. AFS, pers. comm.; Barbara Burrow, "Thirty-Two Years on a Job; She Stays Young," *TN*, Dec. 29, 1950, 8; 1920 USFC.

17. Hubbs, *Tuscaloosa*, 57; "Holt, Alabama, in 1918," photograph AIS.2006.06, Rust Engineering Company Records; "For Export: Utilizing the Great Warrior River Waterway to the Gulf," photograph Q9658, ADAH Digital Collections.

18. Flynt, *Alabama*, 382; Bristow, *American Pandemic*, 43–45; Tompkins, *Cotton-Patch Schoolhouse*, 12–13; Blackman, *Brow of the Hill*, 42–43.

19. Photograph, "Stallworth Lake, circa 1925," in Betty Slowe, "Looking Back:

Stallworth Lake," *TN*, May 21, 2010. For a detailed description of the dummy line, see Singleton and Brown, *Foundry Life*, unnumbered pages. On the popularity of amusement parks and trolley parks in the 1920s, see Kammen, *American Culture*, 24.

20. University of Alabama, *War Corolla* (1919), 233; U.S. World War I Draft Registration Cards; Owen and Owen, *History of Alabama*, 2:1274; Blackman, *Brow of the Hill*, 42; Hubbs, *Tuscaloosa*, 60; Robert DeWitt, "Construction Reveals Tuscaloosa Trolley Tracks," *TN*, July 8, 2010.

21. Foy, "The Home Set to Music," 71; "Con Conrad," Songwriters Hall of Fame, songwritershalloffame.org. The Findleys' sheet music is part of the AFS Collection, UA Special Collections.

22. Porter, *Pollyanna Grows Up*; Lee, *Mary Pickford*. See also appendix 3, this book. On popular novels and films as evidence about the "ethos" of middle-class housewives in the period 1920–45, see Palmer, *Domesticity*, 19–20; Bernstein, *Racial Innocence*, 11.

23. Ten years earlier Eliza lived with her grandparents and an uncle in Clarke County (1910 USFC).

24. Rauner Special Collections Library, "The Papers of Eleanor H. Porter in the Dartmouth College Library" [finding aid], Dartmouth College, http://ead.dartmouth.edu/html/index_ab.html; Overton, *The Women Who Make Our Novels*, 111. Porter and her husband married in 1892 and lived in Springfield, Vermont, by 1900, so they lived in Chattanooga between 1892 and 1900 (1900 USFC).

25. Cook, "Growing Up," 66, 274, 406; Seaton, "A Pedigree for a New Century," 279; Porter, *Pollyanna Grows Up*, 184–86, 281–82, 292–93.

26. Barbara Burrow, "Thirty-Two Years on a Job; She Stays Young," *TN*, Dec. 29, 1950, 8.

27. A fence in the background of one of Earline's photographs appears identical to the fences in a view of a Holt park, seen from the base of one of the village's steep "short streets," in a photograph taken for Rust Engineering in 1918. The bare-swept yard had a recently built picket fence, and a few tall, spindly trees in the background indicate a recently cleared landscape, just as in the Rust pictures (Rust Engineering Company Records), U. of Pittsburgh Digital Reasearch Library, digital.library.pitt.edu.

28. *Polk's Meridian Directory* (1913–14), 2:165, U.S. Phone and Address Directories; VRMK, pers. comm.; Deaths and Burials Index. Annie's house was at 1511 35th Avenue (1920 USFC).

29. "Queen and Crescent Route," Railroad History, http://railga.com/queencres.html; Matthew W. Clinton, "Building the Dummy Line," *TN*, Feb. 25, 1968, 4; Henderson, *Smith's Alabama*, 220; Robert DeWitt, "Construction Reveals Tuscaloosa Trolley Tracks," *TN*, July 8, 2010.

30. Tuscaloosa County Preservation Society, *Past Horizons*, 8.

31. "Jemison-van de Graaf-Burchfield House"; photographs, "Slave Quarters, Eddins House, 919 Greensboro Ave., Tuscaloosa," Dec. 19, 1934; "University of Alabama President's House," Oct. 16, 1935; "Smoke House and Dairy . . . Slave Cabin No. 2," Oct. 16, 1935; "Slave House, North Side—Martin-Randolph-Marlowe House," Oct. 16, 1935, courtesy HABS; photograph, "Wm. Battle or deGraffenreid House, 1217 Greensboro Avenue," Carnegie Survey of the Architecture of the South. On slave quarters as a

public indicator of a homeowner's status, see Vlach, *Big House*, 153.

32. Davis, Gardner, and Gardner, *Deep South*, 189, 199; *Polk's Meridian Directory* (1956), 12, U.S. Phone and Address Directories; 1930 USFC; Barbara Burrow, "Thirty-Two Years on a Job; She Stays Young," *TN*, Dec. 29, 1950, 8; Paul Davis, "'Amazing Grace' Ends 47 Years of School Work," *TN*, May 26, 1966, 1.

33. The historian Anne Firor Scott suggested that scholars "can only guess" at how southern women felt about joining the workforce, but Earline's subsequent choices make her attitude toward teaching clear. As Kenneth Ames observed, "People are motivated as much by negative drives as they are by positive. . . . To put the matter more prosaically, many cultural accomplishments have been propelled by a strong desire *not* to be confused with or associated with other people." Scott, *Southern Lady*, 213; Ames, introduction, 8.

34. Hundley, *Social Relations*, 74, quoted in Scott, *Southern Lady*, 3, 6.

35. Tuscaloosa High School, *The Black Warrior* (1912); University of Alabama, *Corolla* (1915), unnumbered page; U.S. World War I Draft Registration Cards; Certificate, Field Artillery Central Officers' Training School, Camp Zachary Taylor, HLF Jr. Scrapbook, courtesy of MKF; Alabama National Guard Index Cards; 1920 USFC; "20 Years Ago Today," *TN*, July 28, 1940, 4; *Miller's Tuscaloosa Directory* (1922), 85, U.S. Phone and Address Directories; "Judge Findley Re-Elected," *TN*, March 3, 1938, 1, 2; clipping, "Death Claims Murk Findley," *TN*, April 22, 1941, 1, 2; "Judge Herbert Findley Resigns Court Position," *TN*, Aug. 21, 1946, 1. The stretch of U.S. Highway 11 that runs through Tuscaloosa has been known as the Huntsville Road, the Birmingham Highway, Broad Street, University Avenue, and University Boulevard (Tommy Stevenson, "U.S. 11 History Mirrors Area Needs," *TN*, Aug. 13, 1989, 1B, 8B). At the time Earline and Herbert Findley were married, the section in front of the Findley home was known as University Avenue, as indicated by the 1920 USFC, for which an enumerator labeled the page containing the Findley record "University Avenue" and the following page "Huntsville Road" (1920 USFC, Courthouse Beat, District 120, Sheet 30 of 31). As recently as 1941, it was known simultaneously as University Avenue and the Birmingham Highway, as indicated by addresses on notes written to HLF Jr. on April 27 and May 12: one was addressed to "Mr. Lyman Findley, B'ham Highway, Tuscaloosa, Ala.," and the other to "Mr. Lyman Findly [*sic*], 329 University Avenue, City" (HLF Jr. Scrapbook, courtesy of MKF). I use "University Avenue" because this is the term that the Findleys used during Earline's lifetime.

36. Hilliard, *De Vane*; Foster, "Women and Refinement," 189–90; Atkins, "The Romantic Ideal," 242–44; Massey, *Reminiscences*, 13; Scott, *Ivanhoe*, 78–79, 318, 505–8; Howett, "Graces and Modest Majesties," 88; Howett, *World of Her Own Making*, 30; Hagood, "Rewriting the Frontier," 5–8, 35. On the ubiquity of Scott's work in southern homes and classrooms, see Cook, "Growing Up," 12–13, 226. On the role of Scott's fiction in the development of romantic Highlander culture in the United States, see Ray, *Highland Heritage*, 17–19, 30. That Herbert enjoyed this genre is evident from another volume, *Mistress Wilding* by Rafael Sabatini, that he acquired at the age of thirty-seven. See appendix 3, this book.

37. Shapiro, *Appalachia*, 30; Fox, *Little Shepherd*, 47, 143, 4, 170–71, 192, 197, 308,

317. See appendix 3, this book. On regional reconciliation as a theme of turn-of-the-century popular literature, see Blight, *Race and Reunion*, 211.

38. Richards, *Gene Stratton Porter*, 123–24; Stratton-Porter, *The Harvester*, 12, 16–18, 176, 256. See appendix 3, this book.

39. "Golden Wedding Anniversary," *TN*, Sept. 14, 1970, 8.

40. MKF, pers. comm. Archie Hamby and Grace Shields were married and living in Holt by 1924; Hamby was a mechanic at Semet Solvay Company and Grace was a teacher at West End School. *Miller's Tuscaloosa Directory* (1924), 168, U.S. Phone and Address Directories.

41. Although some records indicate her given name was Loula May Hargrove, Herbert's aunt eventually spelled her name "Lula," so I have used that version throughout. USFC, 1910; *Polk's Tuscaloosa Directory* (1922–23), 146, and (1924–25), 172, U.S. Phone and Address Directories; Lula Hargrove to AFS, April 28, 1953, EFS Collection.

42. HLF Sr. to AFS, May 18, 1955, EFS Collection.

43. Laura Jones to EMF, Oct. 30, 1946 (notes from articles in *Virginia Historical Magazine* and other sources), AFS Collection, UA Special Collections; Applications by Henry Noland Crenshaw and Percy Larkins DeLoach, Application for Membership, U.S. Sons of the American Revolution Membership Applications; Owen and Owen, *History of Alabama*, 1:670; Wiggins and Truss, *Journal of Sarah Haynsworth Gayle*, 3; Lazenby, *Methodism in Alabama and West Florida*, 206; Lanier, "Christopher Chapel," 44; U.S. World War I Draft Registration Cards; Gail W. Rolison, "Sheriffs of Choctaw County," ALGenWeb, algw.org; Tommy Campbell, "Friends, Colleagues Remember a 'Legend' in State Politics," *Choctaw Sun-Advocate*, Jan. 14, 2009, 3A.

44. MKF, pers. comm.; Stratton-Porter, *The Harvester*, 241.

45. Wiggins and Truss, *Journal of Sarah Haynsworth Gayle*, 38; Grier, *Culture and Comfort*, 64; Domosh and Seager, *Putting Women in Place*, 8; Wrenn, *A Bachelor's Life*, xxx; Hattie Porter Collier, "Lovely Wedding Brings the Old South Back to Mind," *TN*, June 17, 1934, 9.

46. "Marriage of Mr. Findley and Miss Moore," *Tuscaloosa News and Times-Gazette*, photocopy of clipping. The soloist's name, Lois Phillips, appears in one of Earline's Alabama Normal School photographs as well as the news article about Earline's wedding. In 1920, Lois was a stenographer in Meridian and boarded in the home of a widow (1920 USFC).

47. USFC, 1920; Walters et al., *Camp Zachary Taylor*.

48. Directory of Deceased American Physicians; Sarah Mozingo, comp., "Christopher Chapel Cemetery," Feb. 1998, Rootsweb.

49. The avenue in front of the Findley house apparently was unpaved in 1921 because when Druid City Hospital opened two blocks to the west in 1923, the hospital administrators received assurances that the avenue to the east would soon be paved. Betty Slowe, "The First Druid City Hospital," *TN*, March 3, 2013.

50. Wolfe, *University of Alabama*, 60, 104. The census record for the Smiths immediately preceded the record for the Findleys in 1910 (1910 USFC).

51. From 1920 to 1925, Murk leased a commercial building on the northeast corner of his University Avenue property to Thomas V. Griffith (Tuscaloosa County Probate

Records). Griffith operated a retail grocery store in the building. *Polk's Tuscaloosa Directory* (1922–23), 144, 307, and (1924–25), 166, 346, U.S. Phone and Address Directories.

52. Eugene Allen Smith to Truman Smith, April 2, 1909, Eugene A. Smith Personal Correspondence, UA Special Collections; "Strolls about the Hospital," *Meteor* 16 (April 1876): 16; "Castle Hill—Daly Bottom Community," Historical Marker Database, hmdb.org. Although I found no other use of the name "Frogbottom," this neighborhood was a fixture on the east edge of town for decades. Most or all of the Findleys' neighbors to the east on University Avenue and Second Avenue in 1940 were black menial workers who indicated to the 1940 census enumerator that they lived in the same houses in 1935 (1940 USFC). Margaret Findley recalled that when she married Lyman in 1949, a neighborhood of black families bordered the Findley property on the east (MKF, pers. comm.). The neighborhood still existed during my childhood in the 1960s. On the proximity of predominantly black and white neighborhoods in southern cities, see Rabinowitz, *Race Relations*, 97–101.

53. Murk gave some of his furniture to his son Preston, probably when Preston and his bride moved into Murk's country home. Anita Kenerson Prickett, pers. comm.; Ila Blackman Findley to AFS, n.d., EFS Collection.

54. "Twenty Years Ago Today," *TN*, July 8, 1931, 4; 1910 USFC.

55. A census enumerator visited Mary Collins's residence immediately before Murk's house in 1920 (1920 USFC).

56. AFS, pers. comm. The Findley tilt-top table is in the collection of the University of Alabama.

57. An anthropologist described a similar arrangement at a small farmer's home, apparently an enclosed dogtrot, in Wilcox County, Alabama: "Off one end of the hall is a back porch where there is a shelf for shaving articles, a wash basin, and wooden buckets which are brought up from the well in the yard" (Rubin, *Plantation County*, 54). The Findley plantation desk is now in the collection of the University of Alabama. It resembles a "post office," circa 1830s, made for a log stagecoach inn in Castalian Springs, Tennessee, although the Findley desk differs from the post office in that the cupboard has a slant lid instead of a pair of hinged doors. The lower section of the Findley desk resembles a slab (Atlanta Historical Society, *Neat Pieces*, 113). It also resembles a Tennessee desk, circa 1850–60, made of walnut with tulip poplar as a secondary wood, with an upper compartment of ledger slots and pigeonholes and a slant lid and a lower section with a single full-width drawer and turned legs (Williams and Harsh, *Tennessee Furniture*, 116).

58. Ida Louise Findley Kenerson, pers. comm. via Anita Kenerson Prickett; Clark, *Pills*, 166; Agee, *Cotton Tenants*, 86, 90–91. One had to "acquire a taste for sorghum," according to a syrup maker in Priceville (Frank Sikora, "Alabamian Continues 30-Year Tradition of Selling Sorghum Syrup," *TN*, Dec. 22, 1996, 3B). Ila's sister-in-law Nancy Dean Callahan Blackman described making sorghum. See Hiestand, *Angela the Upside-Down Girl*, 65–67.

59. Gaines, *Southern Plantation*, 167; Rubin, *Plantation County*, 41–42. On the popularity of daguerreotype portraits, see advertisement in *Mobile Daily Advertiser*, April 18, 1843, quoted in Henninger, *Ordering the Facade*, 35; Burns and National Arts Club,

Forgotten Marriage, 78–79. The portraits of Murk and Ida are part of the AFS Collection, UA Special Collections.

60. MKF, pers. comm. See "Dress, 1-Piece," Number CS*039253, and "Hand-tinted photograph of Emeline Butler Posey in her 'second day' outfit, November 9, 1860, Henderson County, Kentucky," Number 1989.0295.014, Smithsonian Costume Collection, http://amhistory.si.edu/costume. Ella Gertrude Clanton Thomas of Georgia (1834–1907) recruited a friend who was going to New York to select and purchase her "bridal paraphanalia [*sic*]" including "my bridal dress—second day dress—bonnet and velvet cloak" (Burr, *The Secret Eye*, 115). Thomas subsequently wore the second-day dress for a formal portrait (Bleser, *In Joy and Sorrow*, unnumbered page).

61. Ashelford and Einsiedel, *The Art of Dress*, 239. Ida's red dress is in the textile collection of ADAH.

62. Similarly, the antebellum belle Ella Clanton "slept late, read voraciously, visited friends, dressed prettily, and wrote letters." Painter, "Introduction," 4.

63. Stratton-Porter, *The Harvester*, 43; MKF, pers. comm.

64. USFC, 1920; Tuscaloosa County Preservation Society, *Past Horizons*, 72. On the enclosure of the dogtrot and expansion of the Findley house, see Friends of Historic Northport, *Northport*, 36. On the scarcity of "hewd-log" as early as 1886, see E. A. Powell, "Fifty-Five Years in West Alabama," *Tuskaloosa Gazette*, reproduced in *Alabama Historical Quarterly* 4, no. 4 (1942): 490. A photograph attributed to the 1920s shows white-painted clapboard on the house: "The Findley House in the 1920s as viewed from Byler Road (Main Avenue)," in Boyd, "An Old Hill," 8. Preston Findley's granddaughter observed paneling, presumably over the original log exterior, in the center hall on visits to the house in the 1960s (Anita Kenerson Prickett, pers. comm.). On the cultural significance of the dogtrot cabin, see Gamble, *Historic Architecture*, 27–29; Davis, *Way through the Wilderness*, 86–89.

65. MKF, pers. comm. On Otis and Herbert once showing unmarked family graves to another genealogy buff, see Lackey Stevens, "Catherine Murchison Findley," Sept. 26, 2011, Find a Grave Index.

66. *Polk's Tuscaloosa Directory* (1922–23), 38, U.S. Phone and Address Directories; Confederate Pension and Service Records. By 1924, Lula was the assistant principal of Holt Public School (*Polk's Tuscaloosa Directory* [1924–25], 172, U.S. Phone and Address Directories). The Lawn Station stop was in front of Druid City Hospital (Robert DeWitt, "Construction Reveals Tuscaloosa Trolley Tracks," *TN*, July 8, 2010). It was named for the expansive lawn of Bryce Hospital ("Mrs. Jones Is Hostess for Estes Circle," *TN*, May 11, 1933, 5; "Rush Party Is Social Event of L.O.L. Club," *TN*, June 12, 1942, 7; "Social Calendar," *TN*, Oct. 1, 1945, 5). Minerva's house still stood in 2014 and was in use as a clothing shop. Hargrove Alley eventually became known as Grace Street. By 1980, the shotgun houses on Grace Street were extremely dilapidated and two elderly residents died from the heat in their houses on a single summer day (Anne Plott, "Sun Still Hits Tin Roofs on Grace Street," *TN*, July 20, 1980, 3D). Earline and Herbert taught their children to address Murk as "Father Findley," and their daughter-in-law always referred to Earline as "Mother Findley." On the antebellum practice of addressing parents-in-law as "Mother Jones" and "Father Brown," see James C.

Bonner, ed., "Plantation Experiences of a New York Woman," *North Carolina Historical Review* 33 (July 1956): 384–412, quoted in Scott, *Southern Lady*, 29–30; Davis, Gardner, and Gardner, *Deep South*, 115.

Chapter 3

1. Grave marker, "Kenneth Findley," Robertson-Stone Cemetery, Northport, Alabama; Sarah White, "Things Hum All Around, But Old Cemetery's 'Lost,'" *TN*, Dec. 11, 1968, 30. In her excellent genealogical study of the Keesee family of Tuscaloosa, Carolyn Earle Billingsley found the grandchildren of another Tuscaloosa pioneer, Thomas Keesee Sr., passed down the story that he fought in the Battle of New Orleans even though no official record of Keesee's service seems to exist (*Communities of Kinship*, 40).

2. Murchison Findley told a census enumerator in 1880 that his father, Kenneth, was born in Scotland (1880 USFC). Lula repeated this story (Lula Hargrove, untitled handwritten notes, n.d., EFS Collection; AFS, "Family Tree," handwritten notes, n.d., EFS Collection). On the arrival of John Findley and family in Charleston, see McCaskill, *MacAskill/McCaskill History*, 10; *Belfast Newsletter*, Aug. 7, 1767, Irish Emigration Database, www.dippam.ac.uk/ied; *South Carolina Gazette*, extracted in Dobson, *Ships from Ireland*, 31; R. J. Dickson, *Ulster Emigration to Colonial America, 1718–1775* (London, 1966), 55–57, cited in Rogers, Chestnutt, and Clark, *The Papers of Henry Laurens*, 5:630n2; Warren, *Citizens and Immigrants*, 8, 143, 201, 206. On "Canetuck" and "Kentuck," see Claire M. Wilson, "Northport," *Encyclopedia of Alabama*, http://www.encyclopediaofalabama.org [Jan. 12, 2012] Feb. 27, 2013. For Crockett's story, see Crockett, *Narrative*, 127–28; "A Notable," *Tuscaloosa Times*, Oct. 28, 1896, transcript, James Austin Anderson Papers, UA Special Collections; Davis, *Way through the Wilderness*, 85; Rich, "Landscapes and the Imagination," 161–62.

3. Doster, "Land Titles," 112–18; Rothman, *Slave Country*, 45, 183.

4. Thomas B. Clinton, 1916, quoted in Mike Kilgore, "Warrior River Canebrake Has Evolved into a Thriving City," *TN*, July 4, 1976, 12A; Acker, *Franklin County, Georgia Tax Digests*, 2:194; Acker, *Deeds of Franklin County*, 394; Georgia Census. On the enormity of the canebrakes on the Alabama frontier, see Hall, "Landscape Considerations," 222. Billingsley speculated that Keesee passed near the Black Warrior River valley while serving in the War of 1812 and decided to migrate there (*Communities of Kinship*, 40). On the reconnaissance mission of another Alabama pioneer, see Rothman, *Slave Country*, 165.

5. U.S. General Land Office Records; photograph, "The Findley House in the 1920s as viewed from Byler Road (Main Avenue)," in Boyd, "An Old Hill," 8; photograph, "Findley-Stone House; 2320 Main Avenue," in Friends of Historic Northport, *Northport*, 36.

6. A man named John Robertson was within three lines of Kenneth's father, John Findley, on the census roster of 1790 for Pendleton, South Carolina (1790 USFC).

7. Christopher, *Horseshoe Robinson*, 7–8; Werner, "The Old South, 1815–1840," 89–90.

8. Kennedy, *Horse Shoe Robinson*, xii.

9. Grave marker, "Catherine Murchison Findley," Robertson-Stone Cemetery,

Northport, Alabama; Sarah White, "Things Hum All Around, But Old Cemetery's 'Lost,'" *TN*, Dec. 11, 1968, 30.

10. Foster, "Women and Refinement," 220; Alabama Marriage Collection; Tuscaloosa Genealogical Society, *Pioneers*, 84; Find a Grave Index; "History of Tuscaloosa County," Tuscaloosa County Sheriff's Office, https://www.tcsoal.org/about/history. William's father-in-law, Robert Cook, ran unsuccessfully for the state legislature. Powell, "Fifty-Five Years," 592.

11. Clark and Guice, *Frontiers in Conflict*, 250–51; Hubbs, *Guarding Greensboro*, 53; Ellisor, *Second Creek War*, 170–71, 163–64, 209, 222. For more about Dent, see Owen and Owen, *History of Alabama*, 2:1338; Powell, "Fifty-Five Years," 556, 569; "George Dent (1756–1813)," Biographical Directory of the United States Congress, http://bioguide.congress.gov/biosearch/biosearch.asp; Garrett, *Reminiscences*, 169; Sellers and Foster, *First Methodist Church*, 42.

12. Linda S. Ayres, comp., "Some Military Land Grants in Tuscaloosa County Alabama for Soldiers of the Indian Wars," USGenWebArchives, www.usgwarchives.net; Powell, "Fifty-Five Years," 626. For more about A. B. Meek, see Hagood, "'Literature to Him Was a Recreation.'"

13. Christopher, "Autobiography"; Methodist Episcopal Church, *Annual Conferences . . . 1773–1828*, 189, 198; Hamilton, "Alexander Beaufort Meek"; Sellers and Foster, *First Methodist Church*, 26–27; McEachin, *History of Tuscaloosa*, 68–69.

14. Mahon, "Journal of A. B. Meek," 316; Wright, *General Scott*; Mahon, *Second Seminole War*, 160–61; Hatch, *Osceola*, 157; Ellisor, *Second Creek War*, 210, 230–31; "167th Infantry Regiment (Fourth Alabama)," U.S. Army Center of Military History, http://www.history.army.mil/html/forcestruc/lineages/branches/inf/0167in.htm.

15. "From the Pensacola Gazette," *Rutland (VT) Herald*, Aug. 8, 1837, 2, Chronicling America.

16. Callahan, "Garner Murder Case," 9.

17. USFC, 1850; USFC Slave Schedules; USFC Non-Population Schedules; Military Warrant (U.S. General Land Office Records); Barefield, *Old Tuskaloosa*, 64, 133; U.S. Department of Agriculture, *Tuscaloosa County Soil Survey Map* (Washington, DC: U.S. Department of Agriculture, 1911), UA Alabama Maps. William married Nancy Adaline Cook in 1829; Murchison's bride, Rebecca Mahala Cook, was Nancy's sister. Tuscaloosa Genealogical Society, *Pioneers*, 84; Alabama Marriage Collection.

18. Tuscaloosa Genealogical Society, *Pioneers*, 84. On the practice of naming daughters for southern states, see Billingsley, *Communities of Kinship*, 23–24; Rich, "Landscapes and the Imagination," 156.

19. Tuscaloosa Genealogical Society, *Pioneers*, 134; Clinton, *Scrapbook*, 167; 1820, 1830 USFC; Society for the Preservation of Old Mills Mid Atlantic Chapter, spoom.org; "Keene's Mill," Historical Marker Database, hmdb.org; Lundegard, "Mills and Mill Sites in Fairfax County," 8, 27; April Wortham, "Paddling Past the Ruins of Old Mills," *TN*, July 4, 2004, 1A, 19A; Lovett, "Historic Context Evaluation for Mills in Tennessee"; J. Kenneth Major, "The Pre-Industrial Sources of Power: Muscle Power," *History Today* 30, no. 3 (1980), http://www.historytoday.com/j-kenneth-major/pre-industrial-sources-power-muscle-power; Prison Discipline Society, *Sixteenth Annual Report*, 66;

McInnis, *Politics of Taste*, 82; Geoffrey Abbott, "Treadwheel," Encyclopaedia Britannica, http://www.britannica.com/topic/treadwheel. Archaeologists have found remnants of a treadwheel pump that was used to move saltwater through an aqueduct at St. Charles Bay, Texas. Hatchett, "Salt Works," 32.

20. Cooke, *Scottish Songs*, 52; Missy Harris, "Rebel Hearts Beat in Confederate Sons' Breasts," *TN*, Nov. 30, 1986, 1D.

21. MKF, AFS, pers. comm.; Hiestand, *Angela the Upside-Down Girl*, 57. On the significance of goats in Masonic culture, see Moore, "Riding the Goat."

22. The 1855 state census recorded three white girls under the age of twenty-one in Murchison's household. Murchison and Lucy had only two daughters by that time. The 1860 USFC identified Mahala Findley as an occupant of the house.

23. On the name of White's Landing, see Clinton, "Military Operations," 455; Maxwell, *Autobiography*, 116.

24. Gamble, *Historic Architecture*, 57, 60; Reinberger, "Architecture of Sharecropping," 120. In a master's thesis on antebellum Tuscaloosa architecture, Lucy Findley's niece Sydnia Keene Smyth noted Lucy's brother Taylor "was present at the time. He gave this information" ("Ante-Bellum Architecture," 32). The photograph of the house that Smyth took for her thesis is one of two known photographs of the house, which was demolished. The unusual style of the house was an example of what the architectural historian Catherine W. Bishir called "a high-style vernacular architecture of lively individuality" (*Southern Built*, 159).

25. Gamble, *Historic Architecture*, 188; Dana Beyerle, "Glascock House Added to Endangered Site List," *TN*, May 15, 2001, 1B; drawing, "Glascock-Bealle-Foster House, 1109 21st Avenue," Tuscaloosa Area Virtual Museum, https://tavm.omeka.net/items/show/1054. For more on the design of the Alabama Insane Hospital, see Robert O. Mellown, "Bryce Hospital: Historical Significance" (unpublished manuscript, n.d., Bryce Hospital Historic Preservation Project, http://www.mh.alabama.gov/BryceHospitalProject/Documents/BryceHospitalHistoricalSignificance2.pdf); Yanni, *Architecture of Madness*, 14.

26. Smyth, "Ante-Bellum Architecture," 32; "Merchants Want Display Ban Changed," *TN*, April 21, 1966, 1, 2; Lupold and French, *Bridging Deep South Rivers*, 103; Powell, "Fifty-Five Years," 557; Smith, *Reminiscences*, 307; Sellers, *Slavery in Alabama*, 199. Records exist of the University of Alabama renting or "hiring" slaves in the 1830s (Wolfe, *University of Alabama*, 25). See appendix 4, this book. Also see Zaborney, *Slaves for Hire*.

27. Mellown, "Alabama Insane Hospital," 85–87, 94; Mellown, *Historic Structures Report*, 10. Robert Jemison adopted the suffix "Jr." to avoid confusion with his uncle, an alderman in Tuscaloosa and later a real estate developer in Birmingham, Alabama, whose name also was Robert. Maxwell, *Autobiography*, 34; Green, *Tuscaloosa*, 16; Lupold and French, *Bridging Deep South Rivers*, 139.

28. A search of census records for Tuscaloosa County in 1850 finds just one other girl with the name, Cherokee Reynolds. Find a Grave Index; 1850, 1860 USFC.

29. Jemison never entered Murchison's given name in the ledger, instead noting "Findly," "M. Findly," or "M. Findley," but Murchison's house was only a mile from

the hospital and fourteen of the rented slaves were dispatched to work half days on the asylum and half days on the Findley house, making it virtually certain that Murchison Findley was Jemison's rental customer (Robert Jemison Jr., Account Book on Rent of Slaves, 1858–1864, Robert Jemison Jr. Papers, UA Special Collections). Jemison also entered into a contract in 1858 with J. Findley, presumably Murchison's brother, to "rent" five slaves who were carpenters and a blacksmith at a price of five thousand dollars. The terms of the contract are not clear in the partially illegible document. "Record of Robert Jemison, Jr., J. M. Jemison, and J. Findley, January 1, 1858," Robert Jemison Jr. Papers, UA Special Collections.

30. Powell, "Fifty-Five Years," 570–71; Maxwell, *Autobiography*, 20; Clinton, *Tuscaloosa*, 152; "Facts and Legends about the Drish House, Tuscaloosa, Alabama," Historic Houses, Rootsweb. Sarah Gayle suspected Drish's incompetent treatment of her children's nurse caused the woman's death (Wiggins and Truss, *Journal of Sarah Haynsworth Gayle*, 285–87). William Russell Smith recalled that Drish was known for not reading medical texts (*Reminiscences*, 143).

31. Tuscaloosa County Preservation Society, "Drish House," Historic Tuscaloosa, historictuscaloosa.org.

32. Gaines, *Southern Plantation*, 161; Wyatt-Brown, *Southern Honor*, 339–40; Powell, "Fifty-Five Years," 547; Hagood, "Rewriting the Frontier," 76; Smyth, "Ante-Bellum Architecture," 32. On the perception of gambling as the pastime of gentlemen, see Greenberg, *Honor and Slavery*, 135, 141.

33. Clinton, *Scrapbook*, unnumbered page; Windham and Figh, *Thirteen Alabama Ghosts*, 27–28; Sellers, *Slavery in Alabama*, 323.

34. Taylor Keene, "Findley House," memory drawing of floor plan, in Smyth, "Ante-Bellum Architecture," 32; Preston Findley, "Murchison Findley House in Riverview," memory drawing of floor plan, n.d., EFS Collection.

35. AFS, pers. comm.; Smyth, "Murchison Findley House," photograph, in Smyth, "Ante-Bellum Architecture." The Findley chaise longue is now in the collection of the University of Alabama.

36. Green, *Tuscaloosa*, 10; Clinton, *Scrapbook*, 15, 92, 189, 207; W. H. Mitchell to his wife, Jan. 11, 1861, excerpted in Griffith, *Alabama*, 382–83.

37. Missy Harris, "Rebel Hearts Beat in Confederate Sons' Breasts," *TN*, Nov. 30, 1986, 1D; Profile Form for Lewis Bourbon Keene, Alabama Pension Department, March 1, 1921, Alabama Census of Confederate Soldiers; Application by Taylor Keene, Confederate Pension and Service Records. On students enlisting over their parents' objections, see Eckinger, "Militarization of the University of Alabama," 180.

38. USFC, 1860; USFC Slave Schedules. Similarly, Murchison's comrade in the Second Seminole War, A. B. Meek, did not enlist in the Confederate Army "because he was then in his upper forties." Mahon, "Journal of A. B. Meek," 318.

39. Massey, *Ersatz in the Confederacy*, 60–62; Matthew W. Clinton, "Tuscaloosa Scrapbook: Hospital and Civil War," *TN*, April 13, 1968, 4; Clinton, *Scrapbook*, 156; Maxwell, *Autobiography*, 16; Atkins, *The Valley and the Hills*, 36. On older men on the home front assisting women with their farms, see Fleming, "Home Life," 85; Harris, *Plain Folk and Gentry*, 154.

40. Hoole and McArthur, *The Yankee Invasion*, 32–33, 40, 55; Conrad, *The Young Lions*, 143–44, 148; Eckinger, "Militarization of the University of Alabama," 184; Tuscaloosa County Preservation Society, *Past Horizons*, 64; Massey, *Reminiscences*, 138; "Kate Keene Seay," *TN*, March 30, 1980, 15A; Hubbs, *Tuscaloosa*, 44–45; Matthew W. Clinton, "Tuscaloosa Scrapbook: Hospital and Civil War," *TN*, April 13, 1968, 4; Sellers and Foster, *First Methodist Church*, 283–85; Dowling, "Tuscaloosa, Alabama," 9–10. James Anderson, a local history buff, recorded without attribution that "all his life" Taylor Keene "deplored the fact that he had to leave behind in the burning buildings a pair of new handmade boots. He was in the thick of the ensuing skirmish, acting as a courier during the fight" ("Keene Family," 3). On distances between rural homes in antebellum Tuscaloosa County, Billingsley noted "a mile is not a significant distance at all; it can be walked in less than fifteen minutes and, on a horse or mule, ridden in far less time" (*Communities of Kinship*, 72).

41. Anderson, "Keene Family," 3; Clinton, "Military Operations," 455; Hoole and McArthur, *The Yankee Invasion*, 40. A woman from Tuscumbia, Alabama, recalled in an interview in 1908, "unless you have experienced it, one cannot know . . . the unspeakable horror . . . of having the negroes run in the house and say: 'The Yankees are Coming!' . . . The sound . . . will follow me like a nightmare to the end of my days.'" Rebecca Thompson Bayless, "Yankee Raids on the South Side of the Tennessee," *Montgomery Advertiser*, May 3, 1908, quoted in Sterkx, *Partners in Rebellion*, 168.

42. Ila Blackman Findley to AFS, notes on hand-drawn floor plans, n.d., EFS Collection; Maxwell, *Autobiography*, 284.

43. Palmer, *Register*, 291; "Death Claims Murk Findley," *TN*, April 22, 1941, 1, 2.

44. Maxwell, *The King Bee's Dream*, 95–98. See appendix 3, this book.

45. USFC, 1870; Alabama State Census, 1820–1866, www.ancestry.com.

46. Roark, *Masters without Slaves*, 173, 150. For the economic adjustments of post-Emancipation planters in Alabama, see Wiener, *Social Origins*.

47. "Proclamation to Robert Jemison Jr.'s Slaves, circa 1865," Robert Jemison Jr. Papers, UA Special Collections. On this sort of control over former slaves, see Foner, *Reconstruction*, 61.

48. Andrea, *Findley-Finley*, 32; 1860, 1870 USFC; MKF, pers. comm.; Clinton, *Scrapbook*, 133; Blackman, *Brow of the Hill*, 47; U.S. IRS Tax Assessment Lists.

49. USFC, 1870. Murchison's nephew John Findley also named a daughter, born in 1866, Flora (Deaths and Burials Index). On the history and legends of Flora MacDonald, see Toffey, *A Woman Nobly Planned*.

50. USFC, 1870.

51. On engineers as part of the new urban elite, see Roark, *Masters without Slaves*, 151; Morsman, *The Big House*, 161–62; Case, "Historical Ideology," 620.

52. U.S. Army Corps of Engineers, Black Warrior and Tombigbee Lakes, sam.usace.army.mil/bwt/history.htm, retrieved December 20, 2011.

53. University of Alabama, "History: Engineering at UA," University of Alabama, https://www.ua.edu/about/history, News of the Alumni," *University of Alabama Alumni News* 24 (June 1941): 141.

54. "Dr. W. J. Vaughn and his engineering class," photograph 2007 .001 .004146,

Box 35, Collection 2007 .001, UA Photograph Collection, UA Special Collections. On conversation pictures, see Brilliant, *Portraiture*, 96–98.

55. "Death Claims Murk Findley," *TN*, April 22, 1941, 1, 2; Railroad Commission of Alabama, *Twenty-Second Annual Report*, 506; Palmer, *Register*, 291. Although the census enumerator identified Murchison and Murk as "farmers" in 1880, Billingsley found "at any one given point in time, one or more individuals may not meet the explicit definition of 'planter,' but they were still members of the planter class by virtue of their affiliation with family members who did meet such a definition" (1880 USFC; Billingsley, *Communities of Kinship*, 115). Also see Henry, introduction, vii–viii.

56. Matthew W. Clinton, "Tuscaloosa Scrapbook: Remember Lake Lorraine?" *TN*, Feb. 18, 1968, 5; Frank Gamble Blair, "1900–1909: A New Century," interview, *Perspectives* (Winter 2000), Chamber of Commerce of West Alabama. A local family labeled a photograph, taken in the early twentieth century, of a waterfall "on branch below Dam Lake Lorraine near the old Findley's Mill site." "Illustrated Letter from Mr. and Mrs. Julian Perkins to Edwin C. Perkins," photograph, Perkins Family Papers, UA Special Collections.

57. Paine, *Life and Times of William McKendree*, 248; Tuscaloosa Genealogical Society, *Pioneers*, 106; 1870 USFC; Knight, *History of Georgia*, 5:2422; Abstracts of Graves of Revolutionary Patriots; Abernethy, *Formative Period*, 31; Davis, *Way through the Wilderness*, 84; Charles E. Boyd, "Liberty Church Has Rich Heritage," *TN*, June 6, 1974, 4; Charles Edward Boyd, "Preface with Some Notes," in Lambert, *Tuscaloosa County*, 1:v; Tuscaloosa Genealogical Society, *Pioneers*, 106; West, *Methodism in Alabama*, 154–58; Lazenby, *Methodism in Alabama and West Florida*, 92; Sellers and Foster, *First Methodist Church*, 35.

58. Cartwright and Wallis, *Autobiography*, 6, 9, 135; West, *Methodism in Alabama*, 154–58; Galloway, "Bishop Robert Kennon Hargrove," 628; Mathews, *Slavery and Methodism*, 46–51. Sellers alluded briefly to Dudley Hargrove's resistance but made no clear statement of his opinion of the issue (*Slavery in Alabama*, 325–26). On the uncritical nature of Methodist historiography, see Mathews, *Slavery and Methodism*, 314.

59. Alabama Marriage Collection; 1850 USFC; Barefield, *Old Tuskaloosa*, 38; U.S. General Land Office Records; Gandrud, *Alabama Records*, 99:44, 109:62.

60. Gandrud, *Marriage Records*, 12; Tuscaloosa Genealogical Society, *Pioneers*, 106; Hendrix, *Old Cemeteries*, 28; "Hargrove Family Cemetery, List of Interments," Find a Grave Index; Boyd, "Preface with Some Notes," in Lambert, *Tuscaloosa County*, 1:v; obituary, "Andrew Coleman Hargrove," in American Bar Association, *Twentieth Annual Meeting*, 527–29; Billingsley, *Communities of Kinship*, 108; Gandrud, *Marriage Records*, 55, 88, 89, 106, 115, 118, 122, 136; Smith, *Reminiscences*, 60; Sudduth, *Tuscaloosa County . . . Will Book*, 57–58. On the function of such commissioners, see Deyle, *Carry Me Back*, 167.

61. Muster Rolls of Alabama Civil War Units; Alabama Civil War Service Database. On unenthusiastic Confederate soldiers eventually enlisting alongside brothers, cousins, and neighbors, see Noe, *Reluctant Rebels*, 156–58.

62. Maxwell, *Autobiography*, 270–71; Application by Minerva E. Hargrove, Nov. 29, 1924, Confederate Pension and Service Records; "Mrs. Minerva Hargrove Passes Away

at Age of 96," *TN*, Dec. 4, 1932, 1. On glorification of Confederate wives, see Fleming, "Home Life," 85; Massey, *Ersatz in the Confederacy*, 27; Faust, *Mothers of Invention*, 33.

63. References to Ida's full name are scarce. Minerva and Tenedus identified her as "Belle" to census enumerators in 1870 and "Ida B." in 1880. In his will, Tenedus referred to her as "Ida Bell," perhaps because by then Ida, almost eighteen years old, preferred that spelling (Gandrud, *Alabama Records*, 41:43). For the 1900 census, she identified herself as "Ida B." Murk spelled her name "Ida Bell" on her grave marker: "Ida Bell Hargrove Findley; John Emmet Findley," Evergreen Cemetery, Tuscaloosa.

64. USFC, 1870, 1880, 1900. Tenedus Hargrove produced one thousand bushels of Indian corn in 1870; the next largest producer in his precinct of forty farmers produced seven hundred. He reported expending one thousand dollars in cash and "board" to pay employees. USFC Non-Population Schedules, 1870.

65. MKF, pers. comm.; "Death Claims Murk Findley," *TN*, April 22, 1941, 1, 2; Palmer, *Register*, 291; "Our History," First United Methodist Church [of Knoxville], firstunitedmethodistchurch.org; Whittle, "Knoxville, Tenn., Methodism"; "The Epworth League," *Outlook* (July 13, 1895): 66, Google Books; "The Epworth League," *World Almanac* (1898), 307, Google Books.

66. Carnes, *Secret Ritual*, 48; Bullock, *Revolutionary Brotherhood*, 243. At least eight boys born in Tuscaloosa around 1890 were given Preston as a first or middle name (1900 USFC). There is scant evidence of Sydnia Findley's life and death, but she was the namesake for two other members of Murk's family: his uncle Eli Taylor Keene's daughter born in 1880 and his cousin Simpson Keene's daughter born in 1910 (1880, 1920 USFC).

67. MKF, pers. comm.; *Maryville (TN) Times*, April 23, 1904, quoted on GenForum, www.genealogy.com.

68. Knight, *History of Georgia*, 5:2422. Dennis Dent, the military officer and state legislator in Tuscaloosa, also named a son for Kennon, and in a twist that demonstrates the friendships of these Tuscaloosa families, Dudley's son John Hargrove and his wife named a son, born in 1838, Dennis Dent Hargrove. Jones, *A Complete History of Methodism*, 2:203; 1850 USFC.

69. USFC, 1900; grave marker, "Ida Bell [*sic*] Hargrove Findley; John Emmet [*sic*] Findley," Evergreen Cemetery; Huey, *Alabama Division*, 339–40; G. Ward Hubbs, "Civil War in Alabama," encyclopediaofalabama.org, [Jan. 10, 2008] March 4, 2015.

70. Affidavit by Hargrove, Preston, and Herbert L. Findley, Feb. 25, 1963, Tuscaloosa County Probate Office Records; Ila Blackman Findley to AFS, n.d., EFS Collection; AFS, pers. comm.; guest editorial, Nancy Callahan, "Six Months Later," *TN*, Oct. 23, 2011; Callahan, "Personnel," 13. On plantations retaining the names of earlier owners, see Burr, *The Secret Eye*, 71n3.

71. Preston Findley, "Murchison Findley House in Riverview," memory drawing of floor plan, n.d.

72. Minerva Hargrove's brother Matthew Thomas and his wife, whose records were adjacent to Minerva's on the census report, had two live-in black servants, ages eighteen and thirty-two. Mrs. A. C. Hargrove's next-door neighbors had two live-in black servants, one a twenty-eight-year-old woman identified as a cook and the other a

seven-year-old girl. George (28) and Ada Long (20) and their two-year-old child Clarence lived in Manningham (Butler County) in 1900. By 1910, George Long's wife identified herself as "Ada Long Sr." Their children "Ada Long Jr." (18) and Sam Long (15) lived with them in Manningham and all of the members of the family were farm laborers (1900, 1910 USFC). On white families taking in black children, ostensibly to help the children's parents, see Tompkins, *Cotton-Patch Schoolhouse*, 6; Clayton, *White and Black*, 184–85, 191.

73. Reid, "The Negro in Alabama," 277–78; Kolchin, *First Freedom*, 63–67; Myers, "Black Human Capital," 58–59, 66–69; Gutman, *The Black Family*, 402–3; Bardaglio, *Reconstructing the Household*, 161–62; Hunter, *To 'Joy My Freedom*, 10, 35–36; Zaborney, *Slaves for Hire*, 46–47.

74. Compilation of Choctaw County Records, Roll #S2005–0347, ADAH; 1900, 1920 USFC.

75. Myers, "Black Human Capital," 219; ADAH, *Alabama Official and Statistical Register* (1915), 206; Will George, "Remember When: County Roads Got Little Attention in Early Days," *TN*, April 25, 1969, 25F; Tommy Stevenson, "Days of Road Camps, Buggies Now Memories," *TN*, Aug. 13, 1989, 9B. For more on the convict lease system in Alabama, see Blackmon, *Slavery by Another Name*.

76. Henderson, *Smith's Alabama*, 141. For more on black child servants as playmates for white children, see Cook, "Growing Up," 327; Clark-Lewis, *Living In*, 31, 41–47; Burr, *The Secret Eye*, 359n3; Clayton, *White and Black*, 270; Louise Pyrnelle, *Diddie, Dumps and Tot, or Plantation Child-Life* (New York: Harper and Bros., 1882), 14, quoted in Cook, "Growing Up," 250–51; Williams, *A Literary History of Alabama*, 101. On Pyrnelle's popularity, see Kirk, *Locust Hill*, 89.

77. Escott, *Slavery Remembered*, 30–31; Clark-Lewis, *Living In*, 42; Van Wormer, Jackson, and Sudduth, "Annie Victorian Johnson."

78. On privileged white children questioning white supremacy, see Ritterhouse, *Growing Up Jim Crow*, 11–13, 20.

79. Victoria V. Clayton, "Here We Lived in This Quiet Country Home," in Jones, *Plantation South*, 267–72.

80. Tuscaloosa County Probate Office Records; Tuskaloosa Coal, Iron and Land Co., *Map of City and Suburban Land Belonging to the Tuskaloosa Coal, Iron and Land Co.* (Tuscaloosa, AL, 1887), UA Alabama Maps. The 1907 construction date for Murk and Ida's house on University Avenue is family lore. The basic two-story, L-shaped house with a two-sided porch was popular as early as 1890, when Shoppell's Modern Houses published a plan called Design 646; in 1903, when the Radford Architectural Company published a similar design; and in 1911, when Sears, Roebuck & Company offered a similar plan as Modern Home Number 119. Reiff, *Houses from Books*, 149, 155–56.

81. UA, *Catalog for the Academic Year 1906–1907*, 166. William Scears of Eutaw, Alabama, owned a plantation three miles from town but built a house, known as Magnolia on Main, in town in 1904 "as a townhouse for his family to make it more convenient for his children attending school." See Welcome to Rural Southwest Alabama, www.ruralswalabama.org.

82. Maxwell, *Autobiography*, 46.

83. Dawson, *A State*, 56–57; *Atlanta Constitution*, Sept. 15, 1907, www.genealogybuff.com; Marie Ball, "Water-Powered Grist Mills Are Historical Reminder," *TN*, June 15, 1979, 2C; "Colonel Finnell Will Take Office Next Week," *TN*, July 30, 1937, 1; 1900 USFC; Green, *Tuscaloosa*, 51; Betty Slowe, "Looking Back," *TN*, July 20, 2010; Henderson, *Smith's Alabama*, 205; clipping, "Funeral of Mrs. Murk Finley and John Finley"; "Pneumonia," MayoClinic.org; "Transmission of Measles," Aug. 31, 2009, Centers for Disease Control and Prevention, cdc.org. Ida's mother, Minerva, and sister Lula Hargrove lived together at 1218 University Avenue. Her brother Thomas, a bookkeeper in a bank, lived next door to Minerva, or in a wing of the same house, with his wife, Collette Barnes Hargrove, their two children, and an African American domestic servant who "lived in." Her older brother William Hope lived two blocks away from their mother with his wife and six daughters, the youngest of whom was named Ida (1910 USFC).

84. Lula Hargrove to HLF Sr., Dec. 16, 1957, EFS Collection. See Sellers, *Slavery in Alabama*, 129.

85. USFC, 1870. On slave and white women engaged in spinning and weaving, see Maxwell, *Autobiography*, 39–40; Escott, *Slavery Remembered*, 65; Kierner, *Beyond the Household*, 171–72; Fox-Genovese, *Plantation Household*, 137–38; Vlach, *Big House*, 19.

86. Elaine Greek, "Woven Coverlets," [Sigal] Museum and Northampton County [Pennsylvania] Historical and Genealogical Society, sigalmuseum.org, March 29, 2012; "Woven for Comfort and Joy: Nineteenth-Century American Coverlets," Philadelphia Museum of Art, philamuseum.org; "Centennial Coverlet," Collections, National Museum of American History; Lita Solis-Cohen, "A Coverlet That Celebrated the Centennial," *Philadelphia Inquirer*, March 6, 1987; "Harmony Mills," National Historic Landmarks, www.nps.gov/nhl.

87. Tenedus's father had nine slaves in 1840 and forty-six, including women ages fifty and sixty-one years, by 1860. The census enumerator did not include Tenedus in the 1860 survey of slave ownership but recorded that his brothers and even his teenage cousins Dicy and Henrietta Hargrove held from nine to twenty-two slaves (1840, 1860 USFC, Mortality Schedules). On James Hargrove's incarceration, see Alton Museum of History and Art, "Confederate Prisoner Page," Alton in the Civil War, http://www.altonweb.com/history/civilwar/confed/#search; "Ruins of First State Prison in Illinois," historical marker, http://www.waymarking.com/waymarks/WM927_First_State_Prison_in_Illinois; "Alton Military Prison Site," Civil War Discovery Trail, http://www.civilwar.org/civil-war-discovery-trail/sites/alton-military-prison-site.html.

88. On the custom of referring to elderly African Americans as "Aunt" and "Uncle," see Lambert, *Tuscaloosa County*, 1:38; Powdermaker, *After Freedom*, 44; Ritterhouse, *Growing Up Jim Crow*, 30.

89. USFC, 1870; Brown and Taylor, *Gabr'l Blow Sof'*, 17.

90. Kolchin, *First Freedom*, 4–5; Foner, *Reconstruction*, 35; Faust, *Mothers of Invention*, 74–75; Hunter, *To 'Joy My Freedom*, 25; Blair, *Cities of the Dead*, 34; Brown and Taylor, *Gabr'l Blow Sof'*, 82, 96. On former slaves' dependence on former masters, see Escott, *Slavery Remembered*, 13, 130–37.

91. "Proclamation to Robert Jemison Jr.'s Slaves, circa 1865," Robert Jemison Jr. Papers, UA Special Collections.

92. Myers, "Black Human Capital," 88.

93. Kirk, *Locust Hill*, 40–41, 85; Burr, *The Secret Eye*, 216. On former slaveholders in Alabama typically offering freedmen no more compensation than they received as slaves, see Doss, "Religious Reconstruction," 257–60.

94. Roland McMillan Harper, diary entry for March 5, 1943, Roland Harper Papers, UA Special Collections; "Negro Soldier Dies of Illness," *TN*, March 4, 1943, 2. On white families participating in black servants' funerals, see Thurber, "Development of the Mammy Image," 105.

95. A list of grave markers in the Hargrove family cemetery, compiled in 1981, does not include any graves of slaves or former slaves, or other individuals named Hargrove who died between 1875, the year the coverlet was made, and the death of Tenedus Hargrove in 1882, after which Minerva and her children moved to Tuscaloosa (Hendrix, *Old Cemeteries*, 28–30). However, a list compiled in 2000 includes two unmarked graves ("Hargrove Cemetery," AIGenWeb Project, www.iagenweb.org).

96. Kolchin, *First Freedom*, 57–58.

97. Sterkx, *Partners in Rebellion*, 184; Faust, *Mothers of Invention*, 60–61.

98. Fox-Genovese, introduction, x–xi.

99. See Brundage, *Southern Past*, 119; Trefousse, *Toward a New View*, vii.

Chapter 4

1. AFS to VRMK, April 2, 1977 (carbon), EFS Collection; AFS, pers. comm.; James B. Sellers, letter of recommendation, Aug. 18, 1924, EFS Collection.

2. Ila Blackman Findley to AFS, notes on hand-drawn floor plan of The Old Place, n.d. For the cultural significance of ancestral homes, see Davis, Gardner, and Gardner, *Deep South*, 193. For "the highly formalized layout" of showplace plantations, see Vlach, *Big House*, 8.

3. Smyth, "Murchison Findley House," photograph, "Ante-Bellum Architecture."

4. William "Plain Bill" Brandon, "1920–1929: The Roaring Twenties," interview, *Perspectives* (Winter 2000), Chamber of Commerce of West Alabama; 1930 USFC.

5. Boucher, "Wealthy Planter Families," 84. Three months after his marriage, Murk's parents sold part of their Riverview property to him for a token price of five dollars; they made a similar gift later that year to their daughter Sydnia, who also was married. Murk Findley to Herbert Lyman Findley, Feb. 8, 1922 [deed], and Murchison and Lucy Findley to Murk Findley, April 17, 1891 [deed], Tuscaloosa County Office Probate Records.

6. On the middle-class view of the family residence as the wife's domain, see Robertson, "Male and Female Agendas," 141. On houses as reflections of the homeowner's aspirations, see Miller, *Stuff*, 79–109.

7. Morgan Woodwork Organization, *Building with Assurance*, unnumbered pages (see appendix 3, this book); Betsky, "Inside the Past," 266; Rybczynski, *Home*, 10. Margaret Findley later referred to the catalog in planning the house she built with Lyman (MKF, pers. comm.).

8. See photographs of houses in Livingston, HABS.

9. Post quoted in Marling, "From the Quilt," 7; Stickley quoted in Gowans, *This Comfortable House,* 202; Smith, *Five Hundred Small Houses,* 3; King, *The Bungalow,* 134, 152, 154; Cohen, "Embellishing," 263; Gowans, *The Comfortable House,* 202; Brooks, "Clarity, Contrast," 38–39; Bryden and Floyd, *Domestic Space,* 7. On descendants of slaveholders feeling little need in the 1930s to trace, much less flaunt, their ancestry, see Davis, Gardner, and Gardner, *Deep South,* 84; Brownell, *Urban Ethos,* 212. For a recent treatment of houses as sites for formation of racial identity, see Harris, *Little White Houses.*

10. HLF Sr. to HLF Jr., Aug. 12, 1929, HLF Jr. Scrapbook, courtesy of MKF.

11. Bennett Lumber Co., *Small House Catalog*; "What Is a Sears Modern Home?," Sears Archives, http://www.searsarchives.com/homes/index.htm, and "The Walton," Sears Archives, http://www.searsarchives.com/homes/1927-1932.htm. Later in the 1920s the *TN* ran articles about stock house plans that were for sale, placing advertisements for local building suppliers and insurers around the articles. See "Here's a House That Shingles Built," *TN,* July 1, 1929, 5. Also see Schlereth, "Country Stores," 368–69; Harvey, "Mail-Order Architecture."

12. Gowans, *The Comfortable House,* 195–97; Reiff, *Houses from Books,* 282.

13. Photograph, "Anne and Lyman Findley with the pasteboard houses," in Shores, *On Harper's Trail,* unnumbered page.

14. AFS, MKF, pers. comm. On longleaf pine as the dominant old-growth tree in Tuscaloosa County, see Smith, *Cotton Production,* 113; Hall, "Landscape Considerations," 223. Herbert's cousins Bernice and Samuel Stone were carpenters in Northport, apparently in business together, in 1920 and 1930 (1920, 1930 USFC). Another cousin, L. Van Hook Keene, was a carpenter in Holt in 1921. Lewis Bourbon Keene, application for a Confederate pension, Alabama Census of Confederate Soldiers.

15. Stratton-Porter, *The Harvester,* 54.

16. Schlereth, *Victorian America,* 93; Gottfried and Jennings, *American Vernacular,* 188.

17. MKF, pers. comm. For the importance of traditional garden plants to middle-class women, see Gordon and McArthur, "Interior Decorating," 108; Seaton, "Making the Best of Circumstances," 97.

18. Cothran, *Gardens and Historic Plants,* 245; Welch et al., *Heirloom Gardening,* 394–95.

19. EMF to AFS, Dec. 1951, EFS Collection.

20. Sara Haardt, "Each in Her Own Day," in *Southern Souvenirs,* ed. Henley, 259–60.

21. W. Kirk Wood, "Clarence Cason," www.encyclopediaofalabama.org, [Sept. 17, 2009] July 11, 2013; Matthews, "Clarence Cason," 5–6; Cason, *90 Degrees,* 39–40.

22. Robertson, "Male and Female Agendas," 134–35.

23. Cromley, "American Beds and Bedrooms," 183–84.

24. Stickley, *Craftsman Houses,* 17, 27, 29.

25. On a Dutch door at an antebellum house in Union Springs, see Varian Feare, "Historic Union Springs, in Bullock," *BNAH,* Sept. 15, 1935, 10.

26. Hunter, *To 'Joy My Freedom*, 4; Rybczynski, *Home*, 87; Vlach, *Big House*, 9, 190. A furniture maker in Tuscaloosa advertised "House Bells, with strings, wire and crank," in 1845. Adams, "Mortised, Tenoned," 212.

27. Robertson, "Male and Female Agendas," 130; Volz, "The Modern Look," 27–30.

28. Clark, "The Vision of the Dining Room," 142, 146; Kasson, "Rituals of Dining," 119–31.

29. MKF, pers. comm.; advertisement, "Eden by Haviland," www.replacements.com; Long and Seate, *Fostoria Value Guide*, 188; advertisement, "Theodore Haviland," www.ebay.com.

30. U.S. Public Records Index, https://familysearch.org; Miller's Tuscaloosa Directory (1922), 131, U.S. Phone and Address Directories.

31. "Legal Notice in the Matter of the Estate of Olive K. Findley, Deceased," *TN*, Jan. 27, 1968, 6; "Graphite Industry in Alabama," *Engineering and Mining Journal* (Feb. 9, 1918): 282; grave marker, "Murchison H. Findley," Evergreen Cemetery, Tuscaloosa.

32. Raines, "Introduction," xiii; Beidler, "Yankee Interloper," 29.

33. Carmer, *Stars Fell*, 28–30. Ironically, considering Carl Carmer's informal, shifting blend of fact and fiction, his host and guide for much of his exploration of west Alabama was Ruby Pickens Tartt, the writer in Livingston who strove for meticulous accuracy in her transcripts of interviews with freedpeople. Raines, "Introduction," xv; Brown and Taylor, *Gabr'l Blow Sof'*, vii–viii.

34. Chalmers, *Hooded Americanism*, 79; Tindall, *Emergence of the New South*, 190–91; Lisa C. Maxwell, "Hiram Wesley Evans," Texas State Historical Association, tshaonline.org, June 12, 2010; McWhirter, *Red Summer*, 65; Pegram, *One Hundred Percent American*, 27; Wilson, *Baptized in Blood*, 116–17; Wiggins, *From Civil War*, 320; 1920 USFC.

35. "Ku Klux Klan gathering in Tuscaloosa, Alabama," photograph Q20361, ADAH.

36. Smith, "Lynching Photographs," 18; Apel, "Lynching Photographs," 44. Also see Hale, "Meaning of Progress," 66; Mazzari, *Southern Modernist*, 91.

37. Robert DeWitt, "Remembering the Trolley Line," *TN*, July 19, 2010.

38. MKF, pers. comm.

39. Keith S. Hébert, "Ku Klux Klan during the Reconstruction Era," *Encyclopedia of Alabama*, http://www.encyclopediaofalabama.org [Sept. 14, 2010] Aug. 15, 2012. See also Myers, "Black Human Capital," 157–59; Escott, *Slavery Remembered*, 155; Wilson, *Baptized in Blood*, 112; Carnes, *Secret Ritual*, 8; Foner, *Reconstruction*, 184.

40. Hubbs, *Searching for Freedom*; Horn, *Invisible Empire*, unnumbered pages between 4 and 5, 117, 130, 140. See also Lester and Wilson, *Ku Klux Klan*, 43.

41. William S. Mudd and Newton L. Whitfield, "Testimony Taken by the Joint Select Committee to Inquire into the Condition of Affairs of the Late Insurrectionary States: Alabama," in U.S. Congress, *Second Session of the Forty-Second Congress*, 4:1751, 4:1971–72. The family buried Murchison in Old Liberty Cemetery in Coker, a community slightly west of Tuscaloosa. The inscription on his grave marker is "Our brother has gone to a better land."

42. Colored Citizens of Tuscaloosa to [William H.] Smith, April 22, 1869, Governor William H. Smith Papers, 1868–1870, ADAH.

43. *Pulaski (TN) Citizen*, May 7, 1869, 2, Chronicling America; Robert Jemison Jr. to Andrew Coleman Hargrove, May 27, 1869, Robert Jemison Jr. Papers, UA Special Collections.

44. Callahan, "Personnel," 21; "Alabama State Treasurers: Charles McCall" and "Alabama Attorneys General: Charles McCall," ADAH; Chalmers, *Hooded Americanism*, 83; Feldman, *Politics*, 150. See also Thornton, "Alabama Politics," 13–21.

45. Letters of recommendation, R. E. Parker, July 8, 1924, and T. W. Smith, July 21, 1924, EFS Collection; Department of Education, Division of Teacher Training, Certification and Placement, State of Alabama, July 1, 1924; T. W. Smith to EMF, Dec. 16, 1924, EFS Collection.

46. Schlereth, *Victorian America*, 273–74; "Infant Daughter of Mr. and Mrs. W. B. Fluker," in Sarah Mozingo, comp., Shorts Baptist Cemetery, June 1998, Rootsweb; Kirby, *Rural Worlds Lost*, 163; "DCH Health System History," DCH Health System, https://www.dchsystem.com/about_us/history.aspx.

47. Smith, *American Archives*, 120, 122.

48. "Miss Sarah Elizabeth Hamner Becomes Bride of Mr. Faucett," *TN*, Feb. 15, 1934, 5.

49. "Lyman Findley in George Washington costume, July 10, 1932," photograph courtesy of MKF.

50. Davis, Gardner, and Gardner, *Deep South*, 109–10; Kasson, "Rituals of Dining," 130, 131; AFS, pers. comm.

51. Hayes, *Colonial Woman's Bookshelf*, 59.

52. Dryden, *Etiquette*, 130–31. See appendix 3, this book.

53. HLF to AFS, Aug. 21, 1941, EFS Collection.

54. University Society, *Home University Bookshelf*, 1:123. See appendix 3, this book.

55. The doll bed linens are in the textile collection of ADAH.

56. *Miller's Tuscaloosa Directory* (1922), 131, and (1924), 152, U.S. Phone and Address Directories.

57. AFS, pers. comm.

58. Margaret Robb Shook Cooper, "Father Finley [*sic*]" (unpublished manuscript, 2002).

59. HLF Sr. to HLF Jr., Aug. 12, 1929, HLF Jr. Scrapbook, courtesy of MKF.

60. Davis, Gardner, and Gardner, *Deep South*, 113; Emmett, "I Wish I Was in Dixie's Land"; George M. Cohan, "Over There," Songs for Our Times.

61. AFS, pers. comm.

62. Nancy Dean Callahan Blackman remembered that in Holt, "almost every house had more than one family living in it" (*Brow of the Hill*, 54).

63. Gene Ahern, "Our Boarding House" (cartoon), April 10 and April 11, 1930, *TN*, 10.

64. Annie Elizabeth Moore to Viola Moore, April 17, 1932, courtesy of CBS.

65. Doss, "City Belles," 12. When a Georgia woman took in boarders in 1884, she "suffered a long, debilitating illness, which she suspected was related to the lack of privacy and . . . emotional strain that . . . boarders entailed" (Painter, "Introduction," 15–16). Ruby Pickens Tartt, who had been well-to-do, also resorted to renting rooms

during the Depression and wrote it "hurt" not to have room for guests; the rent payments were "life-saving, soul-destroying checks" (Brown and Owens, *Toting the Lead Row,* 25). See Schlereth, *Victorian America,* 104 on the impact of boarders and Seale, *Tasteful Interlude,* 272 for the use of back bedrooms as informal parlors or family sitting rooms.

66. AFS, pers. comm. Earline's aunt Bettie Moore referred to "roomers" in a 1932 letter. Bettie Moore to Viola Moore, May 14, 1932, courtesy of CBS.

67. AFS, MKF, pers. comm.

68. AFS, pers. comm.

69. Shores, *On Harper's Trail,* 165. The Santa Claus cartoon is part of the AFS Collection, UA Special Collections.

70. Anne made small batches of Earline's toffee cookies at Christmas for many years after Earline died.

71. AFS, pers. comm. The Tuscaloosa Curb Market "always" sold Christmas trees. "Curb Market in 16th Year," *TN,* Feb. 21, 1940, 12.

72. Similarly, in the early twentieth century the youngest child in the Goode family of Gastonburg (Wilcox County) believed "at Christmas [that] brownies sat on every twig and roof and chimney." Liddell, *Southern Accent,* 26.

73. Clark, *Pills,* 125–26.

74. Strother, "Sixth Paper," 282.

75. Denny Chimes was dedicated in 1929. "History of UA," UA, https://www.ua.edu/about/history.

76. Kirk, *Locust Hill,* 81–82; Cook, "Growing Up," 73; Tompkins, *Cotton-Patch Schoolhouse,* 128–29; Morsman, *The Big House,* 21; Wiggins and Truss, *Journal of Sarah Haynsworth Gayle,* xxi, 36, emphasis in the original. The painter Carroll Cloar remembered witnessing a small black girl, a friend during his childhood in Earle, Arkansas, in the second decade of the twentieth century, exclaim "Christmas gift!" when she was overcome by the excitement of being baptized (Thomas, *The Crossroads of Memory,* 159). For more examples of the "Christmas gift!" ritual, see Burr, *The Secret Eye,* 94; Van Buren, "Cotton Growing State," 372; Kane, *Southern Christmas,* 63–64; Greenberg, *Honor and Slavery,* 66; Pleck, *Celebrating the Family,* 52.

77. Burr, *The Secret Eye,* 214; Clark, *Pills,* 132.

78. Deutsch, *Housewife's Paradise,* 40. A graduate student administered a questionnaire in 1930 to women in Tuscaloosa about how they used leisure time, dividing the responses between "business and professional" women and "homemakers." Asked, "What five things do you enjoy most in life?" the women noted many different activities. For homemakers, cooking was behind every activity except swimming, indicating that homemakers did not view cooking as enjoyable (Springer, "A Study of the Use of Leisure," 20). On the shopping and supervisory routines of elite white women in Wilcox County, Alabama, in the later 1940s, see Rubin, *Plantation County,* 116.

79. Advertisement, "Bargains!" *TN,* Aug. 30, 1929, 6; advertisement, "Hill Grocery Co.," *TN,* Aug. 30, 1929, 7; advertisement, "Saturday Specials," *TN,* Aug. 30, 1929, 8; advertisement, "Piggly Wiggly All Over the World," *TN,* Aug. 30, 1929, 12; advertisements, "Serve Sunday's Dinner" and "Modernized for Modern Housewives," *TN,*

Sept. 13, 1929, 3; Deutsch, *Housewife's Paradise*, 68; Davis, Gardner, and Gardner, *Deep South*, 175–76.

80. In 1930, a census enumerator recorded that two buildings on the northeast corner of the block were occupied by tenants, one of them the assistant manager of a grocery store and the other a salesman for a grocery store (1930 USFC). By 1934, Anders Grocery Company was in operation at 807 Third Avenue (*Tuscaloosa White Pages* [1934], U.S. Phone and Address Directories). William D. Anders of Tuscaloosa and his family operated the store until 1954 (1940 USFC; obituary, "George Macon [Bill] Anders," *TN*, April 10, 2002). It was still open during my childhood.

81. Powdermaker, *After Freedom*, 8–9; Rubin, *Plantation County*, 4; Sellers, *Slavery in Alabama*, 146–47; Daniel, "The Arrest and Trial," 128–29; Wyatt-Brown, *Southern Honor*, 328–29; Deyle, *Carry Me Back*, 168.

82. Dorothy Graham Gast, "Grandma at the Curb Market," Days Gone By, http://daysgoneby.me/grandma-at-the-curb-market/, Feb. 14, 2014; Mrs. John L. Seay, "11 Years Valuable Service for Local Curb Market," *TN*, March 27, 1935, 4; Mrs. John Seay, "Fruitful Year Reported by Tuscaloosa Curb Market," *TN*, March 10, 1938, 16; obituary, "Kate Keene Seay," *TN*, March 30, 1980, 15A; Deutsch, *Housewife's Paradise*, 26–27, 46. A 1937 survey of 200 families in rural Tuscaloosa County and Northport found that about half of the rural mothers went to the curb market two or three times per week. Partrich, "A Study of the Living Rooms," 128.

83. Cason, *90 Degrees*, 144–45; "Sorghum, Muscadines Sold at Curb Market," *TN*, Aug. 12, 1934, 13.

84. Photograph, "Greensboro Avenue Looking North c. 1925," Alabama Photographs and Pictures Collection, AFS Collection, UA Special Collections; Dollard, *Caste and Class*, 7; Katzman, *Seven Days a Week*, 185.

85. EMF, clippings and ephemera, in Turner, *Holland's Cook Book*, AFS Collection, UA Special Collections (hereafter EMF Cookbook). See appendix 3, this book. On cookbooks as artifacts of domestic life, see Theophano, *Eat My Words*, 8–13; Bertelsen, "Daily Life." On kitchens and cookbooks as reflections of women's interpersonal relationships, see Miller, *Stuff*, 87.

86. "Mrs. W. D. Rollison Arrives for Visit," *TN*, June 29, 1941, 9; "Miss Eugenia Latimer," *TN*, April 7, 1977, 5. Eugenia Latimer gave Anne a wedding gift in 1957 (wedding gift and address lists, AFS Collections, UA Special Collections).

87. Clayton, *White and Black*, 169; Fox-Genovese, *Plantation Household*, 118; Bentley, *Eating for Victory*, 105; Jabour, *Scarlett's Sisters*, 23. This point is contrary to that of the historian Tracey Deutsch, who commented that the personal meaning that women like Earline derived from their everyday domestic responsibilities is largely a mystery (*Housewife's Paradise*, 10).

88. Shapiro, *Perfection Salad*, 92.

89. AFS, pers. comm.

90. Herbert wrote to Lyman, "Annie Mary said that she wanted to see you and sister and for you to hurry up and come home" (HLF Sr. to HLF Jr., Aug. 12, 1929, HLF Jr. Scrapbook, courtesy of MKF). No woman with the name Annie Mary Peoples appeared in the 1920 or 1930 Tuscaloosa census, but in 1922 a black cook named Ola

Peoples and a black laborer named Virgil Peoples lived in Tuscaloosa, and there were no residents of either race named Peeples, so it can be surmised that Annie Mary's last name was spelled with an "o" (*Polk's Tuscaloosa Directory* [1922–23], 45, U.S. Phone and Address Directories). A woman named Annie Peoples, who was born Feb. 4, 1896, died in Tuscaloosa in 1980 (U.S. Social Security Death Index).

91. AFS, MKF, pers. comm. On the similarities of smokehouses to small cabins, see Vlach, *Big House*, 66. On the commutes of domestic servants who "lived out," see Dollard, *Caste and Class*, 5; Powdermaker, *After Freedom*, 39, 117–19; Sharpless, *Cooking in Other Women's Kitchens*, 15.

92. Dickens, "Time Activities," 11; Katzman, *Seven Days a Week*, 184; Bentley, *Eating for Victory*, 62–63.

93. Thurber, "Development of the Mammy Image." Also see Hale, *Making Whiteness*, 100, for a view of black domestic workers as status symbols.

94. Cason, *90 Degrees*, 110–11.

95. Hiestand, *Angela the Upside-Down Girl*, 79.

96. Bettie Moore to Viola Moore, May 14, 1932, courtesy of CBS.

97. Advertisement, "Murk Findley for Board of Revenue," *TN*, Feb. 14, 1932, 11; "County Politics Warms Up as Cold Wave Ends," *TN*, March 20, 1932, 2; "Barnes, Clements Appear Elected," *TN*, May 4, 1932, 1; "Appointments to Commerce Faculty Made," *TN*, July 24, 1932, 12. On the revenue board as the governing board of the county, see U.S. Bureau of the Census, *U.S. Census of Governments*, 2.

98. Hoeckel and Van Itallie, *Images of America*, 69; Schwieterman, *When the Railroad Leaves Town*, 22–23; "Island History," Boca Grande Real Estate, www.bocagranderealestate.com/island-guide/island-history. Roland McMillan Harper may have recommended Boca Grande; he had visited several locations near the resort town. See Shores, *On Harper's Trail*.

99. Annie E. Christopher Moore to AFS, April 8, 1934, EFS Collection.

100. "Aunt Sally Tucker Victim of Illness," *TN*, July 27, 1933, 1.

101. AFS, pers. comm.

102. Katzman, *Seven Days a Week*, 199; Palmer, *Domesticity*, 66, 68, 74; Clark-Lewis, *Living In*, 62, 148; Johnston-Miller, "Heirs to Paternalism," 399; Valk and Brown, *Living with Jim Crow*, 84.

103. Rybczynski, *Home*, 156; Marks, *Farewell, We're Good and Gone*.

104. Dollard, *Caste and Class*, 374–75; Powdermaker, *After Freedom*, 23–24; Sharpless, *Cooking in Other Women's Kitchens*, 154. On theft as a form of black resistance, see Escott, *Slavery Remembered*, 166.

105. MKF, pers. comm.

106. On the deceptive relations of white and black women, see Powdermaker, *After Freedom*, 119, 331. On antebellum white women's shock at the departure of freedpeople, see Painter, "Introduction," 36; Faust, *Mothers of Invention*, 76.

107. Dollard, *Caste and Class*, 383–84; Powdermaker, *After Freedom*, 24–25; Bruce, *Violence and Culture*, 17; Morsman, *The Big House*, 25–26, 38–39.

108. Gaines, *Southern Plantation*, 191.

109. Henderson, *Smith's Alabama*, 175–76; "Woman and Four Children on Porch of Eugene Allen Smith Home," UA Photograph Collection, UA Special Collections.

Chapter 5

1. MKF, pers. comm.; 1910 USFC; "Twenty Years Ago Today," *TN*, Oct. 22, 1933, 4; Robert DeWitt, "Bill Newt Hinton, Friend of FDR, Dies at 77," *TN*, Jan. 13, 2006; "Laurel Class Will Give Picnic," *TN*, July 26, 1933, 5; "Church Services," *TN*, Sept. 17, 1933, 11; "Called Meeting of P.T.A. Executive Board," *TN*, Sept. 12, 1933, 5; "Crowds Throng Streets for 'Blue Eagle Day,'" *TN*, Sept. 22, 1933, 1; Deutsch, *Housewife's Paradise*, 97. Earline's handwritten recipes included Gingerbread (Hatchett), Torte (Hatchett), and Nut Cake (Hatchet) (all in EMF Cookbook).

2. "Fine 1933 Game Season Foreseen for This Area," *TN*, Sept. 21, 1933, 1.

3. "Negro Is Lured from His Home Then Murdered," *TN*, Sept. 25, 1933, 1. An independent investigation of the Dennis Cross case found that he was generally known by whites as Old Cross and that whites who knew him were "surprise[d] and disgust[ed]" that the woman had made such an accusation. Southern Commission on the Study of Lynching, *Plight of Tuscaloosa*, 27.

4. "Negro Shot in Eye by Section Foreman," *TN*, June 28, 1933, 1; "'United against Crime'—Judge Urges," *TN*, Oct. 9, 1933, 1, 2; "Militia Guards Three Negroes in Hale County," *TN*, Sept. 11, 1933, 1; "Two Negroes Seized in Pressing Shop Robbery," *TN*, Sept. 12, 1933, 2.

5. Editorial, "Do Not Kill the Dog," *TN*, June 25, 1933, 4; "Two Little Girls Want to Work in Nice Home," *TN*, June 21, 1933, 2; "William Ford Shot, Arm to Be Amputated," *TN*, Sept. 8, 1933, 1.

6. "Negro Jailed as Attack Suspect," *TN*, June 16, 1933, 1; "Jail Gathering Will Be Probed by Grand Jury," *TN*, June 22, 1, 9; "Three Indicted in Maddox Case," *TN*, June 25, 1933, 1.

7. "Court Appoints Counsel to Aid Negroes' Defense," *TN*, July 30, 1933, 1; Callahan, "Personnel," 9. Demonstrating the complicated network of professional ties in the local bar, one of the three lawyers Foster appointed had recently represented Herbert and his brother Hargrove, along with their aunt Elizabeth Hargrove Countess and several cousins, in an unsuccessful suit against their aunt Lula Hargrove and uncle Thomas A. Hargrove over their grandmother Minerva Hargrove's will. "Hargrove Will Upheld by Jury in Court Here," *TN*, July 14, 1933, 7.

8. Editorial, "To Prevent Lynching, Remove the Cause—Crying 'Shame' Not Enough," *TN*, Aug. 25, 1933, 4; "I.L.D. Says It Will Continue Fight in Case," *TN*, Aug. 2, 1933, 1; "Grand Jury Recesses, Praises Judge Foster," *TN*, Sept. 7, 1933, 1, 3; "Pippen Murder Trial Continued," *TN*, Aug. 1, 1933, 1, 7; "I.L.D. Interference Costs State and County $1,500," *TN*, Aug. 3, 1933, 1, 7. The historian Glenn Feldman interpreted this episode differently, suggesting without attribution that Foster "sought to coerce two of the three defendants into firing their Communist lawyers. . . . Foster, a confirmed opponent of labor, engaged in questionable conduct during the following weeks. . . . The judge refused to allow ILD lawyers to represent the blacks" (*Politics*, 251–52). Related to Feldman's suggestion that Foster was anti-labor, the sociologist John Dollard wrote that in Indianola, which he studied two years after the Maddox murder, "when white people did not know what a northern man was doing in the town, they suspected him of being [a labor] organizer" (*Caste and Class*, 9–10; see also Adams and Gorton, "Southern Trauma").

9. Dray, *At the Hands*, 319.

10. Hall, *Revolt against Chivalry*, 224, 226. Also see Griffin, Clark, and Sandberg, "Narrative and Event," 26–27.

11. "Jury Called to Probe Lynching," *TN*, Aug. 14, 1933, 1, 2.

12. Pearl Hargrove lived in southeastern Tuscaloosa County, the area that the Hargroves originally settled, in a small community called Vance, about eleven miles from another small community called Pearl that was situated on Hargrove Road, east of the Hargrove Branch of Big Sandy Creek. Greg and Charesa Hester, "Vance Family Cemetery," IAGenWeb, iagenweb.org.

13. Southern Commission on the Study of Lynching, *Plight of Tuscaloosa*, 21; "Clark Tells Miraculous Escape from Killing," *TN*, Aug. 15, 1933, 1, 3.

14. AP, "I.L.D. Wires Miller, Demanding Arrests," *TN*, Aug. 14, 1933, 2; Raper, *Tragedy of Lynching*, 19; "Jury Called to Probe Lynching," *TN*, Aug. 14, 1933, 1, 2.

15. Southern Commission on the Study of Lynching, *Plight of Tuscaloosa*, 22; "Grand Jury Recesses, Praises Judge Foster," *TN*, Sept. 7, 1933, 1, 3; "Evidence Is Not Thought Enough for Indictment," *TN*, Oct. 2, 1933, 1; Callahan, "Segregated Society," 11; "Festus Shamblin Thanks News and Sees Aroused Public as Great Benefit," *TN*, Oct. 2, 1933, 1.

16. "Negro Man Held as Suspect for Hit-Run Crash," *TN*, July 6, 1933, 1.

17. "New Clue Found in Crosby Case," *TN*, July 16, 1933, 1; "Negro Confesses Crosby Murder," *TN*, July 17, 1933, 1, 3; AP, "Georgia Lynching Probe Causes Death Threats," *TN*, June 28, 1933, 7; AP, "Fifteen Arrested on Mob Violence Charge," *TN*, July 13, 1933, 1; AP, "Negro Lynched by Mississippi Gang Is Report," *TN*, July 23, 1933, 1; AP, "Negro Man Shot by Officers, Mob Takes His Body," *TN*, Aug. 28, 1933, 1; AP, "Mob Lynches Negro in Louisiana Case," *TN*, Oct. 12, 1933, 2.

18. Armstrong, *Mary Turner*, 27.

19. "Negro Shot in Eye by Section Foreman," *TN*, June 28, 1933, 1; AP, "Negro Saved by Solicitor from Deatsville Mob," *TN*, Aug. 4, 1933, 2.

20. AP, "Negroes Sought for Attack on Girl, Companion," *TN*, Sept. 6, 1933, 1; AP, "Officers Search for Negroes in Attack of Girl," *TN*, Sept. 7, 1933, 1.

21. "R.F.C. to Curtail Activities Here, Funds Near End," *TN*, May 31, 1933, 1; AP, "Negro Menaced with Lynching by Gotham Mob," *TN*, Sept. 11, 1933, 1; Southern Commission on the Study of Lynching, *Plight of Tuscaloosa*, 27; 1930 USFC; Deaths and Burials Index; Cason, *90 Degrees*, 118–20; "Negro Is Held Here in Attack on Woman," *TN*, Sept. 13, 1933, 1; "Negro Is Lured from His Home Then Murdered," *TN*, Sept. 25, 1933, 1; editorial, "Work of Claude Hinton Helped Many People," *TN*, April 20, 1969, 4. See also Ames, *The Changing Character*, 34.

22. "'United against Crime'—Judge Urges," *TN*, Oct. 9, 1933, 1, 2; "Reward of $400 Posted by State in Cross Death," *TN*, Sept. 27, 1933, 1; editorial, "Shall We Accept the Challenge?" *TN*, Sept. 27, 1933, 1; "Ministers Urge All Citizens to Enlist in Crime Crusade," *TN*, Oct. 2, 1933, 1; "Negro Chorus Will Be Heard in Program Here," *TN*, Oct. 1, 1933, 2; "Ministers Issue Statement," *TN*, Sept. 25, 1933, 1; "Citizens Organize to Wage Crusade against Crime Here," *TN*, Oct. 1, 1933, 1; Southern Commission on the Study of Lynching, *Plight of Tuscaloosa*, 32. Powdermaker observed in Mississippi that while

most whites thought mistreatment of blacks was "too bad," they did not consider mistreatment a moral fault (*After Freedom*, 27).

23. Carmer, *Stars Fell*, 271.

24. "City May Obtain Bloodhounds to Check Criminals," *TN*, Sept. 26, 1933, 1. On black fear of white violence as "one of the major facts of life," see Dollard, *Caste and Class*, quoted in Hoelscher, "Making Place," 675.

25. "Three Men Arrested for Attack on Negro," *TN*, Oct. 1, 1933, 2; Mrs. James G. Snedecor, letter to the editor, *TN*, Oct. 8, 1933, 4; Deaths and Burials Index; Nancy DuPree and Robert DuPree, "Stillman College," *Encyclopedia of Alabama*, http://www.encyclopediaofalabama.org, April 24, 2013.

26. "Murder Case against Honey Clark Dismissed," *TN*, May 24, 1934, 1.

27. In 1969, the *TN* published a long feature article summarizing the history of the city and referred to the murders of Pippen and Harden as "one of Tuscaloosa's few lynchings," overlooking the murder of Dennis Cross (Matthew W. Clinton, "City's Growth Begins," *TN*, April 24, 1969, 1, 13, 22–23). For a discussion of when and why white residents tended to recall details of lynchings, see Baker, "Under the Rope," 324–25. A few details of the 1933 murders in Tuscaloosa—the low socioeconomic status and suspicious father of Vaudine Maddox; the low mental capacity of Alice Johnson; the withered arms of Honey Clark and Dennis Cross—resemble details in Harper Lee's iconic novel *To Kill a Mockingbird*. B. J. Hollars noticed these similarities while literary scholar James A. Miller suggested that Lee based her book on "the historic Scottsboro trials and on a 1930 case in Sumter County, Alabama, involving a black defendant named Tom Robinson" (Hollars, *Thirteen Loops*, 35; Miller, *Remembering Scottsboro*, 222). Lee could have drawn from all of those events if she happened to find the 1933 report *The Tragedy of Lynching* by the sociologist Arthur Raper. Raper described the 1933 murders in Tuscaloosa and the lynching of Robinson in Sumter County. An editorial that the *TN* published on the same day as a report in the Maddox case, urging readers not to kill dogs without clear evidence of rabies, could have inspired her central metaphor, Atticus Finch's shooting of a rabid dog. Editorial, "Do Not Kill the Dog," *TN*, June 25, 1933, 4; "Three Indicted in Maddox Case," *TN*, June 25, 1933, 1.

28. Marie Ball, "Garner Stayed Involved," *TN*, June 14, 1981, 2C; MKF, pers. comm.; Mrs. Archie Hamby, "Alberta City News," *TN*, Jan. 11, 1940, 5, and Feb. 8, 1942, 8; 1920 USFC; *Polk's Tuscaloosa Directory* (1916–17), 92, and (1922–23), 109, U.S. Phone and Address Directories; Horton, *Family Quilts*, 129. The society editor for the *Birmingham News* in 1940 was Sue M. Markell, the elderly wife of a retired lawyer (1940 USFC).

29. Cason, "Middle Class and Bourbon," 499.

30. "Billy Bland Plans Party," *TN*, July 21, 1933, 5; "Reception for Auxiliary Is Much Enjoyed," *TN*, July 26, 1933, 5; *Polk's Tuscaloosa Directory* (1932), 275, U.S. Phone and Address Directories; "Miss Kirk Observes Fifth Birthday," *TN*, Oct. 6, 1933, 5; "Plantation Supper for Miss Snow and Leslie Dee," *TN*, Oct. 13, 1933, 6; "Ye Old Plantation Luncheon Planned," *TN*, July 17, 1933, 5.

31. Gordon, *Saturated World*, 5, 66, 77; "Miss Mackereth Celebrates Birthday," *TN*, Sept. 26, 1933, 5; AFS, pers. comm. Again in 1936, the *TN* described a party where

"blue ribbons extended from the centerpiece to each cover and held corsage bouquets of candy which served as favors" ("Luncheon Is Given by Miss Searcy for Miss Deal," *TN*, Feb. 9, 1936, 9). On articles about parties as "a dynamic feedback loop," see Gordon, *Saturated World*, 74–75.

32. "Tom Thumb Wedding Music Planned," *TN*, Dec. 6, 1933, 5; program, "Tom Thumb Wedding"; "Tom Thumb Wedding Is Huge Event," *TN*, Dec. 8, 1933, 5; Coleman, *We're Heaven Bound*, 29; "Lilliputian Wedding," *Palestine (TX) Daily Herald*, May 11, 1910, 5.

33. "Lundi Bleu Club Gives Shower," *TN*, Dec. 22, 1931, 5.

34. Maxwell, *Autobiography*, 8, 13, 315.

35. Sellers, *Slavery in Alabama*, 323. On mock weddings for slaves, see Hague, *Blockaded Family*, 7–9; Pleck, *Celebrating the Family*, 210; Roberts, *Confederate Belle*, 151–52; Cleveland, "Social Conditions in Alabama," 12; Burr, *The Secret Eye*, 115; Kirk, *Locust Hill*, 85.

36. "The Mischievous Nigger," *The Meteor*, Dec. 25, 1879, 3; "At the Theater Unique," *TN*, Sept. 27, 1910, 3. For more about mock weddings and black and blackface minstrelsy, see Cauthen, *With Fiddle*, 13; Sotiropoulos, *Staging Race*, 3; Abbott and Seroff, *Ragged But Right*, 11, 209; Henninger, *Ordering the Facade*, 41; Prince, *Stories of the South*, 168–203. On African American athletic stars as minstrel-type performers, see Doyle, "On the Cusp of Modernity," 203–4.

37. *Scrambled Courtship, Whar's de Groom?* and *Coon Creek Courtship* (Chicago: T. S. Denison and Company, 1901, 1928, 1929); "Minstrel Planned," *TN*, June 28, 1933, 7; "Minstrel at Coaling," *TN*, July 5, 1933, 5; "Mock Wedding Enjoyed at Community Singing," *TN*, June 16, 1933, 3; "Taylorville to Stage Negro Minstrel Show," *TN*, March 19, 1931, 2.

38. "Mock Trial Planned," *TN*, Aug. 16, 1933, 2.

39. Mrs. Archie Hamby, "Alberta City News," *TN*, Feb. 8, 1942, 8. Southside Baptist Church also produced a womanless wedding a few months later. "Womanless Wedding," *TN*, May 15, 1942, 7.

40. Bob Kyle, "Cop Turns Preacher, 'Hitches' Negro Pair," *TN*, Dec. 27, 1944, 2.

41. Hoelscher, "Making Place," 673; Prince, *Stories of the South*, 170.

42. "New Home Is Dedicated by BP&W Club," *TN*, Sept. 11, 1933, 5; "Pageant Feature of Stafford P.T.A. Fathers' Night," *TN*, March 6, 1938, 11; "Mrs. Harrison Hostess for Kettledrum," *TN*, Oct. 15, 1933, 7; "Mrs. Jones Is Host to 20th Century Club," *TN*, Oct. 8, 1933, 7.

43. Clipping, "Legion Members Entertain Auxiliary at Joint Meeting," *TN*, May 15, 1941, 6; Hattie Porter Collier, "Herbert Caldwell's Success in Music Pleases Tuscaloosa Folk," *TN*, Aug. 14, 1936, 6; Hattie Porter Collier, "Tuscaloosa Is Fortunate to Have Real Musical Artists in Midst," *TN*, Aug. 18, 1940, 5; advertisement, "Herbert Caldwell Vocal Studio," *TN*, Sept. 2, 1940, 5; "Clement Wood," *Alabama's Literary Landscape: This Goodly Land*, Alabama Center for the Book, http://alabamaliterarymap.lib.ua.edu/authors; Wolfe, "Three Negro Poems" and "Short'nin' Bread." Wood was a prolific writer in several genres. The African American intellectual Alain Locke considered that Wood's work, including *Nigger* and numerous "Negro poems," helped bring "the

materials of Negro life out of the shambles of conventional polemics, cheap romance and journalism into the domain of pure . . . art" ("Negro Youth Speaks," 184).

44. When an elderly woman in Tuscaloosa played the piano at a family reunion in October 1933, the *TN* noted she was "recognized as a musician without peer [and] the personification of genuine aristocracy" ("Twenty Years Ago Today," *TN*, July 17, 1934, 4; "Family Reunion in Perkins Home," *TN*, Oct. 15, 1933, 6). On artistic talent as a requirement for the belle, see Gaines, *Southern Plantation*, 175–76; Bleser and Heath, "The Clays of Alabama," 135; Kearney, *Slaveholder's Daughter*, 23, 40; Burr, *The Secret Eye*, 264, 306.

45. Ila Blackman Findley to AFS, n.d., EFS Collection; "Extended Illness Fatal to Beloved Matron," *TN*, Nov. 14, 1930, 1.

46. "Forty Present Piano Recital," *TN*, Aug. 13, 1933, 6; advertisement, "Miss Mary Lee Strickland," *TN*, Aug. 29, 1933, 5; advertisement, "Mrs. I. N. Hobson," *TN*, Aug. 29, 1933, 5; advertisement, "Paul Lavier Newell," *TN*, Sept. 1, 1933, 2.

47. Kate Cooper, "Of Grandmothers, Bookshops, and Private Tragedies," https://kateantiquity.com/2013/12/15/of-grandmothers-bookshops-and-private-tragedies, Dec. 15, 2013; AFS, pers. comm.; 1930 USFC.

48. AFS, pers. comm. Louisiana M. Keene, a sister of Lucy Virginia Keene Findley, was the second wife of Virginia Moore's maternal grandfather, Daniel Goree. See 1870 USFC; Tuscaloosa Genealogical Society, *Pioneers*, 134; Gandrud, *Alabama Records*, 57, "Newspaper Extracts," 79.

49. On Virginia Moore's lineage, see Gandrud, *Marriage Records*, 11; Edgar Abernethy, "The Forneys," *The State*, March 11, 1944 (facsimile), USGenWebArchives, usgenweb.org; U.S. Congress, "Peter Forney (1756–1834)" and "Daniel Munroe Forney (1784–1847)," Biographical Directory of the United States Congress, http://bioguide.congress.gov/biosearch/biosearch.asp; Garrett, *Reminiscences*, 121; Cullum, *Biographical Register*, 1:543; Owen and Owen, *History of Alabama*, 3:758.

50. AFS, handwritten notes; AFS pers. comm.

51. Sara Haardt, "Each in Her Own Day," in *Southern Souvenirs*, ed. Henley, 106.

52. *Atlanta Constitution*, Sept. 15, 1907; "Educational Reports of U.S. Consuls," *School Journal* 74 (Feb. 16, 1907): 169, Google Books. Jennie registered at the American Consulate in Leipzig, Germany, on Oct. 28, 1907, indicating that she had previously lived in Chattanooga and had moved to Leipzig for the purpose of "studying music" (Certificate #2341, U.S. Consular Registrations).

53. Wilkinson, *Liszt*; Walker, *Franz Liszt*, 3:241.

54. Deaths and Burials Index; 1930 USFC; *Miller's Tuscaloosa Directory* (1924), 232, U.S. Phone and Address Directories.

55. "Forney Moore, Widely Known Resident, Dies," *TN*, July 5, 1934, 1; AFS, pers. comm. Margaret Koster Findley recalled that the house was green (MKF, pers. comm.).

56. Watson, *Liszt*, 10–11; Rellstab, "Life Sketch."

57. AFS, Elna Bolding Shugerman, pers. comm. On mothers seeing music lessons as a step into the upper class, see Davis, Gardner, and Gardner, *Deep South*, 187; Ames, *Dining Room*, 156nn4.6, 4.7, 164; Roell, "The Piano," 87, 96.

58. Roland M. Harper, "Anne and Emily Having a Lawn Party" (cartoon), Nov. 3,

1933, AFS Collection, UA Special Collections; "Weather," *TN*, Nov. 2, 1933, 1.

59. "Three Clinics Are Scheduled for This Week," *TN*, Nov. 5, 1933, 8.

60. USFC 1920, 1940; "13,239 Receive Inoculations in Recent Months," *TN*, Oct. 9, 1933, 3.

61. "Miss Hinton Returns from Warm Springs," *TN*, April 18, 1934, 9; Robert DeWitt, "Bill Newt Hinton, Friend of FDR, Dies at 77," *TN*, Jan. 13, 2006; Oshinsky, *Polio*, 47; Hattie Porter Collier, "First of Series to Be Presented on Monday Night," *TN*, Nov. 25, 1934, 5; EMF to AFS, June 12, 1938, EFS Collection. The forecasted high temperatures in Tuscaloosa between Monday, Oct. 30, and Sunday, Nov. 5, 1933, ranged from 82 to 86 degrees. On Halloween, when "a dozen or more parties" took place around town, the forecast high was 86 degrees ("Weather," *TN*, Oct. 27–Nov. 5, 1933, 1; "Market Has Big Sale on Hallowe'en Trimmings," *TN*, Oct. 31, 1933, 3). On the widespread fear of polio in the mid-twentieth century, see Wilson, *Living with Polio*.

62. Annie E. Christopher Moore to AFS, April 8, 1934, EFS Collection.

63. "Weather," *TN*, March 20, 1934, 1; "Weather," *TN*, March 29, 1934, 1; photographs, Ormond-Little House and Scott-Moody House, March 29, 1934, HABS.

64. "Negro Given 20-Year Term in Attack Case," *TN*, July 22, 1934, 1.

65. "Twenty Years Meted to Young Negro in Assault Case," *TN*, Aug. 2, 1934, 1, 2.

66. AP, "Berlin Tense as Squads of Police Patrol Streets," *TN*, July 1, 1934, 1.

67. Cason, *90 Degrees*, 118–20.

68. Raper, *Tragedy of Lynching*, 20.

69. Hall, *Revolt against Chivalry*, 160–61; Southern Commission on the Study of Lynching, *Plight of Tuscaloosa*, 22.

70. "Publishers of Book by Cason Relate His Worry," *TN*, May 9, 1935, 1. On the spate of books about the South and southern culture that appeared in the 1930s, many published by the University of North Carolina Press, see Egerton, *Speak Now*, 133, 147–48.

71. Cason, *90 Degrees*, xiii.

72. Ibid., 113–20; Matthews, "Clarence Cason," 18; "the North was relatively right, while the South was relatively wrong": Enoch M. Banks quoted in Blight, *Race and Reunion*, 296; McGovern, *Anatomy of a Lynching*, ix. On younger whites approving of "nigger hunts," see Powdermaker, *After Freedom*, 54.

73. Drew Pearson and Robert S. Allen, "Merry-Go-Round," *TN*, May 7, 1935, 3; Ball, *Hugo L. Black*, 74.

74. Beidler, "Yankee Interloper," 29; Raines, "Introduction," xv.

75. "Junior Council Officers Chosen," *TN*, Oct. 15, 1939, 3; "Clarence Cason Ends Own Life with Pistol," *TN*, May 8, 1935, 1, 2.

76. "Publishers of Book by Cason Relate His Worry," *TN*, May 9, 1935, 1; W. Kirk Wood, "Clarence Cason," encyclopediaofalabama.org, [Sept. 17, 2009] July 11, 2013.

77. "Clarence Cason Ends Own Life with Pistol," *TN*, May 8, 1935, 1, 2; Flynt, introduction, x; Thomson, "Clarence Cason," 64. For more on Cason's fears, see Rose, *Psychology and Selfhood*, 87–88.

78. Advertisement, "90 in the Shade," *TN*, May 12, 1935, 6.

79. Hamner Cobbs, "A Critical But Fair Study of Dixie," *TN*, May 12, 1935, 12. Cobbs

was the namesake of the first Episcopal bishop in Alabama and an editorial writer for the *TN* from 1931 to 1940 who "won wide recognition as a spokesman for the conservative viewpoint in this section of the country." In 1943 he revived a Greensboro newspaper, the *Southern Watchman*, saying it would be "pro-South" and a voice for "White Supremacy." "Nicholas Hamner Cobbs Papers" [finding aid], UA Special Collections; "The Southern Watchman Revived by Hamner Cobbs," *TN*, March 10, 1943, 8.

80. Cason, *90 Degrees*, 113–20.

81. University of Alabama, *Corolla* (1915), unnumbered page; MKF, pers. comm.

Chapter 6

1. Govan, *Those Plummer Children*, i, 1. See appendix 3, this book. Eggleston, born in 1856, was a lawyer in Franklin. He and his wife, Julia Plummer Eggleston, had at least six children, including a daughter, Julia, who was born the same year as Govan and was the inspiration for Govan's character Judy Plummer (1900, 1910 USFC).

2. Govan, *Those Plummer Children*, 5–6. Similar characters in two of Lyman's books, Booth Tarkington's *Penrod and Sam* and *Penrod Jashber*, were named Verman and Sherman. Mildred Spurrier Topp, a memoirist in Mississippi, perpetuated this patronizing form of humor in a 1948 memoir, naming African American sister-and-brother twins who were live-in servants Lovey and Dovey (*Smile Please*, 125). The cultural historian Robin Bernstein proposed that Tarkington made Verman and Sherman "insensate," unable to feel pain inflicted by whites (*Racial Innocence*, 52).

3. Govan, *Narcissus*, 33; Govan, *Those Plummer Children*, 49, 51, 56. On the use of "maum" or "mom" as a synonym for "mammy," see Cook, "Growing Up," 75; Clayton, *White and Black*, 268.

4. Govan, *Those Plummer Children*, 51–52. On the "thousands of black women [who] spent their aging lives trying to reassemble lost families dislocated by emancipation's diaspora," see Blight, *Race and Reunion*, 312.

5. Govan, *Narcissus*, 103. On the supposed infatuation of African Americans with bright shades of pink, see Powdermaker, *After Freedom*, 10. The association by whites of the color pink and African American culture also appears in the work of another Tennessee writer who used the phrase "nigger pink." Evelyn Scott, *Background in Tennessee* (New York: R. M. McBride, 1937), 216, quoted in Cook, "Growing Up," 251.

6. Govan, *Those Plummer Children*, 21, 88–90, 192; Govan, *Narcissus*, 68, 141, 142, 140–41. On the ancestor portrait in American popular fiction as a sign of "intentional and unintentional snobberies," see Betsky, "Inside the Past," 269.

7. Seidel, *Southern Belle*, 157; Wyatt-Brown, *Southern Honor*, 366.

8. Dawson, *A State*, 10–14, 30–31, 27–28; Marie Ball, "City Elections Have Always Been Colorful," *TN*, July 12, 1981, 2C; Brown, *John McKinley*, 47–48.

9. Clipping, "Funeral of Mrs. Murk Finley and John Finley," n.d.; clipping, Herbert Findley, "To the People of Tuscaloosa County."

10. Obituary, "Hope Hargrove, Widely Known Citizen, Dies," *TN*, June 12, 1932, 1, 3.

11. Callahan, "Personnel," 13; Lee N. Adams, "William W. Brandon (1923–27)," *Encyclopedia of Alabama*, http://www.encyclopediaofalabama.org, Oct. 7, 2012.

12. "Twenty-Six Cases Beer Confiscated by Police in Raid," *TN*, July 26, 1933, 1;

"Bonds Are Forfeited in 'Beer Raid' Case," *TN*, July 28, 1933, 7; "Beer Trial Delayed," *TN*, July 31, 1933, 7; Howington, "John Barley Corn," 217–21; Sellers, *The Prohibition Movement*, 219.

13. "Further Firms Join NRA Drive in Tuscaloosa," *TN*, Aug. 1, 1933, 1. A genealogist indicated Henry Foster and Richard Foster shared a relative, Josephine F. Foster Patton, who was Henry's cousin and Richard's aunt ("Josephine F. Foster Patton," Find a Grave Index).

14. Wolfe, *University of Alabama*, 160; "New Year Begun by Legion Post in Tuscaloosa," *TN*, Sept. 14, 1933, 7; "R. C. Foster Named Party Head," *TN*, Jan. 21, 1934, 1.

15. "Judge Herbert Findley Resigns Court Position," *TN*, Aug. 21, 1946, 1; "Festus Shamblin Thanks News and Sees Aroused Public as Great Benefit," *TN*, Oct. 2, 1933, 1; "Tuscaloosa Agog as Hot Races Draw Close to Balloting Stage," *TN*, April 29, 1934, 1; Dumenil, *Freemasonry*, 130; Carnes, *Secret Ritual*, 2–3; "Masonic Lodges to Consolidate Tomorrow Night," *TN*, Oct. 13, 1934, 1.

16. "Judge Findley Re-Elected," *TN*, March 3, 1938, 2.

17. Cauthen, *With Fiddle*, 35; Brown, *John McKinley*, 49; Wiggins and Truss, *Journal of Sarah Haynsworth Gayle*, 38; obituary, "Alfred David (A. D.) Hamner," *TN*, July 20, 2005; Foster, "Women and Refinement," 220. For fiddling in pioneer Alabama, see Cauthen, *With Fiddle*, 3–4. Also see Harris, *Plain Folk and Gentry*, 82, on "fiddling schools" in Georgia.

18. "Special Features at Square Dance Planned" and advertisement, "Old Fashioned Square Dance," *TN*, Jan. 21, 1937, 2; J. L. Newman, "Alberta City News," *TN*, Feb. 27, 1938, 2; "Halloween Dance Planned Friday at Senior High Gym," *TN*, Oct. 20, 1938, 6; advertisement, "Boss Hinton Asks for Promotion," *TN*, May 29, 1938, 13; "Dance for Roy Smith to Be Given Tonight," *TN*, March 17, 1939, 1; "Dance at Taylorville," *TN*, Oct. 20, 1941, 8.

19. Editorial, "Square Dance and Fiddlers' Contest Return to Tuscaloosa," *TN*, March 19, 1937, 4; Cauthen, *With Fiddle*, 137; "Repeal Rally to Be Held at Holt High," *TN*, June 26, 1933, 7; Sellers, *The Prohibition Movement*, 219; "Fiddlers' Convention," *TN*, Dec. 9, 1934, 2.

20. Nancy Callahan, "Bring Back the Personal Touch of County Politics," *TN*, Oct. 15, 2006; editorial, "Tonight's Climactic Rally," *TN*, May 3, 1940, 4; "Supper-Rally Changed," *TN*, April 23, 1934, 5; "Holman Rally Planned," *TN*, April 22, 1934, 3; "Box Supper at Sterling," *TN*, April 23, 1934, 7; "Women of Duncanville Plan Entertainment," *TN*, April 25, 1934, 2.

21. "Rally at Brownville," *TN*, March 25, 1940, 3; "First 'Free' Rally Goes Over in a Big Way," *TN*, March 26, 1940, 1; editorial, "Tonight's Climactic Rally," *TN*, May 3, 1940, 4.

22. Callahan, "Personnel," 1; Marks, *Southern Hunting*, 94. On the more "democratic" nature of Deep South foxhunts as compared to Virginia hunts, see Cobb, *Away Down South*, 137.

23. Bruce, *Violence and Culture*, 198; Brown and Taylor, *Gabr'l Blow Sof'*, 79; Proctor, *Bathed in Blood*, 39, 42, 72–73, 109, 119; Marks, *Southern Hunting*, 24, 28. For a vivid description of a hunt with hounds on an 1838 Alabama plantation, see Gosse,

"Possum-Hunting," 88–89. For the aristocratic image of antebellum hunts in Mississippi, see Van Buren, "Cotton Growing State."

24. Fox, *Little Shepherd*, 171, 110–11. On bestowing the tail or "brush" as a ritual in foxhunting, see "Foxhunting," Encyclopedia Britannica, http://www.britannica.com/sports/foxhunting.

25. Smith, *Reminiscences*, 53–59; Matthew W. Clinton, "Tuscaloosa Scrapbook: Powell Won Us Capital," *TN*, April 9, 1967, 5.

26. "Twenty Years Ago Today," *TN*, Aug. 10, 1937, 4; "Beautiful Wedding Held at Presbyterian Church," *TN*, Aug. 12, 1931, 5; "Looking Back," *TN*, Feb. 17, 1981, 3; "Guide to the Little Family Papers, 1857–1950," UA Special Collections; clipping, "Funeral of Mrs. Murk Finley and John Finley"; Callahan, "Personnel," 1–2; Bill Plott, "Harwood and Coleman: Retiring Justices Honored Here," *TN*, Oct. 11, 1974, 1; "Community Mourns Glenn Foster's Death," *TN*, April 3, 1939, 1; Betty Slowe, "Nov. 12–18: One Hundred Years Ago," *TN*, Dec. 2, 2012; "Walker Will Take Over Probate Office Monday," *TN*, Nov. 15, 1936, 1; "Army Trucks to Pass through Tuscaloosa," *TN*, Aug. 1, 1940, 5. Even the magazine *Field and Stream* noted the political connections in Alabama's foxhunting network (Rodney Random, "With Fox and Hound in Alabama," *Field and Stream* 87 [Jan.–Dec. 1917]: 112, 142, Google Books). On the political value of foxhunts in the twentieth-century South, see Marks, *Southern Hunting*, 96.

27. Brown and Taylor, *Gabr'l Blow Sof'*, 9; Gohdes, *Hunting in the Old South*, xvi; Proctor, *Bathed in Blood*, 119.

28. "Yesterday's News," *Mobile Press-Register*, Jan. 18, 2009; "The Hospital Farms," *TN*, July 30, 1937, 4; "Dr. Faulk Resigns from Bryce Staff," *TN*, Aug. 19, 1945, 14; Tuscaloosa County, Alabama Historical Association Historical Markers, www.alabamahistory.net/historical-markers.html. On comic strips as another intergenerational tie, see Kammen, *American Culture*, 86.

29. MKF, pers. comm.; editorial, "Fox Hunting—Two Styles," *TN*, Jan. 22, 1939, 4; Herbert Findley to Charles G. Crawford, Oct. 7, 1946, EFS Collection. The midcentury blues singer Alex Miller, known professionally as Sonny Boy Williamson the Second, reenacted the chatter of men listening to the sound of baying hounds in a minstrel-style novelty song with ironic echoes of southern manhunts: "Old Buck . . . come from a long generation of coondogs. . . . Turn him aloose! Turn him aloose there! . . . You know that hound is singing that song, boy. . . . That sound like Old Buck. . . . He's on the trail of something." Sonny Boy Williamson the Second, *The Real Folks Blues: More Real Folks Blues* (MCA/Chess, [1960] 2002).

30. "Patton's Hounds Win Four Prizes," *TN*, July 6, 1933, 10; "Many Plan to Attend Fox Hunt, Barbecue," *TN*, Oct. 9, 1932, 2; "Fox Hunt at Romulus," *TN*, Oct. 31, 1933, 7; "The Gasper," *TN*, June 22, 1934, 10; "William Woodward Brandon," Alabama Governors, ADAH. See scenes of similar hunts and barbecues in Barbour County, Alabama, in photographs Q2258 and Q2261, ADAH Digital Collections.

31. Advertisement, "A Message to the Voters of Tuscaloosa County from Herbert Findley," *TN*, April 29, 1934, 8; "Shamblin Named Sheriff, Tucker Chosen Senator," *TN*, May 2, 1934, 1; "Democrats Poll Lopsider Ballot over the County," *TN*, Nov. 7, 1934, 1.

32. "J. A. McCollum Chosen as Assistant Solicitor," *TN*, Jan. 10, 1935, 1; Marie Ball,

"Our Town: City Elections Have Always Been Colorful," *TN*, July 12, 1981, 2C.

33. Rubin, *Plantation County*, 116; "Masonic Lodge Oldest in State," *TN*, April 17, 1940, 3; "Verner School P.T.A. Has Interesting Session," *TN*, Oct. 22, 1933, 6; "Laurel Class Plans Social Meeting," *TN*, May 22, 1934, 6; "Laurel Class to Meet Tomorrow," *TN*, Nov. 19, 1936, 11; "Poppy Day Observed in Tuscaloosa," *TN*, April 14, 1935, 11; "Calendar of Social and Club Events," *TN*, April 8, 1935, 5; "American Legion Auxiliary to Meet," *TN*, Dec. 6, 1936, 12; "'The American Home' Will Be Topic of Que [*sic*] Vive Club," *TN*, Sept. 3, 1936, 5; "Community Fair to Open April 6," *TN*, March 16, 1937, 7; "Chester Walker Dies Suddenly at Home Here," *TN*, Sept. 3, 1965, 1. Schoolchildren in Czechoslovakia wrote a letter, dated Feb. 29, 1936, to "dear friends across the ocean," which the Junior Red Cross in Tuscaloosa somehow received. They thanked the recipients for "your friendly letter and pictures of your university." Earline labeled a carbon copy "Copy," in red pencil, folded it in quarters, and tucked it in her cookbook (EMF Cookbook).

34. U.S. Headstone Applications for Military Veterans.

35. "Ectopic Pregnancy," MayoClinic.org.

36. EMF to AFS, June 6, 1938, EFS Collection; MKF, pers. comm.; clipping, "Mrs. Herbert Findley Reported Better," *TN*, Oct. 29, 1937, 5.

37. B. R. Holstun, "For the Farmer," *TN*, Nov. 8, 1942, 3; editorial, "Resolutions," *TN*, Jan. 1, 2003, 6A.

38. "Rose Bowl Bid Remains Secret, Rumors Abound," *TN*, Nov. 29, 1937, 1; Doyle, "On the Cusp of Modernity," 194; "University of Alabama versus Stanford University 1927 Rose Bowl football game," UA Photograph Collection, UA Special Collections; "Thousands Welcome Tide Home," *TN*, Jan. 5, 1931, 1; "History," Rose Bowl: America's Stadium, www.rosebowlstadium.com/about/history; "California Overpowers 'Bama, 13–0," *TN*, Jan. 2, 1938, 1.

39. "Hargrove Van de Graaff Dies at Veterans Hospital in Gulfport, Miss.," *TN*, Jan. 3, 1938, 1, 2.

40. Beardsley, "River Island," 22–23; Bates, "Comfort," 59. See Myers, "Black Human Capital," 129, for another Alabama proponent of this vision of white yeomen farmsteads.

41. University of Alabama, *Corolla* (1915), unnumbered page; "Adrian Van de Graaff Dies of Heart Attack; Prominent Attorney, First of Famous Football Trio at the University, Succumbs While Seated in Office Chair," *TN*, March 15, 1936, 1, 2; Wolfe, *University of Alabama*, 150.

42. Porter, *Biographical Dictionary*, 683–84.

43. Callahan, "Personnel," 10–11.

44. "Funeral Services Set for Mrs. Asa Rountree," *TN*, March 22, 1934, 2; Joan Ladd, "Visit to Mansion Recalls Old Times," *TN*, March 12, 1992, 6A.

45. "Adrian Sebastian Van de Graaff Papers, 1851–1967" [finding aid], UA Special Collections; "Hargrove Van de Graaff Dies at Veterans Hospital in Gulfport, Miss.," *TN*, Jan. 2, 1938, 1, 2; Woofter, *Land Lord and Tenant*, 21.

46. Kathryn Tucker Windham, "Bill Jones," transcript of interview, excerpted in Bates, "Comfort"; Fleischhauer and Brannan, *Documenting America*, 147; Beardsley, "River Island," 23–24.

47. Advertisement, "Announcement: Van de Graaff Coal Co.," *TN*, Nov. 29, 1931, 2; "Van de Graaff Awarded Riverview Park Lease," *TN*, April 18, 1933, 7; "Alabama Legion Forces Convene Here July 24–26," *TN*, April 14, 1933, 1.

48. *Christian Century* article mentioned in Renwick C. Kennedy, "Life at Gee's Bend," cited in Fleischhauer and Brannan, *Documenting America*, 148–49. See also Nelson, "Welfare Capitalism," 225; Henninger, *Ordering the Facade*, 29; Bates, "Comfort," 62.

49. "Van de Graaff Memorial Exercises to Be Held," *TN*, March 17, 1936, 1; "Memorial Tribute Paid to Adrian Van de Graaff," *TN*, March 19, 1936, 1; editorial, "University's New President," *TN*, Oct. 12, 1936, 1.

50. Mellown, *Historic Structures Report*, 20; Joan Ladd, "Visit to Mansion Recalls Old Times," *TN*, March 12, 1992, 6A.

51. O. B. Keeler, "Hargrove Van de Graaff," *TN*, Jan. 17, 1938, 4; editorial, "Hargrove Van de Graaff," *TN*, Jan. 4, 1938, 4; Arthur Rothstein, "Tenant Farmers," Library of Congress Prints and Photographs Online Catalog; Roy Stryker, quoted in Fleischhauer and Brannan, *Documenting America*, 146–47. On the quilts, see Beardsley et al., *Quilts of Gee's Bend*.

52. A black man named Hargrove Pettway gave an interview to researchers (Arnett and Arnett, "On the Map," 36). A young black woman named Cherokee Parker Pettway appeared in a photograph taken at Gee's Bend by Arthur Rothstein in 1937 (Photograph #USF34T01–25365-D, Library of Congress Prints and Photographs Online Catalog). Hargrove Kennedy of Gee's Bend told an interviewer he was named for Hargrove Van de Graaff, "the owner of the Gee's Bend estate, and worked for him as a young man" ("Nettie Jane Kennedy," SoulsGrownDeep.org). For the "tradition of dependence" by which poor black farmers relied on "a solid and sympathetic paternalism," see Johnson, *Shadow of the Plantation*, 27; Rubin, *Plantation County*, 25–27.

53. Beardsley, "River Island," 24, 26–27; editorial, "Hargrove Van de Graaff," *TN*, Jan. 4, 1938, 4.

54. "Tide Returns Home to Thunderous Applause of Five Thousand," *TN*, Jan. 5, 1938, 1; "City Plans Noisy Welcome for Tide," *TN*, Jan. 4, 1938, 1.

55. "Rites Set for Van de Graaff," *TN*, Jan. 4, 1938, 1; "Tribute Is Paid to Van de Graaff," *TN*, Jan. 5, 1938, 1.

56. "Qui Vive Club Plans Business Meeting," *TN*, Feb. 27, 1938, 5; "Mrs. Newton Hinton Ill in Birmingham Hospital," *TN*, March 6, 1938, 11. Earline turned the front bedroom over to Anne around the time of Anne's tenth birthday, in February 1938 (AFS, pers. comm.). Daffodils were blooming that week and Earline cut daffodils and narcissi for a meeting at the bungalow in the spring of 1947. "Mrs. Howard Maxwell Lovely Hostess for 20th Century Club," *TN*, March 6, 1938, 9; "Rodes Chapter Is Entertained," *TN*, Feb. 23, 1947, 10.

57. "Lovely Bridge Shower Staged in Honor of Miss Edna Wood," *TN*, March 6, 1938, 12. Earline so favored Boston brown bread for chilled sandwiches that Anne made them as special treats in the 1960s.

58. "Judge Findley Re-Elected," *TN*, March 3, 1938, 1, 2.

59. "Murray Pate Bound Over on 'Homicide' Charge," *TN*, July 23, 1939, 1. After two mistrials, a circuit court jury, presided over by Herbert's political foe Charles

Warren, finally convicted Pate of murder in 1941 and sentenced him to three years in prison. Pate unsuccessfully appealed the conviction and finally entered prison in 1943 but was paroled after one year. "Mistrial Ends Murder Hearing," *TN*, Oct. 17, 1940, 1; "Pate Sentenced to Three Years," *TN*, April 13, 1941, 1; Alabama Convict Records.

60. "52,000 See Green Wave Roll over Crimson Tide, 13 to 0," *TN*, Nov. 12, 1939, 10; "Judge Henry Foster Dies Suddenly at Age of 76," *TN*, Nov. 12, 1939, 1, 2; "Community Mourns for Judge Foster," *TN*, Nov. 13, 1939, 1; "Governor Interviews Judgeship Applicants," *TN*, Nov. 17, 1939, 1; "Tom B. Ward Designated Circuit Judge by Dixon," *TN*, Nov. 19, 1939, 1.

61. "Dodson Enters Candidacy for Solicitor Post," *TN*, Jan. 29, 1934, 1, 2; "Dodson Enters Race for House," *TN*, March 1, 1942, 1; "Fifth Legislature Candidate Announces," *TN*, Feb. 17, 1946, 1; "99 Candidates Qualify for Local May 7 Races," *TN*, March 3, 1940, 1; editorial, "Tonight's Climactic Rally," *TN*, May 3, 1940, 4; "Methodist W.M.S. Meets Monday," *TN*, March 10, 1940, 13; "Record Crowd Attends County High Rally," *TN*, May 5, 1940, 1; "Today's Early Voting Exceeds 1938 Record," *TN*, May 7, 1940, 1; "Hughes, Warren Lead in County Court Races," *TN*, May 8, 1940, 1; "Two New Circuit Court Officers Are Chosen; Elledge Is Constable Victory," *TN*, June 5, 1940, 1; "Legion Auxiliary Wins Honors at State Convention," *TN*, Aug. 1, 1940, 7. Several of Anne's friends in Girl Scout Troop 16, including Cherry Austin, Jane Cason, Dorothy Fleetwood, Mary Louella Foley, Lylla Jean Kirk, Marion Parker, Joy Pearson, and Bebe Lewis, went to Camp Cherry Austin for an overnight camping trip, but Anne's name was not on the list that the *TN* published. "Many Girls Visit Camp," *TN*, May 9, 1940, 3.

62. Harwell, *Gone with the Wind as Book and Film*, 13; Haskell, *Frankly, My Dear*, 5, 23; Pierpoint, *Passionate Minds*, 98, 105.

63. "Women's Club Sponsors Book Review," *TN*, Nov. 8, 1936, 12; "Study Group Meets at Doster Hall," *TN*, Oct. 25, 1936, 12; "Alathean Class Holds Social Session," *TN*, Nov. 26, 1936, 5.

64. Advertisement, "Gone with the Wind," *TN*, Feb. 1, 1940, 5; Mitchell, *Gone with the Wind: Movie Picture Edition*; "'Gone with the Wind' to Be Here Next Week," *TN*, March 17, 1940, 1; advertisement, "Gone with the Wind," *TN*, March 24, 1940, 7; "At the Churches," *TN*, March 22, 1940, 8; "29-Degree Weather Attends Easter Here," *TN*, March 25, 1940, 1. On new Easter dresses as de rigueur for middle-class mothers and daughters, see Pleck, *Celebrating the Family*, 83. On going to the movie theater as a glamorous experience, see Marling, "Fantasies in Dark Places," 16–18. Earline and Anne also could have seen the film during a week of repeat screenings a year later. Advertisement, "Gone with the Wind," *TN*, March 2, 1941, 13.

65. Mitchell, *Gone with the Wind*, 80th printing, 349. On Foster's song as a lament for a slave who was sold downriver, see Clark, "The Slavery Background," 15–16. Mitchell considered using Foster's phrase "Tote the Weary Load"—the phrase Prissy sings at the height of her maddening resistance to Scarlett's authority—as the title of her novel (Charles McGrath, "A Piece of 'Gone with the Wind' Isn't Gone After All," *New York Times*, March 29, 2011). She created the character of Prissy as "'shiftless' but not as 'stupid'" and "was disappointed" in McQueen's portrayal of her as vapid and incompetent (Harwell, *Gone with the Wind as Book and Film*, 170). Nell Battle Lewis

observed, "Never once did Butterfly McQueen really get into this part, and I doubt that she ever understood what was expected of her." Nell Battle Lewis, "Scarlett Materializes," quoted in Harwell, *Gone with the Wind as Book and Film*, 172. Also see Ritterhouse, *Growing Up Jim Crow*, 14.

66. Govan, *Narcissus*, 193–94, 226.

67. MacKethan, *Recollections of a Southern Daughter*, xviii, on Thomas Nelson Page.

68. See appendix 3, this book. Page, *In Ole Virginia*, 37–38, 45, 67, 77. On "Unc' Edinburg's Drowndin'" containing "virtually all the significant elements of the social rapture which marked the old epoch," see Gaines, *Southern Plantation*, 78; Blight, *Race and Reunion*, 222. For a more recent review of Page's influence, see Prince, *Stories of the South*, 145–52.

69. Twain, *Favorite Works*. See appendix 3, this book.

70. AFS, pers. comm. A friend asked Anne in December 1952, "Have you been hunting yet?" Dave P. to AFS, Dec. 26, 1952, EFS Collection.

71. On *Gone with the Wind* as "a training manual" for belles, see Haskell, *Frankly, My Dear*, 15.

72. MKF, pers. comm.

73. "Death Claims Murk Findley," *TN*, April 22, 1941, 1, 2; "Rites Planned Today for Murk Findley," *TN*, April 23, 1941, 2; "Alberta City News," *TN*, Jan. 29, 1939, 6. For the use of photographs in mourning jewelry, see Batchen, *Forget Me Not*, 32–35.

74. Kennedy, "Alas, Poor Yorick," 405–9; 1940 USFC.

75. "Dentists Honored at Lovely Supper," *TN*, July 4, 1947, 5; editorial, "Those Who Met Defeat," *TN*, May 17, 1938, 4; "Court Appoints Counsel to Aid Negroes' Defense," *TN*, July 30, 1933, 1; "Hargrove Rites Set Saturday; Beloved Resident Dies One Week after Her 98th Birthday," *TN*, Jan. 3, 1941, 1; "Courthouse Closed for Maxwell Funeral," *TN*, March 8, 1951, 2; "Officers Entertained at Barbecue Here," *TN*, Nov. 10, 1939, 2; "20 Years Ago Today," *TN*, Feb. 24, 1933, 4; "Burks-Abbott Vows to Be April Event at First Baptist," *TN*, March 7, 1954, 15; 1910, 1940 USFC. Verner Robertson was a namesake of his uncle Verner Robertson Sr. and descended from Horse Shoe Robertson ("J. Verner Robertson, Sr., Is Buried This Morning," *TN*, n.d., Find a Grave Index). Henry T. Burks's daughter or granddaughter Margaret Amanda later married a son or grandson of Charles E. Abbott ("Burks-Abbott Vows to Be April Event at First Baptist").

76. "Funeral of Little Child," *TN*, Sept. 26, 1910, 2; "Sickness Proves Fatal to 80-Year-Old Resident," *TN*, Sept. 19, 1933, 1. On home funerals, see Burr, *The Secret Eye*, 224; Hall, *Revolt against Chivalry*, 3; Farrell, *Inventing the American Way*, 174–76; Schlereth, *Victorian America*, 291; Jalland, *Death in the Victorian Family*, 210; Laderman, *Rest in Peace*, 1–31; Horton, *Family Quilts*, 139; Hamlett, *Material Relations*, 181.

77. Henderson, *Smith's Alabama*, 226–27.

78. "Extended Illness Fatal to Beloved Matron," *TN*, Nov. 14, 1930, 1; "Mrs. Minerva Hargrove Passes Away at Age of 96," *TN*, Dec. 4, 1932, 1.

79. Walter C. Scott was the minister of First Methodist Church in Tuscaloosa from November 1939 to November 1941. "New Minister Preaches Today," *TN*, Nov. 12, 1939, 2; "11 Changes Announced in Local Methodist District," *TN*, Nov. 10, 1941, 1.

80. "Judge Brandon Goes to His Final Rest as Friends from All Walks Pay Tribute,"

TN, Dec. 9, 1934, 1, 2; obituary, "Thomas W. Shields," *Linden Democrat Reporter*, July 8, 1937. On funeral processions, see Schlereth, *Victorian America*, 291.

81. Lula Hargrove, handwritten notes, n.d., EFS Collection; "News of the Alumni," *University of Alabama Alumni News* 24, no. 8 (June 1941): 141.

Chapter 7

1. Southern Association of Student Government program, 1940, HLF Jr. Scrapbook, courtesy of MKF; "Findley Wins Unopposed in Student Elections," *Hi-Life*, May 30, 1941; "Boy's State Planned June 5," *TN*, May 11, 1941, 14; "Legion Members Entertain Auxiliary at Joint Meeting," *TN*, May 15, 1941, 6; "Twenty Attend Boys' State," *TN*, June 5, 1941, 2, HLF Jr. Scrapbook, courtesy of MKF.

2. Clippings, "N.A.T. Club Entertains at Country Club," *TN*, May 15, 1941, 6, and "N.A.T. Club Gives Dance at Country Club," *TN*, May 16, 1941, 7; "Tuscaloosa Town Topics," *TN*, June 16, 1947, 1; "N.A.T. Club Fetes Throng with Dance at Country Club," *TN*, May 18, 1941, 10. Items from Anne's scrapbook are in the AFS Collection, UA Special Collections.

3. "The Reunions," *University of Alabama Alumni News* 24, no. 8 (June 1941): 130–31.

4. Dryden, *Etiquette*, 138. See appendix 3, this book.

5. "Social Calendar," *TN*, April 7, 1942, 5; clipping, "Girl Scouts Hold Anniversary Tea Honoring Founder," *TN*, April 12, 1942, 13.

6. "Social Calendar," *TN*, May 18–22, 1942; "Laurel Class Is Entertained in Chapman Home," *TN*, May 24, 1942, 6.

7. USFC, 1940; clipping, "N.A.T. Seniors Are Entertained by Bebe Lewis," *TN*, June 4, 1942.

8. Roberts, *Confederate Belle*, 30; Agee, *Cotton Tenants*, 103. On clothing as not merely a representation or reflection of identity but part of one's identity, see Miller, *Stuff*, 20, 38–40.

9. L.O.L. Club invitation; clipping, "Rush Party Is Social Event of L.O.L. Club," *TN*, June 12, 1942, 7; clipping, "Miss Kirk Fetes Miss Anderson at Bridge Party," *TN*, Sept. 1, 1942, 5; clipping, "L.O.L. Club Rush Party Is Held in Jones' Home," *TN*, Sept. 9, 1942; clipping, "Miss Harden Visits in Lewis Home," *TN*, July 8, 1943, 5.

10. Helvenston and Bubolz, "Home Economics," 306. Anne often used the term "store-bought" to refer to clothing not made at home, so Earline probably used the term too.

11. "Twelfth Annual Fashion Walk Set at University," *TN*, May 1, 1941, 6; "University Consumer Group Plans Schedule," *TN*, April 5, 1942, 6.

12. Clipping, "Local Leaders Attend Hi-Y Meeting," *TN*, April 21, 1944; Hi-Y conference program and Whitley Hotel brochure, AFS Collection, UA Special Collections.

13. Patricia Amos, pers. comm.

14. The quotes in this paragraph and the previous one are from EMF to AFS, June 14, 1938, Aug. 17, 1941, and Aug. 19, 1941, EFS Collection.

15. Cronenberg, *Forth to the Mighty Conflict*, 5; "Efforts to Curb Paralysis Urged," *TN*, July 29, 1936, 2.

16. "Collins Requests Delay in Start of State Schools"; "Playgrounds Closed"; "Infantile Paralysis Toll Reaches 454 in Georgia"; "Iron Lung Rushed to Selma Girl"; "Polio May Delay Start of Knoxville Schools"; "State FFA Meeting Set at Auburn Cancelled," *TN*, Aug. 19, 1941, 1, 2, 3. Earline's letters to Anne quoted in this paragraph and the previous one are from EMF to AFS, June 6, 1938, and Aug. 17, 19, and 26, 1941. Mary Louise Shook to AFS, n.d.; HLF to AFS, Aug. 21, 1941, all letters in EFS Collection. Stowe provides a similar example of an early nineteenth-century jurist's doting pleasure in his daughter's musical ability (*Intimacy and Power*, 179).

17. Commencement program, Tuscaloosa Junior High School, June 4, 1942, AFS Collection, UA Special Collections.

18. "Blackout Here 99.99 Per Cent," *TN*, May 29, 1942, 1; "State Guard Mobilizes within Ten Minutes," *TN*, May 29, 1942, 1; "Consumer Goods Shortages Told to 20th Century," *TN*, Feb. 6, 1942, 6; Flynt, *Alabama*, 400; Thomas, *Riveting and Rationing*, 94–103; Bentley, *Eating for Victory*, 14–15, 102; Deutsch, *Housewife's Paradise*, 45, 159–60; advertisement, Mackey Gro. Co., "Cool Foods That Beat the Heat," *TN*, June 15, 1945, 6; "Zeigler Meats," www.buyalabamasbest.com/members/rl-zeigler-company; editorial, "Food Made Here Deserves Support," *TN*, Sept. 26, 2007. The recipe for Earline's traditional Christmas toffee cookies, which Anne passed down to me, shows that she used shortening, a hydrogenated vegetable oil that remained solid at room temperature, instead of butter, which was the traditional ingredient. This undoubtedly was a wartime sacrifice. Flexner, *Out of Kentucky Kitchens*, 268; Kleber, "Marion K. (Weil) Flexner."

19. "Power Blackout Observed Here," *TN*, Nov. 4, 1941, 1; "30 Selectees Chosen Here," *TN*, Nov. 4, 1941, 1; "Findley Home Is Scene of Meeting of Auxiliary," *TN*, Nov. 5, 1941, 6.

20. "75 Apply Here for Enlistment," *TN*, Dec. 10, 1941, 1.

21. "Throng Attends Inspiring Rally," *TN*, Dec. 11, 1941, 8; "Graduating Exercises Set for Tonight," *TN*, June 4, 1942, 5.

22. "City Blackout Takes Effect," *TN*, May 28, 1941, 1; "Defense Corps Units Set for Blackout Tonight," *TN*, May 28, 1942, 1; "Civil Defense Plan Set Up," *TN*, Dec. 11, 1941, 1, 2. On county defense councils, see Thomas, *Riveting and Rationing*.

23. "Junior High PTA Enjoys Delightful Yule Program," *TN*, Dec. 14, 1941, 14; "At the Churches," *TN*, Dec. 12, 1941, 8; "Christmas Party Planned for RAF Cadets at Airport," *TN*, Dec. 23, 1941, 5; "British Cadets Shop Early," *TN*, Dec. 24, 1941, 17; "Campus Christmas Tree to Be Lighted," *TN*, Dec. 12, 1941, 6; Clark, *Pills*, 137; clipping, "37 Inducted by Honor Society," *TN*, Dec. 17, 1941, 3; "Laurel Class Plans Christmas Party," *TN*, Dec. 17, 1941, 5; "Yule Pageant Planned Today," *TN*, Dec. 21, 1941, 20; "High School Set Enjoys L.O.L. Christmas Party," *TN*, Dec. 26, 1941, 6; advertisement, "Your Tuscaloosa County Officials," *TN*, Dec. 24, 1941, 12. For more on the cadets, see Flynt, *Alabama*, 393–94. For community tree-lightings, see Pleck, *Celebrating the Family*, 54.

24. "Masonic Rites Planned for Walter Smith Today," *TN*, Jan. 25, 1942, 1, 2; Mrs. Archie Hamby, "Alberta City News," *TN*, Feb. 8, 1942, 8; "Vote Broadcast-Matinee Starts at 6:30 O'clock," *TN*, May 5, 1942, 1; "Tucker Congratulates Congressman Jarman," *TN*, May 8, 1942, 1.

25. AP, "Houston Cole Says U.S. Cities May Be Bombed," *TN*, Dec. 14, 1941, 10; AP, "Posse Hunts Negro Slayer," *TN*, Dec. 21, 1941, 1; AP, "Negro Slayer Is Believed Surrounded," *TN*, Dec. 22, 1941, 2; "Relative of Hambys Killed in War Zone," *TN*, Dec. 22, 1941, 3; Mrs. Archie Hamby, "Alberta City News," *TN*, Dec. 7, 1941, 6.

26. "Legion Auxiliary Meets Tuesday," *TN*, Jan. 3, 1943, 6; clipping, "Judge Findley Will Lead War Bond Campaign Here," *TN*, Feb. 25, 1943, 1; clipping, "North Alabama Girds to Aid U.S. War Loan Drive," April 3, 1943; "Congressman Jarman Is Proud of Bond Record," *TN*, May 6, 1943, 4; "Special Bond Effort Urged," *TN*, Sept. 26, 1943, 1; "Bond Show Caps 'Salerno Day,'" *TN*, Sept. 17, 1943, 1; "County Nears Halfway Mark on War Loan Goal," *TN*, Sept. 19, 1943, 1; Cronenberg, *Forth to the Mighty Conflict*, 30; Helen Schulz, "Safe Flight Is Wish for Plane," *TN*, Oct. 1, 1943, 3; clipping, "Third War Loan Bombers Take the Air," *BNAH*, Oct. 3, 1943.

27. Tuscaloosa High School, *Black Warrior* (1945).

28. "Juniors Start Member Drive," *TN*, Nov. 3, 1942, 3; "Junior Red Cross Member Drive Set," *TN*, Oct. 24, 1943, 9; "Red Cross Officials Meet Today," *TN*, May 17, 1944, 6.

29. Tuscaloosa High School, *Black Warrior* (1945); obituary, "Alleen Rhodes," *TN*, March 16, 1988, 24; Caroline Cepin Benser, "Ottokar Čadek," *Encyclopedia of Alabama*, http://www.encyclopediaofalabama.org, July 11, 2013; 1940 USFC.

30. Elna Bolding Shugerman, pers. comm.; "Girl Scout Day Camp Concluded at End of Successful Year," *TN*, Aug. 14, 1938, 8; HLF Jr. to AFS, July 30, 1945, EFS Collection; Hiestand, *Angela the Upside-Down Girl*, 23. See Rosen, *Arnold Schoenberg*.

31. "Tom Thumb Wedding Is Huge Event," *TN*, Dec. 8, 1933, 5. See also "Tuscaloosa B.P.W. Club Brings Back State Prize," *TN*, May 20, 1940, 1, 3; "At the Churches," *TN*, Dec. 20, 1940, 3; "Pageant of Alabama Features Meeting of Study Club," *TN*, Nov. 22, 1937, 5; "U.D.C. Does Excellent Work in Caring for Confederate Markers," *TN*, Oct. 14, 1934, 6; "Miss Slaughter Is Wed to Mr. Bridgers in Columbus, Miss.," *TN*, June 11, 1939, 5. For more about tableaux vivants, see Sterkx, *Partners in Rebellion*, 56–57; Brownell, *Urban Ethos*, 192, 196–97, 204, 214; Glassberg, *American Historical Pageantry*, 16, 252–53; Cook, "Growing Up," 16, 261; Faust, *Mothers of Invention*, 26–28, 227; Kierner, *Beyond the Household*, 133; Hoelscher, "Making Place," 658–59; Bishir, *Southern Built*, 268. For staged photographs, see Gordon, *Saturated World*, 130–35.

32. Bailey, "Patrician Cult," 516; Brundage, "White Women," 132; Case, "Historical Ideology," 604, 626; Cox, *Dixie's Daughters*, 160; McElya, *Clinging to Mammy*, 50–52.

33. Clipping, "Funeral of Mrs. Murk Finley and John Finley"; *Polk's Tuscaloosa Directory* (1922–23), 24, U.S. Phone and Address Directories; Little and Maxwell, *Lumsden's Battery*; Hendrix and Reese, *Tuskaloosa's Own*, 77, 81, 88; Maxwell, *Autobiography*, 281; Massey, *Reminiscences*, 105; "Guide to the Andrew Coleman Hargrove Papers, 1858–1896," UA Special Collections; obituary, "Andrew Coleman Hargrove," in American Bar Association, *Twentieth Annual Meeting*, 527–29; Thornton, *Politics and Power*, 441; R. E. Rodes Chapter, United Daughters of the Confederacy, *Year Book, 1935* (pamphlet retrieved from www.ebay.com); "R. E. Rodes Chapter U.D.C. to Meet," *TN*, Oct. 4, 1933, 5; "R. E. Rodes Chapter to Sponsor Southern Picture," *TN*, Nov. 24, 1935, 1; "U.D.C. Unit Holds Year's First Social," *TN*, Sept. 22, 1933, 5; editorial, "Daughters of the Confederacy," *TN*, May 6, 1941, 4. Herbert's sister-in-law Olive Findley also was

a member, although perhaps not during Earline's lifetime. "Calendar of Events," *TN*, Feb. 14, 1965, 28.

34. Radford, "Identity and Tradition," 99; Brundage, "White Women," 119.

35. Choctaw County Probate Judge W. H. Lindsey, Feb. 17, 1923, attachment, in Application by Earline Moore Findley, April 7, 1945, United Daughters of the Confederacy; E. S. Adams to Mrs. Jennie F. Brown, Sept. 7, 1940, EFS Collection.

36. On the range of southern opinions about secession, see Roark, *Masters without Slaves*, 3, 9; Berends, "Confederate Sacrifice," 100; Noe, *Reluctant Rebels*, 10, 13, 15, 48–49, 66.

37. The 1860 USFC Slave Schedules show the following numbers of enslaved workers by owner: C. E. DeLoach (28), J. C. Christopher (6), M. C. Thompson (5), A. T. [Nancy Ann] Christopher (7), T. H. Christopher (4), M. J. Fitch (10), A. E. Fitch (2), and L. S. [Laura Louise] Fitch (2).

38. U.S. Civil War Soldier Records and Profiles; application by Annie Elizabeth Fitch Christopher, Confederate Pension and Service Records; Wynne and Taylor, *This War So Horrible*, xiv–xv; Smith and Neel, preface, ii.

39. Noe, *Reluctant Rebels*, 50–52, 113–17, 132–39. On white opposition to arming slaves, see Myers, "Black Human Capital," 14.

40. Noe, *Reluctant Rebels*, 113–14; Widow's Original Application by Ann Elizabeth Christopher, Confederate Pension and Service Records. John Chiles Christopher's substitute was William Bolick, who was mustered into the Fortieth Regiment of Alabama Volunteers on Dec. 31, 1862, in Mobile (Company F, 40th Regiment, Alabama Civil War Muster Rolls). On antebellum women wanting their husbands nearby during delivery, see McMillen, *Motherhood*, 62–63.

41. Liddell, *Southern Accent*, 38; Sterkx, *Partners in Rebellion*, 42–44.

42. "U.D.C. Leaders to Attend General Convention," *TN*, Nov. 18, 1940, 5; "R. E. Rodes Group Is Complimented in Francis Home," *TN*, Dec. 21, 1941, 17; Application by Edward Judson Finnell, Sons of the American Revolution Membership Applications; "U.D.C. Names Delegates for State Session," *TN*, April 13, 1932, 5; "Tuscaloosa Chapter of U.D.C. Wins Trophy," *TN*, Dec. 8, 1935, 14; "Twelfth Annual Fashion Walk Set at University," *TN*, May 1, 1941, 6; clipping, "120 Years of Tuscaloosa History in a Family Name," *TN*, Nov. 26, 1941, 4.

43. Certificate of admission for EMF, United Daughters of the Confederacy, EFS Collection.

44. "Rodes Chapter Is Entertained," *TN*, April 21, 1946, 15; "Second U.D.C. Group Is Formed in Tuscaloosa," *TN*, Sept. 12, 1940, 6; clipping, "Mrs. Findley Returns from Meridian," *TN*, Aug. 23, 1942, 6; AFS, pers. comm. Annie returned to Meridian at some point before she died in 1946. Clipping, "Mother of Local Resident Succumbs," *TN*, Sept. 3, 1946, 2; *Polk's Meridian Directory* (1946), 364, U.S. Phone and Address Directories.

45. "Judges Sure of Election May 7," *TN*, March 3, 1946, 1; "Walker, Mize, Callahan, Shelton Win; Parker, Suther in Run-Off," *TN*, May 8, 1946, 1, 2.

46. "Legion Installs New Officers," *TN*, July 21, 1943, 1. A letter that Herbert wrote in 1924 indicates that he was familiar with Tenedus's Confederate record. The Pension

Division of the office of the state auditor had rejected Minerva's application for a Confederate widow's pension on the grounds that Tenedus hired a substitute in order to be relieved of military duty. In his letter Herbert wrote, "Your records should show that soldier T A Hargrove within a very short time after being discharged by reason of substitute on June 1st 1863 re-enlisted in Lumsdem's [*sic*] Battery [and] served with this battery until termination of war" (H. L. Findley to Pension Division, Oct. 18, 1924, Confederate Pension and Service Records). On Herbert's interest in history, see the books he received as gifts from Anne in appendix 3, this book. On men of his age and class having little interest in Civil War commemoration, see Powdermaker, *After Freedom*, 30–31; Brundage, "White Women," 123; Case, "Historical Ideology," 623.

47. Tuscaloosa High School, *Black Warrior* (1945); "Junior Music Club Holds Afternoon Meeting," *TN*, Feb. 6, 1942, 7; clipping, "Junior Musicians Hold Meeting with Miss Harris," *TN*, April 2, 1942, 7; clipping, "Jr. Music Study Club Entertains Clionian Group," *TN*, May 6, 1943, 6; clipping, "Miss Findlay [*sic*] Heads Junior Music Club," *TN*, Oct. 7, 1943, 6; "Junior Music Club Presents Program," *TN*, May 4, 1944, 6; clipping, "THS Graduating Students Tapped," *TN*, May 25, 1945, 5; AFS, "GONE Det. West" (list of stolen items written for police detective), EFS Collection; clipping, "Legion Members Entertain Auxiliary at Joint Meeting," *TN*, May 15, 1941; clipping, "Laurel Class Is Entertained in Hackney Home," *TN*, Jan. 27, 1942, 5; "Answers to Questions," *The Etude* 27, no. 5 (May 1909): 354; 1940 USFC; "Findley Home Is Scene of Meeting of Auxiliary," *TN*, Nov. 5, 1941, 6; "Clionian Study Club Meets with Mrs. Jackman," *TN*, May 6, 1942, 5; "Mrs. W. J. Samford Is Guest of Honor at Meeting," *TN*, May 3, 1936, 1; 1930 USFC; "Rodes Chapter Elects Delegates," *TN*, Oct. 21, 1945, 10; McDowell and Jones, *History of the Alabama Division*, 159.

48. Alabama, WWII Military Dead and Wounded, 1944–1946, http://www.ancestry.com; "The Home Front," *Huntsville Times*, April 26, 1995, B3; John C. Hall, pers. comm.; U.S. World War II Army Enlistment Records.

49. MKF, pers. comm.; Col. William S. Mullins, ed., "Medical Department, United States Army, Medical Training in World War II" (Washington, DC: Office of the Surgeon General, Department of the Army, 1974), U.S. Army Office of Medical History, http://history.amedd.army.mil; Office of the P.M.S.&T., University of Alabama, General Orders No. 17, July 23, 1942; W. D. Partlow, letter of recommendation, May 4, 1943, courtesy of MKF; Chester Walker to Director of Naval Officer Procurement, May 13, 1943, all letters in HLF Jr. Scrapbook, courtesy of MKF.

50. "Verner School Features Health," *TN*, Nov. 23, 1932, 5; obituary, "Hazel P. Jones," Madison County, Alabama, Obituary Collection, www.genealogybuff.com; MKF, pers. comm.

51. Clipping, "Medical Student Transfers Set," *TN*, May 17, 1945, 8; Allen T. Cronenberg, "World War II and Alabama," *Encyclopedia of Alabama*, http://www.encyclopediaofalabama.org, [Sept. 14, 2007] Nov. 7, 2013; HLF Jr. to AFS, July 30, 1945, EFS Collection. Lyman was a member of the third-year class in the period July 1945–March 1946. "School of Medicine, Third Year Class, 1945–1946," photograph #RG-30/1/10/011, University of Virginia Visual History Collection.

52. "Walker, Mize, Callahan, Shelton Win; Parker, Suther in Run-Off," *TN*, May

8, 1946, 1, 2; clipping, "Judge Herbert Findley Resigns Court Position," *TN*, Aug. 21, 1946, 1; "Difficult Position to Fill," *TN*, Aug. 22, 1946; "Committee to Nominate Judge," *TN*, Aug. 22, 1946, 1; "Eugene Bailey Selected as Judgeship Nominee," *TN*, Aug. 26, 1946, 1, 2. Coincidentally, Bailey's son Donald Eugene Bailey married Herbert's widowed granddaughter, Louise Findley Labosier, in 2008.

53. Clipping, "Lawyers, Courthouse Workers Honor Findley; Inferior Court Judge Receives Gifts at Unusual Ceremony," *TN*, Sept. 15, 1946, 1, 2.

54. Advertisement, "The Tuscaloosa County Executive Committee Endorses the Boswell Amendment," *TN*, Nov. 3, 1946, 4; Key, *Southern Politics*, 571, 634–35; Goldfield, *Black, White, and Southern*, 45; Scotty E. Kirkland, "Boswell Amendment," *Encyclopedia of Alabama*, http://www.encyclopediaofalabama.org, [June 2, 2011] Aug. 10, 2013; "Boswell Amendment," Alabama Moments in American History, http://www.alabamamoments.alabama.gov/sec53.html.

55. When the 1908 courthouse, which was built during Murk Findley's tenure as county engineer, was demolished and a new one constructed in 1964, the County Commission rehung the portrait of Herbert in the new Courtroom Number Four ("1900–1909: A New Century," *Perspectives* [Winter 2000], Chamber of Commerce of West Alabama; Betty Slowe, "Looking Back," *TN*, July 20, 2010; Donna J. Siebenthaler, "Tuscaloosa County," EncyclopediaofAlabama.org, [Aug. 22, 2007] Nov. 7, 2013). The portrait is now part of the AFS Collection, UA Special Collections, and a duplicate hangs in the courthouse.

56. Olan Mills established the first Olan Mills Studio in Tuscaloosa in 1932. "Amazing Growth Shown by Olan Mills Studio," *TN*, July 3, 1938, 5; "Olan Mills Studio Opens Here in Former Plant," *TN*, June 7, 1943, 1; "Mills to Speak at Convocation," *TN*, May 15, 1946, 5. For the cultural significance of oil portraits, see Ames, *Dining Room*, 185; Halle, *Inside Culture*, 87; Wajda, "The Artistic Portrait Photograph," 167–68; Smith, *American Archives*, 54; West, *Portraiture*, 136–37. Rubin observed in Wilcox County, Alabama, in 1947 that within the upper and upper-middle classes "physical attractiveness is the main criterion for marriage or mating" (*Plantation County*, 176–77).

57. "Walter Blackman, Cartoonist, Dies," *Washington Post*, Dec. 31, 1939, excerpted in "Ghoul News-Cartoonist Death Notices," http://strippersguide.blogspot.com/2006/04/ghoul-news-cartoonist-death-notices.html; "Mrs. Findley to Have Art Show in Birmingham," *TN*, Nov. 1, 1942, 5; "Local Woman's Art Works on Exhibit," *TN*, April 25, 1945, 5.

58. Clipping, "Funeral of Mrs. Murk Finley and John Finley"; "Joe Searcy Has Pneumonia," *TN*, Dec. 27, 1945, 5; "Rites Held for Joe A. Searcy," *TN*, Jan. 2, 1946, 1; obituary, "Joseph Alexander Searcy, Jr.," *TN*, March 2, 2008, 2B; "Miss Nina Ross Searcy Weds Lawrence Struss," *TN*, Nov. 17, 1938, 6; Henry Cunningham, "Portrait Artist Uses Her Talent to Illustrate Alabama's History," *TN*, Oct. 28, 1984, 1C; "Dinner Party Given Especially in Honor of Bridal Couple," *TN*, Nov. 17, 1938, 6; "Miss Nina Ross Searcy Weds Lawrence Struss," *TN*, Nov. 17, 1938, 6; "Larry Struss Is Birthday Host," *TN*, Aug. 19, 1945, 6; "Lieut. Struss Aids in Rescue," *TN*, Jan. 31, 1945, 3. The Tuscaloosa County Preservation Society installed a small portrait that Struss painted, a copy of a picture on the cover of the memoir of Virginia Clay-Clopton, in the

Battle-Friedman House Museum in 1984. Teenage members of the Tuscaloosa Belles, wearing "antebellum hoop skirts," participated in the ceremony. Henry Cunningham, "Gifts Received at Ceremony," *TN*, Oct. 23, 1984, 4.

59. Certificate of Membership for AFS, Eta Chapter, Alpha Delta Pi, Feb. 2, 1946; address book, Eta Chapter, Alpha Delta Pi, 1945–46; dance card, Eta Chapter, Alpha Delta Pi, July 1946, all EFS Collection.

60. This portrait also is in the AFS Collection, UA Special Collections. On tension between reality and the envisioned ideal of southern womanhood, see Henninger, *Ordering the Facade*, 87.

61. AFS, pers. comm.; Seidel, *Southern Belle*, 131.

Chapter 8

1. "Rodes Chapter Is Entertained," *TN*, Feb. 23, 1947, 10; "Miss Emmett Lewis Entrances Audience of Music Lovers," *TN*, Oct. 12, 1939, 5; "Personal Mention," *TN*, Dec. 19, 1948, 26; "Pilots Enjoy Novel Entertainment," *TN*, March 13, 1935, 6; "Tuscaloosa DAR Chapter Adds Three New Members to Roster," *TN*, Oct. 13, 1953, 6; Bill Edwards, "David Wendel Guion," Rag Piano, http://www.perfessorbill.com/comps/dguion.shtml. "Juba: Dance" is from *In the Bottoms* by the African American composer R. Nathaniel Dett. Historian Marian Winter revived the reputation of William Henry Lane, the freedman who created juba, with her 1947 article "Juba and American Minstrelsy."

2. Sterkx, *Partners in Rebellion*, 158.

3. Earline and Herbert probably did not attend this party, which was for contemporaries of the son and new daughter-in-law of Herbert's hunting friend Wilson Patton, but Earline could have heard about it from her friends ("Evening Party Honors Couple in Patton Home," *TN*, Jan. 12, 1941, 7). For other references to charlotte russe at parties in Tuscaloosa, see "Lundi Bleu Club Gives Shower," *TN*, Dec. 22, 1931, 5; Marie L. Hagler, "Northport News," *TN*, Dec. 22, 1935, 1; "Evening Party Given for Bride-Elect," *TN*, Jan. 9, 1944, 6; "Parties Honor Miss Strickland," *TN*, Oct. 30, 1946, 5.

4. Van Duzor, *Fascinating Foods*.

5. "Club Opening Is Brilliant Event," *TN*, Feb. 24, 1947, 5; Writers' Program of the Work Projects Administration, *WPA Guide*, 249; Hubbs, *Tuscaloosa*, 24; Mellown, *University of Alabama*, 186–87; Max Heine, "Gulf States Marks Its Centennial Year," *TN*, Jan. 29, 1984, 11A; Lydia Seabol Avant, "University Club Turns 60 Today," *TN*, Feb. 23, 2007; "History," University Club, http://www.universityclub.ua.edu/history.html.

6. Little, "The University Club," 64, 66.

7. Gamble, *Historic Architecture*, 24–29.

8. Varian Feare, "Rosemount, Gem of Black Belt Area," *BNAH*, Dec. 29, 1935; Ausherman, *The Photographic Legacy*, 172; "E. Walter Burkhardt Award," College of Architecture, Design and Construction, Auburn University, http://cadc.auburn.edu.

9. E. Walter Burkhardt, "Alabama Possessor of Rich Heritage," *BNAH*, June 24, 1934.

10. Varian Feare, "University Ante-Bellum Charm Lingers," *BNAH*, Aug. 12, 1934.

11. E. Walter Burkhardt, "West Alabama Rich in Old Homes," *BNAH*, Sept. 9, 1934.

12. On newspaper-reading habits in Tuscaloosa County, see Partrich, "A Study of the Living Rooms," 128. Earline saved a page of grocery advertisements from the May 2, 1941, issue of the *Birmingham Age-Herald*. The family also saved the front page of the newspaper on the day following Japan's attack on Pearl Harbor.

13. "Legislature Restricts Powers of Local Justices," *TN*, July 8, 1945, 1; "Livingston Added to Faculty of University," *TN*, Sept. 17, 1945, 3.

14. Vlach, *Big House*, 8–9.

15. Gamble, *Historic Architecture*, 107.

16. These renovations were complete when Margaret Koster Findley first visited the house in 1949. MKF, pers. comm.

17. Arsenault, "The End of the Long Hot Summer," 608–10.

18. The breezeway at a home in Tuscumbia, Alabama, was "the scene of many and varied activities and a gathering place for all the children and servants" (Kirk, *Locust Hill*, 22–23). A similar breezeway linked the kitchen and main house at a historic house in Talladega County in 1935. Vlach, "Detached kitchen and covered walkway," photograph 4.14, in *Big House*, 55.

19. Varian Feare, "'Before-the-War' Home Goes Modern," *BNAH*, March 8, 1936, 12; E. Walter Burkhardt, "Tennessee Valley Plantation Homes," *BNAH*, Sept. 23, 1934, 13; Varian Feare, "Rosemount and Three Musketeers," *BNAH*, Jan. 19, 1936, 8.

20. Gregory, "Alabama's Endangered Historic Landmarks," 38–39; Varian Feare, "Charm of Old Mobile Holds Visitors," *BNAH*, Sept. 2, 1934, 13; Varian Feare, "Barton Mansion in Colbert," *BNAH*, Dec. 6, 1936, 5; Varian Feare, "Wrought Iron Recreates Old Charm," *BNAH*, Sept. 16, 1934, 12; Clinton, *Scrapbook*, unnumbered page; MKF, pers. comm. The Battle (de Graffenreid) House at 1217 Greensboro Avenue had elaborate wrought-iron trim on its front exterior. The Nicholson House at 1011 Greensboro Avenue had wrought-iron trim on a small front porch. See Frances Benjamin Johnston, "Wm. Battle or de Graffenreid House," photograph, Carnegie Survey of the Architecture of the South. The features that the Nicholson House had in common with the renovations of the Findley bungalow were in place when the architectural photographer Frances Benjamin Johnston documented the house for the Carnegie Survey of the Architecture of the South in 1939. Frances Benjamin Johnston, "Nicholson House," photograph, Carnegie Survey of the Architecture of the South.

21. "Bird of Paradise," image of a casting pattern, Artistic Iron, www.artisticusa.com; Robert Amos, pers. comm.

22. AFS, pers. comm.

23. "The Story of Magnolia Cemetery," www.cityofmobile.org; Sledge, *An Ornament to the City*, 86; "Ornamental Ironwork Plays Vital Role in Building; Furnished by Strickland," *TN*, June 5, 1950, 12. Goodbrad Iron Works was founded in Theodore, Alabama, in 1945 and made custom ornamental ironwork for houses and businesses, but the company changed ownership several times over the years and has no records of sales or advertising during 1945–53 (telephone interview with Goodbrad employee, Oct. 18, 2011). Margaret and Lyman Findley removed the cast-iron trim before the bungalow was demolished in 1973, reinstalling it at their house in a Tuscaloosa subdivision and purchasing an additional section, in the same pattern, from a local supplier. MKF, pers. comm.

24. See Clark, "The Vision of the Dining Room," 157–58, on the guest as "a detective . . . trying to understand the symbolic meanings of the furnishings."

25. "Bates Style Bedspreads," P. C. Fallon Co., www.pcfallon.com.

26. EMF to AFS, June 14, 1949, EFS Collection. On general stores selling furniture, see Clark, *Pills*, 307; Schlereth, "Country Stores," 342–44; Agnew, "A House of Fiction," 139.

27. Anne's musical powder box resembled numerous boxes, now available through online auction sites, which had Swiss movements and were distributed by the Silverite Company of New York. Burkhalter's Jewelers in Tuscaloosa sold "musical powder boxes" in 1957. "Wide Selection of Christmas Gifts to Choose from at Burkhalter Jewelry," *TN*, Dec. 15, 1957, 10.

28. AFS, pers. comm.; Ames, *Dining Room*, 227, caption 5.33.

29. Kenneth Ames observed hall chairs "were not intended for prolonged sitting" and typically "embodied . . . visual appeal and utility, not comfort" (*Dining Room*, 32–34).

30. Varian Feare, "A Glimpse at Old Montgomery Homes," *BNAH*, Nov. 25, 1934, 12.

31. "Antique Oil Lamps," *Collectors Weekly*, n.d.; "Hurricane Lamp Facts and History—Lighting Homes through the Ages," Emerson Creek Pottery, www.ecreekpotteryandtearoom.com.

32. On objects like the "Gone with the Wind lamp" suggesting "a script for a performance," see Bernstein, *Racial Innocence*, 71–72.

33. The signature on this painting is "Nina Ross Struss—Copy—1948." In 1949, Struss made another floral painting, *Floral Still Life, First Prize*, of an arrangement that a friend entered in the Charleston, South Carolina, Flower Show. "Struss, Nina Ross; Oil on Canvas, Signed, Floral Still Life, First Prize," www.Prices4Antiques.com.

34. Advertisement, "Lewis' Label Adds Much to Your Gift—Nothing to Its Cost!" *TN*, Dec. 14, 1941, 17; advertisement, "This Year . . . Give Something You Would Enjoy Yourself," *TN*, Dec. 14, 1941, 10; advertisement, "Your Gift Problems Vanish When You Shop Lewis," *TN*, Dec. 12, 1948, 14.

35. Marshall and Leimenstoll, *Thomas Day*, 96, caption 5.35; AFS, pers. comm.; Moore Family Bible; E. Walter Burkhardt, "The Charm of Ante-Bellum Interiors," *BNAH*, Nov. 18, 1934, 12. See also Naeve, *Identifying American Furniture*, 32–33.

36. Ronstrom, "Seignouret and Mallard," 79; Jordan, *Ante-bellum Alabama*, 5; Woodman, *King Cotton*, 30–33.

37. MKF, pers. comm.

38. Alex Bush, "Stair on South Wall in Cross-Hall," Aug. 14, 1936, photograph #ALA, 63-TUSLO, 10—5, HABS.

39. Busch, "The French Rococo Revival," 84–89; Williams and Harsh, *Tennessee Furniture*, 43–44; Wolfe, *University of Alabama*, 24.

40. Maxwell, *Autobiography*, 43; Adams et al., *Made in Alabama*, 206, 211.

41. AFS, MKF, pers. comm.

42. McLendon was in business in Montgomery from as early as 1940 until years after Earline's death (*Polk's Montgomery Directory* [1940], 447, and [1955], 351, U.S. Phone and Address Directories). Druid Furniture Company advertised "Carlton McLendon hand made" furniture that had "18th century styling . . . with flawless workmanship"

(advertisement, "Druid Furniture Co.," *TN*, June 5, 1949, 16). The historic properties curator at Old Alabama Town in Montgomery recalled that McLendon reportedly made copies of Seignoret chairs as well as his better-known Victorian reproductions. Carole A. King, pers. comm.

43. Rubin, *Plantation County*, 41; Varian Feare, "Ante-Bellum Bird's Nest Being Revived," *BNAH*, Sept. 8, 1935. The anthropologist Daniel Miller discusses tension between collectors of genuine and reproduction antiques in *Stuff* (95–96).

44. Six of Earline's assorted dining chairs, including three of the Seignoret-style chairs, are now in the collection of the University of Alabama.

45. Advertisement, "Tuscaloosa News Fancy Work," *TN*, Jan. 28, 1951, 16; advertisement, "Display Your Flowers to a Real Advantage!" *TN*, May 10, 1942, 8; "Rehearsal Party Is Lovely Event," *TN*, April 27, 1947, 14. For other examples of *TN* reports of crystal bowls with openwork tablecloths, see "Lovely Evening Party Given in Honor of Mrs. Dennis," Jan. 25, 1937, 5; "Mrs. George Truett Is Honor Guest for Beautiful Tea," May 5, 1937, 5; Mrs. G. A. Smith, "News from Holt," March 27, 1938, 1; "20th Century Club Meets with Mrs. McFarland," Feb. 22, 1942, 6.

46. MKF, AFS, pers. comm.; Adams et al., *Made in Alabama*, 298–99, 312–13.

47. MKF, pers. comm.; Helaine Fendelman, "Vintage Serving Trays," www.countryliving.com/shopping/antiques/a509/vintage-serving-trays-0607/.

48. The lines of Earline's chair are more graceful and evocative than the squared-off corners that were popular in rattan furniture by 1949 and the ubiquitous rattan furniture manufactured by the Heywood-Wakefield Company in the 1940s and 1950s. Its Campeche lines and sectional cushion resemble a pre–World War II piece made by Rattan Art & Decorations of Manila. The chair also resembles the "evolved *butaque*" by Clara Porset, a Cuban-born designer. Gontar, "The American Campeche Chair," 89; Schwartz and Waters, *Rattan Furniture*, 12, 76.

49. "Parker-Summerville Wedding Held," *TN*, July 24, 1949, 13; Blake Godfrey to AFS, July 31, 1949, and Charles Moore to AFS, May 21, 1951, EFS Collection.

50. EMF to AFS, Jan. 1952, EFS Collection.

51. "Musical Program at Harris Studio," *TN*, April 6, 1944, 8.

52. "Miss Kirk Becomes Bride of Mr. Woody," *TN*, Sept. 5, 1948, 14; 1940 USFC.

53. "Clionian Study Club Meets with Mrs. Jackman," *TN*, May 6, 1942, 5; "Yule Pageant Planned Today," *TN*, Dec. 21, 1941, 20; "Services at Churches in the Tuscaloosa Area," *TN*, Aug. 23, 1947, 2; "N.A.T. Club Fetes Throng with Dance at Country Club," *TN*, May 18, 1941, 10; "37 Inducted by Honor Society," *TN*, Dec. 17, 1941, 3; clipping, "N.A.T. Seniors Are Entertained by Bebe Lewis," *TN*, June 4, 1942; "Musical Program at Harris Studio," *TN*, April 6, 1944, 8; "Dance Leader" (caption), *TN*, April 19, 1945, 5.

54. "Miss Graves Becomes Bride of Sgt. Grady in Church Ceremony," *TN*, July 29, 1945, 7; "Mothers Honored at Pretty Banquet," *TN*, May 4, 1944, 5; University of Alabama, *Corolla* (1950); "17 Beauties to Meet for Contest Rehearsal," *TN*, Aug. 9, 1948, 1; "Talented Beauty Entry" (caption), *TN*, Aug. 8, 1948, 20; "Miss Lowery Named Jaycee Beauty Queen," *TN*, Aug. 14, 1948, 1; "745 in Swim School Here, Begin Tests This Week," *TN*, July 10, 1947, 1.

55. Dryden, *Etiquette*, 22–23, 39–43; "Pearson-Dendy Plans Complete," *TN*, Dec. 12, 1948, 24; "Capstone No. 1 Beauty Is Mayor's Daughter," *TN*, Dec. 12, 1948, 6; "Party Series Entertains Bride-Elect," *TN*, Dec. 21, 1948, 7; "Friends Set Dates to Fete Miss Pearson," *TN*, Dec. 12, 1948, 25.

56. Advertisement, "For 48 Years . . . The Symbol of Christmas," *TN*, Dec. 17, 1948, 2.

57. Migliario et al., *The Household Searchlight Recipe Book*. For these examples, I consulted Jane Beachboard's well-used copy of *The Household Searchlight*, which is missing the covers and front matter, so I don't know its edition.

58. Kleber, "Marion K. (Weil) Flexner"; the references to Flexner's *Out of Kentucky Kitchens* in this paragraph and the previous one are from p. 29; EMF Cookbook, 263–64, 191–92, 193–96, 167, 185.

59. Van Duzor, *Fascinating Foods*, 26, 59, 61, 63.

60. Flexner, *Out of Kentucky Kitchens*, 29, 203, 268.

61. Davis, Gardner, and Gardner, *Deep South*, 145.

62. Dryden, *Etiquette*, 41–42.

63. Tucker, *Telling Memories*, 278; Bentley, *Eating for Victory*, 77–78.

64. "Weather Forecast," *TN*, Dec. 22, 1948, 1.

65. "Wedding Party Honored at the Patton Home," *TN*, Aug. 12, 1931, 5. On children's birthday parties as tests and displays of etiquette for middle- and upper-class children, see Pleck, *Celebrating the Family*, 141–42, 148. The *TN* noted in 1933 that a little girl at a birthday party "welcomed her friends with marked cordiality." "Little Miss King Celebrates Birthday," *TN*, Nov. 23, 1933, 5.

66. "'The American Home' Will Be Topic of Que [*sic*] Vive Club," *TN*, Sept. 3, 1936, 5; "Social Calendar," *TN*, June 9, 1938, 9; "Interesting Meeting Held by Legion Auxiliary," *TN*, Feb. 13, 1935, 5; "Legion Auxiliary Wins Honors at State Convention," *TN*, Aug. 1, 1940, 7; "Dentists Honored at Lovely Supper," *TN*, July 4, 1947, 5; "Dr. John Crowder to Tour State for Candidacy," *TN*, Oct. 30, 1950, 1.

67. Dryden, *Etiquette*, 41–42.

68. Rybczynski, *Home*, 107–8; Jones, "Event Analysis." On women's parties as "domesticated pageantry" and dainty refreshments as symbols of the elite class, see Gordon, *Saturated World*, 79, 96.

69. "Pearson Home Is Scene of Luncheon," *TN*, July 21, 1946, 12; "Wedding Party Honored at the Patton Home," *TN*, Aug. 12, 1931, 5.

70. On society editors taking reports of parties over the telephone, see Horton, *Family Quilts*, 129.

71. "Morning Party Fetes Miss Joy Pearson," *TN*, Dec. 24, 1948, 6; 1940 USFC; "Miss Pearson Is Honored at Afternoon Tea," *TN*, Dec. 24, 1948, 9.

Chapter 9

1. VRMK to the author, April 4, 2012, and JCM to the author, April 2014, both in EFS Collection; C. H. Christopher, Inc., Mississippi Secretary of State Business Services, www.sos.ms.gov/BusinessServices/Pages/default.aspx; Velma Barber to AFS, May 28, 1953, EFS Collection; U.S. Bureau of the Census, *Classified Index to Occupations*, 77. Charles Christopher lived at Thirty-Ninth Avenue and Fifth Street. Alva's

widow, Annie Moore, lived on Thirty-Third Avenue. Velma and Gene Barber lived on Thirty-Ninth Avenue. J. C. and Virginia Moore lived at 2241 Thirty-Ninth Avenue in 1959. *Polk's Meridian Directory* (1946), 364, and (1959), 14, 210, 212, U.S. Phone and Address Directories; 1940 USFC.

2. Reba Hammond, "Seen in the Shops around Town," *TN*, May 31, 1949, 2; "Laurel Class Meets with Mrs. G. Rhodes," *TN*, May 29, 1949, 16; "C. Otis Moore Loses Life at Rail Crossing," *Meridian Star*, Aug. 14, 1942, 1; "Margaret Koster Weds Dr. Findley," *TN*, Dec. 1, 1949, 6; VRMK to the author, April 4, 2012, EFS Collection; *Polk's Meridian Directory* (1946), 40, 365, U.S. Phone and Address Directories; "Miss. Distrib Tosses Phono Ops Barbecue," *Billboard*, Sept. 13, 1947, 108; "Miss. Phono Ops Hold Oct. Meet; Aid Cancer Fund," *Billboard*, Oct. 25, 1947, 120; AFS, pers. comm.

3. "Labor Day Observance Slated for Tuscaloosa," *TN*, Sept. 3, 1944, 1, 2; "Tuscaloosa Town Topics," *TN*, Sept. 25, 1948, 1; "Tuscaloosa Town Topics," *TN*, Feb. 19, 1949, 1; classified advertisements, "Eating Establishments," *TN*, Dec. 27, 1949, 7 and May 28, 1950, 26; MKF, pers. comm.

4. U.S. Department of Veterans Affairs BIRLS Death File; HLF Jr. to AFS, Aug. 10, 1949, EFS Collection.

5. "High School Set Enjoys L.O.L. Christmas Party," *TN*, Dec. 26, 1941, 6; "Rush Party Is Social Event of L.O.L. Club," *TN*, June 12, 1942, 7; Tuscaloosa High School, *Black Warrior* (1943); MKF, pers. comm.; Deaths and Burials Index; "Dr. J. Emil Shirley Dies at Northport," *TN*, April 1, 1949, 1.

6. Commencement program and diploma, University of Alabama, 1945; "U. of A. Reception Held at Mansion," *TN*, June 9, 1949, 6; "Schedule of Coming Events at the University of Alabama," *TN*, June 5, 1949, 1; "Personal Mention," *TN*, June 9, 1949, 7; "Begins Internship," *TN*, June 5, 1949, 16; 1940 USFC.

7. AFS to EMF, Nov. 25, 1951, EFS Collection; "History," Office of the Dean, School of Medicine, UAB University Archives. The university had moved the medical school from Tuscaloosa to Birmingham in 1945, taking over two municipal hospitals, Jefferson and Hillman, to create a new academic hospital, Jefferson-Hillman. Fisher, *University of Alabama at Birmingham*, 2, 17.

8. "Klan Has Been Using County Building," "Report Says Klan to Ride Here Tonight," "KKK Mask Is Off," and editorial, "Will It Happen in Tuscaloosa," *TN*, May 27, 1949, 1; "Klansman Hits 'Dirty' Talk at KKK Meeting," *TN*, May 28, 1949, 1; "Klan Afraid of 'Bad Man'; The Mask Is Off," *TN*, May 29, 1949, 1; "Klan Looks Forward to Time When It Can 'Run the Town,'" *TN*, May 30, 1949, 1; editorial, "Who Are Our Klansmen in Tuscaloosa," *TN*, May 31, 1949, 4; L. M. Evans, "No Place for the KKK," and H. T. Cockrell Sr., "KKK and Upholding Free Speech," letters to the editor, *TN*, June 3, 1949, 4. Like *TN* reports of the 1933 lynchings, these articles could have inspired Harper Lee, who referred, in the first draft of her novel, to the character of Atticus Finch infiltrating a local Klan meeting in order to identify the group's members (*Go Set a Watchman*, 229). For another view of the Tuscaloosa Klan in this period, see Feldman, *Politics*, 292–93.

9. AP, "Officers Will Probe Beating of Woman; Cafe Also Attacked by Cloaked Invaders," *TN*, June 12, 1949, 1; "Hooded Mob Marches in Tuscaloosa," *TN*, June 12,

1949, 1; "Hooded Band Parades through City" (caption), *TN*, June 12, 1949, 1.

10. EMF to AFS, June 14, 1949, EFS Collection; United Press, "Robed Night Riders Flog Veteran," *TN*, June 15, 1949, 1; "51 Stories of Violence Told in Three Southern States; KKK Blamed in Many; No Convictions," *TN*, June 27, 1949, 1, 2; "Anti-Mask Measure Becomes Law," *TN*, June 28, 1949, 1.

11. Wedding invitation, MKF; HLF Jr. to AFS, Aug. 10, 1949, and HLF Jr. to AFS, Nov. 20, 1949, both in EFS Collection.

12. "Social Calendar," *TN*, Sept. 1, 1947, 6; "Party Series Fetes Margaret L. Koster," *TN*, Nov. 27, 1949, 27; "Social Calendar," *TN*, Nov. 27, 1949, 27; "Margaret Koster Weds Dr. Findley," *TN*, Dec. 1, 1949, 6; Dryden, *Etiquette*, 135. On stand-ins for brides during rehearsals, see Andrew MacBeth. *Dearly Beloved: Navigating Your Church Wedding* (New York: Seabird Books, 2006), 65.

13. "Personal Mention," *TN*, Dec. 6, 1949, 6, and Jan. 24, 1950, 6; MKF, pers. comm.; "Marine Corps Base Camp Pendleton," United States Marine Corps, http://www.pendleton.marines.mil.

14. Hattie Porter Collier, "Annual Flower Show Here Proves Brilliant," *TN*, April 26, 1936, 9; "Flowers in Abundance Make of Tuscaloosa a Garden," *TN*, June 10, 1934, 9; "Chairman for Garden Pilgrimage," *TN*, April 30, 1941, 3; "Garden Pilgrimage Leaders Named," *TN*, April 27, 1947, 14; "Garden Pilgrimage Has Flower Show," *TN*, March 29, 1949, 6; Brundage, *Southern Past*, 322.

15. "'Glorify Tuscaloosa' Slogan Begins Work for Pilgrimage," *TN*, March 26, 1950, 15; "Garden Members Announce Final Pilgrimage Plans," *TN*, May 4, 1950, 6; "Flower Festival Opens Pilgrimage at Pool," *TN*, May 5, 1950, 1; "Thousands Visit Hospitals Here; Many Receive Service Awards," *TN*, May 8, 1950, 1; Dan Meissner, "Days Are Now Numbered for Northington Campus," *TN*, Aug. 17, 1975, 4A.

16. The society editor Hattie Porter Collier encouraged her readers to drive about and view front gardens. "Annual Flower Show Here Proves Brilliant," *TN*, April 26, 1936, 9.

17. Welch and Grant, *Heirloom Garden*, 260–62; Stout, *Daylilies*, 56; American Hemerocallis Society, "'Caballero' (Stout, 1941)," Online Daylily Database, daylilies.org. An aerial photograph taken in 1956 confirms my recollection that the hedges lined the eastern edge of the driveway and the southern edge of the backyard. Aerial photograph, Tuscaloosa North Central, 1956, UA Alabama Maps.

18. MKF, pers. comm.

19. HLF Jr. to AFS, April 18, 1951, EFS Collection; MKF, pers. comm.; "Rupertus," Oct. 21, 2005, Naval History and Heritage Command, www.history.navy.mil.

20. "Lieut. Struss Aids in Rescue," *TN*, Jan. 31, 1945, 3. Photographs taken of Edward in 1919 and Lyman in 1946 reveal they had the same broad forehead, aquiline nose, prominent ears, and steady gaze. University of Alabama, *War Corolla* (1919), 244; HLF Jr., National Board of Medical Examiners Candidate's Identification Form, May 1946.

21. MKF, pers. comm.; "Chairman for Garden Pilgrimage," *TN*, April 30, 1941, 3; "Garden Pilgrimage Leaders Named," *TN*, April 27, 1947, 14; "Garden Pilgrimage Has Flower Show," *TN*, March 29, 1949, 6; Kent, *The Hooked Rug*, 49–56, 205, 173. Varian

Feare referred to "a lovely hooked rug made . . . nearly 100 years ago" ("Prattville Has Charming Old Homes," *BNAH*, June 2, 1935, 3). On women's decorative crafts as a strategy for brightening their world, see Gordon, *Saturated World*, 13.

22. U.S. Department of Veterans Affairs BIRLS Death File.

23. MKF, pers. comm.; HLF Jr. to AFS, April 18, 1951, EFS Collection.

24. EMF to AFS, March 16, 1952, EFS Collection.

25. MKF, pers. comm.; Burgin Mathews, "Ezell's Fish Camp Is a Family Tradition," http://arts.alabama.gov/traditional_culture/folkwaysarticles/EZELLSFISHCAMP.aspx.

26. "Negro Man Held as Suspect for Hit-Run Crash," *TN*, July 6, 1933, 1; "'Mr. X' Found to Be Brother of Local Man," *TN*, Feb. 8, 1939, 1; "Mr. X 'Comes Home' to City with Relatives," *TN*, Feb. 10, 1939, 1.

27. Affidavit by Hargrove Findley, Preston Findley, and Herbert L. Findley, Feb. 25, 1963, Tuscaloosa County Probate Office Records; EMF to AFS, Feb. 22, 1952; EMF to AFS, March 17, 1952; EMF to AFS, April 4, 1952, all in EFS Collection.

28. MKF, pers. comm.; "Personal Mention," *TN*, March 6, 1950, 4, and March 7, 1950, 7. The letters Earline and Anne sent to each other that are quoted in this paragraph and the previous one are AFS to EMF, Nov. 25, 1951; EMF to AFS, Dec. 1951; EMF to AFS, Feb. 22, 1952, all in EFS Collection.

29. *Polk's Tuscaloosa Directory* (1932), 186, U.S. Phone and Address Directories; 1940 USFC. On African Americans who served "in the household of the child's grandfather and who took part in training the child's parent" as "a direct link to the past," see Davis, Gardner, and Gardner, *Deep South*, 92. The Alabama memoirist Mary Wallace Kirk demonstrated this attitude in referring to her mother's longtime laundress "who washed for Mother before I was born, even as her mother, Ellen, had washed for my grandmother" (*Locust Hill*, 26–27).

30. EMF to AFS, Feb. 4, 1952, EFS Collection; "This Week," *TN*, Feb. 10, 1952, 13; EMF to AFS, Feb. 22, 1952, EFS Collection.

31. EMF to AFS, March 16, 1952, EFS Collection; 1940 USFC; *Polk's Tuscaloosa Directory* (1950), 3, U.S. Phone and Address Directories.

32. EMF to AFS, March 16, 1952, EFS Collection.

33. Sheet music, Bert Fitzgibbon, "Eeny, Meeny, Miny, Mo" (New York: F. B. Haviland, 1906), Duke University Libraries Digital Collections. A trade journal reported when Herbert was about eleven that Fitzgibbon's "new coon song" was a hit. "Haviland & Co. Continue to Score," *Music Trade Review* 43, no. 26 (1906): 50.

34. Powdermaker, *After Freedom*, 46–47; Rubin, *Plantation County*, 155; Katzman, *Seven Days a Week*, 185; Tucker, *Telling Memories*, 9; Ritterhouse, *Growing Up Jim Crow*, 68.

35. EMF to AFS, April 4, 1952, EFS Collection. For the "kind of mistress-servant relationship" in which nurses, maids, and cooks pretended "to be unintelligent, subservient, and content with their positions [because] they know the position[s] could be lost," see Rollins, *Between Women*, 225–27.

36. "Tuscaloosa Town Topics," *TN*, Feb. 29, 1952, 2; "Klan Leaders Charged," *TN*, Feb. 29, 1952, 2.

37. EMF to AFS, Sept. 26, 1952, EFS Collection; Samuel L. Webb, "John Sparkman,"

Encyclopedia of Alabama, http://www.encyclopediaofalabama.org, [Jan. 24, 2008] Sept. 20, 2012; Morgan, *A Time to Speak*, 28; Bartley, *Massive Resistance*, 12–17; Egerton, *Speak Now*, 525, 588; "Campus Landmarks: Bidgood Hall," University of Alabama, www.dialog.ua.edu/2012/07/campus-landmarks-bidgood-hall.

38. Key, *Southern Politics*, 559. In *Sweat v. Painter* (1950), the court ruled that segregated law schools in Texas were unequal. On the same day, the court ruled in *McLaurin v. Oklahoma Board of Regents of Higher Education* against the University of Oklahoma, which had admitted a black doctoral student but required him to sit separately from white students ("History of Brown v. Board of Education," www.uscourts.gov; search for "history brown"). Amendment No. 5 on Alabama ballots Dec. 11, 1951, to require applicants for registration "to be able to read and write, be of 'good character,' embrace the 'duties and obligations of citizenship,' take a written questionnaire, and sign an anti-Communist oath," passed although a majority of voters in Tuscaloosa County opposed it. AP, "Alabama Voters Will Perform Biggest 'Operation' on Constitution Tuesday," *TN*, Dec. 9, 1951, 3; "Road Bonds Approved by 3–2 Vote" and "Road Bonds Win in This County by 457 Votes," *TN*, Dec. 12, 1951, 1.

39. James P. Kaetz, "Autherine Lucy," www.encyclopediaofalabama.org, [Nov. 9, 2009] Dec. 13, 2010; "2 Negro Women Refused Admittance to U. of A.," *TN*, Sept. 21, 1952, 1; Clark, *The Schoolhouse Door*, 21; interview, George A. LeMaistre, "1950–1959: Good Times and Challenges," *Perspectives* (Winter 2000), Chamber of Commerce of West Alabama; "Tuscaloosa Town Topics," *TN*, May 29, 1951, 1; obituary, "George LeMaistre, 83, Banker and Ex-Chairman of F.D.I.C.," *New York Times*, Sept. 29, 1994.

40. Egerton, *Speak Now*, 601–4.

41. Bob Kyle, "'Divinest' Affinity Exists between Fox-Hunter, Hound," *TN*, Dec. 10, 1952, 1, 2; Karl R. Bauman, "Supreme Court Hearing 'Trial' of Segregation," *TN*, Dec. 10, 1952, 2.

42. "Mother of Local Resident Succumbs," *TN*, Sept. 3, 1946, 2; "What Is Angina?" National Heart, Lung, and Blood Institute, www.nhlbi.nih.gov/health/health-topics/topics/angina; "First Ladies of Kiwanis" (caption), TN, Jan. 8, 1950, 13; EMF to AFS, Sept. 26, 1952, EFS Collection.

43. William Eugene Barber, U.S. Headstone Applications for Military Veterans.

44. "Lewis-Gunn Vows Pledged in Impressive Afternoon Rites," *TN*, Dec. 7, 1952, 17; "Fund to Honor Dr. Fred Lewis," *TN*, April 18, 1982, 27A.

45. Dave P. to AFS, Dec. 26, 1952, EFS Collection.

46. Shapiro, *Perfection Salad*, 86–87. Anne later passed the recipe for pot roast on to her mother-in-law, Hazel Graham Shores, who wrote it in a blank area of her own cookbook (*Better Homes and Gardens Cook Book*, 23rd ed. [Des Moines, IA: Meredith Publishing, 1951], courtesy of Linda S. Shores). Tuscaloosa grocery stores offered canned salmon, the key ingredient in salmon croquettes, at fluctuating prices through the 1940s. Advertisement, "Quality Food Values," *TN*, Feb. 9, 1940, 7; advertisement, "Values in Polson's Market," *TN*, Jan. 5, 1945, 2; advertisement, "Plan Now to Be Thrifty in 1950—the Dixie's Way," *TN*, Jan. 6, 1950, 9.

47. VRMK to the author, n.d., EFS Collection.

48. Blake W. Godfrey to AFS, Dec. 27, 1950, EFS Collection.

49. VRMK passed on recipes for muscadine wine and blackberry wine, written in Earline's hand, and "Egg Nog (Erline)," written in Velma's hand.

50. MKF, pers. comm.

51. Arsenault, "The End of the Long Hot Summer," 608–10.

52. Dave P. to AFS, Dec. 26, 1952, EFS Collection.

53. "The Bedroom and Its Individuality," *The Craftsman* 9 (Feb. 1906): 694–704, 595–96, quoted in Cromley, "American Beds and Bedrooms, 1890–1930," 128.

54. Ida B. Longley to AFS, Feb. 22, 1952, EFS Collection.

55. AFS, pers. comm. The Moore chaise meridienne is in UA's collections.

56. JCM, pers. comm.; EMF to AFS, Feb. 6, 1953, EFS Collection.

57. Ida B. Longley to AFS, April 18, 1953, EFS Collection.

58. AFS, pers. comm.

59. The Greek key lamp closely resembled the Icicle lamp that was advertised by the Fostoria Glass Company in 1899 and the Daisy lamp manufactured by Westmoreland Specialty Company in the 1890s. Thuro, *Oil Lamps II*, 10, 119.

60. "How It All Got Started," www.patternglass.com; Laura Evans, "American Sun Purple Colored Glass," www.life123.com, retrieved Oct. 16, 2012.

61. Jordan-Bychkov, *Texas Graveyards*, 21; Jeane, "The Upland South Folk Cemetery Complex," 108; Gundaker and Cowan, *Keep Your Head to the Sky*, 17; Baumann, "Bottle Trees," 77.

62. Agee, *Cotton Tenants*, 202–3.

63. AFS, pers. comm.; "Brookwood Eyeing New City Hall," *TN*, Jan. 28, 1984, 31B; Chare Hester and Chuck Gerdau, "Brookwood Cemetery," 2000, IAGenWeb.org.

64. Agee, *Famous Men*, 44–45, 49.

65. Curtis, *Mind's Eye*, ix, 40–44; Mellow, *Walker Evans*, 323. See Cloar's painting in Thomas, *The Crossroads of Memory*, 161.

66. Gordon, *Textiles*, 118–19; Susan Roach, "The Kinship Quilt: An Ethnographic Semiotic Analysis of a Quilting Bee," in Rosan A. Jordan and Susan J. Kalcik, *Women's Folklore, Women's Culture* (Philadelphia: University of Pennsylvania Press, 1985), 64, quoted in Jones, "Event Analysis," 207.

67. On whole-cloth quilts and crazy quilts, see Horton, *Family Quilts*, 17–19, 97–98.

Chapter 10

1. "Part of Overflow Crowd" (caption), *TN*, Dec. 8, 1952, 1; dedication program, Druid City Hospital, Dec. 4, 1952, Tuscaloosa Area Virtual Museum, https://tavm.omeka.net; Paul Davis, "Institutional Growth Seen in Next 50 Years," *TN*, April 25, 1969, F1; A. J. Wright, "Hillman Hospital and How It Became UAB Hospital," Oct. 4, 2013, DiscoverBirmingham.org.

2. Bob Gunn to AFS, Aug. 20, 1952, EFS Collection; "A Chronological History of the University of Alabama at Birmingham (UAB) and Its Predecessor Institutions and Organizations, 1831," UAB University Archives.

3. MKF, pers. comm.

4. Airmail letter, Mary Luella Foley to AFS, April 21, 1953. All sympathy notes are in the AFS Collection, UA Special Collections.

5. Elna Bolding Shugerman, pers. comm.

6. Telegram, Alice Murphy to AFS, April 21, 1953; Rachel P. Johnson to AFS, May 4, 1953; Marion Parker Summerville to AFS, May 19, 1953; Rachel P. Johnson to AFS, May 4, 1953; Mrs. James Bailey to AFS, April 29, 1953; Martha Pace to AFS, April 29, 1953; telegram, Mrs. T. N. Goode to AFS, April 21, 1953; Truman N. Goode to AFS, April 22, 1953; Carolyn Loy to AFS, May 5, 1953; Estelle Baker to AFS, April 30, 1953.

7. "Mrs. H. L. Findley, Wife of Judge, Dies in B'ham," *TN*, April 21, 1953, 1.

8. Obituary, "Mrs. Herbert Findley," *Birmingham News*, April 21, 1953, 4. Alice was a staff writer for the *Birmingham News* in 1955. "Mrs. Alice Murphy, Rector's Wife, Dies; Rites Today at 5," *TN*, May 2, 1955, 1.

9. Dryden, *Etiquette*, 113.

10. USFC, 1920, 1930, 1940; "Death Claims Murk Findley," *TN*, April 22, 1941, 1, 2.

11. "Mrs. H. L. Findley, Wife of Judge, Dies in B'ham," *TN*, April 21, 1953, 1; "Funeral Is Held for Mrs. Findley," *TN*, April 22, 1953, 2; MKF, pers. comm.; "Weather," *TN*, April 23, 1953, 1.

12. AFS to EMF, Feb. 1, 1952, and Alice Murphy to AFS, April 26, 1953, AFS Collection, UA Special Collections.

13. Dryden, *Etiquette*, 111.

14. AFS, "Flowers sent to Mother's funeral . . . Wednesday, April 22, 1953" (typed list, AFS Collection, UA Special Collections).

15. "Town Topics," *TN*, April 22, 1948, 2; Totsie Jones to HLF, April 23, 1953, AFS Collection, UA Special Collections; "Dr. McBurney Gets Health Group Honor," *TN*, Nov. 16, 1958, 5; "Physical Examination Is Suggested for School Children," *TN*, Aug. 18, 1936, 5; "Clionian Club Holds Meeting in Davis Home," *TN*, Jan. 7, 1943, 8; "Clionian Study Club Meets with Mrs. Jackman," *TN*, May 6, 1942, 5; "Jr. Music Study Club Entertains Clionian Group," *TN*, May 6, 1943, 6; Hazel McBurney to HLF, April 22, 1953; Margaret Shook to HLF, April 27, 1953; Margaret Shook to AFS, May 1953; Ida M. Longley to AFS, May 8, 1953.

16. "Tribute Is Paid to Van de Graaff," *TN*, Jan. 5, 1938, 1; "Last Rites Planned for Mrs. Van de Graaff," *TN*, Nov. 26, 1941, 2; 1880 USFC; Sons of the American Revolution Membership Applications; Dick Looser, "He's Authority on City's History," *TN*, March 20, 1964, 9; Daniel Fate Brooks, "William Rufus King," *Encyclopedia of Alabama*, http://www.encyclopediaofalabama.org, [Dec. 10, 2008] June 28, 2013; Tuscaloosa High School, *Black Warrior* (1912).

17. Devane K. Jones to HLF, April 30, 1953; MKF, pers. comm. Devane's first wife, Alice McLean Jones, died in 1928 (Deaths and Burials Index). The sympathy cards and notes are in the AFS Collection, UA Special Collections.

18. See appendix 3, this book.

19. MKF, pers. comm.

20. Order of Service, Methodist Campus Church, Nov. 22, 1953, AFS Collection, UA Special Collections; photograph of Harpers with roses, Roland Harper Photo Collection, Folder Number 03.903, UA Special Collections.

21. Editorial, "Approach the Problems Calmly," *TN*, May 19, 1954, 4; Egerton, *Speak Now*, 606–8; Rogers et al., *Alabama: The History of a Deep South State*, 569; Durr,

Autobiography, 254, 282–83. Durr echoed John Dollard's description of "a little tide of traffic laps from the Negro to the white side of" Indianola (*Caste and Class*, 5).

22. Wayne Greenhaw, "Like Visiting Old Friends," retrieved May 1, 2011, from Greenhaw's website (link now broken); Hubbs, *Tuscaloosa*, 72; Wolfe, *University of Alabama*, 201; James P. Kaetz, "Autherine Lucy," EncyclopediaofAlabama.org, [Nov. 9, 2009] Dec. 13, 2010; AP, "Autherine Lucy Has Retreated into Obscurity," *Florence (AL) Times*, Sept. 19, 1962, 3; editorial, Buford Boone, "What a Price for Peace," *TN*, Feb. 7, 1956, 1. Boone's editorial won the 1957 Pulitzer Prize in Editorial Writing. The citation read, "For his fearless and reasoned editorials in a community inflamed by a segregation issue" (http://www.pulitzer.org/winners/buford-boone). As of 2015, this is still one of only two Pulitzers ever awarded to the *Tuscaloosa News*.

23. Davis, *Way through the Wilderness*, 128; Doss, "City Belles," 6, 9.

24. Smith, *Reminiscences*, 96.

25. "Alabama," *Burlington (VT) Free Press*, Feb. 4, 1842, 4, Chronicling America; Benjamin Buford Williams, "William Russell Smith," EncyclopediaofAlabama.org, [July 8, 2009] July 19, 2012. It was common in the nineteenth century for newspapers in one part of the country to reproduce humorous material from newspapers in another region. Meine, foreword, xv.

26. "Egg Nog (Erline)," handwritten recipe courtesy of VRMK.

27. AFS, pers. comm.

28. "Judge Findley Honored at UA," *TN*, Jan. 15, 1965, 9.

29. On African Americans in Macon County, Alabama, asking whites for advice on "virtually all those phases of life which are related to the moving world outside," see Johnson, *Shadow of the Plantation*, 3.

Conclusion

1. Bryden and Floyd, introduction to *Domestic Space*, 8. See also Wyatt-Brown, *Southern Honor*, 328–29; Kierner, *Beyond the Household*, 3, 37–38. On comparable antebellum events as "cultural artifacts," see Stowe, *Intimacy and Power*, xviii.

2. Proctor, *Bathed in Blood*, 170; Henneman, *History of the Literary and Intellectual Life of the Southern States*, 337, quoted in Brundage, *Southern Past*, 131.

3. MacKethan, *Recollections of a Southern Daughter*, xxxiii.

4. Ames, *Dining Room*, 7; Reinberger, "Architecture of Sharecropping," 117; Stowe, *Intimacy and Power*, 162, 250.

5. Smith, *Killers of the Dream*, 141.

6. Helfand, *Scrapbooks*, xvii.

7. Maslow, *Motivation and Personality*, 15; Holmes, *John Bowlby*, 9, 20, 42, 116, 120. On the phenomenon of children experiencing displaced parental hostility, see Tuan, *Landscapes of Fear*, 34.

8. Louis Cozolino links insecure early emotional attachment, symptoms of a borderline personality disorder, and a sense that one is "defective, bad, and worthy of rejection. . . . When these patients look within, all they feel is pain. To feel is to feel badly about the self" (*Neuroscience of Human Relationships*, 256–57, 265–66, 322).

9. Charlie Ann McCall Smith died four months after the birth of her daughter

Charlie Annie Smith, who then lived with her maternal grandparents, Charles and Martha McCall. According to the sequence of records in the 1900 census manuscript, the McCalls were one of the three white families living in the closest proximity to Earline's family. Grave marker, "In Memory of Charlie Ann," Mount Sterling Cemetery, Choctaw County, Find a Grave Index; 1900, 1910 USFC.

10. "19 Go Down to Their Deaths," *Keowee (Pickens County, SC) Courier*, June 18, 1919, 1, Chronicling America; Matthew W. Clinton, "City's Growth Begins," *TN*, April 24, 1969, 1, 13, 22–23; "South Suffering, Five States Hit," *Morning Tulsa Daily World*, April 17, 1921, 1, 13, Chronicling America; "Warrior River Leaps to 65.1 Feet," *TN*, Nov. 15, 1929, 1; "Storm Kills 20, Hurts Hundreds," *TN*, March 21, 1932, 1; Friends of Historic Northport, *Northport*, 17; Matthew W. Clinton, quoted in Frank Fitts Sr., "1930–1939: Progress Follows the Depression," interview, *Perspectives* (Winter 2000), Chamber of Commerce of West Alabama.

11. Cash, *Mind of the South*, 115–16, quoted in Cobb, *Away Down South*, 175; Wilson, *Baptized in Blood*, 101. Also see McGovern, *Anatomy of a Lynching*, 8.

12. Tuan, *Landscapes of Fear*, 34, 104, 132, 139, 206–7, 209. For real and imagined threats acting as triggers for "a state of terror," see Cozolino, *Neuroscience of Human Relationships*, 256–57.

13. Maslow, *Motivation and Personality*, 23–25.

14. Gordon, "Woman's Domestic Body," 292; Clark, "The Vision of the Dining Room," 157–58; Pleck, *Celebrating the Family*, 105, 150; Motz, introduction, 5; Howett, *World of Her Own Making*, 3, 26; Bushman, *The Refinement of America*, 242.

15. Gordon and McArthur, "Interior Decorating Advice," 115–16; Marcus, *House as a Mirror of Self*, 20.

16. AFS, pers. comm.; Seale, *Tasteful Interlude*, 167; Gamble, *Historic Architecture*, 107.

17. Gordon, "Woman's Domestic Body," 282, 288. On Goffman's view of interior decoration as the manifestation of the woman or man who made decorating choices, see *Presentation of Self*, 124. The historian Dolores Hayden compared identification with one's house (or "place attachment") to "an infant's attachment to parental figures" ("Urban Landscape History," 112). Also see Marcus, who quoted an interview subject who rejected the idea that his ongoing house remodeling project was a hobby: "Bill reacted with feeling. 'This is not a hobby. This is a fundamental part of our existence. . . . The house is me'" (*House as a Mirror of Self*, 52, 54).

18. Csikszentmihalyi and Rochberg-Halton, *The Meaning of Things*, 22–23.

19. Varian Feare, "Beauty Hides in Post Oak Country," *BNAH*, Dec. 8, 1935, 8, and "'Before-the-War' Home Goes Modern," *BNAH*, March 8, 1936, 12; Rubin, *Plantation County*, 41–42.

20. Eastmond, "Metaphor and the Self-portrait," 656–57; West, *Portraiture*, 199; Gottfried and Jennings, *American Vernacular*, 106, 109–10.

21. Although brooches in the form of floral sprays were common, and the costume jewelry manufacturers Trifari, Coro, Dujay, and DeRosa made many similar pieces, the use of cabochons in Earline's piece was distinctive. It resembles pieces by the jewelry designer McClelland Barclay that included cabochons. Jane Haley Clarke, "McClelland Barclay Sterling Jewelry," www.morninggloryantiques.com/collectMcClellandBarclay.html.

22. Gordon, "Cozy, Charming," 131.

23. MKF, pers. comm. James J. "Jack" Andrews was an illustrator and painter in Tuscaloosa. "3 Artists Featured," *TN*, Dec. 24, 1976, 10; obituary, "James J. Andrews," *TN*, Feb. 16, 2005.

24. That Herbert believed in the innate inferiority of some individuals is clear; he supported compulsory sterilization of female patients at the state facility for people with developmental disabilities. Clipping, "Findley Supports Sterilization," *TN*, April 20, 1945, 1, 2.

25. Rogers quotation in Coplan and Goldie, introduction, xviii–xix. For a clear introduction to the subject of empathy, see Howe, *Empathy*. For a recent review of the psychological literature on the nature of empathy, see Kernberg, *The Inseparable Nature of Love*. For overviews of this research, including the work of Martin Hoffman on the relationship of empathy and moral development, see Coplan and Goldie, introduction; Castano, "Antisocial Behavior."

26. On the mother's lack of empathy causing the child to lack empathy, see Cozolino, *Neuroscience of Human Relationships*, 299; Castano, "Antisocial Behavior," 419, 427; Mikulincer et al., "Attachment, Caregiving, and Altruism"; De Fruyt and De Clercq, "Childhood Antecedents of Personality Disorders," 174–75; Fonagy and Luyten, "Psychodynamic Models."

27. On the role of play in social-emotional development, see Howe, *Empathy*, 38.

28. On the perception of a dangerous world, see Hooley, Cole, and Gironde, "Borderline Personality Disorder," 420; Bateman and Fonagy, "Mentalization-Based Treatment," 771; Castano, "Antisocial Behavior," 427.

29. Holmes, *John Bowlby*, 150. On the relationship of empathy and "self narrative," see Goldman, "Two Routes to Empathy," 39; Bateman and Fonagy, "Mentalization-Based Treatment," 771; Cozolino, *Neuroscience of Human Relationships*, 209, 304–6. On the tendency of people with Borderline Personality Disorder to only tell vague stories of their own lives, see Hooley, Cole, and Gironde, "Borderline Personality Disorder," 424.

30. Christopher, "Autobiography," 7.

31. Laura Jones to EMF, Oct. 30, 1946 (notes from articles in *Virginia Historical Magazine* and other sources), AFS Collection, UA Special Collections; JCM to the author, April 2014.

32. Lee, introduction, 4.

33. Holmes, *John Bowlby*, 9, 85.

34. Rosselin, "The Ins and Outs of the Hall," 53–54; Ames, *Dining Room*, 43; Beckham, "The American Front Porch," 72, 75; Volz, "The Modern Look," 27–30; Cromley, "American Beds and Bedrooms, 1890–1930," 125, 128; Cromley, "American Beds and Bedrooms," 185; Gordon, *Saturated World*, 1, 13. The literary scholar Rachel Watson suggested that in the novel and film *To Kill a Mockingbird*, porches are zones where empathy can develop ("The View from the Porch," 423, 432, 438). On privacy as an attribute of post–World War II housing design, see Harris, *Little White Houses*, 111–57; Tuan, *Landscapes of Fear*, 6.

35. AFS to Ila Blackman Findley, May 18, 1981.

36. AFS, untitled typed manuscript, EFS Collection; "Services at the Churches," *TN* April 4, 1953, 4. J. C. Penney's in Tuscaloosa advertised "rough-woven straw" hats with net veils, "so very, very becoming," and "pastel beauties in fine strawcloth [were] fit to lead the Easter parade." Brown's Department Store had "over 1,000 hats." Advertisement, "Penney's," *TN*, April 1, 1953, 5; advertisement, "Easter Bonnets," *TN*, April 1, 1953, 6.

37. Devane K. Jones to HLF, April 30, 1953.

38. Maslow, *Motivation and Personality*, 18–19; AFS, pers. comm.

39. Leaflet, Chase Nursery Company, "Foundation Plantings"; Glen B. Fain, "Ornamental Nursery Crops Production," *Encyclopedia of Alabama*, http://www.encyclopediaofalabama.org, [Feb. 26, 2009] July 30, 2013.

Bibliography

Digital Archives and Resources

ADAH Digital Collections. www.digital.archives.alabama.gov

ALGenWeb. www.algw.org

Ancestry.com. www.ancestry.com

Born in Slavery: Slave Narratives from the Federal Writers' Project, 1936–1938. https://memory.loc.gov/ammem/snhtml/snhome.html

California Digital Newspaper Collection. cdnc.ucr.edu

Chronicling America. http://chroniclingamerica.loc.gov

Digital Library on American Slavery. https://library.uncg.edu/slavery

Duke University Libraries Digital Collections. http://library.duke.edu/digitalcollections

Documenting the American South. www.docsouth.unc.edu

Find a Grave Index. www.findagrave.com

The Free Library. www.thefreelibrary.co.

Google Books. https://books.google.com

Google News. https://news.google.com

Historic Pittsburgh. http://digital.library.pitt.edu/pittsburgh

National Archives and Records Administration. www.archives.gov

National Museum of American History (Smithsonian). http://americanhistory.si.edu

UA Alabama Maps. www.alabamamaps.ua.edu

UA Special Collections. http://acumen.lib.ua.edu

UAB Mervyn H. Sterne Library Oral History Collection. www.mhsl.uab.edu/dc

UAB University Archives. www.uab.edu/archives

University Libraries Division of Special Collections, University of Alabama. www.lib.ua.edu/libraries/hoole

University of Virginia Visual History Collection. http://small.library.virginia.edu/collections/featured/university-of-virginia-visual-history-collection

Primary Sources

Abstracts of Graves of Revolutionary Patriots, www.ancestry.com.

Acker, Martha Walters, comp. *Deeds of Franklin County, Georgia, 1784–1826*. Birmingham, AL: Author, 1976.

———, comp. *Franklin County, Georgia Tax Digests*. 3 vols. Birmingham, AL: Author, 1980–1982.

Agee, James. *Cotton Tenants: Three Families*. Brooklyn, NY: Melville House, 2013.

Agee, James, and Walker Evans. *Let Us Now Praise Famous Men*. Boston: Houghton Mifflin, [1941] 2001.

Alabama Board of Health. *Transactions of the Medical Association of the State of Alabama*. Montgomery, AL: Brown Printing, 1892.

Alabama Census of Confederate Soldiers. www.ancestry.com.

Alabama Civil War Service Database. ADAH.

Alabama Convict Records. www.ancestry.com.

Alabama Department of Archives and History. www.archives.alabama.gov.

———. *Alabama Official and Statistical Register.* Montgomery, AL: Brown Printing, 1915.

Alabama Marriage Collection. www.ancestry.com.

Alabama National Guard Index Cards. www.ancestry.com.

Alabama Photographs and Pictures Collection. ADAH.

Alabama State Bar Association. *Proceedings of the Thirteenth Annual Meeting of the Alabama State Bar Association.* Montgomery, AL: Brown Printing, 1891.

American Bar Association. *Report of the Twentieth Annual Meeting of the American Bar Association.* Philadelphia: Dando Printing and Publishing Company, 1897.

Ames, Jessie Daniel. *The Changing Character of Lynching: Review of Lynching, 1931–1941, with a Discussion of Recent Developments in the Field.* New York: AMS Press, [1942] 1973.

Anderson, James A. "Sketch of Keene Family and Keene's Mill." Unpublished manuscript, Tuscaloosa, circa 1940, UA Special Collections.

Andrea, Leonardo, comp. *Findley-Finley.* Columbia, SC: Author, 1949.

Baker, Daniel. "Practical Methods of Dealing with the Liquor Traffic." In *Proceedings of the Third Ecumenical Methodist Conference*, 402–6. London: Eaton and Mains, 1901.

Barefield, Marilyn Davis, comp. *Old Tuskaloosa Land Office Records and Military Warrants, 1821–1855.* Easley, SC: Southern Historical Press, 1984.

Bennett Lumber Co. *Bennett's Small House Catalog, 1920.* New York: Dover, 1993.

Berney, Saffold. *Handbook of Alabama: A Complete Index to the State; With a Geological Map and an Appendix of Useful Tables.* Mobile, AL: Mobile Register, 1878.

Blackman, Nancy Dean. *Brow of the Hill above the Warrior: History of Holt First Baptist Church, Holt, Alabama, 1904–1974.* Holt, AL: Holt First Baptist Church, 1976.

Born in Slavery: Slave Narratives from the Federal Writers' Project, 1936–1938. Library of Congress.

Boyd, Hayse. "An Old Hill, an Old House, an Old Cemetery, and an Old Road." *Friends of Historic Northport* 14, no. 2/3 (2009): 7–10.

Brantley, Mary E. *From Cabins to Mansions: Gleanings from Southwest Alabama.* Huntsville, AL: Strode Publishers, 1981.

Burkhardt, E. Walter, Varian Feare Burkhardt, and Alabama Historical Commission. *Alabama Ante-Bellum Architecture: A Scrapbook View from the 1930's.* Montgomery: Alabama Historical Commission, 1976.

Burr, Virginia I., ed. *The Secret Eye: The Journal of Ella Gertrude Clanton Thomas, 1848–1889.* Chapel Hill: University of North Carolina Press, 1990.

Callahan, Artemas K. "The Napoleon B. Garner Murder Case." Unpublished manuscript, courtesy of MKF.

———. "The Personnel of the Tuscaloosa Bar When I Graduated from Law School in 1926." Unpublished manuscript, courtesy of MKF.

———. "The Segregated Society," 1980. Transcript of interview. Birmingham, AL:

UAB Mervyn H. Sterne Library Oral History Collection.

Campbell-Everden, William Preston. *Freemasonry and Its Etiquette: With Which Is Incorporated "The Etiquette of Freemasonry."* Rev. ed. New York: Weathervane Books, 1955.

Card Index of Personal Corporate Names and Subjects. ADAH.

Carmer, Carl. *Stars Fell on Alabama.* Tuscaloosa: University of Alabama Press, [1934] 1990.

Carnegie Survey of the Architecture of the South. Library of Congress.

Cartwright, Peter, and Charles Langworthy Wallis. *Autobiography of Peter Cartwright.* Nashville, TN: Abingdon Press, 1956.

Cason, Clarence. "Middle Class and Bourbon." In *Culture in the South,* ed. W. T. Couch, 478–500. Chapel Hill: University of North Carolina Press, 1935.

———. *90 Degrees in the Shade.* Westport, CT: Negro Universities Press, [1935] 1970.

Choctaw County Records. ADAH.

Christopher, Ralph Griffin. "Autobiography." Unpublished transcript, AFS Collection, UA Special Collections.

Chronicling America. Library of Congress.

Clay-Clopton, Virginia, and Ada Sterling. *A Belle of the Fifties: Memoirs of Mrs. Clay of Alabama, Covering Social and Political Life in Washington and the South, 1853–66.* Tuscaloosa: University of Alabama Press, [1905] 1999.

Clayton, Victoria Virginia Hunter. *White and Black under the Old Regime.* Milwaukee, WI: Young Churchman, 1899.

Clear Creek Baptist Church Historical Society Committee. "Clear Creek Baptist Church." In *Church Histories of Choctaw County,* ed. Choctaw County Historical Society, 150–51. Butler, AL: Choctaw County Historical Society, 1980.

Clinton, Matthew William. *Matt Clinton's Scrapbook.* Tuscaloosa, AL: Bernice Blackshere Clinton, 1979.

———. *Tuscaloosa, Alabama: Its Early Days, 1816–1865.* Tuscaloosa, AL: Zonta Club, 1958.

Confederate Pension and Service Records. www.ancestry.com.

Cooke, Nathaniel. *The Illustrated Book of Scottish Songs: From the Sixteenth to the Nineteenth Century.* London: Illustrated London Library, 1854.

Crockett, David. *A Narrative of the Life of David Crockett by Himself.* Lincoln: University of Nebraska Press, [1834] 1987.

Cullum, George Washington. *Biographical Register of the Officers and Graduates of the U.S. Military Academy from 1802 to 1867.* Bedford, MA: Applewood Books, 1879.

Davis, Allison, Burleigh B. Gardner, and Mary R. Gardner. *Deep South: A Social Anthropological Study of Caste and Class.* Chicago: University of Chicago Press, 1941.

Dawson, Lemuel Orah. *A State, a Father and a Son.* Tuscaloosa, AL: Weatherford Print Co., 193–?.

Deaths and Burials Index. www.ancestry.com.

Dickens, Dorothy. "Time Activities in Homemaking." Bulletin 424. State College: Mississippi State College, Agricultural Experiment Station, 1945.

Directory of Deceased American Physicians. www.ancestry.com.

Dobson, David. *Ships from Ireland to Early America, 1623–1850*. Baltimore: Genealogical Publishing, 1999.

Dollard, John. *Caste and Class in a Southern Town*. Madison: University of Wisconsin Press, [1937] 1988.

Dowling, Herndon Glenn. "Tuscaloosa, Alabama 'The Druid City': A Brief Sketch of the History Back of This Thriving City." Pamphlet. Tuscaloosa, AL: Tuscaloosa Chamber of Commerce, 1939.

Dryden, Ellen. *Essentials of Etiquette: Complete Rules of the Social Game*. New York: Carey Craft Press, 1924.

Durr, Virginia Foster. *The Autobiography of Virginia Foster Durr: Outside the Magic Circle*. Tuscaloosa: University of Alabama Press, 1985.

Emmett, Dan D. "I Wish I Was in Dixie's Land." New York: Firth, Pond, 1860.

Fleming, Walter L. *Civil War and Reconstruction in Alabama*. New York: P. Smith, [1905] 1949.

———. "Home Life in Alabama during the Civil War." *Southern History Association Publications* 7 (1904): 81–103.

———. "The Servant Problem in a Black Belt Village." *Sewanee Review* 13, no. 1 (Jan. 1905): 1–17.

Flexner, Marion. *Out of Kentucky Kitchens*. New York: Bramhall House, 1949.

Fox, John, Jr. *The Little Shepherd of Kingdom Come*. New York: Charles Scribner's Sons, [1903] 1931.

Friends of Historic Northport. *Northport in the 20th Century*. Northport, AL: Friends of Historic Northport, 2005.

Fry, Anna M. Gayle. *Memories of Old Cahaba*. Nashville, TN: Publishing House of the Methodist Episcopal Church, South, 1908.

Galloway, Bishop Charles B. "Bishop Robert Kennon Hargrove." *Methodist Quarterly Review* 54 (Oct. 1905): 627–38.

Gandrud, Pauline Jones, comp. *Alabama Records*. Multiple volumes with sections with individually numbered pages. Easley, SC: Southern Historical Press, various years.

———, comp. *Marriage Records of Tuscaloosa County, Alabama, 1823–1860, Being Transcribed and Indexed from the Original Marriage Books at the Court House of Tuscaloosa Alabama*. Memphis, TN: Milestone Press, 1968.

Garrett, William. *Reminiscences of Public Men in Alabama for Thirty Years*. Atlanta: Plantation Publishing Company and Press, 1872.

Gay, Ann H., ed. *Choctaw Names and Notes: Alabama's Choctaw County*. Butler, AL: A. H. Gay, 1993.

Georgia Census. www.ancestry.com.

Gosse, Philip Henry. "Possum-Hunting in Alabama." In *Hunting in the Old South: Original Narratives of the Hunters*, ed. Clarence Gohdes, 87–93. Baton Rouge: Louisiana State University Press, 1967.

Govan, Christine Noble. *Narcissus an' de Chillun*. Boston: Houghton Mifflin, 1938.

———. *Those Plummer Children*. Boston: Houghton Mifflin, 1934.

Griffith, Lucille. *Alabama: A Documentary History to 1900*. Tuscaloosa: University of Alabama Press, 1968.

Hague, Parthenia Antoinette. *A Blockaded Family: Life in Southern Alabama during the Civil War.* Lincoln: University of Nebraska Press, [1888] 1991.

Henderson, Aileen Kilgore. *Eugene Allen Smith's Alabama: How a Geologist Shaped a State.* Montgomery, AL: NewSouth Books, 2011.

Hendrix, Beasley S., Jr. *Old Cemeteries Found in Tuscaloosa County, Alabama, with Inscriptions Taken from Headstones.* Tuscaloosa, AL: Author, 1981.

Hendrix, Beasley S., Jr., and June Orr Reese. *Tuskaloosa's Own: A Short History and Muster List of Confederate Units from Tuskaloosa County, Alabama.* Tuscaloosa, AL: Colonial Press, 1988.

Hiestand, Emily. *Angela the Upside-Down Girl and Other Domestic Travels.* Boston: Beacon Press, 1998.

Historic American Buildings Survey. Library of Congress.

Hoeckel, Marilyn, and Theodore B. Van Itallie. *Images of America: Boca Grande.* Charleston, SC: Arcadia Publishing, 2000.

Horn, Stanley F. *Invisible Empire: The Story of the Ku Klux Klan, 1866–1871.* Montclair, NJ: Patterson Smith, [1939] 1969.

Hundley, Daniel R. *Social Relations in the Southern States.* Baton Rouge: Louisiana State University Press, [1860] 1979.

Johnson, Charles Spurgeon. *The Shadow of the Plantation.* Chicago: University of Chicago Press, 1934.

Joint Select Committee on the Condition of Affairs in the Late Insurrectionary States. 42nd Cong., 2nd Sess. *House Report 22.* Washington, DC: U.S. GPO, 1872.

Jones, John Griffling. *A Complete History of Methodism as Connected with the Mississippi Conference of the Methodist Episcopal Church, South.* 2 vols. Nashville, TN: Publishing House of the Methodist Episcopal Church, South, 1908.

Kearney, Belle. *A Slaveholder's Daughter.* Chapel Hill: University of North Carolina Press, [1900] 1997.

Kennedy, John Pendleton. *Horse Shoe Robinson.* New York: John B. Alden Company, [1835] 1852.

Kirk, Mary Wallace. *Locust Hill.* Tuscaloosa: University of Alabama Press, [1975] 1976.

Knight, Lucian Lamar. *A Standard History of Georgia and Georgians.* 6 vols. Chicago: Lewis Publishing, 1917.

Lanier, Louise B. "Christopher Chapel United Methodist Church History." In *Church Histories of Choctaw County,* ed. Choctaw County Historical Society, 44–46. Butler, AL: Choctaw County Historical Society, 1980.

Lazenby, Marion Elias. *History of Methodism in Alabama and West Florida; Being an Account of the Amazing March of Methodism through Alabama and West Florida.* Nashville, TN: Methodist Publishing, 1960.

Lee, Harper. *Go Set a Watchman.* New York: HarperCollins, 2015.

———. *To Kill a Mockingbird.* Philadelphia: Lippincott, 1960.

Lester, J. C., and D. L. Wilson. *Ku Klux Klan: Its Origin, Growth and Disbandment.* New York: Neale Publishing, 1905.

Liddell, Viola Goode. *With a Southern Accent.* Norman: University of Oklahoma Press, 1948.

Little, George, and James R. Maxwell. *A History of Lumsden's Battery, C.S.A.* Tuscaloosa, AL: R. E. Rodes Chapter, United Daughters of the Confederacy, 1905.

Little, Robert Irving. "The University Club." Unpublished manuscript, Tuscaloosa, 1955. UA Special Collections.

Masello, David. "I Love My Bed: Temo Callahan." *House Beautiful* (March 2012): 42.

Massey, John. *Reminiscences, Giving Sketches of Scenes through Which the Author Has Passed and Pen Portraits of People Who Have Modified His Life.* Nashville, TN: Publishing House of the M. E. Church, South, 1916.

Maxwell, James Robert. *Autobiography of James Robert Maxwell of Tuskaloosa, Alabama, 1850–1926.* Baltimore: Gateway Press, [1926] 1996.

Maxwell, Thomas. *The King Bee's Dream: A Metrical Address Delivered before the Druid City Literary Club of the City of Tuskaloosa, Alabama, by Thomas Maxwell, May 12, 1875.* Tuscaloosa, AL: G. A. Searcy, 1875.

McCaskill, Dixie Miller, comp. *The MacAskill/McCaskill History, 1770–1984.* Irmo, SC: A. & D. McCaskill, 1985.

McDowell, Caroline Dent, and Mollie Hollifield Jones. *History of the Alabama Division; United Daughters of the Confederacy.* Opelika, AL: Post Publishing Company, 1952.

McEachin, Archibald Bruce. *The History of Tuscaloosa, 1816–1880.* Tuscaloosa, AL: Confederate Publishing Company, 1977.

Methodist Episcopal Church. *Minutes of the Annual Conferences of the Methodist Episcopal Church, for the Years 1773–1828.* New York: T. Mason and G. Lane, 1840.

Migliario, Ida Rigney, Harriet Wright Allard, Zorada Zerna Titus, and Irene Westbrook. *The Household Searchlight Recipe Book.* Topeka, KS: Household Magazine, 1931, 1937, 1943, 1946, 1952, 1955, 1977.

Mitchell, Margaret. *Gone with the Wind.* 80th printing. Toronto: Macmillan, 1969.

———. *Gone with the Wind: Movie Picture Edition.* New York: Macmillan, 1939.

Moore, George F., Esq. "The Justice of the Peace." In *Proceedings of the Forty-Fifth Annual Meeting of the Alabama State Bar,* by Alabama State Bar Association. Montgomery, AL: Brown Printing, 1891.

Morgan, Charles, Jr. *A Time to Speak.* New York: Holt, Rinehart and Winston, 1964.

Muster Rolls of Alabama Civil War Units. ADAH.

Natural Resources Conservation Service. *Soil Survey of Choctaw County, Alabama.* Washington, DC: U.S. Department of Agriculture, 1998 [?].

Owen, Marie Bankhead, comp. *Alabama Official and Statistical Register.* Montgomery, AL: ADAH, 1927.

Owen, Thomas McAdory, and Marie Bankhead Owen. *History of Alabama and Dictionary of Alabama Biography.* 4 vols. Chicago: S. J. Clarke Publishing, 1921.

Page, Thomas Nelson. *Social Life in Old Virginia before the War.* New York: Scribner's, 1897.

Palmer, Thomas Waverly, comp. *A Register of the Officers and Students of the University of Alabama, 1831–1901.* Tuscaloosa: University of Alabama, 1901.

Partrich, Sally Virginia. "A Study of the Living Rooms in the Homes of 200 Families in Tuscaloosa County, Alabama." Master's thesis, University of Alabama, 1937.

Porter, Eleanor H. *Pollyanna Grows Up.* New York: Grosset and Dunlap, 1915.

Powdermaker, Hortense. *After Freedom: A Cultural Study in the Deep South*. New York: Viking, 1939.

Powell, E. A. "Fifty-Five Years in West Alabama." *Alabama Historical Quarterly* 4, no. 4 (1942): 459–641.

Prints and Photographs Online Catalog. Library of Congress.

Prison Discipline Society. *Sixteenth Annual Report, Boston, 1836–1845*. Boston: Press of T. R. Marvin, 1841.

R. E. Rodes Chapter, United Daughters of the Confederacy. *Year Book of the R. E. Rodes Chapter, U.D.C.* Tuscaloosa, AL: R. E. Rodes Chapter, various years.

Railroad Commission of Alabama. *Twenty-Second Annual Report*. Montgomery: State of Alabama, 1902.

Raper, Arthur. *The Tragedy of Lynching*. Mineola, NY: Dover [1933], 2003.

Rootsweb. www.ancestry.com.

Rubin, Morton. *Plantation County*. Chapel Hill: University of North Carolina Press, 1951.

Rust Engineering Company Records, Historic Pittsburgh.

Scott, Sir Walter. *Ivanhoe: A Romance*. New York: Modern Library, [1820] 2001.

Sellers, James Benson. *The Prohibition Movement in Alabama, 1702 to 1943*. Chapel Hill: University of North Carolina Press, 1943.

———. *Slavery in Alabama*. Tuscaloosa: University of Alabama Press, [1950] 1994.

Sellers, James Benson, and Charles William Foster. *The First Methodist Church of Tuscaloosa, Alabama, 1818–1968*. Tuscaloosa, AL: Weatherford Printing, 1968.

Singleton, Paul, and Donald Brown. *Foundry Life: Holt, Alabama*. Tuscaloosa, AL: Tuscaloosa Public Library, 2004.

Smith, Eugene Allen. *Report on the Cotton Production of the State of Alabama, with a Discussion of the General Agricultural Features of the State*. Washington, DC: U.S. GPO, 1884.

Smith, Henry Atterbury. *Five Hundred Small Houses of the Twenties*. New York: Dover, [1923] 1990.

Smith, William Russell. *Reminiscences of a Long Life: Historical, Political, Personal and Literary*. Washington, DC: Author, 1889.

Smithsonian Costume Collection. Smithsonian Museum of American History.

Smyth, Sydnia Keene. "The Ante-Bellum Architecture of Tuscaloosa, Alabama." Master's thesis, University of Alabama, 1929.

Songs for Our Times. Library of Congress.

Sons of the American Revolution Membership Applications. www.ancestry.com.

Southern Commission on the Study of Lynching. *The Plight of Tuscaloosa: A Case Study of Conditions in Tuscaloosa, Alabama, 1933*. Atlanta: Author, 1933.

Springer, Mrs. Elmer Clanahan. "A Study of the Use of Leisure of One Hundred Women of Tuscaloosa, Alabama." Master's thesis, University of Alabama, 1930.

Stickley, Gustav. *Craftsman Houses: The 1913 Catalog*. Mineola, NY: Dover, 2009.

Stratton-Porter, Gene. *The Harvester*. New York: Grosset and Dunlap, 1911.

Sudduth, Maggie Hubbard, comp. *Tuscaloosa County, Alabama, Will Book, 1821–1855*. Tuscaloosa, AL: Author, 1994.

Tompkins, Susie Powers. *Cotton-Patch Schoolhouse.* Tuscaloosa: University of Alabama Press, 1992.

Topp, Mildred Spurrier. *Smile Please.* Boston: Houghton Mifflin, 1948.

Tuscaloosa County Preservation Society. *Past Horizons.* Tuscaloosa, AL: Tuscaloosa County Preservation Society, 1978.

Tuscaloosa Genealogical Society. *Pioneers of Tuscaloosa County, Alabama Prior to 1830.* Montgomery, AL: Herff Jones Division, 1981.

Tuscaloosa White Pages and Yellow Pages. www.ancestry.com.

University of Alabama. *Catalog for the Academic Year 1906–1907.* Tuscaloosa: University of Alabama, 1906.

———. *Corolla.* Tuscaloosa: University of Alabama, various years.

———. *War Corolla.* Tuscaloosa: University of Alabama, 1919.

UA Photograph Collection, UA Special Collections.

U.S. Bureau of the Census. *Classified Index to Occupations.* Washington, DC: U.S. GPO, 1921.

———. *U.S. Census of Governments* (1957). Washington, DC: U.S. GPO, 1959.

U.S. Civil War Soldier Records and Profiles. www.ancestry.com.

U.S. Congress. *Second Session of the Forty-Second Congress, Reports of Committees of the House of Representatives.* 4 vols. Washington, DC: U.S. GPO, 1872.

U.S. Consular Registrations. www.ancestry.com.

U.S. Department of Veterans Affairs BIRLS Death File. www.ancestry.com.

U.S. Federal Census. www.ancestry.com.

U.S. Federal Census Mortality Schedules. www.ancestry.com.

U.S. Federal Census Non-Population Schedules. www.ancestry.com.

U.S. Federal Census Slave Schedules. www.ancestry.com.

U.S. General Land Office Records. www.ancestry.com.

U.S. GPO. *Official Register of the United States.* Washington, DC: U.S. GPO, 1881.

U.S. Headstone Applications for Military Veterans. www.ancestry.com.

U.S. IRS Tax Assessment Lists. www.ancestry.com.

U.S. Phone and Address Directories. www.ancestry.com.

U.S. Social Security Death Index. www.ancestry.com.

U.S. Sons of the American Revolution Membership Applications. www.ancestry.com.

U.S. World War I Draft Registration Cards. www.ancestry.com.

U.S. World War II Army Enlistment Records. National Archives and Records Administration.

University Society. *The Home University Bookshelf.* 9 vols. New York, 1927.

Van Buren, A. De Puy. "Mississippi Is a Cotton Growing State." In *The Plantation South,* ed. Katharine M. Jones, 366–80. New York: Bobbs-Merrill, 1957.

Van Duzor, Alline P. *Fascinating Foods from the Deep South.* New York: Gramercy, 1962.

Walters, Raymond, George Palmer Putnam, John Kirby, Arthur Baer, Homer Dye Jr., Forrest B. Myers, and Others. *F.A.C.O.T.S., the Story of the Field Artillery Central Officers Training School, Camp Zachary Taylor, Kentucky.* New York: Knickerbocker Press, 1919.

Warren, Mary Bondurant, comp. *Citizens and Immigrants: South Carolina, 1768.* Danielsville, GA: Heritage Papers, 1980.

West, Anson. *A History of Methodism in Alabama.* Spartanburg, SC: Reprint Company, [1893] 1983.

Whittle, Charles A. "Knoxville, Tenn., Methodism." *Western Christian Advocate* 75 (April 28, 1909): 10.

Windham, Kathryn Tucker, and Margaret Gillis Figh. *Thirteen Alabama Ghosts and Jeffrey.* Huntsville, AL: Strode Publishers, 1969.

Wood, Clement. *Nigger: A Novel.* New York: E. P. Dutton, 1922.

Wood, Orlyn Hill. "Christopher Family in Choctaw County." In *Choctaw Names and Notes: Alabama's Choctaw County,* ed. Ann Harwell Gay, 82–84. Butler, AL: Ann Harwell Gay, 1993.

Woofter, T. J., Jr. *Land Lord and Tenant on the Cotton Plantation.* Works Progress Administration Research Monograph no. 5. Washington, DC, 1936.

Wrenn, Lynette Boney, ed. *A Bachelor's Life in Antebellum Mississippi: The Diary of Dr. Elijah Millington Walker, 1849–1852.* Knoxville: University of Tennessee Press, 2004.

Wright, General Marcus J. *General Scott.* New York: D. Appleton and Co., 1893.

Writers' Program of the Work Projects Administration. *The WPA Guide to 1930s Alabama.* Tuscaloosa: University of Alabama Press, 2000.

Yerby, William Edward Wadsworth, and Mabel Yerby Lawson. *History of Greensboro, Alabama, from Its Earliest Settlement.* Northport, AL: Colonial Press, [1908] 1963.

Secondary Sources

Abbott, Lynn, and Doug Seroff. *Ragged But Right: Black Traveling Shows, "Coon Songs," and the Dark Pathway to Blues and Jazz.* Jackson: University Press of Mississippi, 2007.

Abernethy, Thomas Perkins. *The Formative Period in Alabama, 1815–1828.* Montgomery, AL: Brown Printing, 1922.

Adams, Bryding, et al. *Made in Alabama: A State Legacy.* Birmingham, AL: Birmingham Museum of Art, 1995.

Adams, E. Bryding. "Mortised, Tenoned and Screwed Together: A Large Assortment of Alabama Furniture." In *Made in Alabama: A State Legacy,* ed. Bryding Adams et al., 190–237. Birmingham, AL: Birmingham Museum of Art, 1995.

Adams, Jane, and D. Gorton. "Southern Trauma: Revisiting Caste and Class in the Mississippi Delta." *American Anthropologist* 106 (June 2004): 334–45.

Agnew, Jean-Christophe. "A House of Fiction: Domestic Interiors and the Commodity Aesthetic." In *Consuming Visions: Accumulation and Display of Goods in America, 1880–1920,* ed. Samuel J. Bronner and Henry Francis du Pont Winterthur Museum, 133–56. New York: Norton, 1989.

Ames, Kenneth L. Conclusion to *The Arts and the American Home, 1890–1930,* ed. Jessica H. Foy and Karal Ann Marling, 183–85. Knoxville: University of Tennessee Press, 1994.

———. *Death in the Dining Room and Other Tales of Victorian Culture.* Philadelphia: Temple University Press, 1992.

———. Introduction to *The Colonial Revival in America*, ed. Alan Axelrod, 1–14. New York: W. W. Norton, 1985.

Apel, Dora. "Lynching Photographs and the Politics of Public Shaming." In *Lynching Photographs*, by Dora Apel and Shawn Michelle Smith, 42–78. Berkeley: University of California Press, 2007.

Apel, Dora, and Shawn Michelle Smith. *Lynching Photographs*. Berkeley: University of California Press, 2007.

Armstrong, Julie Buckner. *Mary Turner and the Memory of Lynching*. Athens: University of Georgia Press, 2011.

Arnett, William, and Paul Arnett. "On the Map." In *The Quilts of Gee's Bend*, ed. John Beardsley, William Arnett, Paul Arnett, and Jane Livingston, 34–49. Atlanta: Tinwood Books in association with the Museum of Fine Arts, Houston, 2002.

Arsenault, Raymond. "The End of the Long Hot Summer: The Air Conditioner and Southern Culture." *Journal of Southern History* 50 (Nov. 1984): 597–628.

Ashelford, Jane, and Andreas Einsiedel. *The Art of Dress: Clothes and Society, 1500–1914*. London: National Trust, 1996.

Atkins, Leah Rawls. "The Romantic Ideal: Alabama's Plantation Eden." In *Perspectives: The Alabama Heritage*, ed. Rosemary Canfield, 240–61. Troy, AL: Troy State University Press, 1978.

———. *The Valley and the Hills: An Illustrated History of Birmingham and Jefferson County*. Woodland Hills, CA: Windsor Publications, 1981.

Atlanta Historical Society. *Neat Pieces: The Plain-Style Furniture of Nineteenth-Century Georgia*. Athens: University of Georgia Press, 2006.

Ausherman, Maria Elizabeth. *The Photographic Legacy of Frances Benjamin Johnston*. Gainesville: University Press of Florida, 2009.

Ayers, Edward L. *The Promise of the New South: Life after Reconstruction*. New York: Oxford University Press, 1992.

Bailey, Fred Arthur. "Mildred Lewis Rutherford and the Patrician Cult of the New South." *Georgia Historical Quarterly* 78 (Fall 1994): 509–35.

Baker, Bruce E. "Under the Rope: Lynching and Memory in Laurens County, South Carolina." In *Where These Memories Grow: History, Memory, and Southern Identity*, ed. W. Fitzhugh Brundage, 319–45. Chapel Hill: University of North Carolina Press, 2000.

Ball, Howard. *Hugo L. Black: Cold Steel Warrior*. New York: Oxford University Press, 1996.

Bardaglio, Peter W. *Reconstructing the Household: Families, Sex, and the Law in the Nineteenth-Century South*. Chapel Hill: University of North Carolina Press, 1995.

Bartley, Numan V. *The Rise of Massive Resistance: Race and Politics in the South during the 1950's*. 2nd ed. Baton Rouge: Louisiana State University Press, 1969.

Batchen, Geoffrey. *Forget Me Not: Photography and Remembrance*. Amsterdam: Van Gogh Museum/New York: Princeton Architectural Press, 2004.

Bateman, Anthony W., and Peter Fonagy. "Mentalization-Based Treatment of Borderline Personality Disorder." In *The Oxford Handbook of Personality Disorders*, ed. Thomas A. Widiger, 767–84. New York: Oxford University Press, 2012.

Bates, Kelsey Scouten. "Comfort in a Decidedly Uncomfortable Time: Hunger, Collective Memory, and the Meaning of Soul Food in Gee's Bend, Alabama." *Food and Foodways* 20, no. 1 (Jan.–March 2012): 55–62.

Baumann, Timothy E. "Bottle Trees." In *World of a Slave: Encyclopedia of the Material Life of Slaves in the United States*, ed. Martha B. Katz-Hyman and Kym S. Rice, 76–77. Santa Barbara, CA: ABC-CLIO, 2011.

Beardsley, John. "River Island." In *The Quilts of Gee's Bend*, ed. John Beardsley, William Arnett, Paul Arnett, and Jane Livingston, 20–33. Atlanta: Tinwood Books in association with the Museum of Fine Arts, Houston, 2002.

Beardsley, John, William Arnett, Paul Arnett, and Jane Livingston. *The Quilts of Gee's Bend*. Atlanta: Tinwood Books in association with the Museum of Fine Arts, Houston, 2002.

Beckham, Sue Bridwell. "The American Front Porch: Women's Liminal Space." In *Making the American Home: Middle-Class Women and Domestic Material Culture, 1840–1940*, ed. Marilyn Ferris Motz and Pat Browne, 69–89. Bowling Green, OH: Bowling Green University Popular Press, 1988.

Beidler, Philip D. "Yankee Interloper and Native Son: Carl Carmer and Clarence Cason: Unlikely Twins of Alabama Exposé." *Southern Cultures* 9, no. 1 (2003): 18–35.

Bentley, Amy. *Eating for Victory: Food Rationing and the Politics of Domesticity*. Urbana: University of Illinois Press, 1998.

Benton, Jeffrey C. *The Very Worst Road: Travellers' Accounts of Crossing Alabama's Old Creek Indian Territory, 1820–1847*. Tuscaloosa: University of Alabama Press, [1998] 2009.

Berends, Kurt O. "Confederate Sacrifice and the 'Redemption' of the South." In *Religion in the American South: Protestants and Others in History and Culture*, ed. Beth Barton Schweiger and Donald G. Mathews, 99–124. Chapel Hill: University of North Carolina Press, 2004.

Bernstein, Robin. *Racial Innocence: Performing American Childhood from Slavery to Civil Rights*. New York: New York University Press, 2011.

Bertelsen, Cynthia D. "Daily Life through Cooking and Cookbooks: A Brief Guide to Using Cookbooks as a Tool in Historical Archaeology." *Artifact* 49 (2011): 2–26.

Betsky, Celia. "Inside the Past: The Interior and the Colonial Revival in American Art and Literature, 1860–1914." In *The Colonial Revival in America*, ed. Alan Axelrod, 241–77. New York: W. W. Norton, 1985.

Billingsley, Carolyn Earle. *Communities of Kinship: Antebellum Families and the Settlement of the Cotton Frontier*. Athens: University of Georgia Press, 2004.

Bishir, Catherine W. *Southern Built: American Architecture, Regional Practice*. Charlottesville: University of Virginia Press, 2006.

Blackmon, Douglas A. *Slavery by Another Name: The Re-Enslavement of Black Americans from the Civil War to World War II*. New York: Doubleday, 2008.

Blair, William. *Cities of the Dead: Contesting the Memory of the Civil War in the South, 1865–1914*. Chapel Hill: University of North Carolina Press, 2004.

Blassingame, John W. "Using the Testimony of Ex-Slaves." *Journal of Southern History* 41, no. 4 (1975): 473–92.

Bleser, Carol K., ed. *In Joy and Sorrow: Women, Family, and Marriage in the Victorian South, 1830–1900*. New York: Oxford University Press, 1991.

Bleser, Carol K., and Frederick M. Heath. "The Clays of Alabama: The Impact of the Civil War on a Southern Marriage." In *In Joy and Sorrow: Women, Family, and Marriage in the Victorian South, 1830–1900*, ed. Carol K. Bleser, 135–53. New York: Oxford University Press, 1991.

Blight, David W. *Race and Reunion: The Civil War in American Memory*. Cambridge, MA: Belknap Press of Harvard University Press, 2001.

Bloom, Harold. *Zora Neale Hurston*. New York: Chelsea House, 1986.

Botkin, Benjamin Albert. *A Treasury of Southern Folklore; Stories, Ballads, Traditions, and Folkways of the People of the South*. New York: Bonanza Books, [1949] 1977.

Boucher, Ann Williams. "Wealthy Planter Families in Nineteenth-Century Alabama." PhD diss., University of Connecticut, 1978.

Brilliant, Richard. *Portraiture*. Cambridge, MA: Harvard University Press, 1991.

Bristow, Nancy K. *American Pandemic: The Lost Worlds of the 1918 Influenza Epidemic*. New York: Oxford University Press, 2012.

Brooks, Bradley C. "Clarity, Contrast, and Simplicity: Changes in American Interiors, 1880–1930." In *The Arts and the American Home, 1890–1930*, ed. Jessica H. Foy and Karal Ann Marling, 14–43. Knoxville: University of Tennessee Press, 1994.

Brown, Alan, and David Vassar Taylor. *Gabr'l Blow Sof': Sumter County, Alabama Slave Narratives*. Livingston, AL: Livingston Press, 1997.

Brown, Steven Preston. *John McKinley and the Antebellum Supreme Court: Circuit Riding in the Old Southwest*. Tuscaloosa: University of Alabama Press, 2012.

Brown, Virginia Pounds, and Laurella Owens. *Toting the Lead Row: Ruby Pickens Tartt, Alabama Folklorist*. Tuscaloosa: University of Alabama Press, 1981.

Brownell, Blaine A. *The Urban Ethos in the South, 1920–1930*. Baton Rouge: Louisiana State University Press, 1975.

Bruce, Dickson D., Jr. *Violence and Culture in the Antebellum South*. Austin: University of Texas Press, 1979.

Brundage, W. Fitzhugh. *Lynching in the New South: Georgia and Virginia, 1880–1930*. Urbana: University of Illinois Press, 1993.

———. *The Southern Past: A Clash of Race and Memory*. Cambridge, MA: Harvard University Press, 2005.

———. "White Women and the Politics of Historical Memory in the New South, 1880–1920." In *Jumpin' Jim Crow: Southern Politics from Civil War to Civil Rights*, ed. Jane Elizabeth Dailey, Glenda Elizabeth Gilmore, and Bryant Simon, 115–39. Princeton, NJ: Princeton University Press, 2000.

———. "'Woman's Hand and Heart and Deathless Love.'" In *Monuments to the Lost Cause: Women, Art, and the Landscapes of Southern Memory*, ed. Cynthia Mills and Pamela H. Simpson, 64–82. Knoxville: University of Tennessee Press, 2003.

Bryden, Inga, and Janet Floyd. *Domestic Space: Reading the Nineteenth-Century Interior*. Manchester: Manchester University Press, 1999.

Bull, Jacqueline P. "The General Merchant in the Economic History of the New South." *Journal of Southern History* 18 (Feb. 1952): 37–59.

Bullock, Steven C. *Revolutionary Brotherhood: Freemasonry and the Transformation of the American Social Order, 1730–1840*. Chapel Hill: University of North Carolina Press, 1996.

Burke, Peter. *Eyewitnessing: The Uses of Images as Historical Evidence*. Ithaca, NY: Cornell University Press, 2001.

———. *A Social History of Knowledge II: From the Encyclopaedia to Wikipedia*. Cambridge: Polity, 2012.

———. *What Is Cultural History?* 2nd ed. Cambridge: Polity, 2008.

Burns, Stanley B., and National Arts Club. *Forgotten Marriage: The Painted Tintype and the Decorative Frame, 1860–1910: A Lost Chapter in American Portraiture*. New York: Burns Press, 1995.

Burr, Virginia I. *The Secret Eye: The Journal of Ella Gertrude Clanton Thomas, 1848–1889*. Chapel Hill: University of North Carolina Press, 1990.

Busch, Jason T. "The French Rococo Revival along the Mississippi River." *Antiques* 166 (Aug. 2004): 84–92.

Bushman, Richard. *The Refinement of America: Persons, Houses, Cities*. New York: Knopf, 1992.

Campbell, John. "The Seminoles, the 'Bloodhound War,' and Abolitionism, 1796–1865." *Journal of Southern History* 72, no. 2 (May 2006): 259–302.

Cardinal, Roger. "Memory Painting." In *Encyclopedia of American Folk Art*, ed. Gerard C. Wertkin and Lee Kogan, 362–64. New York: Routledge, 2004.

Carnes, Mark C. *Secret Ritual and Manhood in Victorian America*. New Haven, CT: Yale University Press, 1989.

Case, Sarah H. "The Historical Ideology of Mildred Lewis Rutherford: A Confederate Historian's New South Creed." *Journal of Southern History* 68, no. 3 (Aug. 2002): 599–628.

Cash, W. J. *The Mind of the South*. New York: Vintage, [1941] 1991.

Castano, Emanuele. "Antisocial Behavior in Individuals and Groups: An Empathy-Focused Approach." In *The Oxford Handbook of Personality and Social Psychology*, ed. Kay Deaux and Mark Snyder, 419–55. New York: Oxford University Press, 2012.

Cauthen, Joyce H. *With Fiddle and Well-Rosined Bow: A History of Old-Time Fiddling in Alabama*. Tuscaloosa: University of Alabama Press, [1989] 2001.

Chalmers, David M. *Hooded Americanism: The First Century of the Ku Klux Klan, 1865–1965*. Garden City, NY: Doubleday, 1965.

Chamber of Commerce of West Alabama, "Frank Gamble Blair: 1900-1909: A New Century" [interview], *Perspectives* (Winter 2000).

———. Frank Fitts Sr., "1930–1939: Progress Follows the Depression," [interview], *Perspectives* (Winter 2000).

———. George A. LeMaistre, "1950–1959: Good Times and Challenges," [interview], *Perspectives* (Winter 2000).

———. "1900–1909: A New Century," *Perspectives* (Winter 2000).

———. William "Plain Bill" Brandon, "1920–1929: The Roaring Twenties," [interview], *Perspectives* (Winter 2000).

Christopher, Thomas Weldon. *What Happened to Horseshoe Robinson? A Study of John P. Kennedy's 1835 Novel, "Horseshoe Robinson."* Greenville, SC: T. W. Christopher, 1955.

Clark, Clifford E., Jr. "The Vision of the Dining Room: Plan Book Dreams and

Middle-Class Realities." In *Dining in America, 1850–1900*, ed. Kathryn Grover, 142–72. Amherst: University of Massachusetts Press, 1987.

Clark, E. Culpepper. *The Schoolhouse Door: Segregation's Last Stand at the University of Alabama*. New York: Oxford University Press, 1993.

Clark, Thomas D. *Pills, Petticoats, and Plows: The Southern Country Store*. Indianapolis: Bobbs-Merrill, 1944.

———. "The Slavery Background of Foster's My Old Kentucky Home." *Filson Club Historical Quarterly* 10, no. 1 (Jan. 1936): 1–17.

Clark, Thomas D., and John D. W. Guice. *Frontiers in Conflict: The Old Southwest, 1795–1830*. Albuquerque: University of New Mexico Press, 1989.

Clark-Lewis, Elizabeth. *Living In, Living Out: African American Domestics in Washington, D.C., 1910–1940*. Washington, DC: Smithsonian Institution Press, 1994.

Cleveland, Gordon Baylor. "Social Conditions in Alabama as Seen by Travelers, 1840–1850; Part I." *Alabama Review* 2 (Jan. 1949): 3–23.

Clinton, Thomas P. "The Military Operations of General John T. Croxton in West Alabama, 1865." *Transactions of the Alabama Historical Society* 4 (1904): 449–63.

Cobb, James C. *Away Down South: A History of Southern Identity*. New York: Oxford University Press, 2005.

Cohen, Lizabeth A. "Embellishing a Life of Labor: An Interpretation of the Material Culture of American Working-Class Homes, 1885–1915." In *Common Places: Readings in American Vernacular Architecture*, ed. Dell Upton and John Michael Vlach, 261–78. Athens: University of Georgia Press, 1986.

Coleman, Gregory D. *We're Heaven Bound! Portrait of a Black Sacred Drama*. Athens: University of Georgia Press, [1992] 1994.

Conrad, James Lee. *The Young Lions: Confederate Cadets at War*. Mechanicsburg, PA: Stackpole Books, 1997.

Cook, Florence Elliott. "Growing Up White, Genteel, and Female in a Changing South, 1865–1915." PhD diss., University of California–Berkeley, 1992.

Coplan, Amy, and Peter Goldie. Introduction to *Empathy: Philosophical and Psychological Perspectives*, ed. Amy Coplan and Peter Goldie, ix–xlvii. New York: Oxford University Press, 2011.

Cothran, James R. *Gardens and Historic Plants of the Antebellum South*. Columbia: University of South Carolina Press, 2003.

Cox, Karen L. *Dixie's Daughters: The United Daughters of the Confederacy and the Preservation of Confederate Culture*. Gainesville: University Press of Florida, 2003.

Cozolino, Louis. *The Neuroscience of Human Relationships: Attachment and the Developing Social Brain*. New York: W. W. Norton, 2006.

Cromley, Elizabeth Collins. *The Food Axis: Cooking, Eating, and the Architecture of American Houses*. Charlottesville: University of Virginia Press, 2010.

———. "A History of American Beds and Bedrooms." In *Perspectives in Vernacular Architecture*, vol. 4, ed. Thomas Carter and Bernard L. Herman, 177–86. Columbia: University of Missouri Press for the Vernacular Architecture Forum, 1991.

———. "A History of American Beds and Bedrooms, 1890–1930." In *American Home Life, 1880–1930: A Social History of Spaces and Services*, ed. Jessica H. Foy and Thomas J. Schlereth, 120–41. Knoxville: University of Tennessee Press, 1992.

Cronenberg, Allen. *Forth to the Mighty Conflict: Alabama and World War II.* Tuscaloosa: University of Alabama Press, 1995.

Csikszentmihalyi, Mihaly, and Eugene Rochberg-Halton. *The Meaning of Things: Domestic Symbols and the Self.* Cambridge: Cambridge University Press, 1981.

Curtis, James. *Mind's Eye, Mind's Truth: FSA Photography Reconsidered.* Philadelphia: Temple University Press, 1989.

Daniel, Mike. "The Arrest and Trial of Ryland Randolph, April–May 1868." *Alabama Historical Quarterly* 40 (Fall and Winter 1978): 127–43.

Darnell, Paula Jean. *Victorian to Vamp: Women's Clothing, 1900–1929.* Reno, NV: Fabric Fancies, 2000.

Davis, William C. *A Way through the Wilderness: The Natchez Trace and the Civilization of the Southern Frontier.* Baton Rouge: Louisiana State University Press, 1996.

De Fruyt, Filip, and Barbara De Clercq. "Childhood Antecedents of Personality Disorders." In *The Oxford Handbook of Personality Disorders,* ed. Thomas A. Widiger, 166–85. New York: Oxford University Press, 2012.

Deutsch, Tracey. *Building a Housewife's Paradise: Gender, Politics, and American Grocery Stores in the Twentieth Century.* Chapel Hill: University of North Carolina Press, 2010.

Deyle, Steven. *Carry Me Back: The Domestic Slave Trade in American Life.* New York: Oxford University Press, 2005.

Domosh, Mona, and Joni Seager. *Putting Women in Place: Feminist Geographers Make Sense of the World.* New York: Guilford Press, 2001.

[Doss,] Harriet E. Amos. "City Belles: Images and Realities of Lives of White Women in Antebellum Mobile." *Alabama Review* 34, no. 1 (Jan. 1981): 3–19.

———. "Religious Reconstruction in Microcosm at Faunsdale Plantation." *Alabama Review* 42 (Oct. 1989): 243–69.

Doss, Harriet E. Amos. Introduction to *Slavery in Alabama,* by James Benson Sellers, ix–xxiv. Tuscaloosa: University of Alabama Press, [1950] 1994.

Doster, James F. "Land Titles and Public Land Sales in Early Alabama." *Alabama Review* 16 (April 1963): 108–34.

Doyle, Andrew. "On the Cusp of Modernity: The Southern Sporting World in the Twentieth Century." In *The American South in the Twentieth Century,* ed. Craig S. Pascoe, Karen Trahan Leathem, and Andy Ambrose, 188–208. Atlanta and Athens: Atlanta History Center and University of Georgia Press, 2005.

Dray, Philip. *At the Hands of Persons Unknown: The Lynching of Black America.* New York: Random House, 2002.

Dumenil, Lynn. *Freemasonry and American Culture, 1880–1930.* Princeton, NJ: Princeton University Press, 1984.

Eastmond, Elizabeth. "Metaphor and the Self-portrait: Frances Hodgkins's *Self Portrait: Still Life* and *Still Life: Self-portrait.*" *Art History* 22, no. 5 (1999): 656–75.

Eckinger, Helen. "The Militarization of the University of Alabama." *Alabama Review* 66, no. 3 (2013): 163–85.

Egerton, John. *Speak Now against the Day: The Generation before the Civil Rights Movement in the South.* Chapel Hill: University of North Carolina Press, 1994.

Ellisor, John T. *The Second Creek War: Interethnic Conflict and Collusion on a Collapsing Frontier.* Lincoln: University of Nebraska Press, 2010.

Escott, Paul D. *Slavery Remembered: A Record of Twentieth-Century Slave Narratives.* Chapel Hill: University of North Carolina Press, 1979.

Farrell, James J. *Inventing the American Way of Death, 1830–1920.* Philadelphia: Temple University Press, 1980.

Faust, Drew Gilpin. *Mothers of Invention: Women of the Slaveholding South in the American Civil War.* Chapel Hill: University of North Carolina Press, 1996.

———. *This Republic of Suffering: Death and the American Civil War.* New York: Knopf, 2008.

Feldman, Glenn. *Politics, Society, and the Klan in Alabama, 1915–1949.* Tuscaloosa: University of Alabama Press, 1999.

Fisher, Virginia E. *The University of Alabama at Birmingham: Building on a Vision; A Fifty-Year Retrospective of UAB's Academic Health Center.* Birmingham: University of Alabama at Birmingham, 1995.

Fleischhauer, Carl, and Beverly W. Brannan, ed. *Documenting America, 1935–1943.* Berkeley: University of California Press, 1988.

Flynt, Wayne. *Alabama in the Twentieth Century.* Tuscaloosa: University of Alabama Press, 2004.

———. Introduction to *90 Degrees in the Shade,* by Clarence Cason. Tuscaloosa: University of Alabama Press, [1935] 1983.

———. *Poor But Proud: Alabama's Poor Whites.* Tuscaloosa: University of Alabama Press, 1989.

Fonagy, Peter, and Patrick Luyten. "Psychodynamic Models of Personality Disorders." In *The Oxford Handbook of Personality Disorders,* ed. Thomas A. Widiger, 257–58. New York: Oxford University Press, 2012.

Foner, Eric. *A Short History of Reconstruction, 1863–1877.* New York: Harper and Row, 1990.

Foscue, Virginia O. *Place Names in Alabama.* Tuscaloosa: University of Alabama Press, 1989.

Foster, Shirley Pribbenow. "Women and Refinement in Antibellum Alabama: Privacy, Comfort, and Luxury, 1830–1860." PhD diss., University of Alabama, 1997.

Fox-Genovese, Elizabeth. Introduction to *A Blockaded Family: Life in Southern Alabama during the Civil War,* by Parthenia Antoinette Hague, ix–xxviii. Lincoln: University of Nebraska Press, [1888] 1991.

———. *Within the Plantation Household: Black and White Women of the Old South.* Chapel Hill: University of North Carolina Press, 1988.

Foy, Jessica H. "The Home Set to Music." In *The Arts and the American Home, 1890–1930,* ed. Jessica H. Foy and Karal Ann Marling, 62–84. Knoxville: University of Tennessee Press, 1994.

Franklin, John Hope, and Loren Schweninger. *Runaway Slaves: Rebels on the Plantation, 1790–1860.* New York: Oxford University Press, 1999.

Gaines, Francis Pendleton. *The Southern Plantation: A Study of the Development and the Accuracy of a Tradition.* Gloucester, MA: Peter Smith, [1924] 1962.

Gamble, Robert. *Historic Architecture in Alabama: A Guide to Styles and Types, 1810–1930.* Tuscaloosa: University of Alabama Press, 1990.

Garvey, Ellen Gruber. *Writing with Scissors: American Scrapbooks from the Civil War to the Harlem Renaissance.* New York: Oxford University Press, 2012.

Genovese, Eugene D. "'Rather Be a Nigger than a Poor White Man': Slave Perceptions of Southern Yeomen and Poor Whites." In *Toward a New View of America: Essays in Honor of Arthur C. Cole,* ed. Hans L. Trefousse, 79–96. New York: B. Franklin, 1977.

Glassberg, David. *American Historical Pageantry: The Uses of Tradition in the Early Twentieth Century.* Chapel Hill: University of North Carolina Press, 1990.

Glover, Lorri. *All Our Relations: Blood Ties and Emotional Bonds among the Early South Carolina Gentry.* Baltimore: Johns Hopkins University Press, 2000.

Goffman, Erving. *The Presentation of Self in Everyday Life.* Garden City, NY: Doubleday, 1959.

Gohdes, Clarence. *Hunting in the Old South: Original Narratives of the Hunters.* Baton Rouge: Louisiana State University Press, 1967.

Goldfield, David. *Black, White, and Southern: Race Relations and Southern Culture, 1940 to the Present.* Baton Rouge: Louisiana State University Press, 1990.

Goldman, Alvin I. "Two Routes to Empathy: Insights from Cognitive Neuroscience." In *Empathy: Philosophical and Psychological Perspectives,* ed. Amy Coplan and Peter Goldie, 31–44. New York: Oxford University Press, 2011.

Gontar, Cybele T. "The American Campeche Chair." *Antiques* 175 (May 2009): 88–95.

Gordon, Beverly. "Cozy, Charming, and Artistic: Stitching Together the American Home." In *The Arts and the American Home, 1890–1930,* ed. Jessica H. Foy and Karal Ann Marling, 124–48. Knoxville: University of Tennessee Press, 1994.

———. *The Saturated World: Aesthetic Meaning, Intimate Objects, Women's Lives, 1890–1940.* Knoxville: University of Tennessee Press, 2006.

———. *Textiles: The Whole Story; Uses, Meanings, Significance.* London: Thames and Hudson, 2011.

———. "Woman's Domestic Body: The Conceptual Conflation of Women and Interiors in the Industrial Age." *Winterthur Portfolio* 31 (Winter 1996): 281–301.

Gordon, Jean, and Jan McArthur. "Interior Decorating Advice as Popular Culture: Women's Views Concerning Wall and Window Treatments, 1870–1920." In *Making the American Home: Middle-Class Women and Domestic Material Culture, 1840–1940,* ed. Marilyn Ferris Motz and Pat Browne, 105–20. Bowling Green, OH: Bowling Green University Popular Press, 1988.

Gottfried, Herbert, and Jan Jennings. *American Vernacular Buildings and Interiors, 1870–1960.* New York: W. W. Norton, 2009.

Gowans, Alan. *The Comfortable House: North American Suburban Architecture, 1890–1930.* Cambridge, MA: MIT Press, 1986.

Graffam, Olive Blair. "'They Are Very Handy': Kitchen Furnishings, 1875–1920." In *The American Home: Material Culture, Domestic Space, and Family Life,* ed. Eleanor McD. Thompson, 217–40. Winterthur, DE: Henry Francis du Pont Winterthur Museum, 1998.

Grantham, Dewey W. *Southern Progressivism: The Reconciliation of Progress and Tradition.* Knoxville: University of Tennessee Press, 1983.

Green, Ben. *A History of Tuscaloosa, Alabama, 1816–1949*. Tuscaloosa, AL: Confederate Publishing Company, 1949.

Green, Fletcher M. "Walter Lynwood Fleming: Historian of Reconstruction." *Journal of Southern History* 2, no. 4 (Nov. 1936): 497–521.

Greenberg, Kenneth S. *Honor and Slavery: Lies, Duels, Noses, Masks, Dressing as a Woman, Gifts, Strangers, Humanitarianism, Death, Slave Rebellions, the Proslavery Argument, Baseball, Hunting, and Gambling in the Old South*. Princeton, NJ: Princeton University Press, 1996.

Gregory, Melanie Betz. "Alabama's Endangered Historic Landmarks: Places in Peril 2012." *Alabama Heritage*, no. 106 (Fall 2012): 32–41.

Grier, Katherine C. *Culture and Comfort: Parlor Making and Middle-Class Identity, 1850–1930*. Washington, DC: Smithsonian Institution Press, 1997.

Griffin, Larry J., Paula Clark, and Joanne C. Sandberg. "Narrative and Event: Lynching and Historical Sociology." In *Under Sentence of Death: Lynching in the South*, ed. W. Fitzhugh Brundage, 24–47. Chapel Hill: University of North Carolina Press, 1997.

Grim, Valerie. "African American Rural Culture, 1900–1950." In *African American Life in the Rural South, 1900–1950*, ed. R. Douglas Hurt, 108–28. Columbia: University of Missouri Press, 2003.

Gulley, Harold E. "Women and the Lost Cause: Preserving a Confederate Identity in the American Deep South." *Journal of Historical Geography* 19, no. 2 (1993): 125–41.

Gundaker, Grey, and Tynes Cowan. *Keep Your Head to the Sky: Interpreting African American Home Ground*. Charlottesville: University of Virginia Press, 1998.

Gunn, Simon. "Analysing Behaviour as Performance." In *Research Methods for History*, ed. Simon Gunn and Lucy Faire, 184–200. Edinburgh: Edinburgh University Press, 2012.

Gutman, Herbert G. *The Black Family in Slavery and Freedom, 1750–1925*. New York: Pantheon, 1976.

Haardt, Sarah. *Southern Souvenirs: Stories and Essays by Sara Haardt*, ed. Ann Henley. Tuscaloosa: University of Alabama Press, 1999.

Hagood, Thomas Chase. "'Literature to Him Was a Recreation': A Life of Writing on the Southwestern Frontier." *Alabama Review* 67, no. 4 (Oct. 2014): 374–406.

———. "Rewriting the Frontier: Making History in Tuscaloosa, Alabama." PhD diss., University of Georgia, 2011.

Hale, Grace Elizabeth. *Making Whiteness: The Culture of Segregation in the South, 1890–1940*. New York: Pantheon, 1998.

———. "Of the Meaning of Progress: A Century of Southern Race Relations." In *The American South in the Twentieth Century*, ed. Craig S. Pascoe, Karen Trahan Leathem, and Andy Ambrose, 56–73. Atlanta and Athens: Atlanta History Center and University of Georgia Press, 2005.

Hall, Jacquelyn Dowd. "Partial Truths: Writing Southern Women's History." In *Southern Women: Histories and Identities*, ed. Virginia Bernhard, Betty Brandon, Elizabeth Fox-Genovese, and Theda Perdue, 11–29. Columbia: University of Missouri Press, 1992.

———. *Revolt against Chivalry: Jessie Daniel Ames and the Women's Campaign against Lynching*. New York: Columbia University Press, 1979.

Hall, John C. "Landscape Considerations for the Creek War in Alabama, 1811–1815." *Alabama Review* 67, no. 3 (July 2014): 219–32.

Hallam, Elizabeth, and Jenny Hockey. *Death, Memory, and Material Culture.* Oxford: Berg, 2001.

Halle, David. *Inside Culture: Art and Class in the American Home.* Chicago: University of Chicago Press, 1993.

Hamilton, Peter J. "Alexander Beaufort Meek (1814–1865)." In *Library of Southern Literature,* ed. Edwin Anderson Alderman, Joel Chandler Harris, and Charles William Kent, 3599–3628. Atlanta: Martin and Hoyt Company, 1909.

Hamlett, Jane. *Material Relations: Domestic Interiors and Middle-Class Families in England, 1850–1910.* Manchester, UK: Manchester University Press, 2010.

Harris, Dianne. *Little White Houses: How the Postwar Home Constructed Race in America.* Minneapolis: University of Minnesota Press, 2013.

Harris, J. William. *Plain Folk and Gentry in a Slave Society: White Liberty and Black Slavery in Augusta's Hinterlands.* Middletown, CT: Wesleyan University Press, 1985.

Harvey, Thomas. "Mail-Order Architecture in the Twenties." *Landscape* 25, no. 3 (1981): 1–9.

Harwell, Richard Barksdale. *Gone with the Wind as Book and Film.* Columbia: University of South Carolina Press, 1983.

Haskell, Molly. *Frankly, My Dear: Gone with the Wind Revisited.* New Haven, CT: Yale University Press, 2009.

Hatch, Thom. *Osceola and the Great Seminole War: A Struggle for Justice and Freedom.* New York: St. Martin's Press, 2012.

Hatchett, Jennifer C. "Archaeological and Historical Investigations of Site 41AS95, a Mid-Nineteenth-Century Salt Works on St. Charles Bay, Texas." Master's thesis, Texas Tech University, 2008.

Hayden, Dolores. "Urban Landscape History: The Sense of Place and the Politics of Space." In *Understanding Ordinary Landscapes,* ed. Paul Erling Groth and Todd W. Bressi, 111–33. New Haven, CT: Yale University Press, 1997.

Hayes, Kevin J. *A Colonial Woman's Bookshelf.* Knoxville: University of Tennessee Press, 1996.

Helfand, Jessica. *Scrapbooks: An American History.* New Haven, CT: Yale University Press, 2008.

Helvenston, Sally I., and Margaret M. Bubolz. "Home Economics and Home Sewing in the United States, 1870–1940." In *The Culture of Sewing: Gender, Consumption, and Home Dressmaking,* ed. Barbara Burman, 303–25. Oxford: Berg, 1999.

Henneman, John Bell, Sr., ed. *History of the Literary and Intellectual Life of the Southern States.* Richmond, VA: Southern Historical Publication Society, 1909.

Henninger, Katherine. *Ordering the Facade: Photography and Contemporary Southern Women's Writing.* Chapel Hill: University of North Carolina Press, 2007.

Henry, Robert Selph. Introduction to *The Plantation South,* ed. Katharine M. Jones, vii–x. Indianapolis: Bobbs-Merrill, 1957.

Herman, Bernard L. "The *Bricoleur* Revisited." In *American Material Culture: The Shape of the Field,* ed. Ann Smart Martin, J. Ritchie Garrison, and Henry Francis du Pont Winterthur Museum, 37–63. Knoxville: University of Tennessee Press, 1997.

Hickman, Nollie. *Mississippi Harvest: Lumbering in the Longleaf Pine Belt, 1840–1915.* Oxford: University of Mississippi Press, [1962] 2009.

Hilliard, Henry W. *De Vane: A Story of Plebeians and Patricians.* New York: Blelock, 1865.

Hoelscher, Steven. "Making Place, Making Race: Performances of Whiteness in the Jim Crow South." *Annals of the Association of American Geographers* 93 (2003): 657–86.

Hollars, B. J. *Thirteen Loops: Race, Violence, and the Last Lynching in America.* Tuscaloosa: University of Alabama Press, 2011.

Holley, Howard L. *The History of Medicine in Alabama.* Birmingham: University of Alabama at Birmingham School of Medicine, 1982.

Holmes, Jeremy. *John Bowlby and Attachment Theory.* London: Routledge, 1993.

Hoole, W. S., and E. H. McArthur. *The Yankee Invasion of West Alabama, March–April 1865, Including the Battle of Trion, the Battle of Tuscaloosa, the Burning of the University, and the Battle of Romulus.* Tuscaloosa, AL: Confederate Publishing, 1985.

Hooley, Jill M., Sadie H. Cole, and Stephanie Gironde. "Borderline Personality Disorder." In *The Oxford Handbook of Personality Disorders*, ed. Thomas A. Widiger, 409–36. New York: Oxford University Press, 2012.

Horton, Laurel. *Mary Black's Family Quilts: Memory and Meaning in Everyday Life.* Columbia: University of South Carolina Press, 2005.

Howe, David. *Empathy: What It Is and Why It Matters.* New York: Palgrave Macmillan, 2013.

Howett, Catherine M. "Graces and Modest Majesties: Landscape and Garden Traditions of the American South." In *Keeping Eden: A History of Gardening in America*, ed. Walter T. Punch, 81–95. Boston: Little, Brown, 1992.

———. *A World of Her Own Making: Katharine Smith Reynolds and the Landscape of Reynolda.* Amherst: University of Massachusetts Press, 2007.

Howington, Arthur F. "John Barley Corn Subdued: The Enforcement of Prohibition in Alabama." *Alabama Review* 23 (July 1970): 212–25.

Hubbs, G. Ward. *Guarding Greensboro: A Confederate Company in the Making of a Southern Community.* Athens: University of Georgia Press, 2003.

———. *Searching for Freedom after the Civil War: Klansman, Carpetbagger, Scalawag, and Freedman.* Tuscaloosa: University of Alabama Press, 2015.

———. *Tuscaloosa: Portrait of an Alabama County.* Northridge, CA: Windsor Publications, 1987.

Huey, Mattie McAdory. *History of the Alabama Division: United Daughters of the Confederacy.* Opelika, AL: Post Publishing, 1937.

Huffer, Lynne. *Maternal Pasts, Feminist Futures: Nostalgia, Ethics, and the Question of Difference.* Palo Alto, CA: Stanford University Press, 1998.

Hunter, Tera W. *To 'Joy My Freedom: Southern Black Women's Lives and Labors after the Civil War.* Cambridge, MA: Harvard University Press, 1997.

Jabour, Anya. *Scarlett's Sisters: Young Women in the Old South.* Chapel Hill: University of North Carolina Press, 2007.

Jackson, Harvey H., III. Introduction to *The WPA Guide to 1930s Alabama*, by Writers'

Program of the Works Progress Administration, vii–xxxv. Tuscaloosa: University of Alabama Press, 2000.

Jalland, Patricia. *Death in the Victorian Family*. New York: Oxford University Press, 1996.

Jeane, D. Gregory. "The Upland South Folk Cemetery Complex: Some Suggestions of Origin." In *Cemeteries and Gravemarkers: Voices of American Culture*, ed. Richard E. Meyer, 107–36. Ann Arbor, MI: UMI Research Press, 1989.

Johnson, Ronald N., and Gary D. Libecap. *The Federal Civil Service System and the Problem of Bureaucracy: The Economics and Politics of Institutional Change*. Chicago: University of Chicago Press, 1994.

Johnston-Miller, Mary Margaret. "Heirs to Paternalism: Elite White Women and Their Servants in Alabama and Georgia, 1861–1874." PhD diss., Emory University, 1994.

Jones, Katharine M. *The Plantation South*. Indianapolis: Bobbs-Merrill, 1957.

Jones, Michael Owen. *Exploring Folk Art: Twenty Years of Thought on Craft, Work, and Aesthetics*. Logan: Utah State University Press, 1993.

———. "How Can We Apply Event Analysis to 'Material Behavior,' and Why Should We?" *Western Folklore* 56, no. 3–4 (Summer–Autumn 1997): 199–214.

Jordan, Weymouth Tyree. *Ante-bellum Alabama: Town and Country*. Tuscaloosa: University of Alabama Press, [1957] 1987.

———. *Hugh Davis and His Alabama Plantation*. Tuscaloosa: University of Alabama Press, 1948.

Jordan-Bychkov, Terry G. *Texas Graveyards: A Cultural Legacy*. Austin: University of Texas Press, 1982.

Kammen, Michael G. *American Culture, American Tastes: Social Change and the Twentieth Century*. New York: Knopf, 1999.

———. *Mystic Chords of Memory: The Transformation of Tradition in American Culture*. New York: Knopf, [1991] 1993.

Kane, Harnett T. *The Southern Christmas Book: The Full Story from Earliest Times to Present: People, Customs, Conviviality, Carols, Cooking*. New York: David McKay Company, 1958.

Kasson, John F. "Rituals of Dining." In *Dining in America, 1850–1900*, ed. Kathryn Grover, 114–41. Amherst: University of Massachusetts Press; Rochester, NY: Margaret Woodbury Strong Museum, 1987.

Katzman, David M. *Seven Days a Week: Women and Domestic Service in Industrializing America*. New York: Oxford University Press, 1978.

Kennedy, Renwick C. "Alas, Poor Yorick." *Alabama Historical Quarterly* 2 (Winter 1940): 405–15.

Kent, Winthrop. *The Hooked Rug*. New York: Tudor Publishing, 1941.

Kern, Susan. *The Jeffersons at Shadwell*. New Haven, CT: Yale University Press, 2010.

Kernberg, Otto. *The Inseparable Nature of Love and Aggression: Clinical and Theoretical Perspectives*. Arlington, VA: American Psychiatric Publishing, 2012.

Key, V. O., Jr. *Southern Politics in State and Nation*. New York: Vintage, 1949.

Kierner, Cynthia A. *Beyond the Household: Women's Place in the Early South, 1700–1835*. Ithaca, NY: Cornell University Press, 1998.

King, Anthony D. *The Bungalow: The Production of a Global Culture*. New York: Oxford University Press, [1984] 1995.

Kirby, Jack Temple. *Rural Worlds Lost: The American South, 1920–1960*. Baton Rouge: Louisiana State University Press, 1987.

Kleber, John E. "Marion K. (Weil) Flexner." In *The Kentucky Encyclopedia*, ed. John E. Kleber, 326. Lexington: University Press of Kentucky, 1992.

Kolchin, Peter. *First Freedom: The Responses of Alabama's Blacks to Emancipation and Reconstruction*. Westport, CT: Greenwood Press, 1972.

Laderman, Gary. *Rest in Peace: A Cultural History of Death and the Funeral Home in Twentieth-Century America*. New York: Oxford University Press, 2003.

Lambert, Alton. *History of Tuscaloosa County, Alabama*. 4 vols. Centre, AL: Stewart University Press, 1977.

Le Guin, Charles A., ed. *A Home-Concealed Woman: The Diaries of Magnolia Wynn Le Guin, 1901–1913*. Athens: University of Georgia Press, 1990.

Lee, Anthony W. Introduction to *Lynching Photographs*, ed. Dora Apel and Shawn Michelle Smith, 1–9. Berkeley: University of California Press, 2007.

Lee, Raymond. *The Films of Mary Pickford*. New York: Castle Books, 1970.

Lewis, Pierce. "Common Landscapes as Historical Documents." In *History from Things: Essays on Material Culture*, ed. Steven Lubar and W. David Kingery, 115–39. Washington, DC: Smithsonian Institution Press, 1993.

Locke, Alain. "Negro Youth Speaks." In *The Works of Alain Locke*, ed. Charles Molesworth, 183–87. New York: Oxford University Press, 2012.

Long, Milbra, and Emily Seate. *The Fostoria Value Guide*. Paducah, KY: Schroeder Publishing, 2003.

Lovett, John N., Jr. "Historic Context Evaluation for Mills in Tennessee." University of Tennessee Transportation Center, 2002. http://www.tdot.state.tn.us/longrange/reports/res-1039.pdf.

Lundegard, Marjorie. "Mills and Mill Sites in Fairfax County, Virginia and Washington, DC." Unpublished paper. Great Falls, VA: Friends of Colvin Run Mill, 2009.

Lupold, John S., and Thomas L. French Jr. *Bridging Deep South Rivers: The Life and Legend of Horace King*. Athens: University of Georgia Press, 2004.

MacKethan, Lucinda H., ed. *Recollections of a Southern Daughter: A Memoir by Cornelia Jones Pond of Liberty County*. Athens: University of Georgia Press, 1998.

Mahon, John K. *History of the Second Seminole War, 1835–1842*. Gainesville: University Presses of Florida, [1967] 1985.

———. "The Journal of A. B. Meek and the Second Seminole War, 1836." *Florida Historical Quarterly* 38, no. 4 (1960): 302–18.

Marcus, Clare Cooper. *House as a Mirror of Self: Exploring the Deeper Meaning of Home*. Berkeley, CA: Conari Press, 1995.

Marks, Carole. *Farewell, We're Good and Gone: The Great Black Migration*. Bloomington: Indiana University Press, 1989.

Marks, Stuart A. *Southern Hunting in Black and White: Nature, History, and Ritual in a Carolina Community*. Princeton, NJ: Princeton University Press, 1991.

Marling, Karal Ann. "Fantasies in Dark Places: The Cultural Geography of the American Movie Palace." In *Textures of Place: Exploring Humanistic Geographies*, ed. Paul C. Adams, Steven D. Hoelscher, and Karen E. Till, 8–23. Minneapolis: University of Minnesota Press, 2001.

———. "From the Quilt to the Neocolonial Photograph: The Arts of the Home in an Age of Transition." In *The Arts and the American Home, 1890–1930*, ed. Jessica H. Foy and Karal Ann Marling, 1–13. Knoxville: University of Tennessee Press, 1994.

Marshall, Patricia Phillips, and Jo Ramsay Leimenstoll. *Thomas Day: Master Craftsman and Free Man of Color.* Chapel Hill: University of North Carolina Press, 2010.

Maslow, A. H. *Motivation and Personality.* 3rd ed. New York: Harper and Row, [1954] 1987.

Massey, Mary Elizabeth. *Ersatz in the Confederacy.* Columbia: University of South Carolina Press, 1952.

Mathews, Donald G. "Lynching Is Part of the Religion of Our People: Faith in the Christian South." In *Religion in the American South: Protestants and Others in History and Culture*, ed. Beth Barton Schweiger and Donald G. Mathews, 153–94. Chapel Hill: University of North Carolina Press, 2004.

———. *Slavery and Methodism: A Chapter in American Morality, 1780–1845.* Princeton, NJ: Princeton University Press, 1965.

———. "The Southern Rite of Human Sacrifice: Lynching in the American South." *Mississippi Quarterly* 61, no. 1–2 (2008): 27–70.

Matthews, John M. "Clarence Cason among the Southern Liberals." *Alabama Review* 38 (Jan. 1985): 3–18.

Mazzari, Louis. *Southern Modernist: Arthur Raper from the New Deal to the Cold War.* Baton Rouge: Louisiana State University Press, 2006.

McCandless, Amy Thompson. "Progressivism and the Higher Education of Southern Women." *North Carolina Historical Review* 70, no. 3 (July 1993): 302–25.

McElya, Micki. *Clinging to Mammy: The Faithful Slave in Twentieth-Century America.* Cambridge, MA: Harvard University Press, 2007.

McGovern, James R. *Anatomy of a Lynching: The Killing of Claude Neal.* Baton Rouge: Louisiana State University Press, 1982.

McIlwain, Christopher Lyle, Sr. "Harry: Faithful Unto Death." *Alabama Heritage*, no. 116 (Spring 2015): 22–29.

McInnis, Maurie D. *The Politics of Taste in Antebellum Charleston.* Chapel Hill: University of North Carolina Press, 2005.

McMillen, Sally G. *Motherhood in the Old South: Pregnancy, Childbirth, and Infant Rearing.* Baton Rouge: Louisiana State University Press, 1990.

McWhirter, Cameron. *Red Summer: The Summer of 1919 and the Awakening of Black America.* New York: Henry Holt, 2011.

Meine, Franklin J. Foreword to *Alias Simon Suggs: The Life and Times of Johnson Jones Hooper*, by W. Stanley Hoole, ix–xix. Tuscaloosa: University of Alabama Press, 1952.

Melius, Louis. *History of the Postal Service from the Earliest Times.* Washington, DC: National Capital Press, 1917.

Mellow, James R. *Walker Evans*. New York: Basic Books, 1999.

Mellown, Robert O. "The Construction of the Alabama Insane Hospital, 1852–1861." *Alabama Review* 38, no. 2 (1985): 83–104.

———. *Historic Structures Report: Jemison-Van de Graaff Mansion*. Tuscaloosa, AL: Jemison-Van de Graaff Mansion Foundation, 1992.

———. *The University of Alabama: A Guide to the Campus and Its Architecture*. Tuscaloosa: University of Alabama Press, 2013.

Mikulincer, Mario, Phillip R. Shaver, Omri Gillath, and Rachel A. Nitzberg. "Attachment, Caregiving, and Altruism: Boosting Attachment Security Increases Compassion and Helping." *Journal of Personality and Social Psychology* 89, no. 5 (2005): 817–39.

Miller, Daniel. *Stuff*. Cambridge: Polity Press, 2010.

Miller, James A. *Remembering Scottsboro: The Legacy of an Infamous Trial*. Princeton, NJ: Princeton University Press, 2009.

Moore, William D. "Riding the Goat: Secrecy, Masculinity, and Fraternal High Jinks in the United States, 1845–1930." *Winterthur Portfolio* 41, no. 2–3 (2007): 161–88.

Morsman, Amy Feely. *The Big House after Slavery: Virginia Plantation Families and Their Postbellum Domestic Experiment*. Charlottesville: University of Virginia Press, 2010.

Motz, Marilyn Ferris. Introduction to *Making the American Home: Middle-Class Women and Domestic Material Culture, 1840–1940*, ed. Marilyn Ferris Motz and Pat Browne, 1–10. Bowling Green, OH: Bowling Green University Popular Press, 1988.

Myers, John B. "Black Human Capital: The Freedmen and the Reconstruction of Labor in Alabama, 1860–1880." PhD diss., Florida State University, 1974.

Naeve, Milo M. *Identifying American Furniture: A Pictorial Guide to Styles and Terms, Colonial to Contemporary*. Nashville, TN: American Association for State and Local History, 1981.

Nelson, Lawrence J. "Welfare Capitalism on a Mississippi Plantation in the Great Depression." *Journal of Southern History* 50, no. 2 (May 1984): 225–50.

Noe, Kenneth. *Reluctant Rebels: The Confederates Who Joined the Army after 1861*. Chapel Hill: University of North Carolina Press, 2010.

Nuwer, Deanne Stephens. *Plague among the Magnolias: The 1878 Yellow Fever Epidemic in Mississippi*. Tuscaloosa: University of Alabama Press, 2009.

Oakes, James. *The Ruling Race: A History of American Slaveholders*. New York: Knopf, 1982.

O'Brien, Michael. *The Idea of the American South, 1920–1941*. Baltimore: Johns Hopkins University Press, 1979.

Oshinsky, David M. *Polio: An American Story*. New York: Oxford University Press, 2005.

Ott, Katherine, Susan Tucker, and Patricia P. Buckler. "An Introduction to the History of Scrapbooks." In *The Scrapbook in American Life*, ed. Susan Tucker, Katherine Ott, and Patricia Buckler, 1–25. Philadelphia: Temple University Press, 2006.

Overton, Grant Martin. *The Women Who Make Our Novels*. Freeport, NY: Books for Libraries Press, 1967.

Ownby, Ted. *American Dreams in Mississippi: Consumers, Poverty, and Culture, 1830–1998*. Chapel Hill: University of North Carolina Press, 1999.

Owsley, Frank Lawrence. *Plain Folk of the Old South*. Baton Rouge: Louisiana State University Press, 1949.

Paine, Robert. *Life and Times of William McKendree, Bishop of the Methodist Episcopal Church*. Nashville, TN: Publishing House of the M. E. Church, South, 1922.

Painter, Nell Irvin. "Introduction: The Journal of Ella Gertrude Clanton Thomas, an Educated White Woman in the Eras of Slavery, War and Reconstruction." In *The Secret Eye: The Journal of Ella Gertrude Clanton Thomas, 1848–1889*, ed. Virginia Ingraham Burr, 1–67. Chapel Hill: University of North Carolina Press, 1990.

Palmer, Phyllis M. *Domesticity and Dirt: Housewives and Domestic Servants in the United States, 1920–1945*. Philadelphia: Temple University Press, 1989.

Paolini, Christopher. Foreword to *The Acts of King Arthur and His Noble Knights*, by John Steinbeck, vii–x. New York: Penguin, 2007.

Pegram, Thomas R. *One Hundred Percent American: The Rebirth and Decline of the Ku Klux Klan in the 1920s*. Chicago: Ivan R. Dee, 2011.

Pierpoint, Claudia Roth. *Passionate Minds: Women Rewriting the World*. New York: Vintage, 2000.

Pleck, Elizabeth H. *Celebrating the Family: Ethnicity, Consumer Culture, and Family Rituals*. Cambridge, MA: Harvard University Press, 2000.

Porter, Roy. *The Biographical Dictionary of Scientists*. 2nd ed. New York: Oxford University Press, 1994.

Prince, K. Stephen. *Stories of the South: Race and the Reconstruction of Southern Identity, 1865–1915*. Chapel Hill: University of North Carolina Press, 2014.

Proctor, Nicolas W. *Bathed in Blood: Hunting and Mastery in the Old South*. Charlottesville: University of Virginia Press, 2002.

Rabinowitz, Howard N. *Race Relations in the Urban South, 1865–1890*. New York: Oxford University Press, 1978.

Radford, John. "Identity and Tradition in the Post–Civil War South." *Journal of Historical Geography* 18 (1992): 91–103.

Raines, Howell. "Introduction: The 'Strange Country.'" In *Stars Fell on Alabama*, by Carl Carmer, xi–xxii. Tuscaloosa: University of Alabama Press, [1934] 1990.

Ray, Celeste. *Highland Heritage: Scottish Americans in the American South*. Chapel Hill: University of North Carolina Press, 2001.

Reid, Robert D. "The Negro in Alabama during the Civil War." *Journal of Negro History* 34 (July 1950): 265–88.

Reiff, Daniel D. *Houses from Books: Treatises, Pattern Books, and Catalogs in American Architecture, 1738–1950*. University Park: Pennsylvania State University Press, 2000.

Reinberger, Mark. "The Architecture of Sharecropping: Extended Farms of the Georgia Piedmont." In *Constructing Image, Identity, and Place: Perspectives in Vernacular Architecture*, vol. 9, ed. Alison K. Hoagland and Kenneth A. Breisch, 116–34. Knoxville: University of Tennessee Press, 2003.

Rellstab, Ludwig. "Life Sketch." In *Franz Liszt and His World*, ed. Christopher H.

Gibbs and Dana Gooly, 341–53. Princeton, NJ: Princeton University Press, 2006.

Rich, John Stanley. "Landscapes and the Imagination: The Interplay of Folk Etymology and Place Names." *Southern Folklore Quarterly* 45 (1981): 155–62.

Richards, Bertrand F. *Gene Stratton Porter.* Boston: Twayne, 1980.

Ritterhouse, Jennifer. *Growing Up Jim Crow: How Black and White Southern Children Learned Race.* Chapel Hill: University of North Carolina Press, 2006.

Roark, James L. *Masters without Slaves: Southern Planters in the Civil War and Reconstruction.* New York: W. W. Norton, 1977.

Roberts, Blain. *Pageants, Parlors, and Pretty Women: Race and Beauty in the Twentieth-Century South.* Chapel Hill: University of North Carolina Press, 2014.

Roberts, Giselle. *The Confederate Belle.* Columbia: University of Missouri Press, 2003.

Robertson, Cheryl. "Male and Female Agendas for Domestic Reform: The Middle-Class Bungalow in Gendered Perspective." *Winterthur Portfolio* 26, no. 2–3 (1991): 123–41.

Roell, Craig H. "The Piano in the American Home." In *The Arts and the American Home, 1890–1930,* ed. Jessica H. Foy and Karal Ann Marling, 85–110. Knoxville: University of Tennessee Press, 1994.

Rogers, George C., Jr., David R. Chestnutt, and Peggy J. Clark. *The Papers of Henry Laurens.* Vol. 5. Columbia: University of South Carolina Press, 1976.

Rogers, William Warren, and Robert David Ward. *August Reckoning: Jack Turner and Racism in Post–Civil War Alabama.* Baton Rouge: Louisiana State University Press, 1973.

Rogers, William Warren, Robert David Ward, Leah Rawls Atkins, and Wayne Flynt. *Alabama: The History of a Deep South State.* Tuscaloosa: University of Alabama Press, 1994.

Rollins, Judith. *Between Women: Domestics and Their Employers.* Philadelphia: Temple University Press, 1985.

Ronstrom, Maud O'Bryan. "Seignouret and Mallard, Cabinet-makers." *Antiques* 46 (Aug. 1944): 79–81.

Rose, Anne C. *Psychology and Selfhood in the Segregated South.* Chapel Hill: University of North Carolina Press, 2009.

Rosen, Charles. *Arnold Schoenberg.* New York: Viking, 1975.

Rosselin, Celine. "The Ins and Outs of the Hall: A Parisian Example." In *At Home: An Anthropology of Domestic Space,* ed. Irene Cieraad, 53–59. Syracuse, NY: Syracuse University Press, 1999.

Roth, Rodris. "Scrapbook Houses: A Late Nineteenth-Century Children's View of the American Home." In *The American Home: Material Culture, Domestic Space, and Family Life,* ed. Eleanor McD. Thompson, 301–20. Winterthur, DE: Henry Francis du Pont Winterthur Museum, 1998.

Rothman, Adam. *Slave Country: American Expansion and the Origins of the Deep South.* Cambridge, MA: Harvard University Press, 2005.

Rybczynski, Witold. *Home: A Short History of an Idea.* New York: Penguin, 1986.

Schlereth, Thomas J. "Country Stores, County Fairs, and Mail-Order Catalogues: Consumption in Rural America." In *Consuming Visions: Accumulation and Display of Goods in America, 1880–1920,* ed. Samuel J. Bronner and Henry Francis du Pont

Winterthur Museum, 339–75. New York: W. W. Norton, 1989.

———. "Introduction: American Homes and American Scholars." In *American Home Life, 1880–1930: A Social History of Spaces and Services*, ed. Jessica H. Foy and Thomas J. Schlereth, 1–22. Knoxville: University of Tennessee Press, 1992.

———. *Victorian America: Transformations in Everyday Life, 1876–1915*. New York: HarperCollins, 1991.

Schwartz, Harvey, and Bruce M. Waters. *Rattan Furniture: Tropical Comfort throughout the House*. Atglen, PA: Schiffer Publishing, 1999.

Schwieterman, Joseph P. *When the Railroad Leaves Town: American Communities in the Age of Rail Line Abandonment, Eastern United States*. Kirksville, MO: Truman State University Press, 2001.

Scott, Anne Firor. *Making the Invisible Woman Visible*. Urbana: University of Illinois Press, 1984.

———. *The Southern Lady from Pedestal to Politics, 1830–1930*. Charlottesville: University of Virginia Press, 1995.

Seale, William. *The Tasteful Interlude: American Interiors through the Camera's Eye, 1860–1917*. 2nd ed. Walnut Creek, CA: AltaMira Press, 1995.

Seaton, Beverly. "'Making the Best of Circumstances': The American Woman's Back Yard Garden." In *Making the American Home: Middle-Class Women and Domestic Material Culture, 1840–1940*, ed. Marilyn Ferris Motz and Pat Browne, 90–104. Bowling Green, OH: Bowling Green University Popular Press, 1988.

———. "A Pedigree for a New Century: The Colonial Experience in Popular Historical Novels, 1890–1910." In *The Colonial Revival in America*, ed. Alan Axelrod, 278–93. New York: W. W. Norton, 1985.

Seidel, Kathryn Lee. *The Southern Belle in the American Novel*. Gainesville: University Press of Florida, 1985.

Semper, Philippa. "'My Other World': Historical Reflections and Refractions in Modern Arthurian Fantasy." In *Medieval Afterlives in Popular Culture*, ed. Gail Ashton and Daniel T. Kline, 173–86. New York: Palgrave Macmillan, 2012.

Shapiro, Henry. *Appalachia on Our Mind: The Southern Mountains and Mountaineers in the American Consciousness, 1870–1920*. Chapel Hill: University of North Carolina Press, 1986.

Shapiro, Laura. *Perfection Salad: Women and Cooking at the Turn of the Century*. New York: Modern Library, [1986] 2001.

Sharpless, Rebecca. *Cooking in Other Women's Kitchens: Domestic Workers in the South, 1865–1960*. Chapel Hill: University of North Carolina Press, 2010.

Shores, Elizabeth Findley. *On Harper's Trail: Roland McMillan Harper, Pioneering Botanist of the Southern Coastal Plain*. Athens: University of Georgia Press, 2008.

Sies, Mary Corbin. "Toward a Performance Theory of the Suburban Ideal." In *Perspectives in Vernacular Architecture*, vol. 4, ed. Thomas Carter and Bernard L. Herman, 197–207. Columbia: University of Missouri Press for the Vernacular Architecture Forum, 1991.

Sisk, Glenn N. "Diseases in the Alabama Black Belt." *Alabama Historical Quarterly* 24, no. 1 (Spring 1962): 52–61.

Sledge, John S., and Sheila Hagler, illus. *An Ornament to the City: Old Mobile Ironwork.* Athens: University of Georgia Press, 2006.

Smith, Lillian. *Killers of the Dream.* New York: W. W. Norton, [1949] 1978.

Smith, Louis R., Jr., and David S. Neel Jr. Preface to *Cush: A Civil War Memoir,* ed. Louis R. Smith Jr. and Andrew Quist, i–iii. Livingston, AL: Livingston University Press, 1999.

Smith, Shawn Michelle. *American Archives: Gender, Race, and Class in Visual Culture.* Princeton, NJ: Princeton University Press, 1999.

———. "The Evidence of Lynching Photographs." In *Lynching Photographs,* by Dora Apel and Shawn Michelle Smith, 10–41. Berkeley: University of California Press, 2007.

Sotiropoulos, Karen. *Staging Race: Black Performers in Turn of the Century America.* Cambridge, MA: Harvard University Press, 2006.

Sterkx, H. E. *Partners in Rebellion: Alabama Women in the Civil War.* Rutherford, NJ: Fairleigh Dickinson University Press, 1970.

Stout, A. B. *Daylilies: The Wild Species and Garden Clones, Both Old and New, of the Genus Hemerocallis.* Millwood, NY: Sagapress, [1934] 1986.

Stover, John F. *The Railroads of the South, 1865–1900: A Study of Finances and Control.* Chapel Hill: University of North Carolina Press, 1955.

Stowe, Steven M. *Doctoring the South: Southern Physicians and Everyday Medicine in the Mid-Nineteenth Century.* Chapel Hill: University of North Carolina Press, 2004.

———. *Intimacy and Power in the Old South: Ritual in the Lives of the Planters.* Baltimore: Johns Hopkins University Press, 1987.

Strother, David Hunter. "Sixth Paper." In *The Old South Illustrated by Porte Crayon,* ed. Cecil D. Eby, 269–92. Chapel Hill: University of North Carolina Press, 1959.

Sudduth, Charletta. "Annie Victorian Johnson." Interview. In *The Maid Narratives: Black Domestics and White Families in the Jim Crow South,* ed. Katherine Van Wormer, David W. Jackson III, and Charletta Sudduth, 89–101. Baton Rouge: Louisiana State University Press, 2012.

Swift, Harriet. "A New Day in Wilcox County: 1978." *Southern Changes* 1, no. 6 (1979): 15–16, 28.

Tadman, Michael. *Speculators and Slaves: Masters, Traders, and Slaves in the Old South.* Madison: University of Wisconsin Press, 1989.

Theophano, Janet. *Eat My Words: Reading Women's Lives through the Cookbooks They Wrote.* New York: Palgrave, 2002.

Thomas, Mary Martha. *Riveting and Rationing in Dixie: Alabama Women and the Second World War.* Tuscaloosa: University of Alabama Press, 1987.

Thomas, Stanton. *The Crossroads of Memory: Carroll Cloar and the American South.* Little Rock: Arkansas Arts Center, 2014.

Thomson, Bailey. "Clarence Cason." In *Southern Writers: A New Biographical Dictionary,* ed. Joseph M. Flora and Amber Vogel, 64–65. Baton Rouge: Louisiana State University Press, 2006.

Thornton, J. Mills, III. "Alabama Politics, J. Thomas Heflin, and the Expulsion Movement of 1929." *Alabama Review* 67, no. 1 (Jan. 2014): 10–39.

———. *Politics and Power in a Slave Society; Alabama, 1800 to 1860*. Baton Rouge: Louisiana State University Press, 1978.

Thurber, Cheryl. "Development of the Mammy Image and Mythology." In *Southern Women: Histories and Identities*, ed. Virginia Bernhard, Betty Brandon, Elizabeth Fox-Genovese, and Theda Perdue, 87–108. Columbia: University of Missouri Press, 1992.

Thuro, Catherine M. V. *Oil Lamps II: Glass Kerosene Lamps*. Toronto: Thorncliffe House, [1983] 1994.

Tindall, George Brown. *The Emergence of the New South, 1913–1945*. Baton Rouge: Louisiana State University Press, 1967.

Toffey, John J. *A Woman Nobly Planned: Fact and Myth in the Legacy of Flora MacDonald*. Durham, NC: Carolina Academic Press, 1997.

Tolnay, Stewart Emory, and E. M. Beck. *A Festival of Violence: An Analysis of Southern Lynchings, 1882–1930*. Urbana: University of Illinois Press, 1995.

Trachtenberg, Alan. *Reading American Photographs: Images as History, Mathew Brady to Walker Evans*. New York: Hill and Wang, 1989.

Trefousse, Hans L., ed. *Toward a New View of America: Essays in Honor of Arthur C. Cole*. New York: B. Franklin, 1977.

Tuan, Yi-fu. *Landscapes of Fear*. Minneapolis: University of Minnesota Press, [1980] 2013.

Tucker, Susan. *Telling Memories among Southern Women: Domestic Workers and Their Employers in the Segregated South*. Baton Rouge: Louisiana State University Press, 1988.

Valk, Anne M., and Leslie Brown. *Living with Jim Crow: African American Women and Memories of the Segregated South*. New York: Palgrave Macmillan, 2010.

Van Wormer, Katherine, David W. Jackson III, and Charletta Sudduth. *The Maid Narratives: Black Domestics and White Families in the Jim Crow South*. Baton Rouge: Louisiana State University Press, 2012.

Venable, Charles L., Ellen P. Denker, Katherine C. Grier, and Stephen G. Harrison, eds. *China and Glass in America, 1880–1980: From Table Top to TV Tray*. Dallas: Dallas Museum of Art, 2001.

Vlach, John Michael. *Back of the Big House: The Architecture of Plantation Slavery*. Chapel Hill: University of North Carolina Press, 1993.

———. "'Snug Li'l House with Flue and Oven': Nineteenth-Century Reforms in Plantation Slave Housing." In *Gender, Class and Shelter: Perspectives in Vernacular Architecture*, vol. 5, ed. Elizabeth Collins Cromley and Carter L. Hudgins, 118–29. Knoxville: University of Tennessee Press, 1995.

Volz, Candace M. "The Modern Look of the Early-Twentieth-Century House: A Mirror of Changing Lifestyles." In *American Home Life, 1880–1930: A Social History of Spaces and Services*, ed. Jessica H. Foy and Thomas J. Schlereth, 25–48. Knoxville: University of Tennessee Press, 1992.

Wajda, Shirley Teresa. "The Artistic Portrait Photograph." In *The Arts and the American Home, 1890–1930*, ed. Jessica H. Foy and Karal Ann Marling, 165–82. Knoxville: University of Tennessee Press, 1994.

Walker, Alan. *Franz Liszt.* 3 vols. New York: Knopf, 1983–96.

Walker, Melissa. "Shifting Boundaries: Race Relations in the Rural Jim Crow South." In *African American Life in the Rural South, 1900–1950*, ed. R. Douglas Hurt, 81–107. Columbia: University of Missouri Press, 2003.

Ware, Susan. "Writing Women's Lives: One Historian's Perspective." *Journal of Interdisciplinary History* 40, no. 3 (Winter 2010): 413–35.

Watson, Derek. *Liszt.* New York: Schirmer Books, 1989.

Watson, Rachel. "The View from the Porch: Race and the Limits of Empathy in the Film *To Kill a Mockingbird*." *Mississippi Quarterly* 63, no. 3/4 (2010): 419–44.

Weaver, Richard M. *The Southern Tradition at Bay: A History of Postbellum Thought.* New Rochelle, NY: Arlington House, 1968.

Welch, William C., and Greg Grant. *The Southern Heirloom Garden.* Dallas: Taylor Publishing, 1995.

Welch, William C., Greg Grant, Cynthia W. Mueller, and Jason Powell. *Heirloom Gardening in the South: Yesterday's Plants for Today's Gardens.* College Station: Texas A&M University Press, 2011.

Werner, Craig. "The Old South, 1815–1840." In *The History of Southern Literature*, ed. Louis Rubin et al., 81–91. Baton Rouge: Louisiana State University Press, 1985.

Wertz, Richard W., and Dorothy C. Wertz. *Lying-In: A History of Childbirth in America.* Expanded ed. New Haven, CT: Yale University Press, 1989.

West, Shearer. *Portraiture.* New York: Oxford University Press, 2004.

Wiener, Jonathan M. *Social Origins of the New South: Alabama, 1860–1885.* Baton Rouge: Louisiana State University Press, 1978.

Wiggins, Sarah Woolfolk. *From Civil War to Civil Rights: Alabama, 1860–1960; An Anthology from the Alabama Review.* Tuscaloosa: University of Alabama Press, 1987.

Wiggins, Sarah Woolfolk, with Ruth Smith Truss, eds. *The Journal of Sarah Haynsworth Gayle, 1827–1835.* Tuscaloosa: University of Alabama Press, 2013.

Wilkinson, Anthony. *Liszt.* London: Macmillan, 1975.

Williams, Benjamin Buford. *A Literary History of Alabama: The Nineteenth Century.* Cranbury, NJ: Associated University Presses, 1979.

Williams, Derita Coleman, and Nathan Harsh. *The Art and Mystery of Tennessee Furniture and Its Makers through 1850.* Nashville: Tennessee State Museum Foundation, 1988.

Williams, Sherley Anne. "Janie's Burden." In *Zora Neale Hurston*, by Harold Bloom, 97–102. New York: Chelsea House, 1986.

Wilson, Charles Reagan. *Baptized in Blood: The Religion of the Lost Cause, 1865–1920.* Athens: University of Georgia Press, 1980.

———. *Judgment and Grace in Dixie: Southern Faiths from Faulkner to Elvis.* Athens: University of Georgia Press, 1995.

Wilson, Daniel J. *Living with Polio: The Epidemic and Its Survivors.* Chicago: University of Chicago Press, 2005.

Winter, Marian Hannah. "Juba and American Minstrelsy." In *Inside the Minstrel Mask: Readings in Nineteenth-Century Blackface Minstrelsy*, ed. Annemarie Bean, James

Vernon Hatch, and Brooks McNamara, 223–44. Hanover, NH: Wesleyan University Press, 1996.

Wolfe, Suzanne Rau. *The University of Alabama: A Pictorial History.* Tuscaloosa: University of Alabama Press, 1983.

Woodman, Harold D. *King Cotton and His Retainers: Financing and Marketing the Cotton Crop of the South, 1800–1925.* Lexington: University of Kentucky Press, 1968.

Wyatt-Brown, Bertram. "The Mask of Obedience: Male Slave Psychology in the Old South." *American Historical Review* 93, no. 5 (1988): 1228–52.

———. *Southern Honor: Ethics and Behavior in the Old South.* New York: Oxford University Press, [1982] 2007.

Wynne, Lewis N., and Robert A. Taylor, eds. *This War So Horrible: The Civil War Diary of Hiram Smith Williams.* Tuscaloosa: University of Alabama Press, 1993.

Yanni, Carla. *The Architecture of Madness: Insane Asylums in the United States.* Minneapolis: University of Minnesota Press, 2007.

Zaborney, John J. *Slaves for Hire: Renting Enslaved Workers in Antebellum Virginia.* Baton Rouge: Louisiana State University Press, 2012.

Ziegler, Edith M. *Schools in the Landscape: Localism, Cultural Tradition, and the Development of Alabama's Public Education System, 1865–1915.* Tuscaloosa: University of Alabama Press, 2010.

Index